THE SECRET LIFE OF
BILL CLINTON

THE SECRET LIFE OF BILL CLINTON:

THE UNREPORTED STORIES

AMBROSE EVANS-PRITCHARD

REGNERY PUBLISHING, INC.
Washington, D.C.

Library of Congress Cataloging-in-Publication Data

Evans-Pritchard, Ambrose, 1957–
    The secret life of Bill Clinton : the unreported stories / Ambrose Evans-Pritchard.
        p. cm.
        Includes index.
        ISBN 0-89526-408-0 (alk. paper)
        1. Clinton, Bill, 1946–   .   2. United States—Politics and government—1993–   .   3.   Political corruption—United States—History—20th century. 4. Oklahoma City Federal Building Bombing, Oklahoma City, Okla., 1995. 5. Foster, Vincent W., d. 1993.   6. Arkansas—Politics and government—1951–   I. Title.
        E885.E93 1997
        973.929'092—dc21   97-36539
                                                                          CIP

Published in the United States by
Regnery Publishing, Inc.
An Eagle Publishing Company
1 Massachusetts Avenue, NW
Washington, DC 20001

Distributed to the trade by
National Book Network
4720-A Boston Way
Lanham, MD 20706

Printed on acid-free paper.
Manufactured in the United States of America

10 9 8 7 6 5 4 3 2 1

Books are available in quantity for promotional or premium use. Write to Director of Special Sales, Regnery Publishing, Inc., 1 Massachusetts Avenue, NW, Washington, DC 20001, for information on discounts and terms or call (202) 216-0600.

DEDICATION

To the people of Arkansas who deserve better,

to the people of Oklahoma who deserve the truth,

and to the people of the United States
who have treated me with such generosity

CONTENTS

"Come to Arkansas.... You Might Even Learn a
Thing or Two"

INTRODUCTION

BLACKWATER

I WRITE THIS BOOK with sadness. By elective affinity I am an American, even if I remain a subject of the Queen. I did not come here with an attitude of haughty disdain, intent on running down the country. It has always been my unquestioned assumption that the United States is a force for good in the world, the final guarantor of liberal civilization.

Nor did I harbor animosity toward Bill and Hillary Clinton when I was sent to Washington as Bureau Chief for *The Sunday Telegraph* at the end of 1992. Although a Tory of Burkean philosophy, I had succumbed to the charm of Bill Clinton years before at a conference of the Democratic Leadership Council in Williamsburg. As for Hillary, I was rather taken by her image of flinty altruism. When I wrote the lead editorial for *The Daily Telegraph* the day after the presidential election in November 1992, I was guardedly optimistic. Little did I know.

The Clintons are attractive on the surface. As Yale Law School graduates they have mastered the language and style of the mandarin class. It is only when you walk through the mirrors into the Arkansas underworld whence they came that you begin to realize that something is horribly wrong. You learn that Bill Clinton grew up in the Dixie Mafia stronghold of Hot Springs, and that his brother was a drug dealer with ties to the Medellin Cartel. You learn that a cocaine distributor named Dan Lasater was an intimate friend, and that Lasater's top aide would later be given a post in charge of administration (and drug testing) at the White House. You learn that Arkansas was a mini-Colombia within the United States, infested by narco-corruption.

And you start to wonder.

In Washington, Clinton moved with ruthless efficiency to take control of the federal machinery of coercion. While the U.S. watchdog press barked and howled with pitiful irrelevance about Clinton's $200 hair cut, he quietly fired every U.S. Attorney in the country and then made his move on the FBI, which would be transformed gradually, one appointment at a time, into a replica of the Arkansas State Police. When he sacked William Sessions in July 1993, it was the first time in American history that a president had summarily dismissed an FBI director. The putsch passed without protest. This is how a country starts to lose a democracy.

I have not lost my faith in the American people. In the end, I believe, it is the ordinary citizens who will cleanse the institutions of the country before they become irretrievably corrupt. They are the heroes of this book. Ultimately, this is an optimistic essay, a paean to the American spirit. But let me tell you, I am astounded by the bullying and deceitful conduct of the U.S. Justice Department, the FBI, and other law enforcement agencies under this administration. No doubt there have been abuses in the past, but I believe that malfeasance has become systemic over the last five years. It is spreading down, by example, lodging itself in the institutional apparatus of government. Whether it is the Internal Revenue Service targeting foes of the president, or the Immigration and Naturalization Service expediting citizenship for "Democratic" voters in time for the 1996 elections, or the prostitution of the Lincoln Bedroom, the

Clinton reflex is in evidence everywhere. To put it with brutal honesty, you can sniff the pungent odors of decay in the American body politic. I expect that this is what it smelt like in continental Europe in the 1920s, even as the boom rolled on.

When you are living through events day-by-day it is hard to know whether you are witnessing an historic turning point in the life of a country, or just mistaking the usual noise of politics for something meaningful. But there can be no doubt that the undercurrents in the era of William Jefferson Clinton are unprecedented. It was driven home to me by a symposium in November 1996 held by Father Richard Neuhaus, a respected Catholic intellectual and editor of *First Things*. Neuhaus warned that the experiment of the founding fathers was in danger of failing, and he pointedly spoke of the "the trail of abuses and usurpations" that set off the first American Revolution. Has it reached the point, he asked, "where conscientious citizens can no longer give moral assent to the existing regime?"

Yes, he said "regime."

Something about Bill Clinton—his ineffable caddishness, perhaps—is changing the political discourse of the country. Every year that he continues in power, he eats a little deeper into the eroded legitimacy of the political order. The importance of this cannot be exaggerated. Three-quarters of the American people now tell pollsters that they do not trust the government to do the right thing. If ever there was a time when a leader of stoic virtue was needed to restore the authority of the national institutions, it is surely now.

It is under this president that domestic terrorism has become a feature of daily life in America. For decades the country was largely free of the political violence that has afflicted much of western Europe. Indeed, Europeans looked across the Atlantic with envy, marveling at the way this huge bustling nation managed to order its affairs with such cohesive goodwill. Not any longer. The actions and character of President Clinton have engendered the most deadly terrorist movement in the industrialized world. I choose the word "movement" advisedly because I do not accept the Justice Department claim that Terry Nichols and Timothy McVeigh were acting alone when they killed 168 people in the Oklahoma federal building in April 1995. There has been a steady campaign of bombing since then: three in Atlanta alone, including the deadly pipe bomb that eclipsed the 1996 Olympics. The attacks are so ubiquitous that they do not make the national news unless somebody is killed. To a foreign eye, America looks like a country that is flying out of control.

Again, it is under Clinton that an armed militia movement involving tens of thousands of people has mushroomed out of the plain, an expression of dissent that is unparalleled since the southern gun clubs before the Civil War. People do not spend their weekends with an SKS rifle, drilling for guerrilla warfare against federal forces, in a country that is at ease with itself. It takes very bad behavior to provoke the first simmerings of armed insurgency, and the militias are unmistakably Clinton's offspring. Would they have happened if America were governed by a President Tsongas or a President Bush? Of course not.

Which compels the question: What is it about the combustible chemistry of Bill Clinton that causes such reaction? What has he been doing to America?

The original sin, I believe, was the FBI assault on the Branch Davidian community in Waco, Texas, on April 19, 1993. At least 76 people were incinerated, most of them women and children, after FBI tanks went smashing through the walls of Mount Carmel. The death toll adds up to the worst tragedy precipitated by government action on American soil this century. You have to go back to the slaughter of 200 Sioux Indians at Wounded Knee in 1890 to find an abuse of power on this scale. Just like Waco, Wounded Knee was designated a "battle" by officials; and just like Waco, the victims were demonized as sexual deviants. Some methods never change.

Infants too young to use masks were subjected to six hours exposure to CS gas, a weapon banned in warfare under the Paris Convention on Chemical Weapons. The Justice Department plan, in effect, was to torture the children to force the surrender of the parents. There is expert opinion that some of the babies would have died from the gas alone, without the fire. So I bristled when Attorney General Janet Reno testified to Congress that the raid would have been a success if the FBI had increased the dosage of chemical poison.[1]

It is my contention that every salient fact put forward by the Clinton administration about Waco is a lie. I do not believe that the Branch Davidians were stockpiling weapons for offensive action, or any action. I do not believe that they "ambushed" the ATF as federal agents were "peacefully" trying to deliver a search warrant. I do not find the FBI account of the final conflagration to be remotely credible.

Nobody has ever lost a day's pay for what happened. I am not suggesting a public flogging for the regular FBI and ATF agents who were just trying to do their job in difficult circumstances. That is not the way to resolve anything. Nor am I suggesting that those responsible be put on trial for negligent infanticide. Not yet, at least. But there has to be a ritual expurgation of some kind if the open wound of Waco is ever to heal. What is missing is any sense of guilt or repentance, any admission that something terrible was done to the Branch Davidians. "I do not think the United States government is responsible for the fact that a bunch of fanatics decided to kill themselves" was how Clinton responded at a press conference two days after the fire.

This, too, was a lie, of course, a posthumous slander. Nothing is more undignified than the attempt by the White House and the Justice Department to exonerate their own conduct by falsely accusing the Davidians of murdering their children. The evidence does not support this outrageous claim. It is far more likely that the inflammable residue from the CS gas was ignited by accident, perhaps by a tank smashing into a fuel lantern (the Davidians had had their electricity cut off) or by flash-bang grenades or other explosive devices used by the FBI. But to admit that the U.S. Justice Department killed these children, albeit by accident, is to change the whole character of Waco.

No, the victims, not the perpetrators, would continue to shoulder all the blame. To compound the injustice, the survivors were subjected to a vindictive prosecution. Some of the Davidians were sentenced to 40 years in prison, even though the jury found them innocent of conspiracy to murder. To the horror of the jurors, convictions on minor charges were misconstrued by the judge to vastly increase the penalties. As jury foreman Sarah Bain said later: "The federal government was absolutely out of control here. We spoke in the jury room about the fact that the wrong people were on trial, that it should have been the ones who planned the raid and orchestrated it and insisted on carrying out this plan who should have been on trial."

Quite so.

It was not the first time, nor the last time, that Bill Clinton would misuse the judicial apparatus to shape political perceptions. He practiced the art as Governor of Arkansas, and he has continued to use it as an instrument of intimidation in Washington. Sending people to prison on false charges—or trying to do so—is his specialty, which is the chief reason why I have come to revile the man. Behind the facade of a roguish *bon viveur*, Clinton conceals a very nasty streak.

As a foreign correspondent, I have been uniquely privileged. I am not beholden to any political or financial interest in the United States. I do not hang on lips of official sources, nor do I fear the loss of access in Washington, or the blackball of my profession.

As I write this I am already sitting 3,000 miles away, in a medieval village, looking out over the Weald of Kent. I can tell it as I saw it, the whole unvarnished truth.

THE OKLAHOMA BOMBING—
"OUR COMMON GROUND"

—Bill Clinton to reporters aboard Air Force One,
November 1996

CHAPTER ONE

THE RESURRECTION OF PRESIDENT CLINTON

R ELAXING ON AIR FORCE ONE after the 1996 elections, Bill Clinton told a pool of reporters that he owed his political revival to the Oklahoma bombing. He was in a reflective mood, looking back at the ups and downs of his turbulent presidency. As so often, his thoughts lingered on those first painful months after the Republicans captured both Houses of Congress for the first time in almost two generations. It had been a stinging rebuke for the White House. But then that bomb went off. "It broke a spell in the country as people began searching for our common ground again," he said.

The searing destruction of the Alfred P. Murrah Federal Building on April 19, 1995, was the most traumatic event in the United States since the assassination of President Kennedy. Had it been carried out by foreign radicals, the impact on the national psyche would have been far less. But this was a homegrown conspiracy. Americans were committing mass murder against other Americans. One hundred and sixty-eight people were dead. A crèche full of infants had been massacred in cold blood, by Americans.

President Clinton's analysis cannot be faulted. The bombing had a catalytic effect, abruptly changing the chemistry of American politics. One has to think back to the mood in Washington in April 1995 to understand what Clinton meant. The Republican Congress was completing its one hundred day march; the Contract with America was being rushed through the House at breakneck speed; and the world was kneeling in obeisance before Speaker Newt Gingrich, even as President Clinton spoke plaintively of being "relevant."

Think back to the triumphalist language of the Republican diehards. The Education Department was going to be abolished before breakfast, the Commerce Department before lunch, Housing and Urban Development before supper, and the Environmental Protection Agency was going to be torched in a spectacular bonfire before bedtime. Rhetoric was leaping ahead of reality, of course, but the tone and manner of the new leadership was deeply unsettling to great numbers of Americans of mellow, conservative views. Things were getting out of hand.

The bombing brought it into sharp focus. The militia movement, right-wing talk radio, the perceived Gingrich onslaught against government, all melded together in the public mind as one rampant movement of extremism.

Clinton seized the moment. He castigated talk radio for broadcasting "a relentless clamor of hatred and division." The Right, he said, was sowing distrust of government institutions and creating a climate that fostered recourse to violence. He did not name the Republicans as co-conspirators; he did not have to. The media clerisy made the connection for him. They all but said that Tim McVeigh was the military expression of the Gingrich agenda. Republicans had failed to understand that rhetoric has consequences, opined the commentators, and now look what had happened.

The Republicans were dumbstruck. A few dared to reply that it was the deployment of tanks by a militarized FBI against women and children in Waco that had set off the deadly spiral. But most were too intimidated, or horrified, to articulate a defense. When Senator Phil Gramm risked a word of polite protest—"I think we all need to be very careful that we keep politics out of this thing"—he was reprimanded for his "mean streak."

President Clinton traveled to Oklahoma and handled the ceremony of grief with consummate skill. He visited the rescue workers. He held the hands of the victims. He said all the right things. His empathy was boundless. The polls noted that four-fifths of Americans admired his human touch. Overall, Clinton's job rating jumped from 42 percent to 51 percent, although this did not begin to reflect the tectonic changes beneath the surface of American politics. Clinton had come back to life, and the Justice Department was riding high. There was overwhelming support for White House plans to enhance the anti-terrorist powers of the FBI.

But what if the Clinton administration has not told the full truth about the Oklahoma bombing, as many of the families now suspect? What if some of the perpetrators are still at large, freely walking the streets and giving remarkably candid interviews to this author, because it is not in the political interests of the White House or the FBI to bring them to justice? I think that would give a different complexion to the matter. I hope that the following chapters will make it clear that these are not idle questions.

I do not wish to revisit the Denver trial of Tim McVeigh. I am convinced that McVeigh was guilty, and his own lawyer admitted as much during the sentencing hearings. But the trial did not bring out the full story. Indeed, it was skillfully managed to ensure that collateral revelations were kept to a minimum.

This was a terrible mistake. The Oklahoma bombing was the most deadly act of terrorism ever committed on U.S. soil. It was no time for a sloppy investigation or a trial that could be considered as expedited, abridged, or rigged in any way. Jurists concurred that it was imperative that the Justice Department conduct itself beyond reproach if this tragedy was to attain closure. It would be profoundly injurious to the republic if it were ever felt that the proceedings were manipulated for the benefit of the executive branch. Retribution was important, of course, but it was even more important to sustain confidence in the American democratic system for decades to come. The President professed agreement. The Attorney General promised to make this an exhibit of American excellence.

It did not happen. In violation of its "Brady" responsibilities,[1] the prosecution withheld material from the defense that was exculpatory or impeached the credibility of government witnesses. It delayed a year in handing over FD-302 witness statements that were critical to the defense. It stonewalled, obstructed, and dragged its feet at every turn.[2] It also told a series of demonstrable lies that will be enumerated in this book. If this is how the Justice Department behaves in a high profile case after the President and the Attorney General have both made explicit promises of transparency, I dread to think how it conducts itself when nobody is paying attention.

As for the FBI, the proven malfeasance of the crime labs in the handling of scientific evidence from the crime scene makes it clear that the "OKBOMB" investigation was rotten from the foundations up. Far from taking extra precautions to uphold the highest standards of forensic evidence, the FBI resorted to methods that cannot be tolerated in a democratic society. The report of the Justice Department's Inspector General lists the Oklahoma bombing case as one of the worst examples of *de facto* evidence tampering by the crime labs.

It is worth dwelling on this point because the FBI has been patting itself on the back for "solving" the Oklahoma bombing, as if it had cause for self-congratulation. In the first place, the FBI had no scientific basis for concluding that the Murrah Building was blown up by an ammonium nitrate fertilizer bomb. The FBI did not know in 1995, and does not know to this day, what actually caused the explosion.[3] The Justice Department report concluded that the explosives unit simply guessed that the bomb was made of 4,000 pounds of ammonium nitrate after "the recovery of receipts showing that defendant Nichols purchased 4,000 pounds of ammonium nitrate."

The labs guessed that the explosive charge was placed in 50-gallon white plastic barrels, without conducting the requisite tests, after the discovery of 50-gallon plastic containers at the house of Terry Nichols.[4] They said that the detonator appeared to be a Primadet Delay system, but no trace of this was found at the crime scene. Primadet was, however, found at the house of Terry Nichols.... You get the picture.

The FBI crime labs sculpted a theory of the bombing that would help the prosecution secure convictions against Tim McVeigh and Terry Nichols—and science be damned. Once it is understood that the FBI behaved this way in handling empirical evidence—where malfeasance is susceptible to exposure—it becomes easier to discern the attitudes that informed the rest of the OKBOMB investigation. It is my contention that the crime labs were no worse than other divisions of the FBI. The only difference is that the technicians were caught red-handed, while certain corrupt field agents and their superiors have yet to be exposed.

In summing up, the Inspector General's report found that the FBI crime labs had "repeatedly reached conclusions that incriminated the defendants without a scientific basis" in the Oklahoma bombing case.[5] I find this quite staggering. In Anglo-Saxon jurisprudence, shared by Britain and America, it is not acceptable to shape the crime to fit the suspect. It is a practice we condemn as "framing." I do not understand why the current director of the FBI is still drawing a paycheck from the U.S. taxpayer after a scandal of this magnitude, especially since he permitted the retaliatory harassment of Dr. Frederick Whitehurst, the chief whistle-blower.[6]

It was the duty of Judge Richard Matsch to prevent the executive branch from conducting a politicized trial that obscured the facts.

Instead he went with the flow, acceding to the prosecution's request that the Inspector General's report be barred as evidence. It was never made clear to the jury that the FBI did not know what kind of bomb really caused the blast, nor that the FBI had forfeited its magisterial authority.

But most serious of all, the judge refused to allow the testimony of an ATF informant with very relevant information indicating that the Oklahoma bombing was a broad conspiracy involving several members of the neo-Nazi movement in Oklahoma, an assertion that the U.S. government had gone to great lengths to suppress. Whether or not Judge Richard Matsch was acting in tacit concert with the Justice Department is a matter that will demand hard scrutiny by historians. Doubtless Judge Matsch is sure that he can justify his decision on technical grounds. No judge likes to commit reversible error. But even if he can do so, I still believe that he betrayed his mission as a U.S. federal judge. There was more riding on the trial than the guilt or innocence of Tim McVeigh. The greater cause of justice was obstructed.

Needless to say, the McVeigh trial was not described in this way by the American media. The outcome was seen as a triumph. Judge Matsch was lionized, praised for restoring confidence in the criminal justice system. The reaction of the press disturbed me deeply. I never imagined that the machinery of coverup could be so oppressively efficient.

McVeigh's mercurial counsel, Stephen Jones, allowed himself a moment of angry passion when he returned home to Oklahoma. If anybody thinks that the full story came out in the trial, he said, he could guarantee them that it most assuredly did not. Jones was bound to silence by the rules of attorney-client confidentiality, while McVeigh was "hanging tough" out of loyalty to his sworn brothers in the Aryan order.

Indebted to the Oklahoma families who have refused to accept the half-truths of the U.S. Justice Department, I offer a fragment of the story that these two men cannot or will not reveal.

CHAPTER TWO

GLENN AND KATHY WILBURN

T HE BOYS WERE the heart and soul of the house. They lived with their mother and grandparents, three generations together in the suburbs of Oklahoma City. Chase was three; Colton was two. They were lively spirits, with faces lifted from the frescoes of Fra Angelico.

On weekdays they would be dropped off at *America's Kids* on the second floor of the Alfred P. Murrah Building. Their mother, Edye Smith, worked as a secretary for the IRS, four blocks away. So did their grandmother, Kathy Wilburn, a training instructor.

The daycare center was an extra perk the two women enjoyed as federal employees. They did not know at the time that none of the law enforcement agents put their own children in the crèche as a matter of policy. Nor did they know that the ATF, the Secret Service, and U.S. Customs had offices in the building.[1]

Glenn Wilburn doubled as father and grandfather. A courteous, gentle, well-fed fellow, aged 44, he had a successful practice as a certified public accountant. He drove a big silver Mercedes 380SE and looked the part of a prosperous citizen of stature, but his tastes were simple. In the evenings after work he would take his grandsons down to the park. On weekends he would take them to a movie. They watched *The Lion King* three times.

Glenn had no interest in politics. He did not listen to talk radio. The word militia had never crossed his lips. He had not given much thought to Ruby Ridge, or Nafta, or anything else that was exercising so many Americans in the heartland, although he had cried watching the fiery denouement of the Branch Davidian siege. The knowledge that there were young children trapped inside was deeply disturbing to Glenn. But by and large he was a contented man, firm in his belief that the U.S. federal government was a force for good.

On Tuesday, April 18, 1995, Edye was sick with strep throat and stayed at home with the boys. The next day, Patriot's Day,[2] she was still feeling ill, but her colleagues had made her a birthday cake so she made the extra effort and struggled in to work.

It was the usual morning ritual. The boys were in Edye's bed, one snuggled up on each side. Glenn and Kathy burst in singing "good morning to you," and the scramble began.

"Glenn was helping with Colton. He had him sitting up on the bar in the kitchen, putting on his little blue sandals," said Kathy. "When he finished, Glenn kissed him on the forehead and said 'You're a good boy. Papa loves you.'"

*   *   *

The bomb went off at 9:02 AM.

Edye was about to blow out the candles on her birthday cake when the shock waves rocked the IRS building.

"I grabbed her and we rushed out into the street," recounted Kathy. "I could see smoke over towards the Murrah Building, and I screamed, 'Edye, the babies, the babies,' and we took off running."

"It was like the twilight zone. Big plate glass windows were still crashing out of the sky. There was this boom, boom, boom, and we saw all this black smoke everywhere. It was the cars going off in the parking lot."

"Then we saw it—the total devastation—and Edye crumbled to her knees. I put my arms around her and told her, 'It'll be alright.' But I knew it wasn't true. I knew already that our babies were gone."

Both boys were killed. A rescue worker had found Colton still breathing in the ruins, but he would not live long. His stomach had been ripped out. Kathy's grownup son Daniel had spotted the tiny two-year-old body laid out on a bench.

Glenn had already heard the news. When the women found him in the mayhem outside the Murrah Building, he was leaning over the hood of a pickup truck crying his heart out.

"That was when it all fell apart for Glenn," said Kathy. "It wasn't pancreatic cancer that killed him in the end. He really died of a broken heart."

That night they huddled together at home, silently watching the TV news. The camera picked out a solitary shoe on the edges of the smoking rubble. It was the blue sandal that Glenn had slipped onto Chase's tiny foot that morning.

Anger, grief, confusion—it was the same for all the families. Glenn and Kathy turned the boys' room into a shrine, untouched from that day forth, the teddy bears stacked neatly on each of the little beds. The most poignant memento was a ticket found in Chase's pocket. It was for a Sesame Street Live show entitled "When I grow up."

Within days of the bombing, the rumors began to circulate. People talked of seeing bomb squads in downtown Oklahoma in the early hours of the morning before the blast. It was said that the ATF did not come to work that morning at the Murrah Building. The families noticed that none of the ATF agents were on the casualty list.

It was the usual sort of talk after a disaster of this scale. Glenn did not pay too much attention at first. He assumed like everybody else that the FBI and the U.S. Justice Department would do all they could to establish the truth. One hundred and sixty-eight people had been killed. It was the most deadly act of terrorism in the history of the United States. If there was a bomb squad on alert that morning, the full story would come out soon enough.

But Edye Smith began to sense that the Justice Department was dissembling. There was a hint of arrogance in the responses of U.S. Attorney Pat Ryan. The man was pleasant enough, but he did not make a serious effort to answer the questions of the families. When Edye asked where the ATF agents were on April 19 he brushed her off with a glib comment that they were playing in a golf tournament at Shawnee. He was mistaken. Some of the DEA were playing golf, but not the ATF.

She contacted the ATF directly, only to hear a babel of improvised spin. There were two ATF agents in their offices on the ninth floor that day, said one message on her answering machine. No, there were four, said another message, left by another official the same day. Edye was being trifled with. Her grief turned to anger. On May 23, 1995, the day the ruined Murrah Building was brought down with demolition charges, she erupted in a live interview on CNN.

"Where the hell was the ATF, I want to know?" she thundered, red hair flying in the breeze. "All fifteen or seventeen of their employees survived, and they were on the ninth floor. They were the target of this explosion, and where were they? Did they have a warning sign? Did they think it might be a bad day to go into the office? They had an option not to go to work that day, and my kids didn't. They didn't get that option. Nobody else in the building got that option. And we're just asking questions. We're not making accusations. We just want to know. And they're telling us: 'Keep your mouth shut, don't talk about it.'"

CNN cut her off soon enough, but the impact was searing. Edye Smith, aggrieved and defiant, had thrown down the gauntlet. There would be no turning back.

Deluged with calls from the media, the ATF issued a press release. "I strongly suspect that these malicious rumors are fueled by the same sources as the negative rhetoric that has been recently circulating about law enforcement officers," said Lester D. Martz, the special agent in charge of the Dallas regional office. "The facts are that the ATF's employees in Oklahoma City were carrying out their assigned duties as they would any workday, and several of them were injured in the explosion."[3]

In fact, the only people in the office to suffer injuries were two clerical workers. None of the ATF's field agents were hurt.

If Lester Martz had stopped there, the matter might have subsided. But he overreached, the instinctive reflex of an agency accustomed to operating without accountability. "We were there, and we were heroes," he said. The ATF claimed that Alex McCauley, the resident agent in charge, was in an elevator when the bomb went off. He survived a free fall from the eighth to the third floor. McCauley escaped by breaking through the thick metal doors, and went on to rescue survivors in the stairwell.

If the ATF thought they could get away with this farrago, they had underestimated the 23-year-old redhead and her affable stepfather. Curiosity piqued, the Wilburns tried their hand as amateur sleuths. With the help of a freelance reporter, John "J. D." Cash, Glenn contacted the Midwestern Elevator Company, the firm that had actually searched the elevators for survivors.

"The first thing we did was split up and check, then double check, each elevator for occupants," explained Duane James, one of the engineers. "We found that five of the six elevators were frozen between floors, and a sixth had stopped near floor level…. We had to go in through the ceilings of the elevators to check for people…. All were empty."

Agent Alex McCauley could not possibly have broken out before the team arrived, said James, "not unless he had a blowtorch with him…. The doors were all frozen shut…. It took several of our men over twelve hours just to get the one elevator [opened]."

None of the elevators had been in a free fall. "That's pure fantasy. Modern elevators have counterbalances and can't free fall unless you cut the cables, and none were. There are a series of backup safety switches that will lock an elevator in place if it increases in speed more than 10 percent."

The Midwestern Elevator Company took extensive photographs to document the inspection. These records were later reviewed by ABC's *20/20* program. The pictures confirmed that all the safety cables were intact.

As the details emerged, the ATF began to back away from its claims, suggesting that the blast created the sensation of a falling elevator. "Well, maybe Agent McCauley just imagined he free fell," said Lester Martz in a taped telephone interview with J. D. Cash.

Agent McCauley was transferred to Kansas City and quietly demoted. The Justice Department, however, clung resolutely to the story of his accomplishments. Joseph Hartzler, the chief prosecutor in the case against McVeigh, repeated the tale in a court filing on November 7, 1996, dismissing any doubts about the matter as "outrageous."[4] At the time, Hartzler already had the FD-302 witness statements given to the FBI by the elevator engineers, all concurring that the story was fabricated. But Hartzler has never been held to account for deliberately misinforming the court.

The Wilburns had walked through the looking glass. They now knew for a fact that the head of the ATF's office in Oklahoma City was a shameless liar. And they were learning that some of the others were just as bad. On May 24, 1995, the day after Edye's outburst on CNN, Glenn was visited by two ATF agents. It was a contentious meeting. Glenn pressed them hard. "Didn't April 19 have any significance to your people? You know, Patriot's Day, the Waco raid?"

"No, there was no alert, or any concern on our part about the significance of that day," replied Luke Franey, an undercover agent who sported long hair and a ring in one ear.[5]

Two hours later Glenn was watching the news. It was a live interview with John Magaw, the director of the ATF, explaining that the agency had taken special precautions on April 19. "I was very concerned about that day and issued memos to all our field offices. They were put on alert," said Magaw.

It was the lies that offended Glenn more than anything else. One lie, after another, after another.

Fresh leads were coming thick and fast. A sheriff's deputy had scribbled a quick note for Edye when he recognized her at the courthouse one day. Slipping the message into her hand, he added *sotto voce*: "God bless you people."[6] The note said that Charles Gaines, chief of operations for the Oklahoma City Fire Department, had received a terrorism alert on Good Friday before the bombing.

Glenn paid the man a visit.

"I understand that the FBI called you," he said, glowering across the desk. "That's correct isn't it, Mr. Gaines?"

"I don't know what you're talking about."[7]

"You know damn well what I'm talking about, you were put on alert five days before the bomb went off, weren't you?"

Gaines grabbed his hat and hurried out the door, saying that he was late for an appointment. Glenn wandered down the hall until he found an open door. It was the office of Harvey Weathers, the chief of dispatchers. He tried again.

"You're right," said Weathers. "We got a message from the FBI on the Friday before the bombing. We were told to be on alert for terrorist activity in the near future. I passed it down the line."

"Well, it looks like Chief Gaines's memory is failing. He said it never happened," said Glenn.

"You asked me, and I told you. I'm not going to lie for anybody."[8]

An alert can mean all kinds of things, but this appeared to go beyond the typical *pro forma* advisories put out on sensitive dates. U.S. Federal Judge Wayne Alley had spilled the beans in a spontaneous interview with *The Oregonian* newspaper a few hours after the blast. Yes, he said, his chambers were just across the street from the Murrah Building. But no, he was not hurt. He had decided not come into work that day. There had been talk.

"Let me just say that within the past two or three weeks, information has been disseminated… that indicated concerns on the part of people who ought to know, that we ought to be a little more careful…. My subjective impression was there was a reason for a dissemination of these concerns."

No doubt his guard was down. The reporter was calling from Portland, where the judge grew up, and Portland was far away. But in the age of the Internet, it does not take long for a revelation in *The Oregonian* to reach the families of the dead in Oklahoma City. When a copy fell into Glenn's hands, he was apoplectic.

"We took babies to that building to be protected and cared for," he said. "If anyone knew there was danger in that area and it was not disseminated, then I am mad. I'm awfully damned mad."

The rumors of a bomb squad started becoming real as witnesses came out of the shadows to tell their story. The Wilburns collected testimony on microcassettes, which were piled up in a box in their kitchen. They amassed more than three hundred hours of interviews, much of it with people who had never spoken to the press.

"People don't want to talk, you know. They're afraid of retribution from the federal government, they're scared for their jobs," said Glenn.

But he and Kathy knew how to draw them out. Glenn would introduce himself and talk about Chase and Colton, and his quest for the truth. Kathy followed, with her forbidding silences, and, when necessary, would seize the throat of a recalcitrant witness and question his manhood—or so she told me. In my company she has always been the model of decorum.

There was no question that there had been a bomb squad truck in downtown Oklahoma before the blast.

"I was coming down for a charity board meeting that I had at 7:30 in the Oklahoma Tower," said Daniel J. Adomitis, an Oklahoma lawyer. "There was this fairly large truck with a trailer behind it. It had a shield on the side of the door that said 'bomb disposal' or 'bomb squad' below it. And I really found that interesting. You know, I'd never seen anything like that in person."

Something was still going on fifteen minutes later when Norma Jolson arrived for work at the county courthouse. "As I walked through my building's parking lot, I remember seeing a bomb squad," she said. "There was some talk in our office. We did wonder what it was doing in our parking lot. Jokingly, I said, 'Well, I guess we'll find out soon enough.'"

At 8:05, Renée Cooper dropped her son Antonio at the day care center. As she was driving away she saw a bomb squad in front of the courthouse. There were six or seven men. It made her a little uneasy, but she was late for work already.

"I quizzed her at length," said Glenn. "I said, 'How do you know this was a bomb squad?'"

"Well, they had 'bomb squad' written across their jackets in huge letters."[9]

Renée Cooper's FBI 302 statement makes it sound as if she had confused the 18th of April with the 19th, as if she would forget the moment that killed her baby boy. It was insulting. She had told this story two weeks after the bombing during a meal at the Wilburn house for all the families who lost children in the day care center.

In any case, the transparent absurdity of the FBI's ruse was exposed when the Sheriff's Department finally admitted, after months of adamant denials by Sheriff J. D. Sharp, that the bomb disposal vehicle had indeed been in downtown Oklahoma City that morning.[10]

The driver was Deputy Bill Grimsley. He said that he set out from the county jail at 7:00 AM, stopped at the courthouse for a few minutes to take care of an errand, then went to McDonald's for an

Egg McMuffin and a coffee, and finally made his way to the bomb training squad ten miles outside Oklahoma City.[11] So, the vehicle was there. The only questions were: What it was doing? Why had the Sheriff's Department refused to acknowledge a plain fact? And why had the FBI tried to obfuscate it?

*   *   *

In the first months after the Oklahoma bombing, I was wary of tackling the subject. There were intriguing stories coming out in the alternative press, as well as the usual mix of planted disinformation and off-the-wall conspiracy theories. I preferred to wait and see, assuming that the Justice Department was essentially still honorable, and that the full story would be forced to the surface in the trial of Timothy McVeigh.

The Oklahoma bombing, after all, was one of the epochal events of U.S. history. The great metropolitan newspapers would ensure accountability. The rest of the world was watching to see how the U.S. system would handle domestic terrorist insurgency. This crime was so big that it had to be prosecuted with total transparency. Or so I thought. It makes me want to blush now, to think I could have been so naive.

But then I met Glenn Wilburn, and I realized at once that this man knew what he was talking about. He was a certified public accountant. He dealt in details. He argued along a chain of logic, inductively, from the facts to the theory, not the other way round. He was empirical. And when he walked me through the evidence, he shattered my last illusions. As a journalist, this was the man I wanted as my source, my guide, my mentor, and he was generous enough to respond—squeezing out every last drop of energy until cancer finally consumed him.

The kidney-shaped table in the kitchen of Glenn and Kathy had become the nerve-center of the Oklahoma dissident movement. Their closest friend and ally was J. D. Cash from *The McCurtain*

Daily Gazette. At Glenn's insistence, Cash had more or less moved in with them as a houseguest, commuting back and forth from his home in Idabel, southeastern Oklahoma.

"When I first met John, I thought he was awful crusty looking, like a member of the militia or something," said Kathy, laughing. "But that's just John…. He fit right into the family soon enough."

A tall, thin man with a scraggly beard, dressed in jeans and cowboy boots, J. D. Cash had once been married to a Cherokee Indian. Now he was a bachelor again, a sort of Knight Templar in the crusade for truth. Cash took pride in his defiant stand against the health fetishism of yuppy culture. His day began with a cigarette. Breakfast was a T-bone steak. By late afternoon he was already opening his first can of beer, to be followed by vodka. This was the sort of conduct I expected from a reporter, a soothing respite from the twitchy, uptight, prissy, desiccated ghastliness of the Washington press corps.

Cash was a retired mortgage banker, aged 43, writing a novel about Nazi gold when the bomb went off. Soon afterward, he heard about seismograph data from the University of Oklahoma indicating that there could have been a secondary blast, and it set him thinking about a time in the late 1980s when the IRS had tried to lease one of his buildings in Tulsa. The deal had fallen through because the IRS Criminal Investigations Division had wanted to store "raid equipment," including C-4 explosives, in the building. "I knew these guys kept some bad stuff around, so I started trying to find out if the Feds were storing C-4 in the Murrah Building."[12]

He soon confirmed his suspicions. "I can assure you, Mr. Cash, there were explosives stored in the building. I saw them carry them out," he was told by a fire marshal. "They threw them in the bomb squad truck, hauled them out to the gun range, and blew them up."

He learned that C-4 can detonate spontaneously, without a fuse, if subjected to intense pressure. It was the genesis of his first article. He went to the local newspaper in Idabel, *The McCurtain Daily*

Gazette, circulation 6,500, and offered his copy. They checked the facts and ran the piece. It won him an award for investigative reporting from the Society of Professional Journalists. "Beginner's luck, I think they call it," he quipped.

Cash never looked back. Within two years he would prove himself to be a reporter of extraordinary skill—a loose cannon, perhaps, a wild man, a transgressor of every rule in the Columbia School codex—but still one of the best investigative journalists of modern times.

"I have the instincts of a banker," he explained. "I've done thousands of loan interviews, and I've the best truth detector in the world. That's the one thing I've got going for me."

Among his friends was Richard Reyna, the court-appointed investigator for Timothy McVeigh. It was a relationship that would lead to an unholy alliance between the Wilburns and the defense lawyers of the man who murdered their grandchildren.

Documents have a habit of leaking when friendships are formed across a broad front, and it was not long before the Wilburns acquired the raw material of the OKBOMB investigation—FBI 302 witness statements, Tim McVeigh's phone logs, surveillance reports, the unfiltered facts. They were no longer competing at a total disadvantage against the U.S. Justice Department.

The alliance made sense. The Wilburns and the McVeigh defense team had parallel interests. Both wanted to know whether the U.S. government was telling the truth. "This is warfare," explained Glenn. "And we'll do anything it takes to get to the truth."

It caused consternation in Oklahoma City. Glenn and Kathy were denounced by the state media as "conspiracy theorists" and tools of the far-right. For a year they endured bitter recriminations from many of the families.

"There was one meeting that got out of control. There were some nuts there, handing out crazy literature. They had such weird extreme views that it scared everybody, and we sort of got mixed up in the pot with them," said Kathy. "The families started yelling at us. They hated us for a long time after that."

But that would change.

When the Wilburns filed a federal tort claim against the U.S. government in April 1997, just in time for the two-year statutory deadline, they were joined by 170 of the Oklahoma family members. It was an avalanche, one of such irresistible force that it may ultimately sweep away much of the political landscape of *fin de siècle* America.

The claim alleges that the U.S. federal government "knew or should have known" that the Murrah Building was a likely target of attack.[13] Their chief counsel, Connecticut lawyer Richard Bieder, brought in three other law firms with specialist expertise in a legal alliance that had very deep pockets and a track record of confronting the government.

Another group of five families signed up shortly afterward with the Los Angeles firm Baum, Hedland, Aristie, Guilford, and Downey. Finally, more than 300 family members joined a third suit with John Merritt in Oklahoma State jurisdiction against the FBI, the ATF, and other agencies of the U.S. government. The Merritt lawsuit alleged outright that the disaster was a failed "sting operation."

The claim stated that the U.S. authorities had "detailed prior knowledge of the planned bombing of the Murrah Building yet failed to prevent the bombing from taking place." It alleged that ATF agents were "alerted not go to work on April 19, 1995."[14]

Civil lawsuits are the great purgative instrument of the American system. They are the safeguard against abuse. The rules of civil litigation are very different from criminal trials. The power to subpoena documents and witnesses under legal discovery is much broader, while the power of tame judges to exclude evidence is much narrower. The truth has a way of forcing itself to the surface.

CHAPTER THREE

JOHN DOE TWO

NOT ALL OF THE 168 victims of the Oklahoma bombing died on U.S. federal property. Some died on the streets and in the buildings of Oklahoma County, victims of murder within state jurisdiction.

It was a small point, lost on most people, but Glenn Wilburn seized on it as a second lever to pry the case loose from the U.S. Justice Department. Teaming up with State Representative Charles Key, he began a long, bitter campaign to force the District Attorney to call a county grand jury.

The endeavor seemed hopelessly quixotic. It was greeted with derision and opprobrium from the entire power structure of the state. "The worst kind of conspiracy pandering," said Drew Edmondson, the Attorney General of Oklahoma. "The very idea that a county grand jury could uncover something that the FBI do not know already is ridiculous," he said. Taxpayers' money should not be spent on a "wasteful witchhunt."

"Drop it, Mr. Key," was the title of an editorial in *The Daily Oklahoman*. Drop this "weird and misguided exercise." But

Representative Key had no intention of dropping it, even if it meant political suicide. A round, voluble, impulsive man, he forged ahead, vilified by his colleagues in the Republican Party, and by Governor Frank Keating, a former Justice Department official and FBI agent.

One step at a time, Charles Key and Glenn Wilburn pushed their initiative through Oklahoma courts. The district judge blocked it twice. "This court sees no reason to reinvent the wheel," he said. Finally, in February 1997, the Oklahoma Supreme Court ruled that Oklahomans have a right to petition for a grand jury if they can collect the requisite number of signatures.

It was a partial victory. District Attorney Bob Macy, who had fought the Wilburns all the way, would be the prosecutor in charge of the grand jury. He could sabotage it easily enough, if he tried. But the mood in Oklahoma was changing. People had been promised that the full truth would come out in the trial of Tim McVeigh, yet none of the outstanding questions had been answered.

For months, KTOK radio in Oklahoma City had been hammering away at the incoherence of the government case. By the summer of 1997, when the first witnesses were called before the Key-Wilburn grand jury, polls showed that 70 percent of Oklahomans no longer believed the U.S. Justice Department. They no longer believed that Tim McVeigh had blown up the Murrah Building on his own on April 19, 1995. Indeed, it had reached a point where people in Oklahoma County were treating the Clinton administration's "lone bomber" theory with open disrespect.

In principle, at least, Representative Key and his allies could now do what the federal grand jury had failed to do in 1995. The last effort had been a "dog and pony show," in the words of Hoppy Heidelberg, a race horse breeder of admirably stubborn temperament who had served on the grand jury in the summer of 1995.

When Heidelberg could endure the stench no longer he stepped forward and launched a blistering attack on the prosecution. The people of Oklahoma had been deceived, he said, when the bombing indictment named Tim McVeigh, Terry Nichols, and "others unknown to the grand jury." The government had no intention of finding out who the "others" were. In fact, it had gone to great lengths to suppress evidence indicating that McVeigh was acting as part of a terrorist team on April 19, 1995.

"I knew it was a coverup when they wouldn't show a sketch of John Doe Two to the witnesses," he said. "They brought in all these people who knew nothing about the bombing, but they wouldn't call the real witnesses who'd seen McVeigh at the crime scene. And why? Because they all saw other men with McVeigh, that's why, and they didn't want the citizens of this country to find out about that."[1]

John Doe Two was the thick-set, swarthy suspect seen at Elliot's Body Shop in Junction City, Kansas, with Tim McVeigh. The two men arrived together to rent the Ryder bomb truck. McVeigh signed the rental contract, using the alias of Robert Kling, and chatted with the staff while John Doe Two waited in silence.

There were actually two different sketches of McVeigh's accomplice. The first one, the one that was published on the front page of almost every newspaper in America, was so inaccurate that it was worse than useless. It was a frontal portrait of a thuggish-looking man with heavy jowls. But the witness had seen only a profile of the suspect, and the FBI artist had used a highly manipulative process of choosing faces from a catalog. An outside sketch artist, Jean Boylan, was asked to try again. She drew a face that was finer, more handsome, with less of the gorilla about him. This was the real, "pretty-boy," John Doe Two.

For almost three months he was the quarry of a massive manhunt by the FBI, or so America was led to believe. Then on June 14, 1995, the Justice Department announced that it had all been a big mistake. One of the witnesses, Eldon Elliot, had been confused when he gave his description of John Doe Two. He had mixed him up with Todd Bunting, a burly army private who came to the office a day later.

(Eldon Elliot had not been the only witness, of course, but the FBI did not mention that at the time.)

The Justice Department could do or say whatever it wanted. That was the prerogative of power. The mystery was why any educated American would believe such self-evident nonsense. It was demonstrably untrue that Tim McVeigh was operating alone in Junction City before the bombing, or that he continued to operate alone in Oklahoma City on April 19. One of the few unassailable facts of this case is that McVeigh was accompanied by other men at every stage. Glenn Wilburn, Charles Key, and J. D. Cash knew it. They lived and breathed it. They had so many witnesses to prove it, that they could only laugh or cry at the preposterous representations of the OKBOMB investigation.

At the risk of being prolix, it is worth listing some of the witnesses who saw the procession of terrorists—John Doe Two, Three, Four, perhaps even more—making their way through Junction City and Herington, Kansas, and Oklahoma City in the ambit and company of Timothy McVeigh. Even those familiar with the case, however, may be surprised to learn of the trail of bitterness and frustration left by the FBI.

KANSAS

In interviews conducted on April 19 and 20, the staff at Elliot's Body Shop told the FBI they saw Tim McVeigh accompanied by another man. They were not vague about it. They were categorical.

The debriefing began within seven hours of the bombing. Their memories were fresh, so fresh that they were able to provide the uncanny look-alike sketch of McVeigh, which led to his arrest. Eldon Elliot even tried to capitalize on this, selling T-shirts with the logo "We Remember Our Customers."[2] Contrary to press accounts, none of these witnesses has retracted the core claim that there were two men.

* Eldon Elliot, owner.

In pre-trial hearings on February 18, 1997, he continued to insist that "another person was standing there. I glanced at him." Elliot went out front with the two men to inspect the truck. He said the accomplice had a "white hat with blue lightning bolts on the side." He had told the FBI earlier that the man was "a white male, 5′ 7″ to 5′ 8″."[3]

* Tom Kessinger, mechanic.

He was taking a break in the rental office at about 4:15 PM, eating popcorn, when the two men came in. He watched them for about 10 minutes. John Doe Two was wearing "a black T-shirt, jeans, and a ball-cap colored royal blue in the front and white in the back." He was "about 5′ 10″, clean-shaven, muscular, large arms, large chest, smooth complexion, thick neck, wide chin... tattoo on his upper left arm, 26 to 27, and white."[4]

A year and a half later, after seven debriefings by the FBI, he said that he had confused the face of John Doe Two with Private Bunting.[5] But this does not pass the smell test. When he was visited by Glenn Wilburn in the summer of 1996 he scoffed at the Bunting canard. "He was laughing about it and said 'I don't know where they came up with that one.'"[6]

In any case, he refused to go through with the deception when questioned under oath. During the pre-trial hearings in Denver in February 1997 he repeated his claim that McVeigh was accompanied by another man. The Justice Department decided to drop him as a trial witness.

* Vicki Beemer, bookkeeper.

She had a friendly chat with McVeigh as he was filling out the rental papers, noting that she had been married longer than he had been alive. She testified at McVeigh's trial that she was "very certain" there was a second man.

She told the FBI on April 19 that she "recalled a second person being along but has no recollection of that individual."[7] But in her appearance before the federal grand jury in Oklahoma she described him as a "stocky-built gentleman... darker complected and much larger" than McVeigh.[8]

It seems that half of Junction City and Herington, Kansas, saw McVeigh consorting with other men over the Easter weekend, from the 14th to the 18th of April. Here is a sampler, by no means the full list.

* Nancy Jean Kindle, seating hostess at Denny's Restaurant.

One of the few witnesses called to the trial, she testified that McVeigh came into Denny's at lunchtime on Easter Sunday with two other men. One of them was "a scraggly looking man, about 5´ 7˝." She remembers McVeigh because she asked him to spell out his name... and she thought he was "cute."[9]

* Elenora Hull, elderly lady from Junction City.

She saw McVeigh with two other men when she was having lunch at Denny's on Friday, April 14. The men were at the next table. One of them looked "very scary." She noticed that there were two Ryder trucks outside.

* Tonya, whose last name remains confidential.[10]

McVeigh and John Doe Two came in on Monday at about midday. She described the man as extremely handsome, wearing a bomber jacket. He wanted a haircut but she was having to rush out to pick up a child at 12:00 PM.

* Jeff Davis, deliveryman for the Hunan Palace Restaurant. (Now a provost marshal at Fort Riley.)

He delivered an order of *moo goo gai pan* and egg rolls to the Dreamland Motel on Saturday afternoon, April 15, at about 5:45 PM. The delivery log said "Kling, Room 25." It was the same room that

McVeigh had rented after haggling down the price to $20 a night. But the man who was standing in the doorway was not McVeigh.[11]

Davis and the man chatted briefly. The man gave him $11 for a $9.65 order. He was at least 6′ 2″, aged 28 or 29, 180 to 190 pounds, with "short hair, real dark blonde" that was "generally unkempt" and "tousled about." He had a "slight overbite," and a marked "regional" accent.[12]

Davis told *The Denver Post* that the FBI tried to talk him into saying the man was McVeigh. "I was frustrated quite a bit because they just didn't seem to want to say, 'Okay, there's somebody we may not have.' A lot of it seemed, 'Damn! I just wish he'd say it was McVeigh so we could be done with it.'"

* Hilda Sostre, maid at the Dreamland Motel.

At 9:00 AM on Monday morning, April 17, she started to unlock the door of Room 25, thinking that McVeigh had already left, when a man appeared and handed her some towels. It was definitely not McVeigh. "He was dark and not so tall, I thought he looked like one of my people," she said, referring to her native country of Puerto Rico. "He had these big strong arms."[13]

* Barbara Whittenberg, runs the Santa Fe Trail Inn in Herington.

McVeigh, Terry Nichols, and a third man came into the diner for a coffee between 6:00 and 7:00 AM on Saturday morning. She already knew Nichols, who used to drop in for a meal from time to time. The third man had a "Hawaiian sort of face" with "no neck, wide lips." He looked like a bodybuilder.

She noticed that they had a Ryder truck and a car with Arizona plates. Since she was from Arizona herself, she started chatting and breezily asked where they were headed.

"Oklahoma," said the third man.

"McVeigh looked at him and you could feel buckets of ice being poured over our conversation," she said. "I got out of it."[14]

Later that day, Whittenberg stopped at Lake Geary on her way up to Junction City. Her aging husband had a bladder problem, so this was one of their regular pit stops.

She saw a Ryder truck, like the one at the diner that morning, parked at the lake. This was significant. The original indictment stated that McVeigh and Nichols had built the bomb in a Ryder truck at Lake Geary, but they said it happened on Tuesday, April 18, the day after McVeigh had rented the truck. Whittenberg saw a Ryder truck at Lake Geary on Saturday.

"The FBI never asked for a composite sketch or anything. They told me my story couldn't be true. They just didn't believe me," said Whittenberg. "They told me not to tell anybody what I knew, but after a year it's time to tell the world what's really going on."[15]

The Denver Post found four other witnesses who had seen the Ryder truck sitting at the lake days before McVeigh was supposed to have rented it. After a six-month investigation *The Post* concluded that two Ryder trucks were involved, not one. This extra Ryder truck, stated the newspaper, "could hold the key to unlocking one of the most enduring mysteries in the case—how many people were involved in the bombing."

* Lea McGown, the fierce but engaging German in charge of the Dreamland Motel, says that McVeigh appeared with a Ryder truck on Sunday, April 16, the day *before* he rented the bomb truck from Elliot's. Her recollection is vivid.

"He backed in jerky, jerky, jerky. Like somebody who doesn't know how to drive a truck," she said. "I thought he was going to smash my roof."

He parked on a soil embankment that could not support the weight. She sent her son Eric to ask McVeigh to move the truck over to the open area in front of the office. The Ryder was light yellow, with a faded appearance. She got a good look at it while she was standing at the counter waiting for customers.

The next day she noticed that McVeigh had a different Ryder truck. This was the one he had rented from Elliot's Body Shop. It was newer, with an orange-yellow color and square cab.

"FBI came in every day for three weeks, asking the same dumb questions over and over again, twisting everything around. I wasted so much time," she said. "They always said I'm not right, because it doesn't fit the picture, see."

"I'm very disappointed with the system, I must say. It's no wonder people turn against the government. I'm not helping them any more, I can tell you that," she said, adding that the FBI seemed to be covering up their own mistakes. "If you did something wrong, admit it, straighten it out. It's very simple, isn't it?"

* David King, a guest at the Dreamland, noticed the same switch. He saw an old "faded yellow" Ryder on Sunday. The next day McVeigh was there with a "brand new, aerodynamic" model, accompanied by two other men attaching a trailer. They blocked the access to his parking spot.[16]

* Herta King, David King's mother.
She testified at McVeigh's trial that she saw the large Ryder truck parked at the Dreamland Motel that Sunday when she was bringing an Easter basket to her son.

* Renda Truong, high school student.
Also called to testify by the defense, she noticed the Ryder truck at the motel when she was having Easter dinner with the McGown family. Again, this was the day before the bomb truck was rented.

THE CRIME SCENE

At the trial in Denver, the prosecution did not call a single witness who could place Tim McVeigh in Oklahoma City on April 19, 1995. This is a rather astonishing fact, when you consider that the

government called 27 phone-company employees to establish that
McVeigh had used a pre-paid phone card bought under the alias of
Daryl Bridges.

But such was the trial: 27 witnesses brought in from all over the
country to support a secondary point, but no crime scene witnesses
from Oklahoma City.

This was not for lack of volunteers. Glenn Wilburn had tracked
down a dozen people who had seen McVeigh between 8:00 and
9:00 AM in the downtown area. But in every case they had seen
McVeigh with other men, apparently operating as part of a terrorist
cell.

The credibility of these witnesses ranged across the continuum,
but several were compelling. Glenn kept his taped interviews in a
box full of microcassettes in the kitchen, close at hand for visiting
journalists in need of education.

* Kyle Hunt, vice-president of a Tulsa bank.

He was arriving for an 8:30 AM meeting when he saw a yellow
Ryder truck on Robinson Street, followed by a four-door sedan with
three men inside. One of the men was looking up, straining his neck.
The group looked lost. As Hunt pulled closer, the driver of the
sedan warned him off.

"I got an icy cold, go-to-hell look from the young man that I now
know to be Tim McVeigh. It was unnerving," he said. "I kept tabs
on the group for a few moments while we were approaching Main
Street. All three men in the truck were caucasians; and how many
may have been in the Ryder, I couldn't tell."[17]

* Dave Snider, warehouse worker.

He was waiting for a delivery in the Bricktown area of Oklahoma
City at about 8:40 AM when he saw a Ryder truck turn the corner. It
was coming toward him very slowly. Thinking it was for him, he
waved the truck down.

As it passed by, very slowly, Tim McVeigh glowered at him from the passenger's seat. The driver was a darker, stockier man.[18]

* Mike Moroz, attendant at Johnny's Tire Service.

A Ryder truck pulled in at about 8:45 AM. Tim McVeigh got out and politely asked directions to 5th Street and Harvey. There was a darker, thicker set, morose-looking man in the cab of the truck.[19]

* Daina Bradley, bombing victim.

It is a gruesome story. On April 19 she went to the Social Security Office on the first floor of the Murrah Building with her mother, her sister, and her two tiny children. As she was filling out documents in front of the Fifth Street window, she saw a Ryder truck pull into a parking place between the two cars. A man got out of the passenger seat facing her, went to the back of the truck, and then strode down the sidewalk very fast toward Harvey Street. "He was acting very mysterious, and very nervous," she said.[20]

"It was an olive-complexion[ed] man with short hair, curly, clean-cut. He had on a blue starter jacket, blue jeans, and tennis shoes and a white hat with purple flames," she said. He had a tanned look, a slim build.[21]

She stepped back from the window and made a comment to her mother about the truck. It struck her as unusual. The next thing she remembered was a feeling of electricity running through her body, then a flash of light, and the sensation of crashing down into the rubble. Her children were killed. So was her mother. She herself was trapped for five hours. A doctor had to crawl into the rubble and amputate her leg with a saw before rescue workers could pull her out. It was too hazardous to use anesthetics so she had to endure unspeakable pain.

In her interviews with the FBI on May 3 and May 21, 1995, she said the man resembled the sketch of John Doe Two. "That was the same guy I seen get out of the truck," she said.[22] She did not see any other man get out of the truck, nor did she recognize the artist's sketch of McVeigh. This was a position she maintained for two years.

The defense team decided to take a calculated risk by calling her as a witness. They underestimated the persuasive power of the U.S. Justice Department.

On May 16, a week before her testimony, she was visited by a member of the prosecution team. Five days later she met with U.S. Attorney Pat Ryan. All of a sudden, she could remember a second man getting out of the driver's side and walking quickly across the street. He had a baby face. She did not see him clearly. It might have been McVeigh. Or, it might not have. She didn't know.

The reaction to Daina Bradley's testimony is a nice exhibit of the deformed media culture in the United States. In a country with an adversarial press—certainly Britain, France, or Spain—the newspapers would have honed in with irreverent zest on the one salient fact of the matter. Ms. Bradley had made a mockery of the government's "lone bomber theory." She was the only crime scene witness called to the stand, and she had testified, categorically, that she saw John Doe Two get out of the Ryder truck.

But no, the U.S. press did not notice this, or feigned not to notice it. Instead, Americans were informed the next day that the subpoena of Daina Bradley was a disastrous own-goal for the defense. It was the usual, exasperating, winner-loser, who's-up-who's-down vacuousness. It was a dubious point anyway. In the end, her testimony had little or no bearing on the outcome of the trial.

With the abdication of the grand press, Americans have had to turn elsewhere for a more illuminating perspective: notably *The John Doe Times*. It is an internet cyber-journal published by a warehouse manager in Birmingham, Alabama—Mike Vanderboegh—dedicated to exposing evidence of a broader conspiracy. It is Vanderboegh's belief that the bombing was carried out by the terrorist wing of the U.S. fascist movement.

He was drawn into the Oklahoma bombing case in late 1995 when he sat down for a coffee with a federal agent in Birmingham, Alabama. It was a cordial meeting. Vanderboegh's militia group had done a favor for the Feds, helping them crack a case involving theft from a military base.

"He pulled out a piece of paper with the name, social security number, and profile of Andreas Strassmeir," recalled Vanderboegh. "He said, 'We've gone as far as we can with this; we've been told to back off. Maybe you guys can do something with it.' Then he told me Strassmeir had been the government-sponsored snitch inside the Oklahoma bombing. He walked me through the whole thing."[23]

Andreas Strassmeir was a former German infantry officer who had gained entry into the U.S. neo-Nazi movement and established himself as the chief of security at Elohim City, the movement's paramilitary headquarters in eastern Oklahoma. At the time, it was not known there might be a neo-Nazi link to the bombing, but it made sense to Vanderboegh. He had been tracking the activities of the white supremacist far-right, which he regarded as an extremely dangerous terrorist movement and a threat to the political stability of the United States.

Vanderboegh did not know what to do with the information about Strassmeir and the terrorist conspiracy at Elohim City. Months later he read an article about Glenn and Kathy Wilburn. (It happened to be a piece I had written for *The Telegraph*, which had been posted on the Internet.) He called them in Oklahoma City and signed on to help them find the truth. "I became their Sancho Panza. It's been the greatest honor of my life to be their friend."

It was a healing process for the portly, 43-year-old warehouse manager to be of service to the victims of April 19. "Imagine what it felt like to be a militia guy when everybody started saying the militia blew up that building in Oklahoma."

Vanderboegh styles himself Brevet Colonel of the *1st Alabama Cavalry Regiment*, one of the more colorful militia squadrons.

"We're light cavalry," he explained, laughing. "We've got a platoon of dirt bikes, and a team of ultra-lights for scouting."

Like a number of militia leaders, he was an activist in the antiwar movement in the 1960s. "I was a Leftist back in my callow youth, a Maoist actually," he said. "I remember cheering when we pulled out of Saigon. Then I learned about the reeducation camps and the killing fields, and that's when I started to change."

It did not take him long to find a crucial role in the Cash-Wilburn campaign. "We were getting all this exciting stuff. J. D. was writing these incredible pieces, and nobody was picking it up," he said. "So I did the only thing I knew how to do. I turned to the poor man's broadcast network."

In June of 1996 he posted the first edition of *The John Doe Times* on the Internet. It was not the only "OKC Bombing" site on the Net, but it was more tightly focused than the other websites. It was designed to propagate the findings of *The McCurtain Daily Gazette* and to expose Elohim City as the nerve-center of the bombing conspiracy. Over time it would acquire great influence.

The John Doe Times has continued to appear, week after week, for almost a year and a half. For Vanderboegh it has been a thankless task. He has made enemies on all fronts. The FBI and the ATF regard him as a menace. The far-right have declared him a mortal enemy of the Aryan cause. The mainstream media call him a crank. "I'm not winning any popularity contests here," he said. "It's tough for your family when you put yourself in a position where nobody loves you."

When Vanderboegh spoke to Glenn Wilburn and J. D. Cash he discovered that they knew all about Elohim City, and that they too were hearing things about the unlikely German infantry officer in charge of terrorist training.

J. D. Cash had been burrowing into Elohim for months, ever since he learned that Tim McVeigh had telephoned the enclave of Odinistic mystics two weeks before the bombing. In itself, the call did not mean much. McVeigh had contacted a large number of people, using the pre-paid telephone card in the name of Daryl Bridges. But this one occurred three seconds after he had telephoned a Ryder rental office in Lake Havasu, Arizona. And the call was for "Andy the German"—according to Joan Millar, who answered the telephone. "Tell Andy I'll be coming through," McVeigh had said.

There was something else that J. D. Cash had found out, a secret that he held very close to the vest. As we shall see, he had extracted a confession from a leader of the White Aryan Resistance, a wild emotional man named Dennis Mahon. During a five-hour whisky binge in January 1996, Mahon had implicated himself and several members of Elohim City in the Oklahoma bombing. It was not information that could be used in a newspaper. Nobody would have believed it. So Cash had to skirt around the edges, using the leads to find corroboration elsewhere.

Over the next year his articles in *The McCurtain Daily Gazette* sketched the outlines of a conspiracy at Elohim City. But it was one of those cases where the details were too arcane for the layman. Only the initiated could make any sense of it. In all likelihood the Cash-Wilburn theory would have remained a minority attraction—much discussed on talk radio, but essentially ignored by the rest of America—had it not been for J. D.'s discovery of an undercover informant for the ATF.

Her name was Carol Howe. In December 1996 she broke silence, telling J. D. Cash that she had infiltrated Elohim City and stumbled on a conspiracy to bomb federal buildings in the state of Oklahoma. The plot was led by Dennis Mahon and Andreas Strassmeir (Andy the German). Furthermore, she said, the main gist of this had been passed on to the U.S. government before the Oklahoma bombing.

He could not ask for more spectacular corroboration than that.

CHAPTER FOUR

ELOHIM CITY AND DENNIS THE MENACE

B IBLICAL SCHOLARS CANNOT agree about the meaning of the word *Elohim*. In the Latin Vulgate of St. Jerome, the Hebrew is translated, simply, as God, and thus was it passed on to western Christendom. But Hebrew purists bridle at such imprecision. They note that *Elohim* is a strictly plural form: Gods, not God. So perhaps it refers to the twin flames of the Godhead, or harkens back to the primordial polytheism of the Jewish tribes. Nobody quite knows, and that is doubtless the source of private satisfaction to Pastor Robert Millar, the founder, patriarch, and theologian of Elohim City.

Is it a Christian cult? Or is it outright paganism, a celebration of the occult practices of Druid, Norse, and Teutonic totemism?

Pastor Millar does not answer such questions. He sits contentedly, stroking his long, white, flowing beard, changing the subject to the less contentious matter of Celtic heraldry. The Highland tribes are his particular passion. He is an ethnic Scot, by way of Canada, and a proud subject of Her Majesty Queen Elizabeth—who is partly Scottish, of course, as well as being a lineal descendant of a Saxon deity on her father's side. A good pedigree.

His eccentric religion is known as Christian Identity, a British import from the 1870s. Drawing heavily on the "ancestral memory" theories of Carl Jung, the movement asserts that the white peoples of Europe are the lost tribes of Israel. Jews are deemed to be "half-devil" descendants of the "serpent seed," a union of Eve and Satan. The Jewish diaspora is the instrument of Satan to achieve dominion over the world—notably, by means of the United Nations.

Blacks do not fare well either in the eschatology of the cult. They are the cohorts of Satan. Before the end of the world in A.D. 2000, there will be a final confrontation between the Aryans and Satan's Jews. Asians are "mud" people.

It is race theology of the most fevered kind, laced with millenarian prophesy from the Old Testament and Wiccan nature worship. But it is not to be confused in any way with the virulent anti-Catholic tradition of the Ku Klux Klan. Pastor Millar holds a special affection for the Celtic fringe, especially the Irish. The Celts are the purest of the Aryan peoples because they were the last to succumb to "Judaic influences." It was Celtic culture that held out against "Nicean Christianity." The Celts were the chosen tribes. And as we shall see, Celtic-Americans would be the shock-troops of Elohim's secret military wing.

J. D. Cash took me to visit Pastor Millar in 1996 after the Elohim new year, which begins at the spring equinox. It took some courage for J. D. to keep going back after he had published stories linking Elohim to the Oklahoma bombing. But his body was already a patchwork of bullet holes and knife wounds from a rambunctious youth, and the risk of more punishment didn't seem to bother him. "Nah, they won't hurt me. They're really very nice people," he said with his characteristic dry wit. "They're actually some of the nicest Nazis you'll ever meet."

He liked to stop by every few weeks to barter information with Grandpa, as Pastor Millar was usually known. Grandpa always wanted the latest news from Satan's world, happily exchanging a useful nugget with J. D. for advance warning on the next story coming out in *The McCurtain Daily Gazette*.

Elohim City is a cluster of huts, caravans, and grubby dwellings at the end of a long dirt road in the wilderness of eastern Oklahoma, just a few miles from the Arkansas state line. It has a lumberyard and a small business leasing trucks. It was also under suspicion of "generating income through the sale of illegal drugs produced and grown on the 400-acre compound," according to surveillance reports by the Oklahoma Department of Public Safety.[1]

The Elohites knew we were coming. They have hidden pressure pads on the access road that sound the alarm.[2] We parked at the entrance to the City, next to a hobgoblin house built in the shape of a boot. Two young men armed with SKS assault rifles came to fetch us. One was wearing a T-shirt adorned with the face of Adolf Hitler. They were members of the "combat" patrol. Every able-bodied man, woman, and child above the age of twelve, I would later learn, was given training for the coming war against the U.S. government. They were divided into "snipers" and "combatants," the latter subjected to the full, excruciating bootcamp of their Prussian instructor, Lt. Andreas Carl Strassmeir.[3]

It was Saturday, the Sabbath at Elohim, so they escorted us up to the cavernous, polyurethane foam Worship House where the twenty-odd families of the commune were singing joyously and reciting poetry in accordance with their Christo-pagan rites. The virgins were performing the sword dance in their long flowing dresses and making eyes at their betrothed. Young children trotted about, and Aryan warriors marched back and forth with martial banners. There must have been a liturgy of sorts, somewhere at the core, but I could not discern the method of it. And all the while Grandpa sat there beside his two wives, pulling on his beard, with a beatific smile, delighted by the exuberance of his kin and his followers.

A virgin offered me lemonade and biscuits. She curtsied grace-fully. No doubt she, too, was a crack shot with an AK-47, but this was worship time. Her manners, the manners of all of them, were decorous.

"We have a guest from England," announced Grandpa as the very, very long service came to an end. "Perhaps he would be so gra-cious as to come forward and tell us about his country."

I was called to the floor, handed a microphone, and subjected to half an hour of polite interrogation. It began gently.

"What do you think of the United Nations?" asked Grandpa.

Knowing that they regarded the U.N. as the font of all evil, the command center of Zionist Occupied Government (ZOG), I con-fessed that my grandfather had been a U.N. ambassador, one of the founding delegates in fact, so perhaps I was not quite politically cor-rect on this subject. There was a puzzled silence while the Lord's cohorts waited to see if I was joking. I was not.

Grandpa came to the rescue, chuckling loudly. Just as J. D. had said, they are some of the nicest Nazis you'll ever meet.

Then the questioning became more pointed. What was I doing? Why was I there? Why did anybody in England care about Elohim City?

I told them that I was investigating the activities of Lt. Andreas Strassmeir, their military guru from 1991 until his flight in the sum-mer of 1995. I wanted to know whether Strassmeir was an authentic vagabond tourist with Aryan sympathies, as he purported to be, or whether he was in fact an undercover agent of the German govern-ment, or the U.S. government, or both. There were indications, I explained, that he may have been involved in the planning of the Oklahoma bombing.

Excuse me for being candid, I added.

"No, no, quite so, quite so," interjected Grandpa.

After the service, he invited us back to his house for a chicken din-ner. Engaging, with a lively, educated mind, he wanted to debate the relative merits of the parliamentary and presidential forms of government. "It's not every day I get a visit from an Oxford man," he said. The sly old fox.

"I'm a tribalist, really. I feel a great sense of kinship with the clans," he said, sitting back in a deep armchair, choosing his words carefully. He was far too shrewd to expose the darker side of his philosophy. "It is inherent in the nature of man that he should wish to mingle with his own kind. That is a lesson we seem to have forgotten, and we do so at our peril.... Don't you agree?"

"Yes, tribalism is indeed a powerful force in the world," I concurred, vaguely.

If one did not know it already, one would not have guessed that this small, round, genial intellectual was the leader of a cult that exalted Adolf Hitler, and by extension endorsed the Holocaust. But then one would not have guessed that he worked for the FBI either. But he did. He had been recruited as an FBI informant several years earlier. That stunning revelation would come out later in a Tulsa courtroom. Whether the FBI got anything useful out of him is another matter. It is my hunch that Grandpa outwitted the Bureau as masterfully as he outwits everybody else.

*   *   *

"I'm a terrorist with words. I terrorize with the truth," said Dennis Mahon, with a wink.

The former Imperial Dragon of the Ku Klux Klan was looking quite ridiculous. A big, strapping, handsome man with a pointed chin, and a comical turn of mind, he was wearing a tight T-shirt with *The Turner Diaries* printed on the front, and a black FBI cap. It was his new fad, this FBI cap.

"If I make a big joke about it—you know—what do you think?"

"I don't know, Dennis. A lot of people are beginning to think you work for the Bureau."

"They are? I wouldn't work for those clowns. They need me in this town, all right. If I go, they'll lose half their staff. I threatened to leave the state and they said, 'No, no, don't go, it'll put us out of business.' So I asked them for a commission."

"I can believe that, Dennis."

"Now the CIA, that's a different matter; that's a good organization," he said, holding his thoughts for a moment while he ordered the biggest plate of food on the menu. We were at Tally's, a Lebanese cafe in Tulsa where he tended to his Iraqi contacts. "You paying for this?"

"Anything you want."

"Just checking, although I'm flush right now. You should see how much money the CIA's putting into my Swiss bank account."

"Yes, Dennis."

"$3,000 a month."

"Really."

"Shit. If I had $300 a month that'd be something. I could live in Russia on that. Maybe I'll go live in Russia. I sure can't live here. I'm going to be indicted if I hang around here."

"What are you going to be indicted for, Dennis? Blowing up federal buildings?"

"Everybody seems to think I did the bombing."

"I can't think why."

"Even the Iraqis think I did it," he continued, freely admitting that he had been on the Iraqi payroll as a propagandist for over three years. "They paid me $100 a month, not much, but it all helps. Then they cut me off, a month after the bombing."

"After all you've done for them?"

"Yeah, bastards. But no, seriously, the only bombs I've ever made are stink bombs. I use bee repellent. You know, if it's some Jew or capitalist getting on our case. I throw it in their car. They can't get rid of the stuff. It stinks for weeks."

"I see."

But for all his bonhomie, the former Imperial Dragon was in a wistful mood. His life had turned into a "Hitchcock movie" since Carol Howe had come forward with her story. He was 47 years old, and his prospects were, well, dim. He had lost a new job at the American Airlines repair shop in Tulsa because of all the fuss. Nine dollars an hour, too. Good money. And now the movement was upset with him. All because of that girl.

"Look, I never cased that federal building. I didn't even know there was a federal building in Oklahoma City," he said. "It's another one of Carol's bald-faced evil lies. The only thing I ever cased with Andy Strassmeir was the nude titty bars in Tulsa. That I did do."

"It looks like Andreas has put you in a bit of a spot, Dennis."

"You think he's an agent?"

"Makes sense."

"Yeah, that little shit's going to get himself killed. You know Andy told me he'd been in GSG-9."

"Strassmeir told you that? He told you he'd worked for German counter-terrorism?"

"Yeah, told me he worked on the Baader-Meinhoff gang in the eighties. This was a guy who could infiltrate, I tell you, he knew his stuff, but I thought he was just going after the Communists," said Mahon, chewing on the inside of his cheek. "Funny thing. He was never curious about the people in my album. His car kept breaking down, and he couldn't travel. Never even had a telephone."

"Good cover."

"You think so?"

"That's exactly what you'd do if you were a deep penetration agent, isn't it, Dennis?"

"Yeah, maybe. I hope to God he wasn't working as an agent over here."

Mahon was undoubtedly in deep water. Things had moved a long way since his days in the Ku Klux Klan, those halcyon, carefree times when all he did was prance about in white regalia, set fire to crosses, wind up the liberal pointy heads—and, he whispered to admirers, firebomb the odd abortion clinic. But then he had decided the Klan was not militant enough for him.

"The Klan are just a bunch of uneducated rednecks with low IQs and green teeth, blaming all their problems on niggers and Jews. I kept telling them to snap out of it. This isn't about niggers, it's about the struggle against the government. I'm tired of hearing about white power. We've got plenty of power. Look at our politicians: they're all white, aren't they?"

"Yes, Dennis, they are."

"I'd rather hang ten rich Aryan corporate bosses for every Jew that I'd hang. Like Carol's father. I'd like to see him hanging from a gibbet.... No, I couldn't get it through to those thickheads in the Klan that this is a white civil war we've got. This is the working class against the capitalists. I've gained so much credibility since I left that fricking Klan."

"You have?"

"Yeah. I can hold my head up now."

Like other diehards, Mahon graduated to the Aryan Nations, the descendant of the fascist Silver Shirts. These gentlemen meant business. He found his niche leading the race commandos of the White Aryan Resistance action squad, calling for the overthrow of the U.S. government by "any means." It was exhilarating. But now it had got him into difficulties.

"That girl. I just knew she was a fricking snitch. No more blonde debutantes for me. It's the last time I fall for that one."

"You told J. D. Cash you wanted to saw Carol's head off?"

"J. D. Cash said that?"

"Sure did. He has it on tape."

"How come that guy's still alive anyway? You know what though, I'd like to put her over my knee and give her a good spanking."

It had all begun in May 1994 when Carol Howe called the "Dial-a-Racist" hotline of the White Aryan Resistance. She followed up with a letter asking for white separatist literature. "I am 23, considered beautiful, and want to defend my race and culture," she explained. They arranged a meeting at the Village Inn at 71st and Yale, and the Imperial Dragon could hardly contain himself as this spectral, alabaster creature hobbled in on crutches.

"What genetics," he said, shaking his head. "I fell in love with that girl, I really did. I wanted us to get married, and make little Aryan babies. With her genetics we couldn't have gone wrong.

"But Carol was out of her mind. You know that, don't you? Totally out of her mind. That girl was always talking about violence and killing. She watched *Natural Born Killers* nine times. Nine times!" he said, with a mixture of awe and reproof.

"Carol only passed her [ATF] polygraph tests because she was on morphine the whole time. She was always popping these pills. I never could reach her soul."

Mahon loved to talk. He would talk all day if you gave him the chance, and I was happy to let him do so. He had me join him on his errands around town, which he carried out in a rickety 1974 truck with a German eagle on the license plate. This was later switched for a CIA Government Vehicle plate, one of those joke tags you can buy for a few dollars at a gun show.

"You're the enemy, of course," he said. The word on the street was that I worked for British MI6. But he didn't care. It was better than working for the Mossad, anyway.

At the Post Office he handed me a large box as he carried his parcels up to the counter.

"This isn't a bomb, is it Dennis?"

"I always deliver my bombs in person, in disguise," he said, with a twinkle. "I can look like an Hispanic, or even a nigger. You should see the stuff I've got. I'm the master of disguise."

The thing about Mahon's spontaneous quips is that they were often true. His old friends in the movement vouched for his makeup skills. They said that he had a whole kit to pass himself off as a Mexican.

"It must have taken a technical genius to build that Oklahoma bomb," I said.

"Yeah. One hell of a bomb, wasn't it."

"Do you think it was an ANFO bomb?"

"How could it be an ANFO bomb if there was no fricking residue of ammonium nitrate? That stuff would be all over the place, and they didn't find any, did they? One fricking crystal, that's all they found. ANFO bomb, my ass. Give me a break. I'll bet you it was a fuel air bomb—two 55-gallon drums, that's all you need. It's very efficient, like a nuke. They used them in the Gulf War to blanket a whole area and set off the anti-tank mines."

"Well, that would get you off the hook, wouldn't it? Carol told the ATF you blew up a truck with a 500-pound ANFO bomb, in Michigan."

"Hmm," muttered Mahon, torn for a moment between a bomber's pride and the risk of incriminating himself. "Nah, I never blew up a truck. I just told Carol that to test her, to see if it came back at me. Then I'd know she was a fricking snitch."

He took me to his house, a rundown rambler on the wrong side of town. He was living in a mixed ethnic neighborhood—one of those indignities he had to suffer every day. "The fricking capitalists, like Carol's father, they're all right, aren't they? And I'm stuck here with niggers on every side."

"Life's not fair, Dennis."

"I can handle it. There's good negroes too, you know. They're not all bad."

Inside, it smelt of urine. Mahon apologized. His scraggly black cat was incontinent, ruining what was left of his threadbare furniture. "I'm going to have him put down. He's had a good life."

He played me a tape of an interview that he and Carol gave to a German film crew in 1994. The two of them are sitting on a park bench, praising Adolf Hitler. At one point the reporter turns to Carol and asks if the movement is penetrated by informants. Undoubtedly, she replies with a deadpan face, undoubtedly it is.

"Jesus, she's good isn't she?"

"Outstanding," I agreed.

"I'll sell you the tape," said Dennis.

"I work for a newspaper. I can't use video."

"Okay, okay, how about this?" he said, pulling out a picture of Carol, half-naked, wrapped in a Confederate flag, carrying a sub-machine gun.

"How much?"

"$1000 bucks."

"Christmas!"

"Okay, $500."

"I can't afford that."

We settled on a cheaper photo of Carol in the uniform of a Russian Air Force officer. To sweeten the deal he threw in his last, treasured copy of *The Turner Diaries*—alleged to be the "blueprint" for the Oklahoma bombing. I got the two for $120, billed to *The Sunday Telegraph*.

"Anything else I can sell you? I've got to get out of this country, soon," he said, winking. "I think I'll go to Argentina."

"Good choice, Dennis."

Before I left, he took me out to a cluttered workshop at the side of his house. It was bedecked with the usual protest posters—"End Organized Crime, Abolish The IRS"—that kind of thing.

"This is where I build my bombs. And this is where I build the detonators," he continued, taking me into the nerve center at the back. "Just kidding. Look, it was a justifiable act to blow up that building, but if I'd been involved I wouldn't have done it at nine in the morning with all those children in there. Anyway, I've got an alibi. I was up at the family farm in Illinois from April 16 to April 23. You talk to my father, he'll tell you."

Alibi or not, Mahon had ensnared himself in his remarkable five-hour confession to J. D. Cash in January 1996. At the time, Cash was in touch with *The Jubilee*, the far-right publication of the Christian Identity movement. He had been invited to speak about the Oklahoma bombing at a *Jubilee* conference, and his picture had appeared in the monthly newspaper next to that of Louis Beam, the *eminence grise* of the Aryan movement. When Mahon saw the picture, he falsely assumed that Cash was an emissary sent by Louis Beam.

"I went along with it. If he was going to be that dumb, that was fine by me," explained Cash. "So I said to him: 'Dennis, why did you blow up the fucking building in broad daylight with a nursery in there? You've no idea how much trouble you've caused the movement, killing all those children.'

"'I know, the whole thing's fucked up.'

"'Dead babies don't cause revolutions. There are some people who are real upset about this.'"

Over the next five hours Mahon worked his way through a bottle of Irish whisky and babbled frantically about the bombing. In the flood of conflicted emotions, he lurched from guilt, to pride, to a perverse jealousy. The former Imperial Dragon could not bear to see an upstart Nazi like Timothy McVeigh hogging the limelight, taking all the *credit* for the bombing.

"The thing you have to understand about Mahon is that he had become a joke in the movement," said Cash. "He was being ridiculed as a talker, and he wanted to prove that he was a 'doer.' It was his middle-aged crisis, I guess."

"It got lively when I told him that Andreas Strassmeir was a government agent. That's when he jumped up and said, 'Oh, sweet Jesus, I'm fucked!'

"Then he told me I had to pass the word on to Michael Brescia and Mark Thomas: 'They're in up to their asses in the bombing.'

And he blurted out that Michael Brescia was the 'pretty-boy' John Doe number two, the one in the side-sketch."

Thomas was the East Coast leader of the Aryan Nations and head of the Posse Comitatus of Pennsylvania. Brescia was one of his protégés. The two had close ties to Elohim City, and Brescia had taken up residence at the commune two years earlier. He shared a house with Andreas Strassmeir.

Cash continued: "Dennis was really quite upset about Strassmeir. He got on the line to Germany and said he wanted Strassmeir checked out. If Andy had betrayed the cause, he was to be shot in both kneecaps, interrogated, given a half-hour trial, and executed. Since it's my duty as a citizen to report death threats, I passed this on to the FBI."

Before leaving, Cash pulled out his tape-recorder and asked Mahon if he wanted to convey any messages to Tim McVeigh in prison. (Cash had a letter from McVeigh's lawyers scheduling an interview with the prisoner.) Mahon fell for the bait. Speaking into the microphone, he exhorted McVeigh to accept his "sacrifice," even if he was guilty by reason of entrapment. Don't forget Waco; don't forget Ruby Ridge; don't forget all the southerners who died for the cause; and don't forget that members of his family were vulnerable to reprisal.

Immediately afterward, J. D. Cash gave a sworn deposition to Stephen Jones, the lawyer of Timothy McVeigh, recording the ramblings of the Imperial Dragon. It was submitted to the court in Denver, where it has remained sealed ever since.

But if it has been kept from public view, the prosecution at least has been able to read it. Apparently it has had no impact. To this day the Justice Department has not seen fit to question Dennis Mahon about the Oklahoma bombing, or treat him as a suspect in any way.

"Yes, I know I'm protected," Mahon told me archly. "It's a nice feeling to have."

CHAPTER FIVE

CAROL HOWE

CAROL ELIZABETH HOWE was recruited as a confidential informant for the U.S. Bureau of Alcohol, Tobacco and Firearms on August 25, 1994. Her task was to gather intelligence on Dennis Mahon and the White Aryan Resistance.

She was 23 years old, with a petite figure, beautifully coifed sandblonde hair, a swastika tattooed on her left shoulder, and a pentagram on her right ankle. Her motive was listed by the ATF as "personal vendetta, public safety."[1]

It was a far cry from the genteel, equestrian pursuits of her caste. Carol was an accomplished hunter-jumper—a gentrified sport known as "point-to-point" in Anglo-American circles. Her family were members of the Southern Hills Country Club, site of the annual PGA Players Championship. Their seven-bedroom residence was just up the road from Southern Hills. It was a discrete, understated home, appraised at $900,000. Genteel, not flashy.

Carol's father had been CEO of Mapco Incorporated, a Tulsa energy conglomerate with 4,500 employees and a ranking on the Fortune 500 list. His position put him at the pinnacle of Oklahoma society. Carol's mother, Aubyn, was an immaculate, effusive philanthropist with short blonde hair and a taste for exotic earrings. They were most definitely Brahmin WASPs. But they were also willful, controlling WASPs, and Carol needed to be given a long rein.

As so often with the highly strung children of privilege, "culture-slumming" was the ultimate rebellion. The lower, the better; the subconscious purpose was to shock. And shock she did. Carol threw herself with zest into the most *verboten* subculture in America. She started to consort with fringe skinheads, neo-Nazis, and punks.

The silliness took a serious turn for the worse in the spring of 1994 when she jumped off a wall to escape a group of black youths and broke both her heels. In retaliation, she called Dennis Mahon's "Dial-a-Racist" hotline. Her flirtation with the White Aryan Resistance would last six weeks. It ended as violently as it had begun, when Dennis Mahon allegedly raped her. She fled to her grandfather's ranch in Texas.

On her return to Tulsa she found a series of threatening messages on her answering machine. "Have you turned on us?" growled Mahon. "We will neutralize you.... We assume you're with the enemy."[2]

Carol filed a complaint with the hate crimes unit of the Tulsa Police on August 22, 1994. "Victim stated she had been a member of WAR (White Aryan Resistance) for two months," said the report. "She has been trying to get out of this organization for the last month. Victim feels that her life is in danger."[3]

Three days later she went to the Tulsa County District Court to file for an emergency protective order. It flagged the Tulsa office of the ATF. They pounced immediately.

Would she like to get even? asked rookie agent Angela Finley, who was not much older than Carol herself.

Most certainly, said Carol. And more than that, she wanted to get these lunatics off the street before they provoked a race war, or blew something up.[4] They signed a two-page contract enlisting her at a pay of $25 a day, plus expenses. Five days later Special Agent Finley submitted the opening report of the ATF's Terrorist/Extremist investigation of the White Aryan Resistance. It outlined her preliminary debriefing of Confidential Informant CI-183, the code number by which Carol would be known.[5]

"WAR has approximately 20–25 active, 50 nonactive and 200 underground members locally. The primary training location is called Elohim City…. Mahon and his organization are preparing for a race war and war with the government in the near future and it is believed that they are rapidly stockpiling weapons."

On August 30, 1994, Carol passed her first ATF polygraph test, as she did every test thereafter. The WAR investigation was designated SIGNIFICANT/SENSITIVE, which meant that it had "potential national interest" and that ATF headquarters in Washington should be kept apprised.[6]

Carol was quite a find for the ATF. Wild, fearless, a talented actress, she was willing to do practically anything. But she was not a "snitch," and that would cause problems. The ATF likes to work with criminal defendants who have "rolled over" to avoid prosecution. Snitches can be controlled. But Carol did not have any criminal record, which is rare. She was a volunteer, performing a public service—and as we shall see—trying to redeem herself in the eyes of her parents.

With her family's millions as the ultimate guarantor behind her, she was not going to be pushed around by low-level agents in the provincial office of a second-tier federal agency. In fact, she was not going to be pushed around by anybody. Not even the FBI elicited the proper sense of deference. Imbued with the prejudices of her class, she tended to view the FBI as jumped-up policemen, perfectly respectable, but not the kind of people you invited to dinner. The Justice Department never understood this, and it would pay dearly for the miscalculation.

Carol reported that Dennis Mahon had promised to teach her how to assemble hand grenades, or "paperweights" as he called them. So her first assignment was to film Dennis Mahon *in flagrante delicto*. She went out shopping with Agent Finley—or just Angie, as she was by then—and bought a trunk. With help of ATF technicians from the Dallas office, they mounted a tiny surveillance camera on the inside, drilled a small hole in the trunk for the lens, and placed it in the living room of Carol's house in Tulsa. Then they picked up four grenade casings from an army-navy surplus store.[7]

"I got Dennis talked into making them real, and he did so on camera. Later we went out to Elohim City and blew them up," she told J. D. Cash.

By now the focus was already shifting from Mahon to Elohim City. Carol's early reports had been so disturbing that the ATF wanted her to infiltrate the cult, find out what kind of weaponry they had, and profile the key radicals. It was an extremely dangerous mission. She learned at worship that execution was the penalty for any informant who caused a member of the group to go to prison.

In September she was given her first taste of "Andy the German." (It would take her three months to discover that he was Andreas Carl Strassmeir, born May 17, 1959.) He made her crawl underneath barbed wire while he fired a .45 caliber pistol at her feet, his idea of a loyalty test.[8]

During worship on the Sabbath, which lasted four hours, Strassmeir would patrol the compound. "If someone—anyone— leaves the meeting during service, he hunts them down and brings them back." He would enforce the 9:00 PM curfew, conduct background checks, and ensure that troublemakers were beaten.[9]

"He believes we cannot outbreed the enemy, so we must use mass genocide against them + of course, the biggest enemy is the U.S. government," wrote Carol in her notes.

Carol was not yet permitted to attend "guerrilla warfare and tactical maneuvers" training, but she would learn that Andy had no tolerance for slackers. He made his troops camp out in 14 degree December weather, and swim through frigid waters in their combat fatigues. No complaining tolerated. When the "troops" let him down, he would have them summoned to the Worship House for a session of vitriolic abuse by the patriarch.[10]

The "troops" were dressed in black jeans, combat boots, and dark blue T-shirts with a badge on the left breast and "Security Officer" in yellow on the back. Every Elohite was required to have gear for "patrols, maneuvers, and combat," with an ammunition stockpile of 400 to 500 rounds per firearm. The full combat load was 200 to 280 rounds per man, worn on a chest pouch. Every male over 17 had to carry a weapon at all times, either a revolver, or a rifle strapped across the shoulder. The standard weapons were Mini-14s, AR-15s, and SKSs. Andy also claimed to have an M-60 heavy machine gun and a 40 mm grenade launcher.

Carol was gaining trust. Grandpa put her on the 3.3.3 test routine, which meant that she was to graduate from a three-day trial stay at Elohim, to a three week stay, to a three month stay, before gaining permanent admission. He wanted her to teach Aryan history at the Elohim school. Approved by the elders, she began her three week probation during the "Pagan Christmas" in December. She moved into a trailer that Mahon kept at the commune, stocked with cans of food and covered with a camouflage net. When it got too cold, she moved in with some of the other families.

By early 1995 Grandpa had started preaching every day, working himself up into a froth about ZOG's storm troopers. "He brought forth his soldiers and instructed them to take whatever action necessary against the U.S. government. He stated that certain groups from Texas, Missouri, Arkansas and Oklahoma will be uniting as one front to fight the government," says an ATF report dated January 11, 1995.[11]

Interestingly, this was not seen as an ethnic uprising. Pastor Millar was in contact with Louis Farrakhan's organization, as well as militant Hispanic and American Indian groups. He explained to Carol that "Elohim City would unite with other races in order to create a more powerful adversary opposing the U.S. government. The white supremacist issues are secondary to the anti-government attitude."[12]

A mood of apocalyptic frenzy was engulfing Elohim City. There were now nightly patrols and daily paramilitary maneuvers. Fully automatic weapons were being stockpiled in anticipation of a Waco-style raid. The flag of the Branch Davidians was hanging in the chapel as a constant reminder of the assault on Mount Carmel on Patriot's Day, April 19, 1993.

But Waco was only part of the drama. The date of April 19, 1995, had multiple significance for Elohim City. It was the ten year anniversary of the federal assault on a white supremacist encampment in Arkansas known as the Covenant, Sword, and Arm of the Lord. The compound had surrendered to federal agents on April 19, 1985, ten years to the day before the Oklahoma bombing.

During the sedition trial of the survivors, it emerged that they had been plotting to blow up the Murrah Federal Building with a rocket launcher in 1983. The conspiracy involved James Ellison, who later married a granddaughter of Pastor Millar and settled at Elohim City. His chief accomplice was Richard Wayne Snell, a neo-fascist cult-hero who edited a newsletter called *The Seekers* and was a member of Elohim's extended family.

It so happens that Snell was executed in Arkansas on April 19, 1995, a few hours after the Oklahoma bombing. He had been convicted of murdering a black state trooper. His supporters dispute this version of events, claiming that Snell shot back in self-defense. Whatever happened, the young bloods at Elohim had worked themselves into a fury as the day of execution drew near. On April 19, a caravan of vehicles drove down to Little Rock for a clemency rally. After the execution they brought the body back for burial on hallowed Aryan ground at Elohim City.

At the Arkansas Department of Corrections, Snell was fulminating about bombs and catastrophic retribution. "He repeatedly predicted that there would be a bombing or an explosion on the day of his death," said prison official Alan Ables, in an interview with *The Denver Post.*

"I moved my wife aboard a federal installation to spend the day and possibly the next night... because I didn't feel safe with her at home." The prison took the exceptional step of transporting Snell to the execution chamber by helicopter.

Pastor Millar ministered to Snell during the final hours before the lethal injection. According to a documentary by the Canadian Broadcast Company, the prison deathwatch log notes that Snell made a request at 12:20 PM that the television in his cell be turned on. He watched the early coverage of the Oklahoma bombing. At 12:30 the log notes: "News 4 special on the situation in Oklahoma. Inmate Snell watching newscast, smiling and chuckling."[13]

*   *   *

As instructed by the ATF, Carol had befriended Strassmeir. She cooked for him; she did his laundry; she cleaned his house—and reported back on the 30 cans of ammunition and grenade casings he kept in storage. This took self-sacrifice. The skinny, buck-toothed fanatic was not exactly her type, and she had could hardly understand his guttural accent anyway. But she succeeded in tempting him.

"Andy and I talked of 'us' and he said he was definitely attracted to me, and I have a chance of being his marriage partner," read her notes from November 24, 1994. This was later followed by a terse notation that the mission was accomplished. "I secured an intimate personal relationship with Andy and am now his girlfriend."

"Sometime in November there was a meeting and Strassmeir and Mahon said it was time to quit talking and go to war.... I reported all this to Angie," she told J. D. Cash.

This is confirmed by Agent Finley's monthly report, dated November 29, 1994, which states that Strassmeir had discussed plans to bring down the United States government with direct actions such as "assassinations" and "<u>bombings</u>" and "mass shootings." The word bombing is underlined in the handwritten notes of Finley's debriefing of Carol.[14]

By Christmas the plot was taking shape. Strassmeir and Mahon, the ringleaders, had picked three possible targets for attack in the state of Oklahoma: the IRS and federal buildings in Tulsa, and the "federal building" in Oklahoma City. Carol has stated under oath that she reported these threats to her ATF case officer. "I wrote down about blowing up federal buildings," she testified. "I relayed it the way we relayed it."[15]

She later said that she informed the ATF, on paper, that something called the "Morrow Building" (sic) had been mentioned as one of the targets.[16]

The ATF denies this adamantly. But Carol is vindicated by an FBI write-up of her debriefing on April 21, 1995, at the FBI's OKBOMB command center in Oklahoma City. It said that Dennis Mahon had discussed "targeting federal installations for destruction through bombings, such as the IRS Building, the Tulsa Federal Building and the Oklahoma City Federal Building."

She said that Strassmeir and Mahon had "taken three trips to Oklahoma City in November 1994, December 1994, and February 1995." She had accompanied the group once, in December 1994.[17]

The government is now claiming that Carol made this story up after the bombing. But this was *their* informant, meeting at *their* request, at the headquarters of the bombing investigation, telling them in strictest confidence what she knew about the most traumatic terrorist event in the history of the United States two days after it happened. It is contained in *their* own internal documents.

Unfortunately, such a large chunk of Angela Finley's ATF notes are missing that it may be impossible to resolve this point with absolute certainty. But here are the transcripts of a closed-door cross-examination of Special Agent Finley, under oath, on April 24, 1997.

Q: "Ms. Howe told you about Mr. Strassmeir's threats to blow up federal buildings, didn't she?"

Finley: "In general, yes."

Q: "That was before the Oklahoma City bombing?"

Finley: "Yes."

Q: "Now, Ms. Howe actually took some of these people from Elohim City at your direction to Oklahoma City, didn't she?"

Finley: "She went with them. She probably did drive."

Q: "She called you before, and said, 'These folks from Elohim City want to go over and look at Oklahoma City.' And she had specific places they were going."

Finley: "It did not include the federal building."

Q: "This trip to Oklahoma City by Elohim City residents occurred before the bombing, actually just by a few weeks, didn't it?"

Finley: "No, it would be months... the fall of '94."

Q: "Are you sure? So, it wasn't the third week of February?"

Finley: "Oh, I'm sorry, we did send her back."

Q: "I'm asking you whether it is a fact that Ms. Howe picked up people from Elohim City... and took them to Oklahoma City in February, the third week, of 1995."

Finley: "I would have to look at my reports again."

Q: "The very next day, you asked Ms. Howe to take you to Oklahoma City and show you the places they visited, didn't you?"

Finley: "I don't know if it was the next day, but yes, I took her to Oklahoma City and asked her the places."

So, the ATF has admitted to the substance of Carol Howe's claims. It knew that Andreas Strassmeir had discussed blowing up federal buildings in Oklahoma. It knew that a party from Elohim City had visited Oklahoma City eight weeks before the Oklahoma bombing. The only dispute is whether the Alfred P. Murrah Building was *specifically* named as one of the targets.

For two years the Justice Department insisted that the U.S. government had no prior warning of any kind that a federal building might be bombed on April 19, 1995. They did not qualify this by saying specific threats, or credible threats. The Justice Department stated categorically that there were no threats, period, and that it was "an outrageous charge" to suggest otherwise.

When Carol Howe came forward, however, it changed the terms of the argument with swift sleight of hand. The operative word was now "specific." Carol Howe did not give a "specific" warning. The ATF records—those parts that have not been shredded already—do not indicate a "specific" warning. The Justice Department holds that unless she can demonstrate otherwise, the information in her debriefings is all mindless chatter. The burden of proof falls entirely on Carol Howe.

But this is indefensible. It is not the job of a confidential informant to cross every "t" and dot every "i." It is the job of the case officer to ensure proper documentation. It is the job of the agency to exploit the tips and leads, using the vast resources of the U.S. federal government. Intelligence rarely comes gift-wrapped in a chocolate box, especially in cases of terrorism. It comes in scraps. A bit here, a bit there. The warnings that Carol provided were, if anything, unusually detailed and precise. If they fell short of absolute specificity, that does not absolve the ATF in any way.

Special Agent Angela Finley has a great deal of explaining to do. But it is unfair to pick on her alone, for she was put in an impossible position by the FBI. The document trail shows that the Tulsa office of the ATF was ready to take action against the White Aryan

Resistance in February 1995. Carol Howe had succeeded in filming Strassmeir preparing hand-grenades, and the ATF was preparing for a possible raid on Elohim City to arrest him. It had requested INS "participation in [the] raid," because Strassmeir was an illegal alien.[18] The Oklahoma Highway Patrol had been alerted that Andreas Strassmeir "carries a .45 auto pistol at all times… if he is stopped and has the gun on him, ATF will file the charges."[19]

But the FBI muscled in and *prevented* the arrest. On February 22, 1995, Agent Finley was notified by the Oklahoma Highway Patrol that the "FBI also had an ongoing investigation at Elohim City."[20] One can imagine the shock of this rookie ATF agent when she discovered that she had unwittingly stumbled on a much bigger sting being conducted by the FBI, probably a counterintelligence operation approved at the highest levels in Washington. For whatever reason, Strassmeir was being protected by the Bureau.

If Agent Finley still had any doubts, they were dispelled the next day. On February 23, 1995, the head of the Tulsa office of the ATF was informed that Bob Ricks, the chief of the FBI regional office in Dallas, wanted to schedule a meeting "to discuss the investigation of Elohim City." The memo made reference to the work of informant CI-183, Carol Howe. On the same day, the ATF Tulsa chief was called in to discuss the problem with the U.S. Attorney for the Northern District of Oklahoma. Major damage control was under way. The Angie-Carol team had stepped on a land mine.

Within days the ATF case against the White Aryan Resistance collapsed. No arrests were ever made. Carol Howe's efforts had been in vain. Less than a month later Agent Finley filed an "emergency request for the removal of Confidential Informant 53270-183." The memo stated that she was "no longer loyal or competent to operate as an informant for ATF." Her accumulated pay had been $4,621.64.[21]

In truth, Carol was in a bad state. She was seriously depressed in February, in part because the ATF had been pressuring her to go back to Elohim City for her three-month probation as a Nazi. It was a terrifying assignment. Elohim was reaching a fever pitch. If anybody had got wind of her activities as an informant she faced kneecapping or the not-so-apocryphal fate of being weighed down with rocks and thrown into a river.

But the notation that she was "no longer competent" was clearly just a bureaucratic formula. It would be forgotten soon enough once they needed her again.

When the bomb went off, Carol was devastated.

"The first thing I thought is that they had done it," she said. "They had taken the next step and done the things they said they were going to do."[22]

Then the guilt set it. She could have stopped it. If she had tried even harder, if she had concentrated properly when they told her these terrible things, if she had been more specific with Angie, perhaps she could have made the difference. But she had failed. Fate had put this matter in her hands, her hands alone, and she had failed.[23]

The day after the bombing she was called by Angela Finley. Would she come down to the OKBOMB command post in Oklahoma City? Would she help identify the sketches of the suspects? Yes, she replied. "I hated to quit prematurely, I wanted to go back and finish the job," she later testified.

The ATF put her back on the informant roster under an "emergency reactivation." The approval request stated that Carol had been reliable in the past, and that she "has shown emotional instability, received treatment and appears to have recovered satisfactorily."

Making a genuine effort to follow up on her information, the ATF increased her pay to $150 a day and sent her back to Elohim City to collect more intelligence and try to identify suspect John Doe Two. She stayed for three days, from the first of May to the third, and reported back that "individuals spoken with were supportive of the bombing." She also learned that "there is a big secret out here."[24]

There were plans to send her back for a second visit in May 1995 to crack open this "secret." But the mission was aborted after the ATF office in Tulsa was informed that Pastor Robert Millar suspected that Carol was a confidential informant. The ATF, of course, had no idea that Pastor Millar was actually working for the FBI.

By this stage the intrigue had become so twisted—with undercover informants from different agencies tripping over each other—that it is almost impossible to disentangle. Reviewing the documents, however, it is clear that the FBI was engaged in major damage control from the first days of the OKBOMB investigation.

The FBI write-up of Carol Howe's debriefing—at the OKBOMB command post on April 21, 1995—omits the surnames of the men identified by Carol as possible suspects in the bombing. After being shown three composite sketches, including one that she had never seen published in the newspapers, Carol identified John Doe One as Peter Ward, the tall blond roommate of Andreas Strassmeir at Elohim City. She said that John Doe Two looked like his brother, Tony Ward.[25] The FBI listed them simply as Pete and Tony, even though Carol had written profiles of them in her ATF reports using their full names.

It was hardly a minor matter. An FBI memo dated April 28, 1995, a week later, states that Officer John Haynie of the Oklahoma Highway Patrol had also suggested that Peter Ward could be one of the bombers. But the FBI, apparently, was not interested. The record shows that they did not speak to Peter Ward for another year and a half. An agent conducted a superficial interview at the Jackson County Jail in Oregon on September 23, 1996.

The Bureau's decision to ignore the Ward brothers, who were last known to be living in New Mexico, cannot be explained by mere oversight or lack of resources. In the days and weeks after the blast, FBI agents were fanning out across the country interrogating street vagabonds about the bombing on the basis of anonymous tip-offs. This had the hallmarks of containment. It is patently obvious that the FBI was willing to go to any lengths to protect its undercover operation at Elohim City, even if that meant allowing suspected bombers to walk free. The only question is why.

Despite the evasions, an April 21 FBI memo confirms that the Bureau was fully aware of Carol's clandestine intelligence within two days of the bombing.

"Mehaun [sic] has talked with Carol about targeting federal installations for destruction through bombings, such as the IRS Building, the Tulsa Federal Building, and the Oklahoma City Federal Building.

"Strasmeyer [sic] has talked frequently about direct action against the U.S. Government. He is trained in weaponry and has discussed assassinations, bombings and mass shootings."

This memo is the smoking gun of the Oklahoma bombing. While the Clinton administration can make an argument, perhaps, that the warnings of the blast were not as clear before April 19, 1995, as they may look in hindsight—much like the disputed warnings before Pearl Harbor—how can it possibly explain the failure to pursue Andreas Strassmeir and Dennis Mahon?

Here were two men under investigation by the ATF for Terrorism/Extremism, who had allegedly threatened to blow up federal buildings in Oklahoma. Yet the FBI is too busy to talk to them? It conducts more than 20,000 witness interviews—most of them inconsequential—but cannot find the time to interview these two gentlemen?

Two and a half years after the bombing, Dennis was still driving the streets of Tulsa in his blue 1974 Chevy pickup. He had never been questioned by any agency of the U.S. government. It is even more staggering when you learn that the handwritten notes of Agent Finley, taken in the September/October 1994 time frame, reveal that Dennis Mahon knew how to make truck bombs out of fertilizer. "He made a 500-pound ammonium nitrate bomb in Michigan about five years ago, put it under a truck and blew it up."[26]

At last, here was somebody who knew how to build an ANFO bomb and detonate it successfully. The FBI crime labs had concluded that the Murrah Building was destroyed by a 4,800-pound ammonium nitrate bomb, and here was one of the few living Americans with the technical expertise to actually do it.

When Tim McVeigh and Terry Nichols tried to blow up a milk jug with a small fertilizer bomb in October 1994, the experiment was a fiasco. "The blasting cap just sprayed the ammonium nitrate everywhere. It didn't work," said Michael Fortier, at McVeigh's trial.[27]

The Justice Department claims that McVeigh improved his technique over the next six months by studying the bomb manual *Homemade C-4*. But the book describes a laborious process of baking ammonium nitrate in small cans. It would take weeks to build a 4,800-pound truck bomb this way, and it would not solve the technical challenge of achieving simultaneous detonation.

Yet the prosecution insists that McVeigh and Nichols built the bomb in one day, on April 18, 1995, and then executed the flawless detonation of the biggest ANFO bomb in the history of U.S. terrorism.

Common sense would suggest that McVeigh had help from an expert, at the very least.

Now we learn that Dennis Mahon—an acknowledged associate of McVeigh[28]—was logged by the ATF as a man capable of detonating large ANFO truck bombs.

The FBI had been told that he had threatened to blow up federal buildings in Oklahoma.

But the FBI was too busy to talk to him.

Really.

There is another clue in that April 21 FBI memo. Every name of significance was misspelled. Special Agent James Blanchard managed to turn Elohim City into Elohm City. Dennis Mahon became Dennis Mehaun. Andreas Strassmeir became Andreas Strasmeyer. Pastor Robert Millar became Bob Lamar.

It is possible, I suppose, that the FBI agents tasked to conduct the most sensitive interviews of the Oklahoma bombing case were imbeciles. But I do not believe it. This ruse of misspelling names is a technique I have encountered before when the FBI wants to jam a computer search.[29] It can backfire, however, for it indicates who may be working undercover for the Bureau. We now know that Pastor Millar was already an FBI informant in early 1995, at the very time that he was inciting "Holy War" against the "Zionist Occupied Government." Was Dennis Mahon on the payroll, or "turned" as a snitch? Was Andreas Strassmeir working in conjunction with the Bureau?

*   *   *

By now Carol was a massive liability to the FBI, the Justice Department, and the Clinton administration as a whole. Even if she remained silent, there was always a risk that McVeigh's defense team would find out about her as it honed in on Elohim City. Indeed, it was likely. FBI agent James Blanchard had slipped up by calling her Carol instead of CI 53270-183 in a memo obtained by the defense team under legal discovery. (In fact, McVeigh's lawyers did not know they had it buried in the 22,111 pages of documents.)

The ATF were apoplectic when they discovered that "the identity of CI 53270-183 had been severely compromised." On April 22, 1996, Agent Angela Finley fired off a "damage assessment" memo reminding her superiors that Carol was "involved with the OKC bomb case" and was "the key in identifying individuals at Elohim City, which is tied to the OKC bomb case."

Noting Carol's concern about reprisals from the neo-Nazis, Finley wrote that "this informant has not been overly paranoid or fearful during undercover operations. This agent believes that s/he could be in serious danger when associates discover his/her identity."[30]

Finley had a clandestine meeting with Carol in a South Tulsa park to tell her that her cover had been blown. It was the FBI that was responsible, said Finley, so Carol should contact the FBI and ask them to deal with it. Carol did as she was told. She called Special Agent Pete Rickel in the Tulsa office of the FBI to request witness protection. He sent her bouncing back like a Ping-Pong ball to the ATF, although he was careful to ensure that there was no paper trail documenting her call or his refusal to refer her request to the proper authorities.[31]

Nobody was going to do anything to protect her. The U.S. government had reneged on a promise, written into her ATF contract, to provide her with witness protection if her life was in danger. It was a foretaste of the full treatment waiting for her.

At this point, she would have been well advised to leave the United States for a few years, studying in Europe, perhaps, or doing volunteer work in some overlooked outpost like Bolivia. Instead she chose to keep going. "I dug myself deeper into the movement, and cloaked myself in it," she said.[32] It was a decision that would be used against her later, but in the back of her tormented mind was a notion that she could still, somehow, prove herself of value to society, perhaps foiling the next act of terrorism by the deranged far right.

Her status as an ATF operative was nebulous. She was still on the "active informant roster," retained for the duration of the OKBOMB investigation. But she had been cut adrift. Angela Finley had stopped using her, stopped paying her, stopped taking her calls. Finley had another informant now, a man, coded CI-196. Carol was, to put it bluntly, the declining member of a *ménage à trois.*

In early December 1996, she was discovered by J. D. Cash, who had been tipped off about her affair with Andreas Strassmeir. Cash called her house and left a message on her answering machine. She did not reply, but the FBI was clearly not going to hazard anything to chance. Days later, on December 13, 1996, the FBI raided Carol's house, alleging that a telephone "hotline" for the Aryan Intelligence Network, registered in her name, had broadcast a bomb threat.

"A letter from a high ranking revolutionary commander has been written and received demanding that action be taken against the government by all white warriors by December 15, 1996, and if this action is not taken, bombs will be activated in 15 major preselected U.S. cities."[33]

It took some imagination to construe this hearsay repetition of a crazed prophesy as an actual bomb threat that Carol Howe was intending to carry out.

Inside the house the FBI found materials that could, theoretically, be assembled into a pipebomb. Most of the material had actually been collected by Carol during her undercover work for the ATF, including the pipe itself, the fuse, and a stash of black powder. The parts were sitting in a box. Nothing had been done to assemble them into a bomb.

The U.S. government was turning Carol's cover against her, the ultimate nightmare for every clandestine operative. The FBI would later claim that they did not know she was still on the active informant roster of the ATF, or that she had ever been an ATF informant for that matter. But the FBI official who orchestrated the raid— Special Agent Pete Rickel—was the same man who had discussed witness protection with Carol eight months earlier. His face flushed red, Rickel would later admit under cross-examination in court that he had rebuffed Carol when she asked for witness protection.[34]

It would later come out in court that the impetus behind the raid had come from the highest levels of the FBI in Washington. It involved not only the chief of domestic terrorism, Kenneth Piernick, but also the head of the national security division, Robert Bryant. This is not the first time that Bryant has surfaced in controversial cases. As head of the Washington Field Office, he had been in charge of the FBI's much criticized response to Vincent Foster's death in 1993.

Carol's live-in boyfriend, James Viefhaus, was indicted on bombing charges, but Carol herself was left hanging, uncertain whether or not they would indict her next. If the purpose was judicial black-mail—as her lawyers have alleged—it was a poor reading of her character. Carol reacted with fury.

Eleven days later she agreed to talk to J. D. Cash, the first time she had ever divulged a word to the press. As they discussed Andreas Strassmeir on the telephone, she dropped a bombshell. Andy never was much of a lover, she said. "All he wanted to do was blow up fed-eral buildings." Cash was flabbergasted. He called me in Washington, flush with excitement, and played the tape. It was a val-idation of everything Cash had been saying for a year about the Elohim conspiracy.

A few days later they met at her house in Tulsa. During the inter-view Cash showed her a document that happened to have Agent Angela Finley's name on it.

"You don't work for *them*, do you?" she shouted at him. Then, beside herself with rage, she fetched a business card with Finley's name on it and said that she used to "work for *those people*."

Throwing caution to the winds in an act of blissful revenge, she explained that she had been an undercover informant for the ATF, infiltrating the White Aryan Resistance, Elohim City, the Aryan Republican Army—and, as it happened, a conspiracy to bomb fed-eral buildings in Oklahoma.

When J. D. Cash published his astounding scoop in *The McCurtain Daily Gazette*, it set off an earthquake. The Justice Department had insisted time and again that no agency of the U.S. government had had an informant at Elohim City. It was a demonstrable lie—for which, by the way, nobody has ever been sanctioned or held to account. Now there was a frantic campaign to prevent any major news outlet from picking up the Cash story. An ABC News segment on Carol Howe was pulled at the last moment on February 5, 1997.[35]

The ABC producers for *20/20* were sitting in the lobby at ABC's KTUL affiliate in Tulsa, waiting to watch the program, only to find that it had been replaced by a segment on New Zealand. When it became clear that the piece was never going to run, the assistant producer, retired Marine Lt. Col. Roger Charles, spoke out in protest. Appearing on the Don Imus radio show, he accused Peter Jennings and the top management of ABC News of caving in to political pressure. He was fired immediately.

"There were two messages," Charles told me later. "The first was that this story would bring the country down, whatever that's supposed to mean. The second was that it would lead to the abolition of the ATF. Machine guns on every street corner. You know the argument."[36]

Abandoning the media as a lost cause, Roger Charles went to work for the defense team of Tim McVeigh. Over the next month, McVeigh's counsel, Stephen Jones, would recast the whole defense strategy, hoping to exculpate McVeigh by suggesting that the Nazis of Elohim were the true perpetrators of the Oklahoma bombing. Carol Howe was going to be the star witness, the linchpin that held it all together.

The Justice Department promptly issued a superseding indictment against Carol Howe on March 11, three months after raiding her house. She was charged with conspiracy, willfully making a bomb threat and possessing a nonregistered destructive device. It tainted her as a witness, and it put her under immense pressure to accept a plea bargain under terms imposed by the political powers in Washington. She told them to go to hell. "If the Justice Department thinks it's going to shut me up, it's going to have the opposite effect," she told J. D. Cash.

Stephen Jones filed a writ of mandamus to the Tenth Circuit Court of Appeals, accusing the "government of engaging in a willful and knowing cover-up of information supplied to it by its informant." The writ asserted that the indictment of Carol Howe was obtained "for purposes of leverage against her in order to keep her mouth shut about the activities of Mahon and Strassmeir."

Jones argued that "there is a high probability that Mahon and Strassmeir are part of a conspiracy that planned to bomb federal buildings, and may in fact have been part of the conspiracy to bomb the Murrah Building.... Our patience is exhausted. We are no longer convinced the documents drafted and furnished to us, after the fact, by bureaucracies whose very existence is challenged, can be relied upon.... Statements by the prosecution that it cannot connect Strassmeir and Mahon to the bombing are hardly surprising. They did not try very hard to connect them because had they been connected, and Carol Howe's previous warning disclosed, the resulting furor would have been unimaginable."

The Appeals Court rejected the writ of mandamus. Then Judge Richard Matsch ruled that Carol Howe could not even be called as a witness in McVeigh's trial. Her testimony was deemed "irrelevant." For Stephen Jones it was a devastating blow. The foundation stone of the defense had been ripped away. The trial became a desiccated exercise and a poor advertisement for the American judicial system. It was the reverse of the O. J. Simpson trial, lurching from one extreme of an overindulgent star-struck judge to the other extreme of a rigid, narrow judge who was overly willing to accommodate executive power.

For the Justice Department it was a victory, of course. Nobody learned anything worthwhile from the McVeigh trial. But it now had to deal with the consequences of indicting the irrepressible daughter of a very wealthy man. Carol's pugnacious lawyer, Clark Brewster, was running rings around the U.S. Attorney's office in Tulsa. And this time the judge was standing up against the executive branch. He compelled the ATF to produce Angela Finley's reports under legal discovery. These would prove that Carol Howe was still a U.S. government operative on December 13, 1996, the day that the FBI raided her house.

Another lie by the Justice Department had been exposed, but this was nothing compared to the rebuke that the prosecutors would suffer when they brought Carol to trial in front of an attentive Tulsa jury in late July and early August of 1997. Eerily pale, with a tragic look about her, she sat motionless in a pink suit as the government attempted to turn her undercover role against her.

Sitting in the court room, I began to feel sorry for the two assistant U.S. Attorneys, decent men following orders to pursue a case they must have known to be an abomination. It was almost pathetic to hear them explain why the constituents of the pipe bomb in the case had been provided to the defendant by the U.S. government in the first place, or explain why Carol Howe was listed on official documents as an active informant of the U.S. government—not a former informant, not a dormant informant—on the day that her house was raided by the same U.S. government.

"The government is not on trial. We did not manufacture this case against the defendant," said Neal Fitzpatrick, plaintively, going through the motions. His efforts at moral outrage were stillborn, because he manifestly did not believe his own words. "To suggest that these charges are retaliatory is absurd."

But everybody in the room suspected that it was exactly that, a retaliatory, manufactured case. On the higher plane of history, it was most certainly the Clinton Justice Department that was on trial, not Carol Howe.

"They ought to be ashamed of themselves. Goodness, how can the government look you in the face and ask you to convict her," thundered Carol's lawyer, Clark Brewster, as he accused the prosecution of trying to destroy his client before she could reveal their terrible secrets. "They want to put Carol Howe away for what she knows, but they need twelve accomplices to do it…. Don't let them. This is wrong!"

The last witness was Carol's white-haired father, Robert Howe. Dressed in a trim grey suit, he was the picture of reassuring respectability. He was asked to read a letter that Carol had written three years earlier, addressed to her family, to be opened in the case of her death or her disappearance into the witness protection program. He had never seen it before.

"Well, I guess by now you may have figured out what happened. Maybe someone's come to see you to explain, maybe you've seen it on the news or in the paper," her father began to read. "Carol Elizabeth Howe no longer exists.

"I don't like America as she is today, but I don't think she is past saving. And if there is something I can do to help this country realize a glimmer of her potential greatness, then I must do it. These people intend to start a war here within the next few years. They have the power, means, and support to do it. This war would especially devastate America. These organizations must be dissembled [sic] one by one....

"Mom, you asked me what I've done to help anyone else. I guess you were right. I've never done anything for anyone else. Now with my actions and with my testimony I am helping every American man, woman, and child. I am helping to avert a war.

"You see, I've always been an idealist, never a realist," continued her father, pausing to wipe away the tears. "I've seen now that I can make a small contribution to my fellow man in the great scheme of things.... I... will live a sacrifice every day for the rest of my life. But I have chosen this path with my eyes wide open and know it is the right one.

"Family, you have done a great job of educating me and preparing me for life. The ATF will now finish where we left off; they will teach me to be responsible, to make good decisions and to take care of myself.... I hope you continue to love me and perhaps respect me and be proud of me."

She was acquitted on all charges on Friday, August 1, 1997. The Clinton administration had fired and missed. Now there would be a settling of accounts.

CHAPTER SIX

LT. ANDREAS STRASSMEIR
PzGren (SPz)

A NDREAS STRASSMEIR MUST lead a charmed life. Two days after the Oklahoma bombing Carol Howe reminded the FBI that Strassmeir was a terrorist instigator who had "talked frequently about direct action against the U.S. government" and had "discussed assassinations, bombings and mass shootings."[1]

The FBI record of her debriefing, dated April 21, 1995, goes on to say that Strassmeir had "taken three trips to Oklahoma City in November 1994, December 1994, and February 1995." It also mentioned the fact that Strassmeir's friend Dennis Mahon had threatened to blow up the Oklahoma Federal Building.

Yet the FBI saw no reason to interview Strassmeir. An illegal alien, he was allowed to leave the country and return to Germany in his own good time in January 1996. The Bureau waited until April 30, 1996, more than a year after the bombing, before conducting a desultory interview over the telephone.

"It was a conference call with my lawyer," he said. "The FBI asked where I was on the day of the bombing. They wanted me to help debunk the rumors spread about me."[2]

Before the McVeigh trial, the Justice Department derided any suggestion that Strassmeir could be linked to the Oklahoma bombing. The chief prosecutor, Joseph Hartzler, even went so far as to state to the court that "at no time did the FBI consider Andreas Strassmeir a subject of the Oklahoma City bombing investigation."

This was not true.

On April 28, 1995, the U.S. Embassy in Bonn sent a cable "TO SECSTATE WASHDC PRIORITY" in reference to the "Oklahoma City Bombing." The teletype transmits the results of a background check on Andreas Carl Strassmeir by German Police Intelligence. It refers to the e-mail and telcon requests of FBI Special Agent Hudspeth made on April 27, 1995.

The cable was sent to the State Department in Washington for distribution to the Counterterrorism Division, and to the office of Deputy Secretary of State Strobe Talbott. Clearly, Strassmeir was under investigation by somebody in the FBI immediately after the bombing. Then the paper trail abruptly stops.

Strassmeir's credentials as a virulent, anti-government warrior in the Aryan resistance are a little shaky, as we shall see. His father, Günter Strassmeir, was a solid, respected member of Germany's ruling Christian Democratic Party (CDU) before his retirement in 1991. During the 1980s the elder Strassmeir served as party chief in Berlin and then as Parliamentary Secretary of State to Chancellor Helmut Kohl from 1989 to 1991.[3] One of Günter's younger sons, Alexander, is currently an elected member of the Berlin assembly. The family is quiet, hardworking, and anything but extremist.

Andreas joined the army. Exactly what he did during eight years in the military is still elusive. He told me that he was a lieutenant in the Panzer Grenadiers, second-in-command of a company of 120 mm mortars on the Helmstedt Highway. This part is true. His papers from the *Kampftruppenshule* in Münster in 1982 list him as an officer cadet in the *PzGren (SPz)*. He also told me that he did a stint as a liaison officer with the British Army of the Rhine. He was placed in the Welsh Guards, which allowed him to cultivate his interest in Celtic folklore.

But he told me other things that are difficult to verify. In the late spring of 1996 we had five long conversations on the telephone. He was living at his parents' home in Wilmersdorf, an affluent sector of West Berlin. It was not easy to get him. He would disappear at times, apparently attending to his affairs at a local *Kneiper*, or an Irish pub he frequented in Berlin. (He said he was besotted with a young Irish woman, who kept breaking his heart.)

But once he was on the telephone line, he enjoyed talking. He would ruminate for hours in his slight guttural accent about life as… as… as what? A Nazi? A spy?

That was never quite clear. At times it was like listening to an organ fugue, billowing up toward a climax as his thoughts raced ahead, then subsiding as he realized he was revealing too much. He should have cut me off, but something impelled him. I believe that the pretense of being a Nazi had become too painful, both for him and for his family. It was horrible, he said, for his parents to pick up the *Tagesspiegel* in Berlin and read that their son was a militant Aryan racist. He wanted to reassure the world that his calling was higher. I was willing to believe him.

"I gained very good knowledge about military intelligence procedures that I can't talk about," he said, and promptly started doing exactly that. He explained that he had served as acting battalion intelligence officer on a regular basis when the designated officer was away on training.

"Military intelligence doesn't have enough young people, so they like to pick junior officers from the field units, to give them some experience…. It doesn't necessarily appear on your papers," he added.

The work involved detecting infiltration by East German agents in the West German Army, apparently a big problem at the time. "If we caught a guy, we'd offer him an amnesty. We'd turn him and use him to feed false information back to the Warsaw Pact."

He also engaged in undercover assignments for the German Police. Under the German *Grundgesetz*, he explained, the police were highly restricted in what they could do. They got around the rules by involving the military. "We did a lot of work with drugs," he said.

So this is the professional background of Lieutenant Andreas Strassmeir, *Panzer Grenadiers*. He also studied at the military university in Hamburg, where he got into a dispute with his superiors. They wanted him to finish a degree in social sciences; he wanted to study English medieval history. In any case, *Wanderlust* was already consuming him. He was thinking of fresh adventures across the Atlantic. During a visit to the United States in 1988 for a Gettysburg Civil War reenactment he got in contact with Lt. Col. Vincent Petruskie, a retired U.S. Air Force officer.

Ostensibly, Petruskie had worked for the Air Force Office of Special Investigations, retiring in 1975. Files at the National Military Records Center in St. Louis list him as having been a "Foreign Intelligence Officer" in Vietnam, deployed to the 1131st U.S. Air Force, Special Activities Squadron, Saigon. In the 1970s he served as Special Projects Officer, Special Activities Branch, Counterintelligence Division in Washington, D.C. During the Gulf War he was reactivated with a sensitive assignment in the Gulf states.[4]

"That I know Colonel Petruskie should be a clue too," said Andreas, coyly, without elaborating,

He said that Petruskie was expecting an appointment to the DEA if George Bush was elected President. The colonel had told Andreas that he might be able to use a German with the right kind of military background.

"I discussed the job when I was in Washington. I was hoping to work for the operations section of the DEA, penetrating the cocaine cartels," said Andreas. "He thought I'd be better with the Hispanics."

The lure was enough. Andreas obtained a discharge from the German army at the age of 27. On April 7, 1989, he flew to Washington, D.C., on a regular B2 tourist visa. However, he already had a Special Status of A O in the INS computers.[5] It was logged in the NIXOBAS data system. McVeigh's defense team was never able to establish what A O meant. Nor was I. The INS professed ignorance, saying they had never heard of it before.

Whatever it was, A O was clearly something sensitive because it was later scrubbed from Strassmeir's computer records. A printout dated April 28, 1995, shows A O on all of his entries into the United States. A year later it had vanished from the records. A printout dated March 18, 1996, shows that somebody had gone back into the system and altered the entries. It is one of those tiny clues.

The job with the DEA fell through. Vincent Petruskie told me that he tried to help Andreas get work at the U.S. Treasury—for Customs, not the ATF, Andreas insists adamantly—but he did not get very far. "We took him under our wing when he first came to the United States, and to be quite honest he's a little immature," said Petruskie. "I mean he's a good kid, but he fantasizes."[6]

Does he?

Andreas is very reticent about his next moves. He went to Texas and started working as a salesman for a computer company. For a while he attended the meetings of the Texas Light Infantry militia, until he was chased off as a suspected undercover agent.[7] From there he apparently drifted into the subculture of the Ku Klux Klan and the Aryan Nations. At some point, he formed a friendship with Kirk Lyons, the strident lawyer for the Ku Klux Klan. Lyons introduced him to Elohim City in 1991. "We had to find a place for Andy where he could live off the land because he didn't have a green card."[8]

There, at the nerve center of the U.S. neo-fascist movement, he established himself as chief of security and weapons training. It would be hard to imagine a better vantage point for gathering intelligence on proto-terrorism—and for helping to shape its activities. An FBI memo reveals some of the information that the Oklahoma Highway Patrol had gained from intermittent surveillance of Elohim City.

"Strassmeir is alleged to train platoon-sized groups consisting of approximately thirty to forty individuals approximately every three months at the Elohim City facility. These individuals are comprised of members of various militia groups throughout the United States.... Sources have indicated the existence of bunkers and weapons storage facilities at Elohim City."[9]

Speaking in his usual, elliptical mode, Andreas noted that the ATF lacked the anthropological skills to infiltrate the ultra-right Christo-pagan militias. "They don't know how to talk to them. These groups are irrational, and it takes a special approach," he said. Of course, he may have misjudged the ATF. They did come up with Carol Howe, after all, and she managed to fool everybody, even Lieutenant Strassmeir himself.

"The right wing in the U.S. is incredibly easy to penetrate if you know how to talk to them," he said, making it clear that he considered himself a gifted artist. "Of course, it's easier for a foreigner with an accent; nobody would ever suspect a German of working for the federal government."

But then he changed tack again, saying that he moved to Elohim City because he loved the outdoor life. It was a carefree time. Money was short, but he made ends meet putting up fences, doing landscape work, helping with the sheep. Every now and then his mother, a former screen actress, sent some deutsche marks to help him out. Andreas stayed at the commune for four years, apparently enjoying the kudos he derived from his time in the German military. They in turn were honored to have him.

He built a house and set his heart on one of the nubile daughters of Elohim, then another, and another. His advances were largely unrequited. But he was showered with affection by everybody else. That was the charm of the place. It was a genuine collective, with ceremonial gatherings every day at noon. Even an eccentric misfit like him could be made to feel at home.

The theological race theory of the movement passed him by, as if it were nothing more than cultural decoration. "I'm pretty tolerant when it comes to religion. I'd go to any church, actually," he said.

As for his politics, he called himself a civil libertarian, with a dash of pastoral romanticism. The Waco raid shocked him. "There was really no political protest from the Left, and that disturbed me. Where were all the hippies who protested Kent State?"

In February 1992 Andreas's Chevy stationwagon was impounded after he was stopped at a roadblock by the Oklahoma highway patrol for a traffic violation. "The police broke the lock on my briefcase and removed the documents, which was a violation of my civil rights," he said.

The incident would elicit a remarkable reaction.

"Boy, we caught hell over that one," said Kenny Pence, the driver who towed Andreas's 1983 maroon Chevy. "Some lawyer in Houston called and said they'd made a bad mistake arresting him. You know, we hear that all the time. But then the phone calls started coming in, from the State Department, from the governor's office, and then someone called and said he had diplomatic immunity."[10]

"When they released the car, he just headed straight for that briefcase…. He was a weird cookie, that boy."

Andreas says the man must be confused about the details. "Some calls did come in to rattle their cage," he said. "Something may have been said about my father's position. I don't know where he got this idea about the State Department."

Inside the briefcase was *The Terrorist Handbook*, which explains how to build an ANFO bomb out of fertilizer and fuel oil, and how to make detonators with a delayed fuse.[11] There were also job application forms for the INS and the DEA, foreign bank statements showing that Andreas was not nearly as poor as he pretended, and a stash of documents in German. One was a letter revealing that he was trying to purchase a Boeing 747 from Lufthansa.[12] This was supposedly part of a scheme by Colonel Petruskie to set up an air cargo service in Latin America.[13] Nothing came of that idea either, apparently.

At Elohim the mood was becoming more apocalyptic. "I don't know whether it was 'Andy,' or whether it was the times. There were a lot of things happening, you know, Ruby Ridge, Waco. We were all starting to feel pretty militant," said Joan Millar, the daughter-in-law of Pastor Millar. "But Andy was stirring things up. He was rounding up the younger kids for his patrols, and in the end we had to tell them to stay away from him."[14]

Zara Patterson, one of the church elders, was much blunter. "From the moment Andy got here, all he wanted to do was illegal stuff," he said. "I had to keep telling him that we were on the defensive, that we didn't want any trouble with the feds."

This is a self-serving version of events, of course. Elohim had in fact been stockpiling fully automatic assault rifles and modified MAK 90 rifles in preparation for the expected assault by the federal government.[15] Grandpa had been inciting his followers to take action against ZOG, preaching in fevered tones about the coming "cataclysm."

But Carol Howe had been saying much the same thing about Andreas Strassmeir in her ATF reports. "Andy leads the young adults in guerrilla warfare and tactical maneuvers training.... [He] makes weapon and firearm purchases for those who cannot buy for themselves," she reported to her ATF handler.[16] "His plans are to forcibly act to destroy the U.S. government."

Even by the standards of Elohim, this Prussian was a firebrand.

It was shortly after the Waco assault, in the late spring of 1993, that Strassmeir met Tim McVeigh at a Tulsa gun show. He sold McVeigh a U.S. Navy combat knife, and bought a pair of camouflage pants in exchange. They shared a few brief thoughts on the FBI's deployment of tanks against the Branch Davidians. "We spoke for five minutes, that's all," said Andreas. But they must have hit it off. He gave McVeigh his telephone number at Elohim.

Two years later McVeigh made the telephone call that would embroil Strassmeir in the Oklahoma bombing mystery.[17] It was recorded at 1:46 PM on April 5, 1995, seconds after McVeigh had telephoned a Ryder truck rental office in Arizona. "Tell Andy I'll be coming through," was all that McVeigh had said. It was enough.

"I don't know why McVeigh was trying to contact me," said Andreas.

Two weeks later McVeigh called the offices of Kirk Lyons, the Klan counsel who had introduced Andreas to Elohim City and who would later give him sanctuary after the bombing at his home in Black Mountain, North Carolina. It was April 18, the day before the blast. McVeigh spoke for fifteen minutes, apparently without identifying himself. He was waxing indignant about the Waco raid. Or at least that is what Kirk Lyons now claims. Dave Holloway, who took the call, says that he cut the conversation short when McVeigh started talking about the need to "send a message to the government."[18]

Andreas insists that the meeting in Tulsa was the only time he ever spoke to Tim McVeigh. But a number of witnesses dispute that assertion. In states as far apart as Idaho, Oklahoma, and Kansas, this skinny, buck-toothed German kept surfacing with McVeigh, or in his immediate circle.

Witness sightings can be notoriously unreliable, but it is hard to discount the claims of Katina Lawson. She got involved with McVeigh during a wild phase in the summer of 1992 after she graduated from high school. It has been reported that she was McVeigh's girlfriend. But Katina vehemently denies this. Tim was just a friend, she insists, part of a group of soldiers from Fort Riley she got to know.

The group used to hang around at a house in Herington, Kansas, that she shared with a dissipated party girl named Lindy Johnson. The scene was so debauched, in fact, that Katina moved out soon afterward and severed her ties with her old roommate. But she was a witness for long enough to observe that the McVeigh crowd was heavily involved in drugs, frequently with high school teenagers.

They liked to hold "pasture parties" on Route 77. "Tim was there, but he never drank. He was always in control," she said. "It was weird that summer. There was always this elder gentleman with Tim, mid 40-ish, with a red sports car. He seemed out of place, but he was always around."[19]

At the time Katina was hoping to work as a youth minister for troubled teenagers, and she found McVeigh's views on life to be repugnant. "He said Hitler would have been a great leader for the world. If he had planned it better it might have worked out, and we'd have had an Aryan world.... At first I didn't know if he was joking with all this scary stuff, but by the end I knew he was really warped. He was always making racial slurs. I thought it was sad to have attitudes like that."

Her account is of great significance. The McVeigh that she describes was an ideological activist in the Aryan Nations movement. This is not quite the same as the portrait sketched by the prosecution of an anti-government radical set on avenging Waco. Indeed, the Justice Department has systematically downplayed the Aryan racist in Tim McVeigh, and the U.S. press has followed suit. The question is why? Why deflect attention from the white supremacist movement?

I showed Katina a photograph of Andreas Strassmeir standing in jeans and a lumberjack shirt in front of an American flag. She recognized him at once. "Oh yes, his name is Andy, and he speaks with a German accent. He came to my house once.... It was either Christmas of '92 or New Years of '93.... He had crooked teeth. I remember he was dressed in black, but he had this very white skin.

He mentioned that his daddy was some big shot in Germany.... I thought he seemed kind of odd."

In the most damning of the witness sightings, McVeigh was seen with Strassmeir and Michael Brescia eleven days before the bombing. The three men were at a strip club in Tulsa called Lady Godiva's. We know that the date was April 8 because the security cameras in the dressing room caught three of the dancers chatting on tape.[20] J. D. Cash discovered the tape and made a copy before the FBI had time to confiscate the original. For once, a critical piece of evidence is available to the public instead of being sucked into the black hole of the official investigation.

The tape shows a cocktail waitress, a winsome brunette with a low-cut dress, walking into the locker room. The wall clock says 9:00 PM. She starts talking about a customer who had clearly made an impression.

"He said, 'I'm a very smart man.' 'You are?' 'Yes I am, and on April 19, 1995, you'll remember me for the rest of your life.'"

"Whooa!" laughs one of the other girls.

"Weirdo," says the brunette as she heads back into the noisy bar.

She returns a little later to discuss business with her colleague Shawn Tea Farrens, who is standing with her back to the camera, wearing nothing but a red G-string and high heels: "What time do you get off?"

"About 10:30."

"You know those guys I'm sitting out there with? Well, one of them says he's looking for a girl to fool around with tonight. Are you interested?"

"No, I don't do that kind of thing all weekend."

"He already knows I'm married. I won't do it."

"Oh, I've got to scam 'em somehow," said Shawn, after thinking about it.

"I kissed his forehead. He's got this real sweaty forehead."

"Oh, gross!" laughs Shawn.

Unfortunately, it is not possible to question Shawn about her night on the town with McVeigh, Strassmeir, and Brescia. She was found dead in her apartment, aged 23, shortly after the existence of the tape became known. The death was ruled a suicide.

But the staff of Lady Godiva's have identified the group of men, first in interviews with J. D. Cash, and then with an investigation team from the Canadian Broadcast Company's *Fifth Estate*. The staff clearly remembered McVeigh sitting in a booth. They could hardly forget him. When he was arrested for the bombing two weeks later his visit was something of a sensation at the club.

But they also picked out Michael Brescia and Andreas Strassmeir from a montage of photos. Brescia, they recalled, was very good looking, but full of himself. He was the one paying for the drinks and flashing hundred dollar bills. Strassmeir was quieter, but they remembered his distinctive narrow face and his buck teeth.

According to the FBI version of events, McVeigh could not possibly have been in Tulsa on April 8, 1995. The records show that he checked into the Imperial Motel in Kingman, Arizona, on April 5 and paid through until April 12. But the telephone logs tell a different story. Shortly after checking in, McVeigh called Elohim City and left his message for "Andy the German" that he would be coming through. There was a steady pace of calls from his motel room for two days. Then it stopped. There was no further telephone activity from his room between April 7 and 11. He vanished from the radar screen.

Andreas says that at the time of the bombing he was at work "clearing a line fence" on the land of an elderly couple near Elohim. He refuses to identify the couple, but insists they kept a schedule sheet that would validate his claim. He says he returned to Elohim an hour and a half later because it was raining. He watched the news about Oklahoma on TV with his housemate and votary, Peter Ward. "I named him as an alibi witness," he said.

Really?

Peter Ward was the tall, fair-haired man named by both Carol Howe and Officer John Haynie of the Oklahoma Highway Patrol as a possible candidate for bombing suspect John Doe One.[21] By the time I learned about this, Andreas had already gone underground. I tried to set up a further series of interviews with the help of his brother, Alexander, but to no avail. The two brothers were not talking to each other much anyway.

"It really is terrible the people he got mixed up with," said Alexander. "All these neo-Nazis and the Ku Klux Klan. I mean, it's quite dreadful."

"It doesn't look good," I agreed. "Especially the bombing."

"Oh God," he groaned.

He is a nice man. All the family are charming. Even Andreas has the mannerisms of a well brought up, polite, late twentieth century Berliner. But there is no escaping the fact that he is now the chief target of McVeigh's defense team. As the appeals process moves its way through the Tenth Circuit Court of Appeals, the petition for a new trial is based largely on the allegation that Andreas Strassmeir and his friends were the true culprits behind the Oklahoma bombing.

In light of this, it is worth exploring what Strassmeir himself told me about the bombing. The series of conversations we had in the late spring of 1996 are probably a unique record of his rambling on the subject. I offer it to the reader as a window into his mind, not as an assertion of fact. He spoke vicariously, alluding to his "very reliable source." He never acknowledged playing any role in the terrorist plot, either as an Aryan warrior or as an undercover agent, informant, or participant observer.

But it was my intuitive feeling that the "very reliable source" was none other than Lt. Andreas Strassmeir of the *Panzer Grenadiers (SPz)*. I sensed that he was in deep anguish about the tragedy and wished to get some of it off his chest without violating any secret protocol he may have signed. Undoubtedly he mixed disinformation with elements of truth. What struck me were the unpredictable surges of passion.

"The different agencies weren't cooperating," he said. "In fact, they were working *against* each other. You even had a situation where one branch of the FBI was investigating and not sharing anything with another branch of the FBI."

Overall, however, he was protective of the Bureau. It was the ATF that evoked intense feelings of bitterness, betrayal, and anger.

"It's obvious that it was a government 'op' that went wrong, isn't it? The ATF had something going with McVeigh. They were watching him—of course they were," he asserted, without qualification. "What they should have done is make an arrest while the bomb was still being made instead of waiting till the last moment for a publicity stunt. They had everything they needed to make the bust, and they screwed it up."

He said that the sting operation acquired a momentum of its own as the ATF tried to "ice the cake" for more dramatic effect. "Whoever thought this thing up is an idiot, in my opinion. I am told they thought it would be better to put a bigger bomb in there. The bigger the better. It would make them more guilty.... McVeigh knew he was delivering a bomb, but he had no idea what was in that truck. He just wanted to shake things up a little; you know, make a gesture."

"According to your source?"

"That's correct. The bomb was never meant to explode. They were going to arrest McVeigh at the site with the bomb in hand, but he didn't come at the right time.... Maybe he changed the time, you never know with people who are so unreliable."

"What time were they expecting the truck?" I asked.

"I have heard that it was the middle of the night, between two and three in the morning. The truck had a transmitter, so they could track it with a radio receiving device. I don't know how they could

have lost contact. I think there was misinformation that the operation had been canceled."

I told Strassmeir outright that the evidence linking him to the
bombing was very strong.

"Either you are a mass murderer, or you are an undercover
agent," I said. "Either you killed all those people, or you risked your
life to penetrate a group of vile, dangerous people. Take your pick,
Andreas, but don't think you can stick your head in the sand and
hope that it will all go away. It won't go away."

"You don't understand," he said.

"You know what I think already," I persisted. "I think you're a
very courageous man. I think you did everything you could to stop
that bombing. You did your part; you got inside the most deadly terrorist conspiracy in the history of the United States; you got these
maniacs to believe in you; your cover was brilliant; and somebody let
you down, didn't they Andreas?"

"You don't understand," he repeated almost plaintively.

"I do understand, Andreas. I understand that it wasn't your fault.
Are you listening to me? It wasn't your fault. So why not just come
out and tell the whole rotten truth, and get it over and done with?
You don't have to cover for the ATF."

"You think it's as simple as that?" he stammered.

"I don't know, Andreas. You tell me. Who were you working for
anyway? Did the Germans send you over?"

"No! No, they would never do that."

"So who was it then? The ATF? The Bureau? Who were you
working for?"

"Look, I can't talk any longer."

"Just listen to me, Andreas. They're going to hang you out to dry.
When this thing comes down they're going to leave you holding that
bomb, or—and you know this as well as I do—you'll fall under a
train one day on the U Bahn, when nobody's looking."

"I've got to go to work."

"There comes a time in every botched operation when the informant has to speak out to save his own skin, and that's now, Andreas."

"How can he?" he shouted into the telephone. "What happens if it was a sting operation from the very beginning? What happens if it comes out that the plant was a provocateur?"

"A provocateur?"

"What if he talked and manipulated the others into it? What then? The country couldn't handle it. The relatives of the victims are going to go crazy. He's going to be held responsible for the murder of 168 people."

"That is true."

"Of course the informant can't come forward. He's scared shitless right now."

"It sounds to me as if you've got a problem, Andreas."

"*Scheise.*"

*   *   *

So who was Andreas Strassmeir working for?

Before the trial in Denver, McVeigh's defense team secured a court order from Judge Richard Matsch compelling the major U.S. law enforcement and intelligence agencies to reveal whether Andreas Strassmeir had ever worked for them as a source, informant, or undercover agent. It is notoriously hard to pin down federal agencies with this type of request. Unless the wording is exactly right, there is usually a way to wriggle out of disclosure without explicitly violating the court order. So it was no surprise when each of the law enforcement agencies came back with denials.

But the response of the CIA remains a secret. The Agency provided its findings to prosecutor Beth Wilkinson, who refused to hand the material to McVeigh's defense team. The Justice Department even ignored a motion to compel, without suffering any sanction from Judge Matsch. At the end of the trial, McVeigh's lawyers still did not know what the CIA had revealed about its ties to the mysterious Andreas Strassmeir.

It is assumed that Strassmeir could not have been a CIA asset because he was operating on U.S. soil. But this is not necessarily the case. He could have been reporting to the domestic services section of the CIA, which has offices all over the country.[22] Under usual procedures, his reports would be passed through them to the CIA's Directorate of Operations. Or alternatively, he could have been an FBI operative working under CIA auspices.

My own conjecture, for what it is worth, is that Strassmeir was a shared asset, on loan to the U.S. government, but ultimately answering to German intelligence. It has been a pet gripe of the Germans for many years that the U.S. neo-Nazis, operating with great freedom under American constitutional protections, have been stirring up the German far right.

FBI Director Louis Freeh alluded to this in December 1993 after a trip to Germany. "We were requested by both the Interior Minister and the Justice Minister to look particularly at several cases where they believe activity by U.S. persons are contributing to the commission of crimes against Germany, and we're going to look at that very seriously and very vigorously."

Freeh's remarks give us a glimpse of the increasingly tight cooperation between the U.S. and German authorities. But I suspect that Strassmeir's operation was already up and running by this stage. I also suspect that there was a more serious purpose than merely stopping the flow of racist propaganda across the Atlantic. It is worth paying some attention to the words of Ron Noble, Undersecretary of the Treasury, who accompanied Freeh on the trip to Germany.

"The FBI Director discussed his concern about the possibility of nuclear materials falling into criminal hands in meetings with Germany's Interior and Justice Ministers."

If I had to bet, I would hazard that Andreas Strassmeir's real purpose at Elohim City was to find out whether the U.S. neo-Nazi movement had the capability and intent to graduate to weapons of mass destruction, particularly biological and chemical devices. A high level counterintelligence operation of this kind would explain why Elohim City was being protected, even though it was engaged in every weapons violation in the U.S. code, not to mention manifest sedition.

CHAPTER SEVEN

THE ARYAN REPUBLICAN ARMY

GLENN WILBURN AND J. D. Cash had amassed enough evidence to convince themselves, if not the FBI, that the bombing was carried out by a team of four to six men, with several others playing support roles in the background. Elohim City was either the headquarters, or at least an integral part of the conspiracy. But what was the organizational structure that tied it together? How was it financed?

Shortly after the bombing, *The New York Times* had reported that McVeigh and Nichols may have been linked to a spree of bank robberies in the Midwest. Most of the press forgot about this after the Justice Department performed one of its nimble pirouettes and issued a new story. J. D. Cash did not.

He discovered that Tim McVeigh's sister, Jennifer, had given a sworn statement to the FBI on May 2, 1995, admitting that her brother had asked her to exchange three $100 bills for clean money. She deposited the three bills at the Federal Credit Union in Lockport, New York, in December 1994.

"He had been involved in a bank robbery but did not provide further details. He advised me that he had not participated in the robbery itself, but was somehow involved in the planning or setting up of this robbery," she said in the affidavit. "I observed at that time that my brother had on his person an undetermined quantity of $100 bills, of which he provided me a small portion. It is my belief that the bank robbery had occurred within the recent past. My brother remarked that the money represented his share of the bank robbery proceeds."

So Cash paid close attention when a group of bank robbers were arrested in Ohio in early 1996, especially when it came to light that the band was a self-described commando cell of the Aryan Republican Army.

The ARA was modeled on the Aryan Resistance Movement, the military arm of a clandestine Nazi organization called *Bruders Schweigen* or simply, *The Order*.[1] In the early 1980s *The Order* was arguably the most dangerous terrorist group in the United States, robbing $3.8 million from a Brinks armored car, planting bombs, and killing, in an escalating guerrilla campaign against the Zionist Occupied Government.

The organization was finally broken by the FBI in 1984 when the leader, Robert Mathews, or "Carlos" as he strangely called himself, chose a fiery "martyrdom" rather than surrender to the FBI. He went up in flames on an island in the Puget Sound as 150 FBI agents watched in awe.

He left behind some very specific instructions on terrorist tactics.[2] "The first rule that must be strictly observed is that cells must be kept separate from other units and then must be broken down into even smaller units called teams. It is recommended that no unit comprise more than six members. This unit is then broken down into two- or three-man teams.

"Every member of the *Bruders Schweigen* is expected to obtain at least one, and preferably two, false identities. No member is to divulge his new identity to anyone, not even his team leader.... All sensitive communications must be made from a pay phone, and often from pay phone to pay phone. Every member should have at least one ten dollar roll of quarters with him at all times...." The document concludes: "This is the strategy of an underground army."

The Aryan Republican Army was clearly an attempt to reconstitute *The Order* for round two of the terrorist war against the ZOG. "Our goal was to open the door to the overthrow of the United States government," admitted Kevin McCarthy, one of the bank robbers.

When the FBI busted two ARA safe houses in Ohio and Kansas in February 1996, they found a recruitment video called the "Armed Struggle Underground." A laconic "Commander Pedro," sitting in a command "bunker" with a ski mask covering his face, explains that the goal of the ARA is the overthrow of the U.S. government, the extermination of America's Jews, the deportation of all blacks, and the establishment of an "Aryan Republic" on the North American continent.

"Linger at your own peril," warns Pedro, with theatrical menace. "We have endeavored to keep collateral damage and civilian damage to a minimum. But, as in all wars, some innocents shall suffer. So be it."

The tape is an interesting exhibit of terrorist cross-pollination in the post-Communist era.

"We call ourselves the Aryan Republican Army because in some of our tactics, and some of our goals, we have modeled the organization after the successful and yet undefeated Irish Republican Army," says Commander Pedro.

"In solidarity with our Serbian brothers, we understand the meaning of ethnic cleansing," says Pedro, briefly digressing into the Balkans, but clearly it is the Provisional IRA that has captured the imagination of the group. This is not entirely surprising. The

"Provos" are the premier terrorist professionals in Europe. And as we have seen, the Christian Identity sect regards the Celtic peoples as the purest survivors of the Aryan race. "The Irish, another tribe of the Aryan people, have fought off the Jewish-inspired elite of the English," says the Commander.

The tape starts with an IRA song, *The Patriot Game*, then moves on to a lively discourse on kneecapping. "We will deal with informers ruthlessly and permanently. For actively working with our enemies, you'll be terminated. If you just like to run your mouth, you'll be kneecapped," warns Commander Pedro, holding up an automatic pistol, and then the feared symbol of the IRA—an electric drill. "Either one, I can assure you, are extremely painful."

Among the items seized from a storage locker belonging to the group was the Irish Republican Army handbook, a terrorist manual known in Ireland as the Green Book. "I gave them that," said Dennis Mahon, who considers himself something of an expert on the Irish cause.[3]

Needless to say, the IRA itself had no idea that it had become a role model for deranged Nazis in the United States. An organization with historic and emotional ties to the Left, it exists in a different ideological universe, though Irish nationalists did indeed flirt with Hitler, at least to the point of official Irish Republic neutrality during the Second World War. In any case, the Provos maintain a strict ban on transatlantic subversion. Any IRA guerrilla who violated this cardinal rule—provoking the wrath of U.S. counterterrorist forces—would probably be court-martialed by the IRA's own military command.

The Aryan Republican Army was equipped for terrorism. In the busts, the FBI captured a shoulder-fired rocket launcher, Semtex explosives, hand-grenade canisters, eleven pipe bombs, and an arsenal of M-14 rifles. It also found high-quality false I.D. badges and drivers licenses in the names of U.S. marshals and FBI agents, along with boxes of books and tapes that included *Say It in Arabic*, a guide to Interpol, a registry of U.S. government radio frequencies, *The Scottish Chiefs*, and *Quotations from Chairman Mao Tse-Tung*.[4]

But this cell was not primarily a terrorist action squad. It appears to have been the fundraising arm of the Aryan revolution. Over a two year stretch, between January 1994 and December 1995, the group netted more than $250,000 in well-planned, pinprick robberies across the Midwest. Wearing Ronald Reagan and Count Dracula masks, they would burst into small town banks, seize the cash on hand—anywhere from $3,000 to $30,000—and get out within 90 seconds, never pushing their luck by trying to get the big haul from the vault. As a decoy for the police, they would leave disarmed pipe bombs in Easter baskets and Christmas stockings.

They were a comical lot. Their special touch was leaving evidence that would track back to legitimate agents of the FBI. Sooner or later, they were bound to make a mistake. It happened when one of the group broke discipline and started freelancing on the side. By the time the FBI cracked the cell, the ARA had carried out a total of twenty-two bank robberies. It was a run that matched the brief career of Jesse James.

One of the commanders, Richard Guthrie, did not last long in police custody. The prison guards found him dangling from an air vent with a sheet around his neck on July 10, 1996. The other commander, Peter Langan, 38, was lucky to survive capture. His white van was shot to pieces by a combined "Safe Streets Task Force" of the FBI, U.S. Marshals, and local police, though he never fired a shot himself. Grazed in the head by a bullet, he managed to crawl out alive.

Langan was high school dropout from suburban Washington, and the son of a CIA agent. It soon emerged that he was the Commander Pedro of the ARA video, though a good deal less menacing without his ski mask. According to a hilarious article by Richard Leiby in *The Washington Post*, Langan had pink varnish on his toenails and a shaven crotch when he was captured by the FBI.

Commander Pedro was a transvestite. He was known as "Donna" at the chapter of Crossdressers and Friends in Kansas City.

This ARA cell might have been no more than a colorful footnote in the history of criminal gangs, except for the fact that all four of the other indicted co-conspirators had close ties to Elohim City. One of them was Pastor Mark Thomas, head of the Posse Comitatus of Pennsylvania and East Coast leader of the Aryan Nations. A former "state chaplain" of the Ku Klux Klan, he had left the organization because it was, he told me, infested with "do-nothing bellyachers."

At his run-down farm in Pennsylvania, he published an intellectual newsletter called *The Watchman*. It offered a rich stew of Odinism, Jungean ancestral theory, and national-socialist anticapitalism—the doctrinal expression of the Aryan Republican Army.

The other three were his protégés, Kevin McCarthy, Scott Stedeford, and Michael Brescia, all former skinheads from Philadelphia who had played together in a speed-metal rock band called Cyanide. Mark Thomas had introduced them to Elohim City, where they had gone through terrorist boot camp under Andreas Strassmeir.

McCarthy and Stedeford used to stay with Strassmeir when they came through for R&R between robberies. In fact, they were with him at Elohim City immediately before the bombing in April 1995, according to McCarthy's statement to the FBI.[5]

Brescia's role seems to have been different. He did participate in the robbery of $9,845 from Bank One in Madison, Wisconsin, on August 30, 1995, waving a 9 mm pistol at customers, and planting a black-powder pipe bomb in the bank. But robbery was not his main function in the ARA. He was a permanent resident of Elohim City, betrothed to Esther Millar, the granddaughter of the patriarch. There, Brescia served as second-in-command of paramilitary operations, apprentice terrorist, and soulmate of Lieutenant Strassmeir.

It was the same Michael Brescia who had been named by Dennis Mahon as the "pretty-boy John Doe Two" when he inadvertently gave away the secrets of the bombing to J. D. Cash.

*   *   *

Glenn Wilburn had a mind like a steel trap. He rarely forgot a name, and this one kept spinning in his head during the early months of 1996. Who was Michael Brescia? Where did he come from?

Mahon's drunken confession had offered a tantalizing lead—yet another one—but it seemed to be going nowhere until a contact in Herington, Kansas, advised him to get in touch with Connie Smith. She was the mother of Katina Lawson, the young woman who had frolicked on and off with Tim McVeigh before she became disgusted by his views.

Glenn called Mrs. Smith on the telephone. J. D. Cash was in the room listening. So was Richard Reyna, the chief investigator for the McVeigh defense team.

Eager to help, she told Glenn about a chance encounter at Cardie's Corner store in Herington, possibly in the summer of 1992. She had run into her daughter, who was hanging out with some new friends. Tim McVeigh was there, accompanied by a very good-looking man called Mike with thick dark hair and a clean-cut, preppie manner. Afterward Mrs. Smith told Katina how handsome this Mike fellow was. Yes, agreed Katina, but he was not as nice as he looked. He was an insufferable braggart, with an undisguised contempt for the peasantry of Kansas.

Connie Smith saw him again in the spring of 1995, around April, getting out of a car.

"Mike? Mike who?" asked Glenn.

"I don't remember. It was a funny name: Braysi or Bresci or something. Mike Bresci, I think."

"Brescia?"

"Yes, that's it, Mike Brescia. I couldn't remember when I spoke to the FBI."

"The FBI? What did you tell the FBI?"

"I told them he looked like John Doe number two.... But they weren't interested."

Glenn couldn't believe his ears. Somebody in Kansas had independently established the link between Tim McVeigh and Michael Brescia. It was imperative, said Glenn, to find a picture of Brescia and show it to the witnesses in Kansas.

J. D. Cash had discovered that Brescia came from Philadelphia. This was closely guarded information. Brescia pretended that he came from the West Coast, and claimed that his father was a Portland lawyer.[6]

Since I lived near Washington, D.C., two hours' drive from Philadelphia, Glenn Wilburn enlisted me in the hunt for a photograph.[7] It did not take long to find out that Michael Brescia's father was an irascible battalion chief for the Fire Department in the Andorra section of Philadelphia. His mother was head of the local civic association, a busybody who had led a campaign to stop construction of a synagogue in their leafy, affluent, very Catholic neighborhood.

They were a pushy family, climbing fast up the social ladder. As for Michael, he was affable, extremely bright, with boyish good looks and, though not tall, a tennis player's body. An Eagle Scout, he had gone on to study finance at La Salle University in Philadelphia. Somehow, blessed with every advantage in life, he turned into a skinhead.

At La Salle he started going to lectures with the sides of his head shaved, a Mohawk buzz over the crown, and a ponytail down the back. Then he tried to set up a white supremacist cell on campus. He stopped going to classes in June 1993. He mentioned something about a "bookkeeping" job in Oklahoma before he vanished. His fellow students had no idea that he had taken the plunge, signing up as a full-fledged warrior in the Aryan Republican Army. All they were left with was a picture of him in the La Salle yearbook holding a corner of the Delta Sigma Pi fraternity flag. It was Brescia in his respectable mode. Coat and tie. Preppie.

"That's him," said Connie Smith, at her home in the farm village of Ramona.[8]

"No question, that's Mike," agreed Katina, leaning over her mother's shoulder.

Katina explained that her housemate, Lindy Johnson, had a brief fling with Brescia after Tim McVeigh had introduced him into their circle in the summer of 1992.[9] "I never found out what he was doing in Kansas. But I remember Lindy saying that he came from Pennsylvania, and I saw the Pennsylvania tags on his car."

Katina had come forward to the FBI after she saw Tim McVeigh undergoing his courthouse "perp walk" in an orange jumpsuit two days after the bombing. The FBI asked if she recognized the sketch of John Doe Two. "I told them he had a tattoo on his arm and his name was 'Mike,' but I didn't know the rest of his name," she said.[10]

Connie said, "I kept telling them that suspect number two was that Mike guy, a nice looking guy, dark skinned; whenever I saw Tim McVeigh he was there.... But they made Katina and I feel ignorant, like we didn't know what we were saying.... When I tried to call in with more information, they wouldn't even talk to me.

"Later the FBI started asking weird questions about Katina. They were sending me a message, a very negative message. That's when I said: 'To heck with this, I'm not going to deal with them any more.' In the end I wouldn't even tell them where Katina was.

"We're not being told the truth here," she said. "It scares me to death as an American citizen. We've got to put a stop to this or we'll lose this country."

J. D. Cash drove up from Oklahoma in his dilapidated brown jeep, and we went to visit Tom Kessinger, the mechanic at Elliot's Body Shop who had provided the FBI with the original sketch of

John Doe Two. I waited outside in the car. Kessinger refused to talk to journalists. He made an exception for Cash because Glenn and Kathy Wilburn had anointed him.

"I think this is the guy we're looking for," he said, excitedly, when J. D. showed him the photo of Brescia. "Where's he from?"

"Italian," said J. D.

"So he tans easily… a real lady-killer. This could be him, but I'll need to look at a color photo."

Months later, after a series of visits by the FBI, Kessinger would self-destruct as a witness. He changed his story abruptly, stating that he had confused John Doe Two with Private Todd Bunting. But the recantation was preposterous. It reflected more on the FBI's methods of coercion than it did on his veracity as a witness. In June of 1996 he was still adamant about his description of the man who had walked into Elliot's Body Shop with Tim McVeigh.

It is possible, I suppose, that Kessinger was spinning yarns, or that Katina Lawson and her mother were both mistaken, or that four women at Lady Godiva's strip club were confused when they said they saw Michael Brescia with Tim McVeigh on April 8, 1995. But there comes a point when accumulated witness testimony reaches critical mass.

At Elohim City, Joan Millar protested that Michael Brescia could not possibly be John Doe Two. "He was right here with us on April 17, helping to prepare the grave for [Richard] Wayne Snell. If he had gone up to Kansas at any time we would have known about it."[11]

Indeed she would. Brescia was part of the family. He was engaged to her daughter, Esther. As for April 19, the day of the bombing, he was supposedly in Little Rock, attending a clemency rally for Richard Snell.[12]

That August he drove to Wisconsin to participate in an ARA bank robbery. After his return, he moved out of the compound, ostensibly expelled for violating the 9:00 PM curfew. For three months Brescia stayed with George Eaton, a neighbor and also the publisher of a radical newsletter called *The Patriot Report*. It was long enough for Eaton to notice the tattoo on Brescia's upper left arm—a marking he shared in common with John Doe Two. It was a circle with four spokes, a neo-fascist symbol.[13]

"He was very difficult to get along with, very secretive," said Eaton. "He wouldn't get a job because he didn't want to use his social security number. Instead he sold military clothing for Civil War reenactments, through magazine ads. He was conducting a whole business, using our washer and dryer, and it got to be a problem. I had to ask him to leave in the end."

For a while he disappeared, much like the others. They had all scattered in different directions. The Ward brothers went to Georgia, then vanished. Peter Ward was later picked up for robbery in Oregon. Strassmeir went to a safe house in Knoxville, Tennessee, then hid out in the Appalachian foothills of North Carolina, and finally made his way back to Germany by crossing the land border into Mexico. (You don't have to show a passport leaving the U.S. across the Rio Grande. All you need is a driver's license. Often they wave you through without looking.)

In the end, Brescia went back to Philadelphia, moved in with his parents, got a job as a bookkeeper at Intelligent Electronics, and enrolled for further classes at La Salle University. On January 30, 1997, he was indicted for his role in the Wisconsin bank robbery by the ARA, and accepted a plea agreement that prevented collateral revelations at trial.

The Justice Department continued to ridicule the notion that the Aryan Republican Army played any role in the Oklahoma bombing. But Glenn Wilburn believed that he had won the argument. He believed that his small circle of followers had solved the crime—the worst mass murder in the history of the United States—and the FBI had failed to do so.

Glenn would go to his grave certain that the bombing was a broad conspiracy involving several men, and that there was some degree of official prior knowledge. The best indications were that the plot was hatched at Elohim City in the fall of 1994 under the guidance of Dennis Mahon and Andreas Strassmeir, two men who are clearly enjoying the protection of the FBI. The attack itself was carried out by the Aryan Republican Army, probably involving more than one terrorist cell. McVeigh was undoubtedly part of the movement. Glenn did not know for sure why the Clinton administration had gone to such lengths to cover this up, but he concluded that the bombing was probably a sting operation that went disastrously wrong. He suspected that the stingers had been outstung at the last moment. But whatever happened, the Justice Department was so fatally enmeshed in the terrorist activities of the ARA that it could not allow the truth to come out. At the very least, the FBI would have to explain why it had ring-fenced a group of virulent Nazis and shielded them from investigation. With time, and with his lawsuit, he believed the truth would force its way into public consciousness.

Consumed by pancreatic cancer, Glenn soldiered on through the early months of 1997. By the end, his voice was gone. Kathy had to interpret his faint utterings as admirers came to pay their last respects. Even *The Daily Oklahoman* found itself paying homage to the man. For two years the dominant newspaper in the state of Oklahoma had been at war with the Wilburns. It had criticized Glenn and mocked his views, but it had never sent a reporter to sit down at that little kitchen table to hear what the leader of the dissident movement had to say.

Two weeks before his death, the call finally came. Glenn, always gracious, made his final heroic effort. Too ill to move, he insisted on being lifted into his wheelchair, his drooping limbs strapped with a sheet, and was taken out to say goodbye to Oklahoma.[14]

"Do you think that the stress of all you've been through the past two years contributed to your illness?" asked the reporter.

Yes, replied Glenn, the emotional trauma had probably suppressed his immune system.

"Knowing that, would you do it all over again?"

"Yes, because I have to look at myself in the mirror."

He died on July 15, 1997, aged 46, an ordinary American who showed great independence of mind. He had been angry with God, bitter at the injustice of the bombing, but he had made his peace. "Lord forgive me that I didn't become all that You wanted me to be," he prayed aloud, in his last conscious act with his wife.

He asked to be buried by Dr. Larry Jones, a family friend and founder of Feed the Children, who had come to see him every day in his agonies.

"What do you want me to tell them?" Jones had asked.

"Just tell them the truth, Larry," replied Glenn.

He did. At the funeral service, Dr. Jones gave a blistering oration. "I don't want us to become a nation, as Alexander Solzhenitsyn said of the Soviet Union, where the lie has become not just a moral category, but a pillar of the state. If I'm not mistaken, we're living in America, and this frustrates me, what is taking place. I am beginning to see that Americans are living under fear of their government."

"I really believe that after the Oklahoma City bombing, if our government had stood up and said: 'This is actually what happened. Something went wrong. And we apologize to Oklahoma City and to the nation. We're sorry for what happened. We want you to forgive us.' Had *that* happened, I don't think we would be here today burying Glenn Wilburn."

"You see, as Huxley said, 'You shall know the truth and the truth shall make you mad.' And as Glenn Wilburn began to find out the truth, it did make him mad. And the load that he carried literally took him to the grave."

The funeral procession circled the haunting, empty site where the Murrah Building had once stood. Among the pallbearers were his greatest admirers: J. D. Cash, State Representative Charles Key, McVeigh defense investigator Richard Reyna, and crime scene witness Bruce Shaw.

For Kathy Wilburn it was a cruel two years. First her grandchildren, then her husband. But she is one of life's stoic souls, raised with the virtues of a different age.

"I will carry it forward," she told me, choking back the tears. "I was Glenn's voice when he couldn't speak any longer, and my mission now is to continue being his voice, for however long it takes, until we know the truth."

VINCE FOSTER AND "THE MOST ETHICAL ADMINISTRATION IN THE HISTORY OF THE REPUBLIC"

—Bill Clinton's promise to the American people,
November 1992

CHAPTER EIGHT

THE TABOO INVESTIGATION

ON JULY 15, 1997, Kenneth Starr issued a terse statement. "Based on investigation, analysis and review of the evidence by experts and experienced investigators and prosecutors, this Office concluded that Mr. Foster committed suicide by gunshot in Fort Marcy Park, VA, on July 20, 1993."

Critics were not allowed to evaluate his arguments or scrutinize his conclusion because the report has not, as I write, been released.

Most people are prepared to accept Starr's conclusion, but before making their judgment they should know that the lead prosecutor appointed to investigate the death came to a very different conclusion. When Starr was presented with the evidence by his own staff, he looked the other way.

Associate Independent Counsel Miquel Rodriguez was summoned to the Washington Office of the Independent Counsel in the fall of 1994 by Kenneth Starr, with the explicit task of reviewing the Foster death. He was not a conservative. He had no ideological investment in the matter. Indeed, when he arrived from California with his ponytail, his earring, and his leather jackets, there were comments among the hard-liners that Kenneth Starr had gone too far in his efforts to recruit Democrats, liberals, and ethnic minorities to his team.

For four months Rodriguez probed the case. He called witnesses before a grand jury to answer questions for the first time under penalty of perjury, and soon discovered serious indications of a cover-up by the FBI. By the early spring of 1995 he was starting to probe a hypothesis that the crime scene at Fort Marcy Park had been staged, that the gun had most likely been planted in Foster's hand, and that a crucial photograph of Foster's neck and head had been falsified.

But Rodriguez believed that the investigation was being sabotaged by prosecutors and FBI agents in his own office. He turned to Starr for support. Nothing was done to resolve the matter. In March 1995 Rodriguez resigned. The only serious investigation ever conducted into the death of Vincent Foster came to an abrupt end.

I do not wish speculate at length about the motives of Kenneth Starr. But one has to wonder about the seriousness of a man willing to abandon a half-completed investigation of the President and seek comfortable refuge as a dean at Pepperdine University in Malibu. The fact that he later reversed himself in panic, after a barrage of press criticism, illustrates the point with brutal clarity. But there is a more important point to understand about Kenneth Starr. He is by character a servant of power, not a prosecutor. One thing can be predicted with absolute certainty: He will never confront the U.S. Justice Department, the FBI, and the institutions of the permanent government in Washington. His whole career has been built on networking, by ingratiating himself. His natural loyalties lie with the politico-legal fraternity that covered up the Foster case in the first place.

While it appears that Kenneth Starr has given more emphasis to investigating Whitewater than to investigating the death of Vince Foster, in my opinion, Whitewater is not a matter of epochal importance. It is a fit subject for news reporting. It is something that the

American people should be told about. It reflects badly on the President and the First Lady. But is it a grievous offense? Should it be allowed to paralyze the executive branch of the world's paramount power? If I were a member of the grand jury in Little Rock, I would be reluctant to indict Bill or Hillary Clinton on anything related to Whitewater, and I believe that a great number of people feel the same way.

The death of Vincent Foster is another matter. He was the highest ranking official of the executive branch to die in suspicious circumstances since President John F. Kennedy; he was handling the private business affairs of the First Family at the White House; and he was Hillary Clinton's closest friend, the one person in the world that she would entrust with the most sensitive problems. His death occurred in July 1993, under this administration. The subsequent conduct of the U.S. Park Police, the U.S. Secret Service, the FBI, the U.S. Justice Department, the Virginia medical authorities, as well as Independent Counsel Robert Fiske and all those who participated in his report indicated that the police and judicial apparatus of this country had been dangerously politicized. Every backstop mechanism had failed. If ever there was a need for a crusading prosecutor to cleanse the institutions of the republic, it was in the case of Vincent Foster.

"Pontius Pilate of the Potomac"—is how Starr was described in a blistering denunciation by James Davidson, the editor of the newsletter *Strategic Investment*. "Starr will fade, but he will not be forgotten. Historians will certainly have something to say about him. When 'The Decline and Fall of the United States' is written, Starr will merit a chapter. He will be seen as a weak, temporizing man who lacked the force of character to confront a corrupt system."

*　　　*　　　*

The Foster case is taboo for American journalists. In private, many concede that the official story is unbelievable, but they will not broach it in print. I have been involved in some contentious matters during my career as a journalist, but I have never seen anything like the irrational fright when the subject of Vincent Foster is raised. It has nothing to do with party affiliation. If anything, Republican journalists are even more susceptible to the spell. Try uttering the words Fort Marcy Park at a gathering of Capitol Hill neo-conservatives and watch the reaction.

I do not entirely understand why this should be so. Unexplained deaths have been a source of fascination for thousands of years, across the globe. What is clear, however, is that the White House has been successful in casting the "Foster crazies" as villains interested in dredging up dirt for partisan advantage without any regard for the feelings of the Foster family. As with all good propaganda, there is an element of truth in this.

Foster left a widow and three children, now grown up. They have been through Purgatory and they linger there still, denied the closure that any normal family would expect. One inquiry after another has kept the controversy alive. It must be exceedingly painful for them.

That said, it is the White House itself that has been exploiting the Foster family, using them as a shield to deflect all legitimate questions about the death. Perhaps they are willing to be exploited in this way for reasons of parallel interest. If so, that is their privilege. But the larger issue needs to be confronted head on. The death of a top official has been covered up by the FBI and the judicial institutions of the U.S. government. It is facile gallantry to silence debate ever after by invoking the name of Lisa Foster.

Americans need to know that within hours of Vincent Foster's death, the White House had stepped in to orchestrate the response of the family. Vulnerable and confused, Lisa Foster surrendered herself totally to the political agenda of James Hamilton, the attorney for the 1992 Clinton-Gore campaign. Let there be no confusion about the allegiances of this man. He is typically described as the

Foster "family lawyer" but an internal White House memo describes him more accurately as a lawyer performing a "surrogate role" for the White House.[1] He was in fact hired by Associate Attorney General Webster Hubbell to handle the fallout from the death. "I knew Jim and asked him to act as counsel," explained Hubbell.[2]

Hamilton was a member of the elite, very expensive K Street firm of Swidler & Berlin. He had never served as Foster's personal lawyer. As the House Travelgate Report makes clear, he was consulted by Vincent Foster shortly before his death as an outside attorney to represent the collective interests of the White House Counsel's Office in the Travelgate affair. He scarcely knew the family.

For the White House, however, he was an ideal "surrogate." He had befriended Hillary Clinton and Bernie Nussbaum, the pugnacious White House Counsel, while serving as Assistant Chief Counsel on the Senate Watergate committee from 1973 to 1974. He had worked on the Clinton transition team, talent scouting for top posts in the new administration, and had continued playing a highly irregular role afterward as leader of a group of private lawyers vetting nominees for the Supreme Court.

There is no question that he did an outstanding job as damage-control handler in the Foster case. For one thing, he did not let the Park Police get anywhere near the grieving family. "We did not interview any of the Foster children. Mr. Hamilton would not make them accessible to us," said Park Police Captain Charles Hume.[3] This is an astounding comment. Foster's children were grown adults, perfectly able to answer questions by the Park Police. Two of them, Laura and Vincent III, accompanied their father to work on the morning of his death. Their insights were critical to the investigation. By what authority can a private lawyer prevent the police from talking to relevant witnesses in the probe of a violent death?

Captain Hume then goes on to say that Lisa Foster had obviously been coached. "She had gone over [the story] with her lawyer [so] that she had it down pat.... I can remember Pete [Markland] having his notebook out and I think he started to question her, you know. We had a hard time to get started because Hamilton wanted to lay out the ground rules."

Lay out the ground rules? It is clear that the U.S. Park Police were deferring to James Hamilton as if he were, indeed, a "surrogate" of the White House.

But there is another reason why Lisa Foster cannot be accorded the last say on all matters concerning her former husband. She must have known, at least intuitively, that Vince was engaged in activities that belied his image of gentlemanly rectitude. This is not to dispute that he was one of life's higher souls, a patron of the Little Rock orchestra, a connoisseur of good wines, a man who enjoyed Tuscany. But that means nothing at all. I have known such people all my life. It is a neutral indicator of moral character.

Foster could also display unusual generosity and consideration. Imagine the pressure he must have been under in November 1992, tying up his work as the star litigator for the Rose Law Firm and preparing for the move to Washington. Yet he found time to take a Swiss exchange student visiting his family to watch the Davis Cup tennis championship in Dallas. A Swiss player was in the final, a rare moment for the little Alpine nation. "Vincent Foster was the kindest person I ever knew. I really loved that man," said Luca Dalla Torre, two years later, speaking from his home in Berne.[4] That is a testimonial worth having, because it is genuine.

But there was a less saintly side to Vincent Foster. One of the things you learn in Arkansas—assuming you move beyond the usual Friends of Bill, and other quasi-official voices of the party apparatus—is that Foster was a man who moved in the shadows. He cultivated an image of propriety that served him well. But it was not entirely authentic, and the act can become a burden in the end. "The reputation you develop for intellectual and ethical integrity will be your greatest asset or your worst enemy," he said in the commencement address to the University of Arkansas Law School a month before his death. "Sometimes doing the right thing will be very unpopular."

His old friend from the Rose Law Firm, Associate White House Counsel William H. Kennedy III, told the FBI that Foster's death had nothing to do with Travelgate, Whitewater, or any of other *scandals du jour* in Washington. It was, he suspected, something he brought with him from Arkansas. Foster had been "fighting his demons" for a long time.[5]

I believe that.

CHAPTER NINE

THE PERIPATETIC GUN

THE "CONFIDENTIAL WITNESS" had been to Fort
Marcy Park at least fifty times over the years, meandering
through its secluded groves on the Virginia heights above the
Potomac.[1] It is known to the initiated as a place for surreptitious
liaisons. Gays go there to score, and to celebrate unusual summer
rites on the ramparts. In the mornings, trainee intelligence agents
use the old Civil War artillery fort to practice their drop-off drills.
The headquarters of the CIA is just up the road.

But for the Confidential Witness it was just a good park. He liked
to stop by on Sunday afternoons on his way back from visits to the
Smithsonian Institution. "It's a great place to sit down for a picnic
with a bottle of wine and a nice young lady," he said, although he
hardly has the look of a swordsman. A short feisty man in his late forties, with a bloodshot face and black spectacles, he earns his living as
a construction foreman. His passion is traveling in Africa, Latin
America, and Europe, when he can afford it, and viewing exhibits of
exotic foreign art when he can't.

This time it was a call of nature. Caught in heavy traffic on the George Washington Parkway with a pint of coffee inside him, he pulled into Fort Marcy Park at about 5:45 PM. It was still suffocatingly hot. That day, July 20, 1993, the temperature had reached 96 degrees. He took off his sweat-soaked shirt and left it to dry in the van, then walked up into the further reaches of the park. About 700 feet into the wooded groves, at the top of an overgrown berm, he caught sight of some trash. It annoyed him, people leaving rubbish on the ground. But as he moved closer, he spotted a body. It was lying in the dense foliage, concealed from view by a berm, more or less in the line of fire of an antique howitzer.

Not a man of squeamish sensibilities, the Confidential Witness went over and peered into the half-closed eyes of the corpse. "He looked as if he'd been dead for a long time, I mean hours," he said. There was no blood on the pristine white shirt; nothing to explain why this elegant figure should be lying dead in the shrub wearing a "$400 or $500 suit" and sparkling "dress shoes," with a bottle of wine cooler at his elbow. The bed of dried leaves below the body had been "very heavily trampled," so something was obviously wrong.[2]

His hands were stretched out, with the palms up. No weapon was visible anywhere. No gun.

"I noticed that there was a tiny bit of dried blood around the mouth and nose, so I thought maybe he'd been hit on the back of the head."

It was eerily silent, so silent that he could hear people talking at the Saudi Ambassador's residence across Chain Bridge Road. The Confidential Witness returned to his white van and drove up the parkway to the Turkey Run outpost of the U.S. Park Service in search of a telephone. Instead he ran into two Park Service employees and decided to let them deal with it. He told them about the body, then drove off without leaving his name. He became the mysterious man in the white van. "Hey, I did my duty. I didn't need the headaches of going to court and all that crap."

The next day his brother told him that the dead man was Vincent W. Foster, the Deputy White House Counsel. The newspapers reported that Foster was a kindergarten playmate of the President, and the former law partner, mentor, and intimate friend of the First Lady. The papers also reported that Foster had committed suicide with a gun. They quoted the Park Police announcing that he had shot himself in the mouth. The weapon had been found in his hand. "That's when I thought, 'Sweet Jesus, this thing's big,' and my brother told me: 'You'd better keep your mouth shut, boy, or you're in trouble.'"

He did exactly that for seven months. Then he heard about an astonishing article in *The New York Daily News*. The newspaper, which has close ties to the Clinton White House, alleged that the man in the white van had never really existed. He was a fiction created by two Park Service workers trying to cover up a bout of truant drinking at Fort Marcy Park.

The Confidential Witness did not relish the implications of this. "I went, 'Wait a minute. Who in the world can put that kind of pressure on two career employees to make them tell that kind of garbage?' That's when I became really concerned about my safety."

The more he thought about it, the more sinister it appeared, so he decided to protect himself by telling his story to the G. Gordon Liddy radio talk show. He was not a Liddy fan, but his brother was, and he knew that the Watergate legend would never betray his identity. Liddy in turn persuaded him to talk to two old veterans in the FBI, believing they would give him a good shake.

The FBI did not take well to the Confidential Witness. By then, April 1994, the Bureau had already decided where it was heading with the investigation of Independent Counsel Robert Fiske. It had also decided that a .38 caliber Colt revolver was going to play the star role in wrapping up the case. One can imagine their annoyance at the sudden appearance of a witness bent on taking the gun away from them.

It was too late to start the investigation all over again. Fiske's office had already leaked to *The Wall Street Journal* that the case was practically closed. On April 4, 1994, *The Journal* reported that investigators "are expected to release a report this month declaring the death of White House aide Vincent Foster a suicide.... The report, to be issued by Special Counsel Robert Fiske, would largely confirm findings by the U.S. Park Police." It was careless of Fiske's staff to leak so prematurely, for it revealed that the conclusion of suicide had been reached before any serious work had actually been done.

The historical record shows that the FBI had not started to interview the key witnesses until late April. They did not talk to Lisa Foster until May 9. The FBI crime labs received the specimens for their firearm tests, chemical analyses, serological analyses, DNA analyses, and mineralogy tests on May 25. They received the "fingerprint card of Vincent W. Foster, Jr.," on May 31.

Verdict first. Interviews later. Tests later. Wonderland on the Potomac.

"It was these two agents, a big guy and a little guy, real smooth they were, and they kept trying to get me to say that the gun could have been hidden, and I kept saying: how many times do I have to keep telling you that there was no gun? It must have happened two dozen times at least.... The next three times they came I made sure there was a witness around, a lady-friend of mine, because I didn't like the way things were going."

But in the end they wore him down. They explained that the weapon had flipped over and was hidden from view beneath the palm of the hand, with nothing visible except the trigger guard. If that was so, the witness allowed, then it was perhaps conceivable that he had failed to see the gun.

But the FBI had tricked him. A few weeks later he was shown a crime scene photo that had been leaked to ABC News. It showed the gun in clear view in Foster's right hand.

"The lying sons of bitches, that was not the picture of what I saw at that scene, point blank," he told me. "Somebody had come after I left and put a gun in the hand."

Two months later, on June 30, 1994, the Fiske Report came out concluding that Foster "committed suicide by firing a bullet from a .38 caliber revolver into his mouth.... The evidence overwhelmingly supports this conclusion, and there is no evidence to the contrary."

The witness obtained a copy of the report and tried to avoid an apoplectic attack as he perused the section entitled "Observations by the Confidential Witness." It stated that "he did not see a gun in the man's hands but said it was difficult to see his hands because of the dense foliage in the area where the body was lying."

"When I saw the Fiske Report, I knew I'd been had," he said. "All you can do with that piece of garbage is flush it down the toilet."

A year later he learned that the FBI had distorted his witness statements. One of his "302" write-ups said that "traces of dry black blood were running from the side of the mouth and nose down the right side of the face."

"Where the hell did they get that from?" he snapped. "There was no blood running down the face... none... absolutely not true. What's more I told them that when they gave me my statement to sign. I underlined it and said take it out.... Goddamn sons of bitches!"

By then he was in touch with Representative Dan Burton (R-Ind.), who was so suspicious about the case that he later carried out a crime scene simulation, firing a .38 caliber revolver into a watermelon to see how far the noise would carry in the suburbs. (A long way.) Burton asked the Confidential Witness to give a sworn deposition. He agreed. When asked under oath if he was sure about the gun, he replied: "As sure as I am standing here. I am absolutely and totally, unequivocally [sure] the palms were up. I looked at both palms. There was nothing in his hands."

Nothing came of it. The Confidential Witness retreated back into the shadows. Reflecting on the event three years later, he suspected that he had disturbed the crime scene before it was "ready" and thought that he was very lucky to be alive.

"The whole thing stinks, he clearly didn't shoot himself there. You can't shoot yourself without a gun. The man had no gun. End of story."

*   *   *

It is not every day that the U.S. Park Police have a dead body on their hands. Perhaps that is why Park Police Officer Kevin Fornshill was so eager to respond when a "DB" alert came over the radio at 6:05 PM and 30 seconds.[3]

He was responsible for guarding the parkway entrance to the CIA, where he had been posted on special assignment. It was not really his job to rush over to the crime scene, or death scene, or whatever it was. That was the task of the beat officer in Car 211, Franz Ferstl, who was patrolling the parkway. But Fornshill took it upon himself to find the body before anyone else.

The paramedics from the Fairfax County Emergency Medical Services were arriving when Officer Fornshill reached the park. Fornshill and the rescue workers fanned out in different directions to search for the body. Fornshill took the upper path into a small clearing. He was joined by rescue workers Todd Hall and George Gonzalez from the McLean Fire Service, Company One. He instructed the two paramedics to go one way while he went off alone, "running at a pretty good clip," to a hidden grove in the top corner of the park.[4]

His instinct was uncanny, for there was the corpse: white male, hazel eyes, grey-black hair, 6′ 4″, 197 pounds, lying in the shrubs by the second cannon. The time was 6:14 PM and 32 seconds. It was almost half an hour after the body had been discovered by the Confidential Witness.

When rescue worker Todd Hall reached the grove a few seconds later, he saw men running away from the scene into the woods. He pointed this out to Park Police Officer Fornshill, but Officer Fornshill did not respond.

The FBI was clearly bothered by this incident. They interviewed Hall twice, first on March 18 and then on April 27, 1994. The first FBI 302 report gave his observations no more than a mild massage. "Hall thought he heard someone else in the woods. He subsequently saw something red moving in the woods. He was unable to determine if it was a person."[5]

But then he was given *the treatment*. The FBI suggested to him that he might have mistaken men for cars moving along Chain Bridge Road. The FBI even took him to Fort Marcy Park and showed him the road. Being a go-along-get-along kind of man, Hall took the hint. His second statement reads: "Upon discovering that there was a road in the area, Hall believes that it is possible that he saw vehicular traffic on route 123."[6]

Well, what was it, he was asked under cross-examination at the Whitewater grand jury in early 1995, was it people running away or was it the flash of cars? It was people, he answered. It could have been cars, he said, but what he saw was people.[7]

By this time a gun had appeared. Todd Hall was about to check the carotid pulse when he noticed the weapon in Foster's right hand, with parts of it tucked under his right leg. He called out to Fornshill, who was already leaving. The Park Police officer came back for a brief look but was unable to see the gun, or so he says: "I sort of strained a little bit, and because of the bushes and the growth on the ground, I couldn't see what he was talking about."[8] However, the Polaroid leaked to ABC News showed that the gun was clearly visible.

Even though Fornshill had lost all curiosity in the crime scene, he still felt confident enough to infer the cause of death. After two minutes, he contacted Park Police communications and announced that it "appeared to be a suicide." Based on what? he was asked later.[9] "Based on the determination the person was dead." Realizing that this was a little thin, he added: "Again, my assumption from the paramedic and that the gun was found in his hand."

The revolver, however, had still not found its final resting place. The crime scene photos show it hopping about in a most animated way in Foster's hand.

"When I went before the grand jury they showed me two Polaroids," I was told by a member of the Fairfax County rescue squad, as we traipsed through the shrub in Fort Marcy Park. "And you know what? You could see blades of grass coming through the forefinger and the second finger in one, and another had grass between the second and third fingers. The prosecutor was real interested in that, real interested."[10]

The grand jury learned a good deal about the revolver in the early months of 1995, during the probe of Associate Independent Counsel Miquel Rodriguez. But the jury was disbanded before it could do any damage. It learned, for instance, that Franz Ferstl, the second Park Police officer to reach Fort Marcy, had questioned the probity of the crime scene photos taken later that evening after he had left. He stated under oath that the gun was in a different position when he saw it. Somehow the right hand had been edging out away from the body.

The set of Polaroids that Officer Ferstl took very early that night, recording the scene when the police first arrived, has disappeared. But that is getting ahead.

At Fort Marcy Park on July 20, 1993, the Foster case was closing down minute by minute. Once Officer Kevin Fornshill had telegraphed news of the gun-in-the-hand-that-he-never-saw, the U.S. Park Police felt that their work was over. The chief detective at the crime scene, Cheryl Braun, was disarmingly frank about the methodology of concluding suicide.

"It seems to me that we made that determination prior to going up and looking at the body," she said. "The gun was in his hand, it was trapped on his thumb. That to me would indicate that he fired the weapon himself."[11]

Having contributed her shafts of insight, Detective Braun then delegated the case to Officer John Rolla. It was his first death investigation, and it showed.

The beauty of using the Park Police to handle the violent death of Hillary Clinton's closest friend is that no other agency could hope to get away with such elliptical logic. Everything they did could be absolved under the capacious rubric of inexperience. But the Park Police have mandatory guidelines, drafted for their Criminal Investigations Branch, which stipulate that "all deaths shall be considered homicides until the facts prove otherwise."

The facts did not prove anything at all at this point. The gun can stay in the hand, due to spasmodic reflex, but typically it does not. The recoil from a .38 caliber revolver usually throws the weapon some distance from the body. Far from establishing suicide, the presence of a gun in the hand is something of a red flag for homicide detectives.

It was not obvious to the paramedics that this DB was a suicide, and the paramedics had far more experience with violent deaths than the Park Police.

Richard Arthur, who had attended to 25 or 30 gunshot deaths in his nine years as a rescue worker, believed it was a homicide. "I've just never seen a body lying so perfectly straight after a bullet in his head," he said.[12]

Back at the McLean Fire Station he pulled up the incident report of his colleague, Corey Ashford, and found that Ashford had coded the death a homicide.[13]

But the Park Police had made up its mind. There was no further need to investigate; no need to canvass the houses around the park to see if anybody had heard a shot; no need to check whether the gun actually worked (the ATF was not asked to do a ballistics check on the gun until August 12, 1993, seven days after the Park Police had already issued its final report); no need to do anything other than dot a few "i"s and cross a few "t"s.

The Park Police ruling of suicide had the effect of crimping further inquiry. It was cited by the Justice Department as grounds for backing off its original pledge to conduct a vigorous investigation. It also kept the FBI at bay. Under the Assassinations Statute, the FBI would have been compelled by law to take over the case if there was any question that it might have been homicide.[14]

The FBI was in turmoil anyway. Director William Sessions had been defenestrated the day before Foster's death in a well-executed Washington putsch. This event passed with remarkably little protest from the U.S. watchdog press, considering the precedent at stake. The Director of the FBI is appointed for a ten-year term, somewhat like a judge, because it has always been understood that a politicized FBI would upset the equilibrium of American government. The most important quality that an FBI Director must have is prickly independence. All else is secondary. Sessions had his faults, but at least he was a man who resisted meddling by the White House in the internal affairs of the Bureau. That, of course, was why he had to go.

Sessions had made himself unpopular with the old-boy network at the FBI because of his aggressive policy of affirmative action for blacks, Hispanics, and women. So to some degree he was the victim of a reactionary backlash within the Bureau.[15] But it was President Clinton who fired him. The pretext was an "ethics cloud," the most memorable cloud being that Alice Sessions, the Director's wife, had transported a bundle of personal firewood on an FBI aircraft.

On Saturday, July 17, Sessions was told by Attorney General Janet Reno that he would be fired by Monday unless he resigned. The meeting took place at the Justice Department, yet White House Counsel Bernie Nussbaum was present in the room.

Sessions refused as a "matter of principle."

On Monday afternoon the President called to tell Sessions he had been dismissed. Clearly in a great hurry, Clinton called a second time minutes later. Sessions was to leave the Hoover Building "effective immediately."[16]

The President appointed Deputy Director Floyd Clarke to take over the Bureau until a successor could be found. It would later emerge that the White House had already been working quietly with Clarke for some time.

The next day, Foster was found dead. Clarke failed to assert FBI jurisdiction, leaving the Park Police in charge. The Foster investigation slipped through the cracks.

If there was no need for a homicide probe on the night of July 20, 1993, there was no need for one later. One after another, the investigators skimmed over the surface of the case. Independent Counsel Robert Fiske, the Senate Banking Committee (twice), Congressman William Clinger (twice), and finally Kenneth Starr—all reploughed the same old ground. They dwelt on evidence that would validate the original finding of suicide, accepting the original premises of the Park Police. The gun sealed it.

*　　　　*　　　　*

Vince Foster had promised to take Lisa out for a "date" on the evening of Tuesday, July 20. At about 5:00 PM she called his office at the White House to find out what his plans were, but was told that he was "unavailable."

She tried again later. This time she was told that the President was appearing on CNN's *Larry King Live* at 9:00 PM, but nobody knew where Vince had gone. She waited at their quaint Georgetown home at 3027 Cambridge Place, where the family was crowded together in circumstances that were very different from the spacious elegance of Hillcrest Heights in Little Rock.

At about 10:00 PM there was a commotion outside. Laura Foster opened the door to find Park Police Detective John Rolla standing on the step. A gaggle of longfaced Arkansas friends and relatives were clustered behind. "Mother," she yelled, up the stairs. "Mother."[17]

Lisa Foster came downstairs and stood on the third step. Detective Rolla broke the news. "I asked her to sit down, it was very rough…. I said, I'm very sorry to tell you that your husband, Vincent, is dead."[18]

In an interview with *The New Yorker*, Lisa later admitted to feeling a twinge of relief that it was her husband who was dead, not her son Vincent III, as she had feared at first. But the blow was hard.

"She was hysterical, screaming, collapsed on the step," said Detective Rolla. "The only question I got to ask was about the gun, did Vincent own a gun. She asked me what does it look like…. Well, it's a black-colored revolver, a .38 revolver. She cut me off, and threw up her hands and said, I don't know what guns look like, and walked into the kitchen away from me."[19]

Nine days later Lisa Foster was interviewed at the K Street law offices of Swidler & Berlin, under the auspices of lawyer James Hamilton, the White House "surrogate" who had been assigned to her. "She was presented with a photograph of the weapon found with Mr. Foster's body but was unable to identify it," states the Park Police interview with Lisa Foster.[20]

The handwritten notes of Park Police Captain Charles Hume were more explicit: "not the gun she thought it must be. Silver six-gun, large barrel."[21] Apparently, she was referring to an old silver gun owned by Vince's late father, which she had seen in a trunk in Little Rock.

There was a cursory effort to see if Vince Foster's sister in Little Rock, Sharon Bowman, could identify the revolver. An outdoors type, she had a better knowledge of the family collection.

"When shown the gun, Sharon Bowman identified it as appearing very similar to the one their father had kept in his bedside table, specifically recalling the pattern on the grip," says the Fiske Report, using this as a key prop in the authentication of the gun.[22]

This is a nice exhibit of Fiske's methods. In fact, the record indicates that Fiske's investigators never showed Sharon Bowman the gun. If they ever to spoke to her at all, they did not leave any paper trail. What the documents reveal is that Ms. Bowman was shown a picture of a gun by a family friend, who then wrote to the Park Police saying that the "pistol in the photograph" looked like a gun she had seen in her father's collection.

In fact, she did not identify it. Her husband, Lee Bowman, told me a very different version of this story. "Sharon thought she would be able to recognize it, but she really couldn't," he said.[23] Fiske's entire identification is built on a *might* or a *perhaps* that was nothing more than hearsay in the first place.

It was their son, Lee Foster Bowman, who had the most detailed knowledge of the guns. He had fired some of his grandfather's collection—three handguns, four shotguns, and two or three rifles— when they used to go duck hunting together at a cabin in Yellowcreek, Arkansas, and he expected to be able to identify the .38 Special with an etched handle that the old man kept by his bed.[24] But the gun found at Fort Marcy Park was an "old piece of junk," nothing like the elegant silver-colored antique he remembered.

"He didn't remember the black handle and the dark color of the metal."[25]

The truth is, no member of the family was ever able to identify the gun found in Foster's hand. Not one. Ever.

The Fiske investigation managed to transcend this. His FBI agents cut the Gordian Knot with a single stroke of Alexandrian audacity by showing Lisa Foster the wrong gun. Back at Swidler & Berlin on May 9, 1994, nearly a year after Foster's death, she gave a long interview to the FBI.[26]

"Lisa Foster believes that the gun found at Fort Marcy Park may be the silver gun which she brought with her other belongings when she permanently moved to Washington," reads the FD-302 write-up of the interview. The black gun was now silver. The widow, who was taking Prozac for depression, finally recognized the gun that she had not been able to identify a year before.

Incurious members of the American press were informed by the Fiske Report that "the gun looked similar to one that she had seen in their home in Arkansas and that she had brought to Washington."[27]

In September 1995, Lisa Foster spoke out for the first time in a *New Yorker* piece by Peter Boyer. Seemingly unaware that she was contradicting her statements to the police, she now talked about the gun as if she had been able to identify it all along. It was a feature article, not a piece of investigative journalism, so I would not wish to fault Boyer for failing to study the source documents. What the records show, however, is that Lisa Foster had been tricked by the FBI—or had allowed herself to be tricked.

The article was extremely influential. It was cited by conservatives as the final word on the Foster case. The editor of my own newspaper in London, *The Sunday Telegraph*, found it so convincing that it made him wary of dissenting views. On Capitol Hill it promoted a feeling of disdain, bordering on disgust, for those who continued to allege a cover-up of the death. Leave the poor family alone! One heard it all the time.

Lisa Foster was building a new life. Three months after the article appeared she married Jim Moody, a kindly lawyer who had just been appointed a U.S. federal judge in Little Rock. Moody moved into the Foster residence at 5414 Stonewall, an unusual thing to do in the South. The spirit of Vincent Foster had been exorcised. "I have found a wonderful man whom I love and who loves me, and who will be good to my children," she told *The New Yorker*. "I can't do anything about the fact that Vince is gone."

*   *   *

So, what do we actually know about this peripatetic gun that was never identified by the family?

It did not have Foster's fingerprints on it, although a print belonging to somebody else was found on the underside of the grip.[28] The FBI crime labs offer one of their deliciously bureaucratic observations about this. "An individual who does not perspire readily" might not leave a print. No doubt true, but July 20 was one of the hottest, muggiest days of the summer of 1993. It then goes on to add that "atmospheric conditions" such as "snow" could destroy any latent prints.

The weapon was a .38 caliber Colt Army Special revolver with two different serial numbers—one was a butt number—both dating back to 1913. It was too old to trace.[29]

It was a workhorse gun. Huge numbers were made. The photos show that it had a four-inch barrel with a big jagged metal sight. The gun supposedly kicked back from the soft palate at the back of Foster's mouth without chipping his teeth or damaging the gum tissue.

Anybody who has fired a .38 Special knows that the recoil is fierce. The one time I tried—courtesy of the central Idaho militia—both my hands were thrown back over my head, and the noise echoed down the Salmon River valley for miles.

There were no visible powder burns inside Foster's mouth, and no signs of gunpowder on his face.[30] "Limited chemical testing" by the FBI Lab did not reveal the presence of any blood on the gun.[31]

The bullet was never found. It should have been close by because it barely forced its way through the back of Foster's skull, if we are to believe the description of the wound in the autopsy report. Inside the cylinder was a second, round-nosed, Remington high-velocity bullet. No matching ammunition was found in Foster's house.

In the Fiske Report there is a passage explaining that "it would have been enormously time-consuming, costly, and in all likelihood unproductive, to have searched the entire park for the bullet."

Quite so. It is hard to fault a single word of that nicely crafted sentence. Nevertheless, the Starr probe decided that this would have to be done before it could hope to close down the exasperating Foster case. By then Kenneth Starr had brought in the renowned forensic expert Henry Lee to review the case. Henry could work wonders, but not with thin air. He was demanding one scrap of evidence that would indicate Foster died where his body was found. Henry wanted that bullet.

So Starr launched a six-week blitz at Fort Marcy Park in the fall of 1995, more than two years after the death, using cranes to scan the big maple trees above the site. When I visited one evening I found that the melancholy groves had been torn to pieces. A wedge-shaped grid had been marked out with cords, and stakes had been posted all over the place indicating the discovery of bullets. Some of them dated back to the Civil War.

Most of all they found snakes. "You wouldn't believe how many snakes there were in there," said one of Starr's prosecutors over dinner at the Occidental Grill. "One of our FBI men got bitten on the arm by a copperhead."

The highest metal-detecting powers of the U.S. federal government had been mobilized, but the elusive Remington had escaped.

No bullet.

No shot either. Nobody heard the shot. Not that the Fiske investigation would have reason to know. When I was sleuthing in the park one day in 1995 I struck up a conversation with an elderly couple walking their dog. They invited me back for coffee at their house, which was well within earshot of the second cannon. To my astonishment they said that the FBI had never dropped by to learn if they had heard that .38 Special on the quiet, sultry afternoon of July 20, 1993.

There are five homes within 570 feet of the spot where Foster's body was found. One of them, 1317 Merrie Ridge Road, belongs to Senator Bennett Johnston of Louisiana. The closest is 660 Chain Bridge Road. It is 300 feet away. With a sand wedge you could pitch a golf ball over the top of it. If you had a 2-iron you could probably put a ball though the front windows of fifty houses.

Nobody heard a shot.

CHAPTER TEN

THE NECK WOUND

"**S**O WHY IS A BRITISH reporter so interested in this when nobody else seems to care?"

"It's the Rosetta Stone," I replied.

"Huh?"

We walked in silence toward the interior of Fort Marcy Park. The path cuts through a breach in the ramparts, then opens into a clearing. It has the overgrown look of an English country garden, one of those decaying Victorian estates that no longer has a groundskeeper. My guide walked through to the upper grove, where the cannon points toward the CIA.

"The body was right here," he said, impassively. "He was straight out with his hands by his side. Funny place to shoot yourself, isn't it, back here in all this shrubbery?"

"Maybe, maybe not. How much blood?"

"Not a lot. It was on the right shoulder, coming down from the neck. That stuff about a trickle out of the mouth, I don't know where that came from because I never saw it."

He scanned the bottom of the park, just in case anybody was watching. But he was not unduly nervous.

"What did the exit wound look like?"

At first he did not answer, as if wondering how much to reveal, then he grabbed me by the shoulder.

"That's all bullshit, man. There was no exit wound."

"Nothing?"

"Listen to me, and listen to me hard, 'cause I'm only going to say this once: Vince Foster was shot right here in the neck," he said, jabbing his finger deep into my flesh, an inch or so below the jawline, about halfway between my ear and my chin.

"Oh."

"Yeah. 'Oh.' We've all been threatened, you know that?"

"I'd heard that."

"Well it's true. We're not allowed to talk to anybody. We're not even allowed to talk to each other. You understand now? This thing's big, man."[1]

*   *   *

Miquel Rodriguez kept holding the photograph up in the light, wondering. He knew there was something wrong with it. The resolution was too blurred, even for a blowup of a Polaroid.[2]

All you could see was a smear of blood on the right side of Foster's neck. It was the mysterious "contact stain" that nobody was able to explain. How had the blood found its way there, against the laws of forensic science, against gravity? It was nagging at him day and night.

The Fiske Report said this blood smear had been "caused by a blotting action."[3] The head must have fallen on the shoulder, and then bounced upright again. But that did not make any sense. There was not enough blood on the upper side of Foster's right shoulder, and the alignment was all wrong for a mirror transfer effect.

Clutching at straws, the forensic pathology panel brought in by the Fiske investigation had concluded that somebody at the crime scene must have moved the head, and was refusing to admit it.[4] But what did the panel know, or care to know?

Dr. Charles Hirsch, chief medical examiner for New York City and the man called to represent the panel in the 1994 Senate hearings, did not speak to the Park Police or the paramedics who attended the crime scene. He did not interview the medical examiner who did the autopsy. He did not even visit Fort Marcy Park.

He relied on autopsy documents, even though the investigation had been fatally compromised by that stage. It was imperative to go deeper into the case. But Dr. Hirsch barely skimmed the surface. This did not stop him testifying in tones of Olympian authority that Foster died where his body was found. "It is my unequivocal, categorical opinion that it was impossible for him to have been killed elsewhere."[5]

Though they were involved in the most important death investigation since the 1960s, the doctors on the Fiske Report's forensic panel were remarkably incurious. Perhaps forensic pathology is a more slapdash profession than we laymen had imagined. Or perhaps it is more attuned to politics. These gentlemen certainly have the most rococo resumes I have ever seen. They go on for 67 pages at the end of the Fiske Report, longer than the report itself.[6]

We learn, for example, that Dr. Charles Stahl attended a one-day workshop at the Quillen-Dishner College of Medicine at East Tennessee State University in Johnson City on May 23, 1984. We also learn that he was the guest speaker at the Kiwanis Club of Bristol, Tennessee, on April 21, 1983.

Their resumes are quite revealing. They show that three of the four experts have close ties to the FBI and the Pentagon. Dr. James L. Luke, who essentially ran the panel and furnished it with the case documents, is Forensic Pathologist to the Investigative Support Unit of the FBI. He has a "Top Secret" security clearance.[7]

Miquel Rodriguez, however, was not a fully signed-up member of the Washington power elite. A man of slight stature, a high-pitched voice, Iberian features, and large, round, Pre-Raphaelite eyes, he does not look the part of a tough prosecutor. But he has an almost reverential passion for his work as an Assistant United States Attorney in Sacramento. Clearly, Kenneth Starr did not know quite what he was getting when this young Hispanic—a child of migrant farm workers and a graduate of Harvard Law School—arrived in Washington in the fall of 1994 to take up his new post of Associate Independent Counsel.

Nonconformist in every way, the man even spelled his name with a dash of Portuguese defiance. No, my name isn't Miguel, it's Miquel. Please be so good as to get it right.

The job of Rodriguez was to reopen the investigation into the death of Vincent Foster. It was generally agreed that the Fiske investigation was so amateurish that the work would have to be done all over again. But this meant very different things to different people. For Rodriguez it meant starting from scratch with an open mind. For Mark H. Tuohey III, the head of the Office of the Independent Counsel in Washington, it meant accommodating the agenda of the U.S. Justice Department. Rodriguez was astounded when Tuohey, his boss, took him aside and told him that it would be ill-advised to challenge the essential findings of the Fiske Report.[8]

This was to be a "friendly takeover." It would be wrong to understand this as an effort to protect the Clintons. Like most Washington lawyers Tuohey happens to be a Democrat, but that is neither here nor there. In my experience, people of his ilk are first and foremost loyal to the group, and the group is an idiosyncratic subculture of like-minded lawyers. They move in and out of the U.S. Attorney's office in Washington, D.C. They clerk for the same

Supreme Court Justices. They are members of the Metropolitan Club. They are Episcopalians and high Catholics. They are alumni of Georgetown Prep. They do not expose each other's dirty linen in public. And there was a great deal of dirty linen in the Fiske Report. It had to be finessed as gracefully as possible.

The mission for Miquel Rodriguez, then, was to produce a better suicide report, one that was not so self-evidently mendacious. Whether or not Tuohey already knew the secrets of the Foster case is something that he will have to answer to his conscience, and to history. But it did not look good when he left the Starr investigation in September 1995 to work for the Houston law firm of Vinson & Elkins. As reported by Christopher Ruddy in *The Pittsburgh Tribune-Review*, this was the same firm that was representing the Rose Law Firm—where Hillary Clinton, Vincent Foster, and Webster Hubbell had been partners—in its dealings with the Office of the Independent Counsel. Vinson & Elkins issued assurances that Tuohey would recuse himself from matters relating to the Rose Law Firm. Very wise. Nobody is accusing Mr. Tuohey of switching sides in the thick of battle, but it goes to show how incestuous this circle of lawyers can be.

At first Rodriguez pretended to be following orders. He went about his business quietly, confiding only in his closest aides at the Washington office of the Independent Counsel. Unlike some of the other prosecutors—aristocratic in their work habits, caught up in the whirl of Georgetown social life—he was spending his evenings combing through the archive of documents in the Foster case, and he did not like what he saw.

It became obvious that the FBI agents who did the nuts and bolts work for the Fiske Report were engaged in a systematic cover-up. Now, a year and a half later, the same FBI agents were still there in

the Office of the Independent Counsel, the gatekeepers who controlled access to the witnesses, the documents, the evidence. Yet
Kenneth Starr had kept them on, allowing them to be the judge of
their own past work.

Rodriguez kept muttering about the photograph. "Is this all there
is?" he asked.

Yes, that's all there is; that's the original, replied his FBI staff.
And so it might have rested if it had not been for the courage of one
person in the Office of the Independent Counsel who managed to
gain access to the locked files. Hidden inside was a folder of crime
scene photographs that had been deliberately withheld from the
prosecutor.

Among them was the original Polaroid of Foster's neck. What it
showed was something very different from the "contact stain" in the
fraudulent picture that had been circulating. Evidently, somebody
had taken a photo of the original and then touched it up to disguise
the incriminating evidence. This second-generation copy had then
been used to create an enhanced "blow up."

It was blatant obstruction of justice. Indeed it was worse.
Whoever had done this was now an accessory after the fact in the
death of the Deputy White House Counsel, and they had made the
mistake of failing to destroy the original.

Wary of entrusting anything to the FBI crime labs, Rodriguez
turned to the Smithsonian Institution for enhancement of the original. The work was done by the Smithsonian's subcontractor, Asman
Custom Photo Service on Pennsylvania Avenue. A set of five
"blowups" of the original were made. They revealed a dime-sized
wound on the right side of Foster's neck (his left side) about half way
between the chin and the ear. It was marked by a black "stippled"
ring—a sort of dotted effect, like an engraving—that was suggestive
of a .22 caliber gunshot fired at point blank range into the flesh.

(Israeli intelligence once had a case like this when they were inter-rogating a Palestinian, gun pressed in the neck, and accidentally shot the man.[9])

One medical examiner who looked at the photo thought that the wound might be the result of a 40,000 volt stun-gun, designed to cause temporary paralysis for about fifteen minutes. Fired at short range it can leave burn marks. But it was more likely to be a low cal-iber gunshot wound. Something had perforated the skin, causing blood to ooze down the side of the neck and into the collar.

The photograph, which I have examined carefully, is one of the few surviving Polaroids taken at Fort Marcy that night. The rest dis-appeared. This includes most of the Polaroids taken by detective John Rolla.

"I mean, I had them in the office that night, I did reports, and I don't know what happened.... I put them in a jacket, I don't know."[10]

All of the seven Polaroids taken by Officer Franz Ferstl disap-peared. He was the first Park Police officer to photograph the crime scene, and his pictures were a unique record of Foster's body as it was during the first ten to fifteen minutes after the police arrived. Ferstl believes that he gave them to Sgt. Bob Edwards. That was the last anybody saw of them.[11]

It has never been explained what Sgt. Edwards was doing at Fort Marcy Park in the first place. (The record shows that the Fiske investigation never talked to him.) He was not the shift commander. He was not one of the detectives assigned to the case. Yet there he was, in the shadows, unaccountable, playing a critical role in the events of July 20. "Usually, there's only one investigator to a scene. This was a little bit unusual as far as I was concerned, four investi-gators at one spot," said Park Police technician Pete Simonello.[12]

Remember, this was supposed to be a "routine suicide." At that stage nobody was supposed to know that Foster was a top White House official.

All of the official 35 mm photos were "underexposed" and deemed useless. The Park Police technician, Peter Simonello, was no beginner. He had attended about 60 gunshot cases in his eleven years with the "identification unit" of the Park Police. But this time something went wrong. The roll was ruined, even though he used a flash for some of the frames. "We can't determine whether it was a malfunction in the camera or not," he said.[13] But Simonello admitted that he had never had the camera fixed afterwards and continued using it without further problems.

The FBI, of course, has the technology to enhance underexposed negatives. In this case the crime labs were in fact able to produce a number of 8-by-10s of extremely high quality on Kodak Ultra print paper. They were not crystal clear but they revealed considerable detail.[14] The FBI withheld this information from the Fiske investigation and the independent panel of forensic experts. Instead, it sent a memo stating that "limited detail could be extracted from each of the selected frames."[15]

All that survives is a motley collection of 18 Polaroids.[16] Five of them depict Foster's grey Honda Accord. The rest are a mix, showing the cannon, the surrounding foliage, Foster's glasses, the gun in Foster's hand, and so forth. There is only one Polaroid close-up showing the right side of Foster's face and neck. It is signed JCR 7/20/93 on the back, indicating that it was taken by Detective John Rolla. This is the polaroid retrieved from the FBI's hiding place at the Office of the Independent Counsel.

It is not some stray piece of evidence that contradicts everything else known about the case. The original report by Dr. Donald Haut, the Fairfax County Medical Examiner and the only doctor to visit the crime scene that night, lists the cause of death as a "self-inflicted gunshot wound mouth to neck."[17]

Neck. Mouth to neck. According to the official version of events, Foster blew a 1 by 1 1/4 inch hole in the upper part of his skull.

"There is no other trauma identified that would suggest a circumstance other than suicide," concluded Fiske's panel of pathologists. "It is exceedingly unlikely that an individual of Mr. Foster's physical stature could have been overcome by an assailant inflicting an intraoral gunshot wound without a struggle and there not to have been some other injury sustained at the time."

Well, gentlemen, evidently there was another injury.

Dr. Haut's report was not included in the documents released by the Senate Banking Committee. It was discovered in June 1997 at the National Archives by my friends Hugh Sprunt and Patrick Knowlton, of whom more later.

So, what did the paramedics see when they arrived from the McLean Station of the Fairfax County Rescue Department?

"I saw blood all over the right side of the neck, from here down, all over the shoulder, and I saw a small—what appeared to be a small gunshot wound here near the jawline. Fine, whether the coroner's report says that or not, fine. I know what I saw," said Richard Arthur in a sworn deposition to the Senate Banking Committee.[18]

"Lt. Bianchi told me from orders higher up that I'm not allowed to talk to anybody about this if I value my job," he continued.

"I said, well, what about the CIA, the FBI, and all that stuff?

"He said, 'You're not allowed to talk to anybody if you value your job.'"

Four of the rescue workers testified in secret before the Whitewater grand jury in the spring of 1995 that they saw trauma to the side of Foster's head or neck.[19] Two of them, including Arthur, described it as a gunshot wound. What they revealed under intensive cross-examination was a far cry from the innocuous observations attributed to most of them in their FBI statements. This information was submitted to Kenneth Starr in a memorandum from Miquel Rodriguez summing up the proceedings of the Whitewater grand jury in Washington.

I look forward to reading the Starr Report, which, as I write, has not been released. His predecessor dismissed eyewitness accounts of trauma to the neck with the following words: "The photographs taken at the crime scene conclusively show there were no such wounds."

A little more ingenuity will be necessary this time.

*   *   *

Corey Ashford had the unpleasant task of moving Foster's corpse from Fort Marcy Park to the morgue at Fairfax Hospital. It was about 8:10 PM by then, still light. The first team of paramedics in Company One had been and gone long ago. His was the cleanup crew.

It can be a horrible business dealing with a gunshot death. A .38 Special will take the back of your head off. Blood everywhere, brain matter. It was not what he was trained for. An Emergency Medical Services technician, aged 24, his metier was saving people's lives. But somebody had to do it.

Funny thing, though. He didn't notice any blood.[20] Ashford picked up the corpse from the shoulders, cradling the head against his stomach as he lifted it into the body bag. Still no blood. He didn't get a drop of blood on his white uniform, or on the disposable gloves he was wearing for the job. There was no blood on the ground underneath the body, either, that he could see.[21] He coded Foster's body a homicide on his incident report.

Roger Harrison didn't see any blood either, as he as helped Corey slide Foster's shoulders into the body bag. No blood on the ground. No blood on the corpse. No blood on anybody who had touched it.[22] The grizzled 19-year veteran of the Fairfax County Fire and Rescue Department did not file a hazardous materials report— which is mandatory if there is blood around.

Nobody filed a hazardous materials report. It was almost as if the blood had vanished from the neck between the time that first team of rescue workers left Fort Marcy Park at 6:37 PM, and the second team arrived at 8:02 PM; almost as if somebody had been cleaning up—which, of course, was impossible.[23]

But one thing they could all agree on when they were recounting war stories back at Fire Station One was that nobody saw an exit wound. Corey Ashford didn't see it.[24]

Richard Arthur didn't see it.[25]

Sgt. George Gonzalez didn't see it.[26]

The head was intact.

None of the paramedics saw the "official" 1 by 1 1/4 inch hole in the back of Foster's skull. They have forensic evidence on their side, too. No bone fragments were ever found behind the head.

Over at the Fairfax County Morgue that night the duty doctor was Julian Orenstein, a charming man who now works as a pediatrician. His job was to verify Vince Foster's death, nothing else. In his FBI statement taken on May 17, 1994, it says that Dr. Orenstein lifted the body by the shoulders in order to "locate and observe the exit wound on the decedent's head."[27]

It is a clever construction. Any normal person reading this document would assume that Dr. Orenstein did indeed see the exit wound. But by this stage I was so suspicious of every FD-302 statement taken by the FBI that I decided to call him up at his home in Falls Church, just to be sure.

What did this exit wound look like, I asked him.

"I never saw one directly," he said, clearly taken aback. "The hair was matted with dried blood, but I didn't get a clear look. I really didn't spend too much time looking back there; my suspicions weren't aroused."[28]

Indeed.

A few months later I obtained a copy of the handwritten notes of the FBI interviews, which Christopher Ruddy had shaken loose after fighting and winning a Freedom of Information Act lawsuit against the Office of the Independent Counsel. There was no mention of Orenstein trying to locate an exit wound.[29] The passage had been inserted into his FD-302 statement. It was another of the clues left by the FBI in the Foster case. Link the little fibs together, and you start to see the anatomy of a cover-up.

There is another clue in the FBI interview of Park Police Detective John Rolla. In the FD-302 write-up provided to the Senate it says "he observed an extensive amount of blood... on the back side of his head."[30] But in the original handwritten notes the description of the back of Foster's head is redacted.[31] Why on earth would the FBI redact that passage? National Security? It is a clear-cut violation of the FBI's obligations under the Freedom of Information Act.

After embalming at the Murphy Funeral Home in Arlington, a Defense Department subcontractor, the body went to the Reubel Funeral Home in Little Rock. There it was prepared for final viewing before burial in Foster's hometown of Hope, Arkansas. The funeral director, Tom Wittenberg, told me that he never looked closely at the body because he was a close friend of Vince Foster's and the whole ordeal was too distressing. "I checked his hair, face, suit, and hands. That's all I saw."

But that is not what he told a private investigator in Arkansas in a taped conversation. "What if there was no exit wound at all," he said. "I'm telling you it's possible there wasn't."[32]

So, what do the X-rays reveal?

Like the crime scene photos, the X-rays have disappeared. It appears that Dr. James C. Beyer, the Deputy Virginia Medical Examiner, did in fact take X-rays. "Dr. Beyer stated that X-rays indicated there was no evidence of bullet fragments in the head," states a Supplemental Criminal Incident Record of the U.S. Park Police.[33]

The X-ray box on the autopsy report had been ticked "yes."[34] In testimony before the Senate Banking Committee, Dr. Beyer said that he had been planning to take X-rays but never did. "I made out that report prior to actually performing the autopsy. We'd been having difficulty with our equipment, and we were not getting readable X-rays. We had a new machine; we had new grids; we had a new processor."[35]

He went on to say that no X-rays were taken in his coroner's office between July 6 and July 26, 1993. In other words, the machine had already been out of action for two weeks. He knew it was not working, but he ticked the box anyway.

"Why didn't you call Fairfax Hospital and arrange for a portable X-ray machine to be brought in for your use in such an important occasion?" asked Senator Lauch Faircloth.

"Because this was a 'perforating' gunshot wound. If it had been a 'penetrating' one, I would have gotten an X-ray of the head."

"Do what, now?"

Beyer went on to bury the Senator in an avalanche of technical jargon. But Faircloth, a North Carolina hog farmer, would not give up. "How did you tell the Park Police the results of an X-ray that you didn't take?"

"I don't recall telling them that statement."

"Well, they do."

"I have no explanation."

"Has Robert Fiske ever talked with you?"

"No, sir."

"How did Robert Fiske decide to believe you instead of the police report? Did he send investigators to the hospital, or to the company that services the X-ray machine?"

"Not that I am aware of."

But by then Senator Faircloth was running out of his allotted five minutes. He was the only Republican on the Banking Committee who asked the relevant questions during the comical one-day show hearings held by the Democrats on July 29, 1994. In a sense Faircloth was "out of order" because the death of Vincent Foster was strictly off limits. Senate Resolution 229 restricted the investigation to questions involving the conduct of the Park Police and "the way in which White House officials handled documents" in Foster's office.[36]

Needless to say, it is a mantra of the American press that "two congressional committees" have investigated the death and endorsed the finding of suicide. But Congress was specifically precluded from investigating any such thing. How many journalists who write about the subject are aware of Resolution 229? How many have read it? Precious few, I would wager.

Dr. Beyer was 75 years old when he conducted the autopsy on Vincent Foster. In his prime he had worked for the U.S. Army doing 8,000 combat autopsies in the Korean War. He had gone on to do weapons research and conduct studies on body armor. But by now he was making serious mistakes.

He was responsible for the ruling that Timothy Easley committed suicide with a self-inflicted stab wound in 1989. Much to his chagrin, the killer later confessed. Beyer had neglected to mention a visible stab wound on the hand.

Beyer also conducted the autopsy in the highly sensitive death of Tommy Burkett in December 1991. The Fairfax County police ruled that Burkett had committed suicide by shooting himself in the head. But the parents had the body exhumed. A second autopsy found extensive signs of trauma, including a badly broken jaw, a bludgeoned right ear, multiple skull fractures. The parents wrote Beyer a public letter calling him a "liar."

"He denied that there were any autopsy photos after my husband had seen them right there in his office," said Beth Burkett, the boy's mother. "As far as we're concerned he's just a stooge for the FBI."[37]

*   *   *

Miquel Rodriguez tipped his hand too soon. He should have watched and waited, quietly amassing such overwhelming evidence that there could be no turning back. But he did not know how to play the two-faced Washington game, and he certainly did not try. He treated his superiors with open contempt.

"I'm not going to take orders from the lapdog of a lapdog," he was heard snapping at John Bates, the bespectacled clerk appointed by Mark Tuohey III to be number two in the Washington office. He made enemies.[38]

The first thing he noticed were little roadblocks left in his path. His requests for subpoenas were being held up. He was unable to call witnesses before the grand jury in a timely fashion. He was even having trouble obtaining Foster's credit card and travel records. Then the campaign of leaks began. In February 1995, planted stories started appearing in the Washington press alleging that he had been badgering the Park Police officers at the grand jury. It was half-true. He had been reading them the perjury statutes in a deliberately pointed manner. With good reason. Their accounts were flatly contradicted by the Fairfax County paramedics, who had no obvious incentive to lie. One Park Police officer ultimately broke ranks under cross-examination and testified that the crime scene had been tampered with after he arrived.

The word was put out that Rodriguez was unstable. It was whispered that his conduct was becoming unprofessional. Drip, drip, drip—news stories started appearing that Kenneth Starr had concluded his investigation into the death of Foster and would soon be issuing a suicide report.

Rodriguez was, of course, being roasted slowly on the Beltway spit. It is how the permanent government of the United States deals with people who refuse to submit. Hundreds have been through the ordeal before him. Even senators. Even the Director of the FBI, as William Sessions can attest.

So Rodriguez went to see Kenneth Starr. This was not an easy thing to do. The Independent Counsel was exceedingly busy representing Hughes Aircraft, Bell Atlantic, General Motors—the whole corporate roster. He has continued to earn about $1 million a year from his private work for Kirkland & Ellis, his Chicago-based law firm.

Starr did not behave according to the precedent set by earlier prosecutors burdened with the unique trust of examining the President. Leon Jaworski had dedicated himself full-time to the Watergate probe. Lawrence Walsh had done the same during Iran-Contra. Even Robert Fiske, for all his sins, had shelved his private practice for the duration of this special task. They all understood, instinctively, that they were called upon to make some sacrifice for the republic and its citizens. Decorum demanded no less.

Not Kenneth Starr. During the Whitewater trial of Susan McDougal, he was defending the interests of the NFL Players Association at the Supreme Court. During crucial grand jury testimony about the First Lady's handling of Rose Law billing records Starr was busy preparing to argue a case for General Motors. He continued to represent Phillip Morris at a time when the tobacco industry was fighting off the threat of regulation by the Food and Drug Administration.

This last case was not exactly a conflict of interest, but as Ralph Nader argues in his book *No Contest: Corporate Lawyers and the Perversion of Justice in America* it stands to reason that the Whitewater investigation gave Starr a degree of suasion over the executive branch of the U.S. government. It strikes me that the criticisms leveled against Kenneth Starr by Nader, *The Nation*, and other voices on the Left are entirely to the point. This is not a man who understands the nature of his duty.

Juggling so many balls in the air left him little time for the Washington office of the Independent Counsel. His thoughts were focused on the Little Rock office of the Whitewater investigation, the one that has secured all the convictions so far: Webb Hubbell, Governor Jim Guy Tucker, and Susan and Jim McDougal, among others. The Washington office has not brought a single indictment. It is an odd appendage, a clique of friends from the U.S. Attorney's office in D.C., known more for their leaks and cozy relationship with the Washington press corps than the conduct of useful business. It was this office that was in charge of the Foster case.

Clearly, Starr had been assured a long time ago that there was nothing to Foster's death. He was none too pleased when Miquel Rodriguez started sending memos warning that there was something deeply wrong. Starr was charming, of course. The son of a Texas, small-town, Church of Christ minister, he is a delightful man, and a devout Christian. But he had no idea what to do when Rodriguez told him that an original Polaroid showed a wound in the neck, and that renegade elements of the FBI were covering up the case.

Rodriguez resigned on March 20. His closest aide resigned in sympathy. He returned to his old job in Sacramento, refusing to give interviews to the press. By all accounts he was philosophical in defeat. There is only so much a single human being can do. Life moves on.

The grand jury was disbanded and sent home. It was replaced by a new jury with no knowledge of the peripatetic gun, or the missing photos, or the wound in the neck.

A second campaign of leaks was launched, this time announcing that the Foster suicide report was ready. It continued for another two and a half years, the longest sustained leak in the history of the Washington Beltway. One after another the major newspapers and TV networks came out with premature stories announcing that the

Starr Report would be released shortly. When it never came, Starr's aides said it had been delayed because of the "Foster crazies" out there. Few reporters stopped to think about this. Why was Starr concerned about the "crazies"? Why would he allow that to influence the timing of his report by one minute, let alone two and a half years?

In March 1997 the Washington Bureau Chief for *The Los Angeles Times*, Jack Nelson, announced that the Starr Report was finally ready. "It puts the lie to that bunch of nuts out there spinning conspiracy theories and talking about murder and cover-ups," said an unnamed source, in the third paragraph.

I wonder if Jack Nelson was even aware of Miquel Rodriguez when he wrote that article. Was the prosecutor who actually investigated the case, and who conducted the cross-examinations in front of the grand jury, reduced to nothing more than a "nut"? Was it really as simple as that?

It sometimes appeared the Starr team had spent more time spinning the media than actually investigating the Foster case. While the Washington office was leaking that the suicide report was coming, the Little Rock office was craftily leaking a very different story. Hickman Ewing, the Deputy Independent Counsel for the South— well-advertised as a Baptist, teetotaler, incorruptible prosecutor— was sent out as an ambassador to the "Foster crazies" to reassure them that the matter was still being investigated seriously.

When this started wearing thin in the spring of 1996, it was announced that a new prosecutor had been appointed to review the whole Foster case. His name was Steven Parker, a Ewing protégé from the U.S. Attorney's Office in Memphis. Much was made of the fact that he was a "homicide expert." Hickman Ewing even ventured so far as to say: "There remain questions about Foster's death.... Was it a murder? Or was it a suicide? Either way, why?"

Talk radio went wild for a few days. Right-wingers toasted Hickman Ewing all over again. It was Hickman this, and Hickman that, and Hickman would save civilization. But it was all eyewash. The case had been closed long before. Hickman Ewing was a team player.

Even as Ewing spoke about remaining questions, the San Diego Medical Examiner, Dr. Brian Blackbourne, was wrapping up his independent review of the case.[39] I asked him if he had been provided with the original Polaroid showing a black stippled wound on the side of Foster's neck.

No, he said, he had not been given anything like that.

The most important piece of crime scene evidence remained locked in a file.

CHAPTER ELEVEN

THE CAR

J OSIE AND DUNCAN were too preoccupied with each other
to notice what was going on in the parking lot at Fort Marcy. But
they did glance up from their adulterous tryst enough times to see
two men tinkering with the old brown Honda at the other end of the
lot.[1]

The Honda was there when they arrived between 5:00 and
5:15 PM on July 20, 1993, and it was still there when they set off on
foot to a secluded knoll inside the park to consummate their affec-
tions half an hour later. Other cars had come and gone. This was the
only other vehicle that was continuously parked in the lot.

A shirtless, dark-haired man was sitting in the driver's seat. The
hood of the vehicle was up and there was a grubby-looking fellow
examining the engine. He was in his mid to late forties, about 6 feet
tall, medium build, dirty, with long blond hair and a beard.

There was a lack of obvious purpose in their actions. Were they
trying to fix the car? Or were they waiting on a drug deal, or what?
Josie and Duncan found it vaguely disconcerting, but then the
bearded blond guy wandered off into the woods.

At one point a dirty, beaten-up sedan came into the parking lot. Josie remembered four doors, lightish color. The driver was a big bruiser in his thirties with long shaggy hair. Not a savory type.

He drove past, looked at Josie and Duncan, then did a U-turn, and went straight back out again onto the George Washington Parkway. Obviously, he didn't want to conduct his business, whatever it was, as long as some yuppie couple was there necking in the car park.

Around 5:45 PM Josie and Duncan went off to have their *affaire du picnic*. They were at the south end when the fire brigade came screeching into Fort Marcy Park, 25 minutes later, followed quickly by the U.S. Park Police.

A man had been found dead, explained Officer Julie Spetz. Had they seen anything? Had they heard a shot? All the usual things. They answered as best they could. The next day they discovered that the victim was Vincent Foster, boyhood friend of President Clinton.

"Wrong place at the wrong time is putting it mildly," said Josie. "This thing could ruin our lives."[2] They were now crime scene witnesses in a death of national importance. They might be called into court. Their names might appear in *The Washington Post*. It would not be easy to explain to their respective spouses what had happened.

They heard nothing for almost a year. Then the FBI interviewed them for the Fiske investigation. That is when Josie and Duncan discovered that the Park Police had made a nonsense of their witness statements. Duncan's surname was misspelled. Not even close. The Park Police had mixed up the cars, mixed up the men in the parking lot, made a minestrone of the whole scene, and concluded that the couple "had not noticed anything unusual."[3]

So Josie and Duncan each sat down with the FBI in April 1994 and tried to set the record straight.

Josie explained that the man without a shirt was sitting in Vincent Foster's brown Honda.

Duncan explained that the long-haired blond fellow had been hovering over the engine of Foster's brown Honda.

This time the authorities got it right. "Our FBI statements are absolutely accurate," said Josie.[4]

So, two men had been observed monkeying with Vincent Foster's car shortly before the body was discovered. One of them had long blond hair. Noteworthy, one would have thought. Blond hairs were found on Foster's undershirt, his trousers, belt, socks, and shoes. [5]

The FBI never tried to identify these hairs. "The source of this hair could have been boundless," said Special Agent Larry Monroe in surreal testimony before the Senate Banking Committee. "It could have been from his residence. It could have been from his automobile, which was used quite often by his children."[6]

The FBI did not deem it necessary to check the hair against samples from the Foster family, or from the staff at the Counsel's Office—surely the obvious way to put the matter to rest. It was a conscious decision by the FBI not to do so. Why not? Were they afraid that the hair samples would not match anybody in Foster's extended circle?

As for Josie and Duncan, they had given the Fiske investigation a wealth of extremely disturbing material. True, they could not recall every detail. Their memories were sometimes contradictory. But they had provided a narrative of events at the crime scene that should have compelled Robert Fiske to go back to the drawing board to start a fresh investigation of the entire Foster case.

Instead, their observations were reduced to this anodyne summary in the Fiske Report: "neither individual heard a gunshot while in the Park or observed anything unusual."[7]

I do not wish to labor the point, but this couple saw two unsavory-looking men handling the car of the dead victim, half an hour before his body was discovered. I cannot see how this could be distilled into nothing "unusual."

"They were going to be my secret weapon," Miquel Rodriguez confided to friends at the Starr investigation. But he never had the chance to call them before the grand jury.

Kenneth Starr concluded his suicide report in July 1997 without taking their testimony under oath. Josie and Duncan were never called before the grand jury. Instead, he sent FBI agents to reinterview them. They were talked into subtle changes that were, cumulatively, enough to dull the impact of their story. This has become a sickening habit of certain FBI agents, in both the Oklahoma bombing case and the Foster case.

The original FD-302s of Josie and Duncan, taken in April 1994, are the pristine documentary record. As Josie said at the time, they "are absolutely accurate." The rest is make-believe.

*   *   *

I had never given much thought to the driver of the Thrifty rental car who dropped into Fort Marcy Park between 4:15 and 4:30 PM. Another weak bladder, apparently.

This man had seen Foster's car, and Foster's suit jacket "folded over the passenger seat," and had then driven away. His cameo role was a single paragraph on page 28 of the Fiske Report. Fine, the man could place Foster's car at the crime scene. But life was too short to chase down every bit player who might, possibly, have an insight into the case. Anyway I did not have the foggiest idea who he was.

But Josie and Duncan's story made me think again. I dug up his FBI 302 interviews and discovered to my astonishment that this witness had seen a threatening man on watch at the entrance to Fort Marcy Park. He described the individual as a "Mexican or Cuban," and said his behavior made him "feel extremely nervous and uneasy."[8]

It appeared as if this Hispanic man had been posted there to dissuade anybody from venturing into Fort Marcy at 4:30 PM on July 20, an hour and a quarter before Foster's body was found. It was another startling piece of crime scene testimony.

I grabbed the Fiske Report and flicked to page 28. Could I possibly have missed a bit about the menacing man? No, I had not. The key passage had been expurgated. It was exactly what Fiske had done to Josie and Duncan.

Finding this witness was no easy matter. His name was redacted in the FBI documents. There was a brief mention of him in a Park Police "incident record": a Patrick Nolton, with a Washington telephone number 296-2339. But nobody at the number had ever heard of him—it appeared to be a doctor's clinic—and it soon became clear that there was no such person as Patrick Nolton in the District of Columbia, and never had been. The Park Police had done a first-rate job of "laundering" the identity of this witness, just as they had "laundered" Duncan's name.

But anybody can be found eventually.

We met for a coffee at the Au Bon Pain near his apartment on Pennsylvania Avenue. He was amiable, worldly, self-assured, wearing clean white jogging shoes and a yachtsman's jersey. Middle American through and through. He was a little over forty, perhaps, with a Celtic face. A registered Democrat. His name was Patrick *Knowlton.*

It was the first time he had ever spoken to the press about Fort Marcy Park. He had never read the Fiske Report or taken any particular interest in the death of Vincent Foster. As far as he was concerned, the matter was closed. He really did not have anything to reveal that he had not said already to the Park Police and the FBI, but he was happy to oblige a Limey. Now what paper was it? The London what?

A jack-of-all-trades, Patrick had been doing some remodeling work on a house in Chevy Chase on July 20, 1993. He left early, had a swim, went to the bank, and then set off for the two hour drive to a cabin he owned in the Blue Ridge Mountains. The traffic was snarled on the George Washington Parkway—as the Confidential Witness would discover an hour later—so Patrick pulled into Fort Marcy Park to find a tree.

There was an old brown Honda on the left, with Arkansas plates. He pulled in to the next space but one. A little further down was a newer blue car, Japanese make by the look of it, facing out into the lot. A man with a manicured appearance wearing a button-down Oxford shirt was sitting in the driver's seat, watching.

The man lowered his window just far enough to glower at Patrick. He had short cropped hair and Hispanic-looking features, although he could have been Middle Eastern. Dark, anyway, and in his late twenties. Patrick did not like the look of him.

"I was worried about getting mugged, so I left my wallet under the seat, just in case." He probably should have driven off straight away, but his knees were knocking by now. He had to find a tree.

"As I got out I heard his car door open and I thought, 'Oh shit, this is it, the guy's coming after me.' But he just stood there, leaning over the roof of the car, watching."

Patrick walked up toward the park. Instead of going into Fort Marcy proper, he took the logging trail to the left where the nearest trees were. That was a fortunate decision. Patrick dreads to think what would have happened if he had walked into the main body of the park.

"When I came back I looked at him and I thought 'Something is going to happen to me unless I get the hell out of here.'"

As an extra precaution on the way down he skirted the far side of the brown Honda. That's when he noticed a jacket draped over the back of the driver's seat, which appeared to be pulled forward.[9] On the passenger seat was a soft leather briefcase. "I remember thinking, these people must be real stupid to leave a briefcase like that in plain view on the front passenger seat."

The next night Knowlton was watching the evening news at his mountain cabin when he heard that Vincent Foster's body had been found in Fort Marcy Park on the afternoon of July 20. "That's when I thought, 'Holy shit.' I couldn't sleep thinking about it."

His girlfriend, Kathryn, told him it was his civic duty to call the police. So he did. It was after midnight. The woman on duty at the Park Police was incredibly rude. They got nowhere. The next morning at about 7:30 AM he called the Park Police again to speak to a detective. He spoke to officer John Rolla, who was friendly enough, but did not seem to think that Patrick's story was very important. There was no follow up. The Park Police never sent a detective to interview him. That was it.

Nine months later he was contacted by the FBI and asked to appear for questioning at the Office of the Independent Counsel. It was another episode of amateur hour, or so it seemed. The FBI agent "kept playing stupid—the whole fricking 'Colombo' routine," he said.

For some inexplicable reason they showed him a photo of a *blue* Honda with Foster's Arkansas tags RCN-504. "They told me right out that this was Foster's blue Honda that he'd driven to work that day. They went over it about twenty times, telling me that this was Foster's car," he said.

"I was quite adamant about it. I walked right next to that goddamn car, and it was *brown*. I saw what I saw, and I wasn't going to change my story."

None of it made any sense. Foster's car was a *grey* 1989 Honda Accord. The registration certificate from the Arkansas Department of Motor Vehicles is quite clear. Color: Grey. "I think they were just trying to screw me around. It pisses me off."

After coffee, Patrick and I adjourned to the *Telegraph* offices at the National Press Building, a few blocks from the White House. By now, he was eager to read his FBI 302 statements to find out what they had said about him. I offered him a deep armchair and then watched out of the corner of my eye as he began to mumble and shake his head.

"Everything's wrong," he said. "Look at this—'a 1988 to 1990 brown or rust brown Honda with Arkansas plates'—I never said that. I told them it was an older model, '83, '84. I was absolutely certain about it. I told them I couldn't believe some hot-shot White House lawyer would be driving a beaten-up old thing like that."

It is hard to believe that the FBI had made an honest mistake. Patrick had been called for a second interview a month later, on May 11, 1994, in order to clear up the dispute about the Honda with Arkansas plates.[10]

The FBI showed him underexposed photos of Foster's Honda— or that's what they said it was—in which the car appeared black. The idea was to convince him that the shade of the trees at Fort Marcy might have distorted the color. Patrick refused to budge.

They went over to the FBI lab in the Hoover Building to examine car brochures and color panels. At one point a lab technician called Frederick Whitehurst walked in and suggested that the FBI check every brown Honda in Arkansas from the early 1980s to see if one of them belonged to somebody with White House ties. The agent brushed him off.

"We're on top of all this," he said.

Patrick Knowlton is convinced that the FBI did not misunderstand him when they wrote up his 302 statement the next day. He believes they knowingly falsified it. And as we shall see, they picked a fight with the wrong man.

Patrick remembered a lot of details about that day at Fort Marcy. He was sure that the Arkansas number plates were not RCN 504. At the time his personal car was a Peugeot 504 and he thinks the number would have stuck in his mind.

Funny thing about his Peugeot. It was vandalized the night before his second interrogation by the FBI. A man followed him for several blocks, parked behind him at the Vietnam Memorial, pulled out a tire iron and smashed the lights. It was done in full view of retired police captain Rufus Peckham.[11]

The man was driving an aging Oldsmobile with Illinois tags that tracked to a Ronald Houston. Fate would have it that the U.S. Park Police was in charge of investigating the crime. They misspelled Patrick's name again. This time it was Knowton. They told him that Ronald Houston could not be found. It was untrue. I located him with no difficulty. He had moved to Hagerstown, Maryland, and was living in an elegant house near the Fountain Head Country Club and was driving an expensive, 4-wheel drive, luxury jeep.

Patrick told the U.S. Attorney's Office in D.C. that the man had been located. The Justice Department looked into it and found that the culprit was in fact Houston's brother-in-law, Scott Jeffrey Bickett. He confessed to the vandalism but the Justice Department refused to take any further action. "It was just a dispute over a parking space," said prosecutor Mary McClaren.[12]

A year later I would discover that Scott Jeffrey Bickett works for the Pentagon and is listed in the federal intelligence data bank with the following designations:

* AGCY=DCII, which stands for Defense Contractor II clearance level.

* FBI-HQ, which indicates that he has been briefed at FBI headquarters and serves as an FBI stringer.

* FBI-T

His security clearance is listed as:

* Active SCI, which is the highest clearance in the U.S. government, higher than Top Secret. It stands for Sensitive Compartmented Information.

He was first "indexed" in 1983 with the number 357DJ61377221P3F with a "retention" for 15 years. His birthplace was listed as Illinois.[13]

So the man who smashed the Peugeot 504 on the night before Patrick's second FBI interview was on the roster of FBI-HQ. No wonder Mary McLaren decided not to press charges.

But this is getting ahead. Sitting in my office, Patrick was now on the brink of a full-blown Irish tempest. "The bastards," he shouted, when he read that he could not "further identify" the menacing man in the park and "would be unable to recognize him in the future."

"That's an outright lie. I want it on the record that I never said that. I told them I could pick him out of a line-up."

I asked him if he would do a police artist's sketch of the suspect. He agreed. "I can close my eyes and visualize this guy like it was yesterday."

I paid an off-duty police artist to do a sketch of Knowlton's suspect.[14] A week later, on October 22, 1995, *The Sunday Telegraph* published the picture, with a cheeky comment that since the U.S. judicial authorities had failed to take the initiative, we would do it for them. *The Telegraph* pointed out that Kenneth Starr had not called Patrick Knowlton before the grand jury. Nor had Starr called the fornicating couple.

Surely the Independent Counsel was not going to issue his suicide report without deposing three of the most important crime scene witnesses in the Foster case. Starr responded quickly. Four days after the article appeared in London he issued a subpoena for Patrick Knowlton to appear before the Whitewater grand jury. It would prove to be a bad miscalculation.

*   *   *

The grey Honda really belonged to Laura Foster. She had driven it up from Vanderbilt University in May. A "Christian University Student" sticker was still on the windscreen. But father and daughter had been sharing the car for a few weeks.[15]

Once her brothers Vincent III and Brugh arrived, everybody was using it. The boys were messy. They left the trunk full of beer cans, cigarette packets, junk of all kinds, after their weekend trip to the beach on July 18.

It was Lisa Foster who got to drive the family's black Lexus 300, apparently. Not that she needed it much in Georgetown. It was easier to take taxis for her errands.[16] But she liked her little luxuries. As Bill Kennedy described her to the FBI, she was a "high maintenance" southern wife.[17]

On July 20, Vince and two children bustled down the steps of their house in Cambridge Place at about 8:30 AM and piled into the Honda.[18] Vince the father dropped Vince the son at the Metro—the son was a staff aide to Arkansas Senator Dale Bumpers—and dropped Laura at work.[19]

Or at least that is what we are told by the Fiske Report. There is no official record of this, so we have to take it on trust. None of Foster's children was interviewed by Fiske's FBI agents—much to their surprise—and the relevant paragraph is redacted in the handwritten notes of Lisa Foster's FBI interview. Why is it redacted? Why, once again, is a passage dealing with Foster's car such an acutely sensitive issue?

Snag. Vincent Foster did not bring his car to work that day. Or if he did, he did not park it in his reserved slot inside the White House grounds, number 16 on Executive Boulevard West.[20] It was never logged in and never logged out.[21]

Nothing seems to make sense about that car. Park Police detective Cheryl Braun took five Polaroids of the Honda at Fort Marcy. Time 7:30 PM. But it is impossible to make anything out, except that the license plate is redacted—yes, redacted—it's just a white box. The close-up shots of the car taken later at the Park Police impoundment lot reveal that there was no White House pass on the windscreen.[22]

It is a legitimate question to ask whether Foster's Honda was in fact at Fort Marcy Park on the late afternoon of July 20, 1993. Four of the original witnesses claim that they saw an old brown Honda, which is very hard to reconcile with Foster's four-year-old grey model. It was not just Patrick Knowlton, and Josie and Duncan. There was the "woman in the blue Mercedes," who went into the Fort Marcy parking lot at around 5:45 in search of a telephone after her car broke down.[23]

What color was the first car on the left? I asked her. "Oh, that was a tannish-brown," she said, spontaneously.

Sure? "Oh, yes, quite sure."

I checked her FBI 302 statement. There is no mention of a "tannish-brown" car. It says "light grey." I then went back to the handwritten FBI notes of the interview. The color is not even mentioned. It is obvious that the FBI inserted the words "light grey" later. Why?

So that made four witnesses who saw a tannish-brown car. What about the paramedics?

The official "narrative report" by Sgt. George Gonzalez of the Emergency Medical Services says: "BRWN HONDA. AR TAGS."[24]

The Medical Examiner?

Dr. Donald Haut saw "an orange compact, a beat-up old thing. I was surprised anybody in the White House would be driving a car like that."[25]

According to their FBI statements, several people observed a car that was consistent with Foster's 1989 grey Honda. The trouble is, some of the official statements are at odds with the agents' original handwritten notes. Park Police Officer Franz Ferstl, for instance, described it as a "late model, light-colored car that he later learned was Foster's vehicle."[26] But the notes do not mention the age or the color. They read: "There was a car parked in ft of lot to left (later learned it was VF's car)." It is not a big change, but it is not quite the same either. The cumulative effect of such distortions is to alter the complexion of the case.

I do not wish to accuse every FBI agent involved in the Foster investigation of distorting evidence. Some of the witness statements are accurate. It appears at least one agent was systematically altering statements, sometimes with little tweaks here and there, sometimes with outright falsehoods, as in the cases of Patrick Knowlton and the Confidential Witness.

The result in this instance was to create enough confusion about Foster's Honda to obscure the facts. But once you are alert to this legerdemain by the FBI, everything comes into focus. The old tannish-brown Honda parked at Fort Marcy between 4:30 PM and 6:37 PM—when the first team of paramedics left the scene—could not have been Vincent Foster's vehicle.

To whom did this car belong? Where was Foster's Honda that afternoon? Was the plate RCN 504 switched? Were the two cars switched at the crime scene as soon as the paramedics had left? These were the questions that Associate Independent Counsel Miquel Rodriguez was about to explore before his investigation was stymied.

*   *   *

Another mystery.

The keys to Vincent Foster's Honda had vanished.

"I searched his pants pockets. I couldn't find a wallet or nothing in his pants pockets," said Detective John Rolla of the U.S. Park Police. "We searched the car, and we were puzzled why we found no keys."[27]

It would be hard to miss them. Foster had a collection of at least six keys on two separate rings. One ring was for the Honda with a tag marked "Vince's Keys."[28] The other had a tag from Cook Jeep Sales, Little Rock, with four cabinet and door keys, including a Medeco-cut high security key with the inscription "U.S. Property Do Not Duplicate."[29]

The likelihood that Detective Rolla could search the trouser pockets of Foster's suit without finding this clump of metal is close to zero.

But two hours later, the keys mysteriously appeared. When detectives John Rolla and Cheryl Braun reached the morgue at the Fairfax County Hospital, the keys were sitting in the front right pocket of Foster's trousers.[30]

By the time they arrived, two men from the White House had already paid a visit to "identify" the body.[31] The White House aides had made themselves unpopular at the Fairfax County Hospital, flashing credentials and acting as if they owned the world. Nurse Christina Tea was not impressed. She refused to let them into the morgue at first, demanding proper authorization from the Park Police.[32] But they got in soon enough. Not only that, they managed to get inside the room itself.

"Many times when you view a body, you are in a separate room and view it through the glass," explained Detective Rolla. "This time, I don't think that happened. They were let in, the room attendant unzipped the body bag, they looked at it, he zipped it back up."[33]

One of the White House aides was Craig Livingstone, the former bar bouncer from Pittsburgh who had risen to White House chief of personnel security under the patronage of Hillary Clinton. It was the same Craig Livingstone who would later emerge as the protagonist of "Filegate," the man who came upon the FBI files of 900 political opponents at the White House as a result of an "innocent snafu."

The other was Associate White House Counsel William H. Kennedy III, friend and protégé of the deceased. Kennedy would have his moment of subpoena glory when he was summoned before the Senate Banking Committee to explain why he had written "Vacuum Rose law files.... Documents never know, go out quietly," in his notes at a White House meeting on November 5, 1993. But this does not do him justice. He is an under-appreciated figure in the Byzantine nexus of the Clintons.

Lugubrious, brooding, abrasive, he was the man who made the trains run on time at the Counsel's office. Where others waffled, he executed. It was his task to comb through the FBI background files and IRS tax-check forms of presidential appointees, and others, too, no doubt. These were not FBI summaries. He was reading the original SF86 raw data files from the "full-field" investigations. Names, places, dates—all the dirt.[34]

When he uncovered something "problematical" he would go to Vincent Foster to talk it through.[35] These two knew all the secrets. Too many, perhaps, for their own good. The two Arkansans went back a long way. Kennedy had first started at the Rose Law Firm in 1976 as an intern for Foster, and for the better part of two decades they had served the same master in Little Rock. Both were bailiffs of Stephens Incorporated, the financial overlord of Arkansas. It was only natural that Foster would tap Kennedy to serve under him at the White House Counsel's office.[36]

The activities of Livingstone and Kennedy on the night of July 20, 1990, do not make sense. They arrived at the morgue separately. But they left together, driving the twenty miles back to Kennedy's home in Alexandria in the same car.

"I drove Mr. Kennedy in my car to his home," said Livingstone in a deposition under oath.[37]

"So you left Mr. Kennedy's car at the hospital?"

"Correct. He was pretty upset."

It strikes me as bizarre for a busy man like Kennedy to leave a car 20 miles away in Fairfax. But Kennedy denied this anyway in his deposition, saying that it was Livingstone who left his car behind.[38]

The handwritten notes of Kennedy's FBI interview read "CL lvs his car at Hospital." The next line is redacted.[39] So are the next four pages. It is clear that the FBI was asking Kennedy questions about his movements that are still so sensitive, years later, that the American people cannot be told.

I do not offer an explanation as to why Livingstone and Kennedy cannot get their story straight on this elementary point. It is part of the inexhaustible mystery of the Foster case. What we do know with near certainty is that somebody slipped those keys into Foster's pocket at the Fairfax County morgue.

It compels a rather sinister question. Whoever had the keys, what were they doing with them in the first place?

CHAPTER TWELVE

STREET FASCISM

"**T**HANK YOU FOR ruining my life," said Patrick Knowlton, calling to announce that he had received a subpoena from the Whitewater grand jury.

It was delivered by FBI Agent Russell Bransford at 10:30 AM on October 26.[1] What happened over the next two days is bizarre beyond belief, but I tell the story because it has had major consequences two years later. The tomfoolery outlined in the following pages is laughable in a way, but it has resulted in a lawsuit that could compel fresh witness testimony through the power of legal discovery. If we ever learn the full truth about Vincent Foster, it may well be because of a childish prank by the political police.

It was Patrick's girlfriend, Kathryn, who noticed it first. They were walking through the avant-garde neighborhood of Dupont Circle that evening when a middle-aged man in a brown suit stopped and stared at Patrick.[2] At first Kathryn did not think much of it. A practical woman, with a Ph.D. in management, she is not the kind to see shadows on the wall. But then it happened again.

The next man was of similar vintage, with a navy blue jacket. His stare lasted about fifteen seconds. It was the same distinctive stare— one designed to provoke fear, confusion, and paranoia. And then it happened again, and again: men cutting in front of them, following them, glowering into Patrick's eyes, fixing him with the look of death wherever he turned.

The harassment was a boiler-plate operation, just the sort of trick played on Communist sympathizers in the 1950s, and Civil Rights activists in the 1960s. Old habits die hard, it seems.

After seven or eight episodes—which are all described in detail in court documents[3]—Patrick and Kathryn were seriously alarmed. The men were becoming more brazen now. They were actually brushing into Patrick, circling like hyenas. Some Middle Eastern types had joined in. Well-groomed. Athletic.

"At this point I was a nervous wreck, I was sweating. It was totally out of control," said Patrick.

He called me up in great distress that night and relayed the details, but was trying hard not to overreact. The next day it began again. My colleague Chris Ruddy, from *The Pittsburgh Tribune-Review*, happened to be visiting Washington. He was extremely skeptical, but agreed to accompany Patrick for a stroll around lunchtime. Half an hour later he called me on his mobile telephone.

"You're not going to believe what's going on here. There's a sur-veillance net of at least thirty people harassing Patrick, I've never seen anything like it in my life."

It was now obvious that they were trying to destabilize Patrick Knowlton before his grand jury appearance, and they did not seem to care whether this was observed by witnesses. It was street fascism in broad daylight, five blocks from the White House.

Patrick had called the FBI, requesting witness protection. Meanwhile Chris Ruddy and I put in a conference call to Deputy Independent Counsel John Bates to inform him that his grand jury witness was being intimidated. His secretary took down a few details. An hour later I called again. She let out an audible laugh and said that her boss had received the message. I can hardly blame her treating it as a joke. The office is no doubt deluged with calls that range from the cranky to the deranged. Bates never called back.

Sometime after midnight, Patrick telephoned me at my home in Bethesda. By now he was on the verge of a nervous breakdown. Somebody had got inside his apartment building and was banging on the door. When he answered, there was nobody there. Outside his window there was a man in a green trenchcoat, staring up at him. The telephone kept ringing. Hang-up calls.

"I can't take it any more. I want out of this," he said.

"Stay calm, don't let these criminals get to you," I said. "I'm going to come down and get you out of there. You're going to stay at my house until this nonsense is over."

On the way down I used my car phone to round up a posse. We met outside Patrick's apartment block, all three of us—a professional clown, accountant Hugh Sprunt (who was visiting from Texas), and myself, trudging through the drizzle, armed with umbrellas.

By then, the harassment had stopped. Patrick had regained his nerve. He decided it was better to tough it out. I told him to disconnect the telephone for the rest of the night. The truth militia would mount a guard outside his apartment building, patrolling the streets of Foggy Bottom with their umbrellas.

Our little foray was just what the FBI wanted. On Monday they told Patrick that "Pritchard and Ruddy" were orchestrating the harassment—to sell newspapers.[4] FBI Agent Russell Bransford finally dropped by the apartment, more than 48 hours after Patrick had requested witness protection. Patrick tried to call his lawyer, but the telephone had gone dead. Agent Bransford was cavalier, ironic, and mocking.

"He had this smirk on his face, as if he thought the whole thing was amusing," said Patrick. "I told him to get the hell out of my house."

*   *   *

"A toast to Kenneth Starr and the cause of justice," I said, acidly.

"To Kenneth Starr," replied Patrick Knowlton, lifting his glass. "The bastard."

We were a foursome—Patrick, his girlfriend Kathryn, Christopher Ruddy, and myself—sitting in one of those mahogany booths at the Occidental Grill, drinking a bottle of very expensive Cakebread Chardonnay. It was strangely jovial. There is always a sense of camaraderie when you find yourselves thrown together, fighting on every front at once: against the White House, against the Republicans, against the FBI, against the Justice Department, against the whole power structure of the United States.

None of us could quite believe that it had reached this point. But it had. The ruling class was going to crush Patrick Knowlton. They were going to trample on the civil rights of an American citizen, rather than let him disturb the settled resolution of Vincent Foster's death. There was nowhere for Patrick to turn. The rule of law was derelict, the press craven.

Patrick was still fuming from his treatment at the Whitewater grand jury that afternoon. It had been another hazing, this time by a young prosecutor named Brett Cavanaugh who attempted to ridicule the witness. Did the menacing man at the park "pass you a note," Mr. Knowlton? Did he "touch your genitals," Mr. Knowlton?[5]

So it went on, surely one of the lowest moments in the life of the Whitewater grand jury. Patrick flew off the handle at the imputation that he was a homosexual. He erupted in fury against the polished yuppy prosecutors, much to the delight of a group of African American jurors who rocked back and forth as if they were at a

Baptist revival meeting. Cavanaugh was unable to reassert his authority. The grand jury was laughing at him. The proceedings were out of control. It had started as a charade; it had ended in farce.

At least Patrick now knew that he could expect nothing from the Starr investigation. He was forced to conclude that the Office of the Independent Counsel was itself corrupt.

We ordered a second bottle of Cakebread, and plotted. Chris Ruddy and Patrick had snapped a few pictures of the street fascists, but identifying these people would take a long time.

We also had the license plate number of one of the cars that had been curb-crawling behind Patrick in a maneuver of overt intimidation. The tags tracked to an Arab living in Vienna, Virginia, close to the headquarters of the CIA. His name was Ayman. Not much to go on, but it was a start. Robustly drunk by now, I suggested that we all pile into a car and drive to the man's house for a surprise visit.

It was after midnight when we arrived at a cluster of mid-market townhouses. The lights were still on.

"Ayman, it's us. Answer the door, Ayman," I called out from the steps. He appeared in the doorway, an affable man of about thirty who spoke educated English. Patrick Knowlton recognized him at once as the driver of the surveillance car.

He explained that he was from Jordan. Not Palestinian. Jordanian. He had studied for a Ph.D. in economics at Oxford University, he said, and was now completing his studies in the United States. What could he do to help us? he asked.

We explained that somebody using his license tags had been conducting a harassment operation related to the death of Vincent Foster.

"Vincent Foster? It has to do with the Foster case?" he spluttered, turning ash white.

"It certainly does, Ayman, old chap. You'd better be more careful with those tags of yours," I advised.

As we spoke, a younger man appeared in the hall. He never said a word, but watched with fierce concentration. "That was him," said Patrick, afterward, "the other guy who was in the car."

Clearly they were stringers of some kind, people who could be called up at short notice to do street jobs for a little extra money. The security forces of every country employ such types for operations that require a degree of deniability. The stringers usually come cheap. If foreign, they tend to have residency problems so they can be induced to work for free.

But who were they working for? Who was Ayman? Oxford University said that they had no record of anybody by his name. But he has an interesting past. During the buildup to the Gulf War in 1990 he worked as the U.S. coordinator for a group called Solidarity International for Kuwait. The group ostensibly represented the civic opposition to the Al-Sabah family. It was making the statement that democracy activists had rallied to support the Kuwaiti monarchy in the face of Iraqi aggression.

In short, Ayman's task was to provide a patina of democratic respectability to the Kuwaiti cause. It was to reassure Americans that young, enlightened, pro-western students were behind the Sheikh. It had intelligence fingerprints all over it. But which intelligence service? Surely not the Jordanians. It could only have been the Saudis, the Kuwaitis, or the CIA.

Most people would have given up at this point. It seemed hopeless for a lone citizen to cut his way through this impenetrable thicket. But Patrick Knowlton was not going to surrender his rights as an American citizen without giving them—whoever they were—a taste of Celtic wrath.

He commissioned a lie detector test from Paul Minor, former chief polygrapher for the FBI, and passed with "no deception indicated" on every question about the events in Fort Marcy Park and the harassment in Dupont Circle.[6] He submitted to a psychiatric examination by Dr. Thomas Goldman who concluded that he was not suffering from mental disorder or paranoia. He underwent a Wechsler Memory Scale test by Dr. Lanning Moldauer, who found that he was in the 90th percentile for his visual memory.

He gave a sworn deposition to Congressman Dan Burton, one of the few stalwarts on Capitol Hill who refused to allow his independent judgment in the Foster case to be swayed by mocking editorials.

Finally he prepared a "Report of Witness Tampering" in the hope that the Starr investigation would be shamed into doing something. It was their responsibility, at the very least, to find out who leaked word of his subpoena. But when Patrick took the report to the Office of the Independent Counsel at 1001 Pennsylvania Avenue, John Bates called security and had him thrown out of the building. That was the last straw.

In October 1996 Patrick Knowlton filed a federal tort claim in the U.S. District Court in the District of Columbia, case number 96-2467, alleging a conspiracy to violate his civil rights, to inflict emotional distress, and to dissuade him from testifying truthfully before the federal grand jury. In the amended complaint he named the United States of America, FBI Agents Lawrence Monroe and Russell T. Bransford, and the two mysterious Jordanians, Ayman and Abdel.

"This case arises from a conspiracy to obstruct justice into investigations of the death of Deputy White House Counsel Vincent W. Foster," began the suit. "Plaintiff avers that overt acts alleged in furtherance of the conspiracy were committed at the direction or with the knowledge or consent of Defendant United States by and through the Federal Bureau of Investigation."[7]

It was a quixotic endeavor. Patrick was in debt. His lawyer and friend, John H. Clarke, had already sold his car to help defray the costs of pursuing the case. They had no money, no well-heeled patrons. Just the little contributions that came in dribs and drabs from around the country for the Knowlton defense fund.

"It's just so reprehensible what they've done—using government agents illegally like that. It's the epitome of everything wrong in this country," said Clarke, explaining why he had sacrificed his law practice to work doggedly on this case. "But I also know in my own mind, as a lawyer, that I can prevail. It's one of the biggest cover-ups in the history of the country, and if they ever give me a day in court I can prove it."

Big if.

CHAPTER THIRTEEN

THE TIP-OFF

T ELEPHONE NUMBER 395-4366. It tracks to the U.S. Secret Service. There it is, in the handwritten notes of Park Police Detective John Rolla on the evening of July 20, 1993.[1]

If it is not proof, it is at least compelling evidence that the White House was tipped off about Foster's death two hours before the official notification.

The sequence is crystal clear. Detective Rolla is contacted at 6:15 PM. In his notebook he writes:

Dead Body
Ft Marcy
Warm Sunny Day

He reaches the crime scene at about 6:35 PM. He is directed to the Honda with Arkansas plates RCN 504 in the parking lot, evidently the vehicle of the victim. Within two minutes a trace reveals that it belongs to Vincent Foster, Jr., 5414 Stonewall Rd, Little Rock, Arkansas, 72202.

Then comes the entry "Lt. Walter 395-4366." This is Lieutenant Danny Walter, U.S. Secret Service.

Detective Rolla was asked about this telephone number in a Senate deposition in June 1994 under penalty of perjury. At first he answered that Danny Walter was "a lieutenant on the Park Police."[2]

When pressed by Counsel Roman E. Darmer III, the detective began a tap dance. "I don't know, maybe this is a Secret Service guy. Maybe I called him. I don't remember.... I say, let's call the number and find out now, then we will know."

Reed Irvine from Accuracy in Media in Washington did exactly that. He called the number. The phone was answered by the Presidential Protection Division of the U.S. Secret Service at room 058 in the basement of the White House.[3]

The notebook indicates that Detective Rolla called the Secret Service at about 6:40 PM, within minutes of arriving at Fort Marcy Park. It would have been surprising if he had done otherwise:

- Foster had a Motorola pager on his belt with the letters WHCA (White House Communications Agency).[4]
- His White House ID was sitting on the front passenger seat of the unlocked Honda.[5]
- And presumably—since this was supposed to be the car he parked in slot 16, West Executive Boulevard, each day[6]—his White House sticker was clearly visible on the windscreen of the car.

The White House, however, has always claimed that it did not learn about the death until closer to 9:00 PM. The official memorandum states that the Secret Service was first notified at 8:30 PM.[7]

"LT. WOLTZ USSS/UD - WHS... ADVISED THAT AT 2030 HRS HE WAS CONTACTED BY LT. GAVIN, US PARK POLICE, WHO PROVIDED THE FOLLOWING INFORMATION: ON THE EVENING OF 7/20/93, UNKNOWN TIME,

US PARK POLICE DISCOVERED THE BODY OF VINCENT FOSTER IN HIS CAR... A .38 CAL. REVOLVER WAS FOUND IN THE CAR."

The body in the car? Gun in the car?

This was just a mistake, apparently. The Park Police accused the Secret Service of not listening properly. "I think he filled in the blanks. I said that his car was found. I didn't mention where the gun was found," said Park Police Lt. Pat Gavin.[8]

The memo then listed the White House officials who were notified by the Secret Service. First in line was David Watkins, identified as "Dir. of Personnel." (In fact, he was Director of Administration.)

*   *   *

"That evening was the earliest I ever got away the whole time I worked at the White House," recounted David Watkins, in his soft Arkansas accent.[9]

He is a very charming man, a former star quarterback, and now a golfing enthusiast. It was golf that proved to be his undoing, for he was fired by President Clinton in May 1994, after taking a Marine helicopter on a scouting trip to a country club near Camp David. To compound the humiliation, Clinton ordered him to reimburse the government $13,679 for the fare. It was rough treatment from a man he had known since childhood in Hope, Arkansas.

Watkins went to work for Calloway Golf, and turned his back on politics. As Rebecca Borders reported in *The American Spectator*, his only political act in the 1996 election campaign was to drive around Little Rock with a Bob Dole sticker on his jeep.

On July 20, 1993, he picked up his wife, Eileen, and went over to the Cineplex Odeon Wisconsin Avenue Cinemas to watch the Clint Eastwood film *In the Line of Fire*. It was showing on Screen A at 6:25 PM and Screen B at 7:10 PM. He cannot remember which screen it was. The credits had rolled through, the film was just starting, when he was beeped by the White House signals office (WACA).

"I thought, damn, I really wanted to watch that film."

He went to a pay phone at the theater. The Secret Service informed him that Vincent Foster was dead, self-inflicted gunshot to the head. It was deeply shocking. Watkins and Foster were not close friends, but they came from the same intimate little world. Both were from Hope. They knew the same people. Watkins had once dated Foster's sister, Sharon.

At the White House, Watkins and Foster talked every day. There were no signs of depression.[10] Eileen Watkins had played tennis with Lisa Foster that morning. Everything seemed fine.

"I was so in shock, I couldn't understand. I kept saying, 'Are you sure it's Vince Foster?'"

Watkins walked out onto Wisconsin Avenue to wait for the Park Police to pick him up. As best he can recall, it was a little after 7:30 PM.

*   *   *

Lt. William Bianchi was at the McLean fire station when the paramedics from Ambulance One and Engine One arrived back. They had left Fort Marcy Park at 6:37 PM.[11]

They were all gossiping about the victim being a White House aide.[12] "One of Clinton's buddies has killed himself," quipped Sgt. Iacone.[13] There was a joke going around that the man had been shot at the White House and dumped in a federal park so the Park Police would be in charge. Give it to the Keystone Cops.[14]

Todd Hall and Rick Arthur were commenting on how strange the whole thing was, the body lying so straight, so clean.[15] Given the circumstances, Lt. Bianchi ordered the unit leaders to fill out a detailed incident report.[16]

Later, Bianchi issued a gag order, as requested by the Office of the County Attorney. It forbade the paramedics from talking to the press about the Foster death "if they were interested in keeping their jobs."[17]

I asked one of the paramedics who logged out of Fort Marcy at 6:37 PM if he was sure they didn't learn of Foster's identity later in the evening. Couldn't there be some confusion?

"We all knew that it was a White House official when we left the park," he said, wearily. "Of course we knew, everybody knew, we were all talking about it on the way back."[18]

The Fairfax County Medical Examiner tells the same story. When Dr. Donald Haut rolled up in his blue Crown Victoria, with his wife, he remembers a whole gaggle of Park Police officers. One of them immediately came over and told him that the victim worked at the White House.

"They all knew right away. Everybody sort of assumed that Foster was one of the underlings the Clintons had brought up from Arkansas," said Haut.[19]

So what time did Dr. Haut arrive? He told the FBI that it was 6:45 PM.[20] But this was probably too early. He had just finished eating supper on the patio at his home when the call came. Reconstructing the chronology with his wife two years later, he thought that it was probably between 7:00 and 7:15 PM by the time they reached Fort Marcy.

This is consistent with the report he filed with the Virginia Office of the Chief Medical Examiner. In the box marked "View of Body" he wrote 7:15 PM.

In one of those revealing little fibs, the Fiske Report claimed that he did not arrive until 7:40 PM. It will be interesting to see if Kenneth Starr tries to stretch the time line, too.

* * *

So how does the Park Police explain the delay of almost two hours in notifying the White House? With great difficulty.

Investigator Cheryl Braun (promoted to sergeant a month later) arrived from the Anacostia station at 6:35 PM. After a quick briefing by the shift commander, she began going through Foster's Honda.

There was a map of the Washington metropolitan area on the floorboard, with no annotations or ink marks. A blue silk tie with swans was lying on top of a suit jacket, which was neatly folded on the front passenger seat. In the inside pocket of the jacket was a brown leather wallet. It contained $292 in cash, Foster's Arkansas driver's license, an American Express gold card, an Exxon card, a Delta Frequent Flyer card, and—this should have set off the alarm bells—a White House Federal Credit Union card.

Finally she noticed Foster's laminated chain ID from the White House Communications Center with Foster's photo lying loose on the seat beneath the jacket.[21]

Strangely, Detective John Rolla told the FBI that he was the one who searched the jacket and wallet, and found the ID.[22] Why can't the two Park Police detectives get their story straight on this? It was not a minor detail. The discovery of the White House ID changed the whole tenor of the case.

I strongly suspect that the ID had in fact been found already, either by Sgt. Jim Edwards or by Lt. Pat Gavin, two Park Police officers of higher rank who were already on the scene. Rescue worker Richard Arthur told the FBI that he saw a group of officers searching Foster's car for an ID before he left the scene at 6:37 PM.[23]

Let us assume that Cheryl Braun is telling the truth. By her own admission she had discovered the White House ID by 7:00 PM, an hour and a half before the White House was told.[24] Why does it take 90 minutes to call the other side of the Potomac River?

Braun says that she asked another officer to relay the message to the shift commander. This officer is not identified in her FBI statement, and for a very good reason.[25] The handwritten notes of her interview reveal that the man was in fact Officer William Watson, a member of the Park Police "Special Weapons and Tactics" team.[26]

What was the Park Police SWAT team doing at Fort Marcy at 7:00 PM on July 20, 1993, attending to a routine suicide? Why was this information withheld from the American people until it was forced into the open by Chris Ruddy's Freedom of Information Act lawsuit?

SWAT Officer Watson forgot to pass on the message, according to Braun. Here was a White House official lying dead in the park, and Officer Watson forgot to carry out the only assignment he was asked to do?

Half an hour later Braun discovered that nobody had notified the shift commander, so she made the call herself.[27] She claims that this was done at 7:30 PM. The FBI later massaged this to 7:30–7:45 in her official statement, but the handwritten notes of the interview say 7:30 PM, period. It is another sign that the FBI was jigging the testimony to close the time gap. Every fifteen minutes helped.

If one believes the story of Cheryl Braun, this still leaves a whole hour unexplained before the Secret Service was notified of Foster's death.

It is no wonder that Associate Independent Counsel Miquel Rodriguez felt the need to read the perjury statutes line by line to the Park Police officers at the grand jury.

*　　　*　　　*

Trooper Roger Perry was on duty at the guard shack of the Arkansas Governor's Mansion when the call came through from the White House. It was Helen Dickey. She was babbling incoherently, quite upset.[28]

Perry tried to calm her down. He knew her well from the days when she was Chelsea Clinton's babysitter. All the troopers on the security detail had grown fond of her. She practically lived with the Clintons. She ate with them, went everywhere with them. She was family, but they had her listed as a security employee on the

Mansion payroll.[29] It was a way for the Clintons to get free nanny care. No social security taxes either. Anyway, she was much grander now: she was Assistant to the White House Social Secretary.

"Vince shot himself," she sputtered. "He walked out to his car and shot himself in the head."

Perry tried to comfort her. He knew that Helen had been a neighbor of the Fosters and looked up to Vince as one of the great gentlemen of life. As she calmed down, Perry went over the details carefully. She repeated that Vince Foster had got off work and shot himself in the parking lot.

Perry relayed the message to Governor Jim Guy Tucker, then telephoned his friend Trooper Larry Patterson. "You ain't going believe what's happened now," he began.

It was early evening. Patterson had not been home all that long. His shift ended at 4:30 PM. He had not even changed out of his uniform. At the very latest it was 6:00 PM central time (7:00 PM eastern time).[30]

Perry also called Lynn Davis, the former commander of the Arkansas State Police.

"It was during the rush-hour, before 6:00 PM our time," said Davis. "He told me they'd found Vince Foster's body in his car, he'd shot himself in the parking lot."[31]

So, three men in Little Rock knew about the death of Vincent Foster before 6:00 PM local time—before 7:00 PM in Washington, D.C.—an hour and a half before the White House was officially notified. Without realizing it, Perry had repeated the version of events that later came to light in the declassified Secret Service memo. He had been told the "body-in-the-car" version that was mistakenly circulating inside the White House during the early part of the evening, which lends a degree of authenticity to his story.

It is possible that they are all confused about the time, but each of them signed a sworn affidavit. Helen Dickey, in turn, issued her own affidavit stating that she did not learn about Foster's death until

10:00 PM—after watching the President on *Larry King Live* in the Solarium at the White House Residence. However, she acknowledges that she made the call to Perry.[32]

The war of the affidavits was under way. Senator Al D'Amato, Chairman of the Senate Whitewater Special Committee, took a brief interest in the matter in September 1995. His office issued a statement announcing that the committee "will try to resolve this discrepancy by calling in Ms. Dickey and Trooper Perry for depositions. We have an obligation to determine the truth."

In his entertaining book, *Fools for Scandal: How the Media Invented Whitewater*, *Arkansas Democrat-Gazette* columnist Gene Lyons saw this as evidence of a "flirtation with the nut right." D'Amato was getting desperate, he alleged. "By late autumn 1995, the revived Senate Whitewater hearings had begun to resemble an absurdist mini-drama."

Something was needed to juice things up, so D'Amato latched on to the "farcical episode" of the Helen Dickey story, which had "started with a story in the London *Sunday Telegraph*" and then snaked its way like a slug into the U.S. press. "It wasn't until February 14, 1996, that the sad little farce came to a predictable end when Helen Dickey testified before the Whitewater committee."

By this, presumably, he meant that she repeated the assertions made in her affidavit. (How could she do otherwise?) Lyons noted that Senator D'Amato was "abjectly apologetic," reminding everybody that it was actually the Democrats who had requested the testimony of Helen Dickey in order to put "this wild speculation" to rest. Neither Trooper Perry, nor Trooper Patterson, nor Commander Lynn Davis—a former FBI agent, and a former U.S. Marshal—were ever called to give their side of the story.

Gene Lyons reached a wide audience with his plucky defense of the Clintons. He wrote long articles for *Harper's* and the ultra-serious *New York Review of Books*, each time alleging that the troopers had refused to testify—as if it were possible to refuse a subpoena.

Over time this came to be accepted as fact. The BBC even came to see me in Washington and started their interview by asking what I had to say for myself now that the whole Dickey story was shown to be a fiction. It was a very interesting insight into the way that consensus is manufactured in the Washington media culture.

But Lyons's olympian pronouncements were ill-informed. The troopers were in fact eager to testify. A "tentative" deposition had been scheduled for October 1995 but it was delayed because both the committee and the lawyer for the troopers agreed that it would make more sense to obtain the telephone records first.[33]

Needless to say, the records were not forthcoming. "The White House has been able to locate no record of a telephone call from Ms. Helen Dickey to the Governor's Mansion in Little Rock on July 20, 1993," associate White House counsel Jane Sherburne informed the U.S. Senate.[34] The call was made through the "Signal Switchboard," she explained, so it could not be traced.

This is very hard to believe. The White House Communications Agency is a high-tech Defense Department outfit run by an officer with the rank of colonel. If it cannot keep track of outgoing calls, America must be slipping into the Third World.

So the testimony of a 25-year-old erstwhile Clinton nanny was accepted as the final word on the matter, while three law enforcement officers with combined service of more than 70 years were not allowed to speak.

Senator D'Amato's acquiescence in this maneuver by the Senate Democrats is all the more remarkable when you learn who Helen Dickey actually is. To call her Chelsea's nanny does not do justice to her wide range of skills. In the first place she is a graduate of the University of Arkansas, and is the daughter of campaign treasurer Robyn Dickey, who signed the checks at the Clinton-Gore headquarters in 1992.

At the White House she worked for Marsha Scott on the illicit "Big Brother" database that has been the subject of an investigation on Capitol Hill.[35] She helped Hillary Clinton write *It Takes a Village*, typing up the pages every day in July and August of 1995. For two years she lived in a suite on the third floor of the Living Quarters of the White House, directly above the Clintons, and went in and out of their kitchen as if it were her own.

This was not some lowly aide to the President and the First Lady. This was their second daughter. Dickey had an obvious motive to dissemble about the events of July 20, 1993, and that is exactly what she did in her closed-door deposition to the Senate.[36]

What time did she get off work? She couldn't remember.

What did she do after work? She couldn't remember.

What did she do for dinner? She couldn't remember.

Did she talk to the First Lady that night? She couldn't remember.

She was alone in the Solarium when she watched the President on *Larry King Live*. Other aides were clustered together in a celebratory mood. But not the gregarious Dickey. Nobody saw her. And on it went, with the help of some very aggressive blocking by the Democratic counsel, James Portnoy.

For the record, the Secret Service logs show that Dickey "went up" to the living quarters from her West Wing office at 19:32. She came down again later at 22:15—although this has been crossed out and replaced with 23:35.[37]

Far from settling the matter, her performance under cross-examination cried out for further investigation. But the Republicans decided to let the issue slide. When Dickey was called before the committee in open hearings two days later she was handled with kid gloves.

All bark and no bite, Al D'Amato.

"Bill Clinton is a crook and a thief," he screamed all of a sudden when I was having coffee in his office. "Hillary Clinton is a crook and a thief, too."[38]

Then he minced his way over to the telephone to take a call from his dear friend Bob. This was Bob Fiske. They had known each other for decades in New York. This meeting occurred during the height of the Fiske investigation, so I asked if he would like me to leave the room.

No, no, he waived, and for the next fifteen to twenty minutes I heard a conversation that helped me understand why Senator Al D'Amato was never going to challenge the findings of the Fiske Report. As he got off the phone, he minced back to the sofa in a state of near ecstasy.

"God that man's tough. Tough, I mean tough. If the Clintons think they've found some patsy who's going to roll over, they've made the biggest mistake of their lives. Bob's going to cut their balls off."

But the real patsy was Al D'Amato. An engaging man, capable of gushing Italian charm, he is also weak, vacillating, and craves the approval of the Washington press corps.

Anybody watching those hearings could see that he was no match for the single-minded Democrats on his committee. The show trial was indeed an "absurdist mini-drama," as Gene Lyons had said. It was an interminable parade of secondary witnesses, talking about secondary issues, for month after month with no theme or purpose. In the end it served to exonerate the White House, giving the impression to the American public that the Clinton scandals had been investigated exhaustively, without result.

Foster's death itself was taboo, so D'Amato confined himself to investigating the seizure of documents from Foster's office that night. But even in this the Senator managed to miss the point. His lawyers honed in on allegations that a raiding party had entered Foster's office at around 10:50 PM to spirit away incriminating documents.

Secret Service officer Henry O'Neill testified that he saw Maggie Williams, the First Lady's chief-of-staff, coming out of Foster's office with a 3- to 5-inch pile of folders in both hands, then disappearing into her office next door, and then coming back out empty-handed.[39]

Ms. Williams denied it under oath, and passed two polygraph tests. She explained that she had wandered into Foster's office out of a Pavlovian reflex. The light was on and she just sort of hoped to feel the presence of Vince one last time.[40] All she did was sit on the sofa and think of Vince and weep her heart out.

Patsy Thomasson was there—the Director of the Office of Administration—sitting at Foster's desk. So Thomasson, too, was grilled by the committee. Senator Faircloth accused her of "rifling through" sensitive documents. She denied it.

"I opened each drawer in his desk, to look if there was something laying in the top. My thought process was if someone left a suicide note, they would leave it where it could be easily found."[41]

Why did she search his briefcase?[42]

"Because it was sitting at the base of his desk, and it just looked like a likely place."

And so it went, on and on, going nowhere. Months later Senator D'Amato had still failed to establish that anything sinister had happened in Foster's office that night.

But of course. He was looking at the wrong raid.

The 10:50 PM excursion into Foster's office was not the one that mattered. There was a reason why the White House has always insisted that it did not learn of Foster's death until 8:30 PM, when it quite obviously learned much earlier. The real mischief in Foster's office occurred between 6:45 and 8:30 PM—that is to say before Foster's set of keys, including that Medeco-cut high security key, made their way back into his pocket at the morgue.

If subpoena power had been used to pull at this string, the cover-up of Foster's death would have unraveled very quickly.

*   *   *

President Clinton was on *Larry King Live* from 9:00 to 10:00 PM, giving a cheerful account of himself. It had been a good day for the

White House. The nomination of Louis Freeh as the new Director of the FBI had been met with approval all round.

If the truth be known, Freeh was not the first choice. Clinton had wanted to appoint his old friend Rick Stearns, by now a judge on the Massachusetts Superior Court, to control the investigative machinery of the Justice Department.

Like the President, Stearns was a Rhodes Scholar from the rambunctious Class of '68, and Clinton's confidant during his maneuvers to evade the Vietnam draft. The two had traveled to Spain together in 1969 on a pilgrimage to the shrines of the Spanish Civil War.

But Clinton's staff had talked him out of appointing Stearns. There were already too many accusations of cronyism flying in Washington. It might have raised suspicions about the way Director Sessions had been disposed of the day before. Louis Freeh was a good compromise. Friend of Bernie Nussbaum. Friend of Bob Fiske. Good recommendations. His Opus Dei background helped, too.[43] It was another power network that Clinton could put to good use.

The president was in such high spirits that he agreed to stay on for another half-hour segment with Larry King. The show was being filmed in the ground-floor library of the White House. Mack McLarty appeared at the door. He waited until the advertisements, then broke in.

"Mr. President, let's quit while we're ahead," he said. "We've done the hour interview. It's been a fine interview."[44]

"Mack, what's wrong? What's up?"

"It's not a national emergency, or a crisis, but it's a very serious matter. Let's go upstairs."

That is when Bill Clinton first learned about the death of his childhood friend Vincent Foster. Or so we are told.

But did Bill Clinton already know something before he appeared on the show? It is hard to imagine that he is such a masterful actor, and such a cynic, that he could have staged this exuberant performance knowing that Foster was already dead. But how are we to account for the events witnessed by the CNN makeup artist sent to prepare the President for his appearance on *Larry King Live* that night? As she was putting the final touches to the President's blotchy yellow skin in the White House Map Room, a man walked in and announced that a note had been found in Vince Foster's office.

She was not able to identify the aide, but remembered that Mack McLarty was in the room. It must have been about 8:50 PM. She came forward to the FBI with some trepidation, for it was obvious that this had dreadful implications. Robert Fiske could not ignore her. She moved in well-connected circles of television. So his FBI agents went through the motions of investigating. They showed her photos of the White House staff to see if she could recognize the mysterious envoy from Foster's office. She could not.

Since then she has eschewed publicity. In a brief comment to Christopher Ruddy, who broke the story in *The Pittsburgh Tribune-Review*, she said: "I usually don't discuss my clients and what goes on. It's not good practice."

The Map Room incident was a closely guarded secret. The Fiske investigation did not provide the makeup artist's FBI 302 statement to the Senate Banking Committee. Like a number of the most incriminating witness reports, it is missing from the archive of documents in the Foster case.[45]

But if the FBI was trying to draw a veil over events that implicated the President of the United States in the Foster cover-up, it slipped up when redacting—or sanitizing—the FBI handwritten notes that were being released under court order. For the Map Room would come up again in the FBI's interview of Bruce Lindsey, the Senior Adviser to the President and the ultimate keeper of the secrets.

"Didn't hear any conversation about finding note that night.... Map Room? Pres never came in. Never shut door. Never talked about note."[46] There it is: the Map Room, the note, apropos of nothing else in the entire investigative record. This was all redacted in the FBI 302 write-up of Lindsey's interview that was provided to the Senate and to the American people.[47]

*   *   *

So what happened at the White House between 6:30 and 8:30 PM on July 20, 1993?

Maggie Williams, the First Lady's chief-of-staff, telephoned Foster at the White House Counsel's office at about 6:15 PM.[48] There was nothing unusual about this. Williams and Foster worked "very closely" together.[49] They had adjacent office suites on the second floor of the White House, and she was always bustling in and out with an armful of folders.

A gregarious, affectionate, voluble African American from Kansas, she even professed to have a crush on her beloved Vince. Couldn't an extra one be cloned, just for her, she used to joke.

The telephone was answered by Betsy Pond, a Clinton loyalist who had worked as a secretary with Hillary Rodham on the Watergate impeachment inquiry. She suggested trying to page Foster. Maggie Williams said: yes, go ahead, have him paged. The call went out through the White House operator at 6:20 PM.[50]

At that time Hillary Clinton was on her way from Los Angeles to Little Rock on a U.S. Air Force flight, accompanied by her mother and her daughter Chelsea.[51] The stop in Arkansas was a chance for the First Lady to drop the elderly Mrs. Rodham off at home and pay a visit to her doctors.

In mid-air, at 7:37 PM eastern time, Hillary Clinton called the White House signals office and was patched through to the apartment of her chief-of-staff at 1730 New Hampshire Avenue. "Maggie, are you at home?" she asked. "I'll call you when I land." The First Lady did not want to discuss details until they had a secure landline.[52]

The aircraft touched down in Little Rock at 8:26 PM eastern time.

Bernie Nussbaum and Betsy Pond left the White House Counsel's suite, room 208, at about 7:00 PM that night. Before leaving, Pond switched on the alarm system—which happened to be located in a box inside Foster's office—and then called the Secret Service Control Center to notify them that the Counsel's suite was being vacated.[53]

If anybody entered that set of rooms later that evening their movements would be picked up by a sensor in the ceiling. They would have two minutes to get out again before the alarm went off in the Control Center—unless, of course, they knew how to neutralize the alarm system. The logs show that at 8:04 PM Tom Castleton, the office intern, accessed the alarm system. It would indicate that he entered the Counsel's suite, but he cannot remember anything about it.[54]

Foster had a locked file cabinet in his office, room 220. Nobody was allowed to touch this cabinet. His executive assistant Deborah Gorham remembers that he kept a file on the Branch Davidian siege at Waco in there, but she did not have a key and never got to look inside.[55]

The most sensitive material was kept in a safe in Bernie Nussbaum's office. Betsy Pond had the combination number taped underneath one of her file drawers, but even with the number she was defeated by the technology of the lock. "I never once was able to get that safe open."[56]

Deborah Gorham was the only person who had mastered the art. She kept the password on the hard drive of her computer in an encoded form so that nobody could make any sense of it, even if they managed to break into her computer files. Foster had asked her to place two binders from the National Security Agency in the encrypted safe in March or April 1993. While the safe was open she noticed two gold envelopes—8 1/2 by 11 inches—inside the safe.

One said "For Eyes Only, Not To Be Opened, William Kennedy." The other said "Janet Reno."[57]

Two floors below, the ubiquitous Patsy Thomasson was hard at work in the Offices of Administration 015–018. At the time she did not have a White House security clearance. Indeed, she was not granted one until March 5, 1994,[58] fourteen months into her tenure at the White House.

David Watkins, her boss, had slipped away early to watch *In the Line of Fire*. The secretaries had gone home.[59] But it appears that Thomasson was not alone. The Secret Service alarm logs—discovered by the indefatigable Hugh Sprunt on page 4214 of Volume XIV of the Senate Whitewater documents—show that Patsy Thomasson checked into the suite at 7:05 PM.

Five minutes later, at 7:10 PM, a unit called the "MIG GROUP"—U.S. Secret Service—was logged into the offices of administration. At 7:44 PM, both Thomasson and the "MIG GROUP" were logged in a second time.[60]

The Secret Service was not very forthcoming about this "MIG GROUP." Mike Tarr, the agency's spokesman, told me at first that he had never heard of it. When pressed about the logs he explained: "It's not our group. We'd be notified they were coming, and we'd process them in."

The next day, polite as always, he corrected himself. "It's us. It's our technical people, our folks who were doing a routine alarm check."

There is no mention of this MIG GROUP in the logs of other offices covering a two-week period in July 1993.

So, what does MIG stand for? "I can't tell you, that's classified. Sorry," said Mike Tarr.

The things they classify. It appears that the unit is the Maintenance and Installation Group. It is part of the Technical Security Division, which handles alarms, locks, safes, surveillance, bugs, and the like. Very high tech. Very capable. If there was any unit in Washington capable of getting into Foster's safe, quickly and cleanly, these were the gentlemen who could do it. They were in the West Wing, between 7:10 to 7:44, with the enterprising Patsy Thomasson.

It is possible that there is an innocent explanation. But if there is, Ms. Thomasson did not offer one. She slammed down the telephone the moment I broached the subject.

On the evening of Foster's death Ms. Thomasson had dinner at the Sequoia Restaurant with a group of visitors from Arkansas. Her set of friends is an unusual one. She spent the 1980s working for Dan Lasater, a Little Rock tycoon who went to prison for cocaine distribution. As we shall see, attempts to investigate Lasater for suspected narcotics trafficking and organized crime were consistently thwarted. Ms. Thomasson was his chief lieutenant. She ran his business affairs while he was in prison, and was still listed as a registered agent of Lasater's Phoenix Mortgage Company after she started work at the White House.

As she came out of the restaurant she was beeped by David Watkins. It was 10:34 PM. She called in from a pay phone and was informed that Foster was dead. Taking a taxi back to the White House, she went directly to Foster's office to look for a suicide note.

The door was open, the lights were on, the cleaning lady was there. Thomasson sat down at Foster's desk and stayed long enough to be seen searching, conspicuously but not in a "purposeful" way, by Maggie Williams, Bernie Nussbaum, and Secret Service Officer Henry O'Neill.[61]

By the time she left the White House Counsel's office, suite 208, her fresh fingerprints were all over Foster's desk, drawers, filing cabinet—and all quite innocently.

CHAPTER FOURTEEN

"COMMUNICATION STREAM OF CONSPIRACY COMMERCE"

*T*HE *DAILY TELEGRAPH* of London was founded in 1855, four years after *The New York Times*. It had a good run covering the American Civil War and the Franco-Prussian War, then settled down as the voice of yeoman England, advancing the purposes of the Anglican Church, the Union, and always, without question, supporting Her Majesty's Dragoon Guards wherever they were deployed.

For a while *The Telegraph* was the newspaper of the Empire, although for some reason it has been more muted on this subject lately. Its historic triumph was to recognize early in the 1930s that fascism was an exceedingly nasty movement, and a threat to the European order. This was not obvious to everybody. *The Times* of London, representing the prevailing mood of the ruling class, belittled such concerns, ridiculed Winston Churchill, and supported the Tory appeasement of Adolf Hitler until the very end.

By the mid-1990s *The Telegraph* was still fighting for Church, Queen, and Country, this time struggling to prevent the United Kingdom from being subsumed into a sort of Vichy II—a European superstate run by the Germans and the French, and administered from Brussels under the terms of the Treaty of Maastricht.

The newspaper is doing very well. Now owned by a Canadian proprietor, Conrad Black (who also owns *The Jerusalem Post* and *The Chicago Sun Times*, among others), the circulation of *The Daily Telegraph* is around 1.2 million, the highest figure for a "quality" newspaper in western Europe. *The Sunday Telegraph* has a circulation approaching 800,000, but no less influence.

Both the daily and the Sunday editions are large broadsheet papers, a fact that is well displayed on the newsstand of any large Washington hotel. So it was with some consternation that I read a 331-page report by the White House Counsel's Office calling *The Sunday Telegraph* a "tabloid."

It is hard to believe that the authors of this remarkable document—"Communication Stream of Conspiracy Commerce"—were so provincial that they did not know the difference between *The Telegraph* and *The Times*, on one side of Fleet Street, and *The Sun* or *The Mirror* with their page three topless girls, on the other. Since this White House is stuffed with Oxonian Rhodes Scholars I have to assume that the smear was deliberate. The authors issued a report at taxpayers' expense, with the full imprimatur of the White House Counsel's Office, that published assertions they knew to be false. It violates the cardinal rule of Washington spin: Never get caught propagating a demonstrable lie, and this one was quite demonstrable. Even under America's forgiving libel laws, it was defamatory.

In clanking prose the report described "the mode of communication employed by the right wing to convey their fringe stories into legitimate subjects of coverage by the mainstream media." At the beginning of the chain is Richard Mellon Scaife, or "the Wizard of Oz," as he is described in the report. Mixing the metaphor, the report then states that "he is nothing less than the financial archangel of the movement's intellectual underpinnings." Whatever that is supposed to mean.

The White House claims that Scaife, 65, uses his $800 million banking fortune to fund the think tanks, foundations, and media outlets that elaborate Clinton conspiracy tales and launch them into cyberspace. Once on the Internet "the story will be picked up by the British tabloids," which launder and return them to the United States as quasi-legitimate news. Then they are picked up by *The Wall Street Journal*, *The Washington Times*, and *The New York Post*. At this point the Congressional Committees start taking an interest and then—*whoosh*—they go mainstream with a vengeance. A busy wizard.

I met Scaife once. When the report came out he invited me to Pittsburgh. Since I was now supposed to be working for him, it was only fitting that we should meet. We had lunch at the old, wood-paneled Allegheny Club, plotting new mischief as we ate homemade peach ice cream. After being told by the White House Counsel's Office that he was a reclusive, shadowy man, I was surprised to find myself with a warm, bubbly extrovert whose greatest joy in life is shooting in the 80s at Cypress Point in Monterrey.

The White House report was hysterical and hopelessly confused but it did sense something real. Matters were, indeed, getting out of hand. The usual levers of control over the media were no longer working properly.

A *Samizdat* media had emerged that resembled the underground network of faxes and newsletters in the Soviet Union in the 1980s— when nobody believed *Pravda* or *Izvestia* any longer. It was comprised of talk radio, the Internet, alternative newsletters, and C-Span, all working in chaotic synergy. The effect was highly subversive, and the White House was having great trouble jamming the broadcast mechanism.

One of the favorite pastimes of mainstream journalists is to comb through the Internet—*Alt.Conspiracy*, etc.—in search of outrageous "posts" that can be used to mock the medium. Amusing. Trite. Above all, uninstructive. If you know where to look, there are real documents to be found on the Internet. When Americans can review the primary material for themselves, they can see with piercing clarity what they long suspected: the American media is incurious, slothful, consensual, pedestrian, biased without acknowledgment, fearful of challenging power, and not particularly honest. In other words, it behaves as the media does in most countries, most of the time, as an adjunct of the governing elite. The guild has done a good job of disguising this with its Pulitzer Prizes and ombudsmen and code of ethics. But that era is coming to an end, I suspect. The reservoir of trust is close to exhaustion, and the market monopoly is breaking.

What was bothering the White House most about the Internet was the enormous amplification it gives to newsletters like *Strategic Investment*, or regional papers like *The Pittsburgh Tribune-Review*, or even foreign publications like *The Sunday Telegraph*. In the 1980s our stories would not have gained any traction. Now they are "posted" within hours of publication, and are then perused by the producers of the radio talk shows, who surf the Net in search of avant-garde material. A good scoop may be picked up by Michael Reagan—the President's son—with 120 radio stations and an audience of millions. (Reagan also breaks his own stories. He has sent investigative staff to go digging in Arkansas.) It might be read on the air by G. Gordon Liddy, Paul Harvey, or Chuck Harder. It might be featured by Blanquita Column, or by Rush Limbaugh, with his 20 million "ditto heads."

Within a week a good news story might have come to the attention of 20 or 30 million people. This would pass unnoticed inside the Beltway, but not inside the White House. Clinton's staff *sensed* what was happening, even if they did not understand how it was happening. The polls were picking up dangerous undertows. Only a third of Americans accepted the official story that Vincent Foster committed suicide, despite the fact that no major newspaper, magazine, or TV station in the United States was questioning the death.

Indeed, most of the media were pouring scorn on the Foster "conspiracists." But word was leaking out.

By the summer of 1995 it was becoming clear that the *Samizdat* media could no longer be ignored as a fringe irritant. Senator Al D'Amato was being ambushed on radio talk shows by the Internet brigade, who were carrying out a spontaneous campaign of guerrilla warfare. Whenever D'Amato, or other Whitewater figures, were scheduled to appear on a call-in show, the troops would issue an alert bulletin over the Net. The snipers would take positions, lie low, and then let off a volley of fire—very accurate, well-informed fire—over the airwaves.

It could cause a skittish politician like Al D'Amato to panic, which is what finally happened when "Carl from Oyster Bay," one of the most ingenious of the rebel pickets, ensnared him on the Bob Grant show in August 1995. Asked about the discrepancies in the case, the Senator started babbling:

"Did [Foster] die in that position? Was he dragged there? Was he carried there?... What about the gun?... And the manner in which the gun was found?"

The Senator had committed himself. He had provided "cover" to the Foster "conspiracists," at least for a while. It was a major rebel advance.

In late June 1995 I had lunch at the Maison Blanche with Joe Gaylord, the chief strategist of Speaker Newt Gingrich. It was a threesome hosted by Mark Melcher, the erudite chief of the Washington research office of Prudential Securities. Gaylord was not loquacious. A lean, wiry man of forbidding intensity, he listened for 45 minutes as I walked him through the backroads of the Foster coverup. He asked a few questions, but did not indicate one way or another what he thought. A few days later he relayed a request for some of the documentary material. I put together a package of articles from the *Samizdat* but did not expect much to come of it.

A month later Gingrich was the guest at one of the informal "Saturday Evening Club" dinners hosted by the editor of *The American Spectator*, Bob Tyrrell. The conversation turned to Foster.

It is easy to forget now, but in July 1995 Gingrich was at the height of his powers. The upper room at La Brasserie was packed. Robert Novak was there; so were Arianna Huffington, David Brock, and Wesley Pruden from *The Washington Times*; John Fund from *The Wall Street Journal* had come down from New York; so had John O'Sullivan, the editor of *National Review*. It was a gathering of the top guns in American conservative journalism. So it created waves when the Speaker said, caustically, that you would have to be "brain dead" to believe the official story about the death of Vincent Foster.

He then blurted out that I had met with Joe Gaylord over lunch and had convinced him that the Fiske Report was a cover-up. Gaylord nearly slithered out of his chair. For my part, I knew at once that this meant trouble. Penn Kemble, the Deputy Director of the U.S. Information Agency and the only administration official to attend these dinners, took out a notebook and started scribbling. Kemble is a good man, but I knew that Newt's comments were going straight to the White House.

There was a heated exchange about Foster—reflecting the deep rift among conservatives over the case—but Gingrich took my side on every point. After dinner, a small group of us withdrew to the "Kennedy Room," where Ted Kennedy had allegedly been interrupted coupling on the table with a female companion.

"I've made up my mind. This evening has sealed it," said Gingrich. "I'm going to appoint an investigator in the House and we're going to go after this."[1]

For the White House, matters were getting dangerously out of hand. The successful, two-year effort to contain the Foster case was suddenly unraveling, and all because of a group of "crazies" that nobody was supposed to be listening to. From what I can tell, the Counsel's Office started putting together the "Communication

Stream of Conspiracy Commerce" report in July 1995 when both Gingrich and D'Amato first began to make their threatening noises about the Foster death.

The report was never intended for public release. It was shown quietly to journalists to discourage them from pursuing the allegations. "Do you realize the provenance of this conspiracy garbage?" the White House would say. "I wouldn't touch it if I were you."[2]

It was also offered as a crib sheet to a few collaborators in the hope that they would write hostile pieces on Scaife and the tiny handful of journalists pursuing the Foster case. A few obviously did exactly that. You can see the outlines of the "Communication Stream of Conspiracy Commerce" report in the work of *Arkansas Democrat-Gazette* columnist Gene Lyons. I kept getting calls from reporters asking the same questions: "Did I know Scaife? Had I ever accepted money from Scaife? So who owned the tabloid I worked for? You mean it's not a tabloid? Oh."

It was only after *The Wall Street Journal* exposed the existence of the report in December 1996 that I was able to confirm my suspicion that all this had been orchestrated behind the scenes by the White House. I found the contents very revealing. What came through strongest was the growing alarm that the investigative journalism on Foster's death was striking close to home.

Clearly somebody was awake at night in the White House fretting that the Helen Dickey story was gaining dangerous momentum. And somebody was worried that a trio of handwriting experts had called the Foster "suicide note" a forgery. The Foster movement was becoming a threat to the Clintons, and the leader—by unanimous acclamation—was Christopher Ruddy, the roving correspondent of *The Pittsburgh Tribune-Review*. He had to be destroyed.

*   *   *

The staff called Ruddy the Lone Ranger at the Adlai E. Stevenson High School in the South Bronx, where he taught social studies to black and Hispanic children. It was one of the toughest schools in the country, a sub-city of 5,000 pupils and 500 staff. By 1992 it was descending into pandemonium. Teachers were being beaten to a pulp in their own classrooms, and nothing was being done about it.

The principal was paralyzed by doubts, and no one would take the initiative to reform the school. So Ruddy ran for election as Chapter Chairman of the American Federation of Teachers on a reform ticket, and won. It was a powerful position. Under New York's "school-based management" system the union chief had a veto on all policy decisions. In effect, Ruddy became co-administrator of the school. Things did not improve. The principal, he realized, was beyond redemption. She had to go.

Ruddy organized his forces for strike action. It caused a minor sensation. TV cameras were all over the school. The strike was the lead story on the New York nightly news. It was years since anybody had challenged the New York school system and successfully toppled a principal. But this time the school bosses backed down. Adlai E. Stevenson High School was given a new principal. Order was restored. Ruddy was 27 years old.

"That's when I learned what it's like to take on the system, make enemies," he said.[3] "It's what has guided me through the morass of the Foster case."

It was never his intention to become a union activist. After finishing a master's degree at the London School of Economics, and briefly studying Middle Eastern policy at the Hebrew University in Jerusalem, he had decided to do a stint of teaching in an inner-city school as a form of social service. He had no money. He was one of fourteen children, the son of an Irish-Catholic police lieutenant in Nassau County. He had the ascetic habits of a monk, at least compared to me. These things are relative, I suppose.

While working as a teacher he wrote articles for *The New York Guardian*, which is what catapulted him into a job as chief investigative reporter for *The New York Post*, a boisterous center-right newspaper owned by Rupert Murdoch. It is what is called a "mid-market tabloid" in Britain: no topless tarts, but less portentous than the Old Grey Lady—*The New York Times*.

In late 1993 nobody was investigating the death of Vincent Foster. The American press had taken the official story on trust, even though the authorities had refused to release the Park Police report, the autopsy report, or a copy of the suicide note.

"A friend of a friend in Washington told me that the gun was found in the hand, which is something that almost never happens in a suicide," said Ruddy. "I thought 'that's interesting' and filed it away in the back of my mind. When I got back to New York I did a Nexus search and found that all the stories were different. Some had Foster draped over a cannon, others had him lying in a ditch. He was all over the place. There was no hard information at all on the crime scene. So I figured it was time to track down somebody who was actually there that night."

Ruddy is portly beyond his years, with an air of impending middle age. He dresses in a stolid coat and tie, like a bureaucrat. The clothes never quite fit; the colors often threaten to clash. Hip is the last word one would ever think of applying to him. But he commands a certain quiet authority, and he has an extraordinary gift of building trust with sources who can see through the usual smarmy deceptions of the press. On a freezing January morning in 1994 he made his first breakthrough with the Park Police.

"Rush Limbaugh's been saying all these bad things about us, but it wasn't our fault," an officer confided over coffee. "We tried to get the truth out but the newspapers covered it up."

A Fairfax County paramedic, George Gonzalez, told Ruddy that he had never seen a gunshot victim like Foster in thirteen years on the job. All so clean, a pristine shirt, no blood to speak of. Then paramedic Corey Ashford said he picked up the body—which was lying straight, "ready for a coffin"—and didn't see any blood.

Ruddy had a story. It was the first of a series that appeared in *The New York Post* in January and February of 1994. They caused a furor. The newly appointed Whitewater prosecutor, Robert Fiske, announced that he would expand his brief to include a review of the Foster case and indicated that this time it would be a genuine homicide investigation. Ruddy became a celebrity.

But there was something strange about the way the rest of the media was responding. Instead of cultivating crime scene witnesses of their own and building on Ruddy's work, they tried to shoot down the story. They wheeled out Major Robert Hines, the public affairs spokesman of the Park Police, accepting his *pro forma* comments as if they were the last word.

The New York Daily News—the chief competitor of *The New York Post*—embarked on a debunking campaign. Their Washington Bureau Chief, Karen Ball, a personal friend of President Clinton, was given access to the autopsy report. In a two-page spread on February 11 she wrote that the gunpowder burns in Foster's mouth were "consistent" with the powder traces found on his right thumb. It sounded good, but in fact it was meaningless. Gunpowder is not manufactured with taggants that allow police labs to establish such a match.

The Daily News then sent its star columnist Mike McAlary down to Washington to talk to the Park Police. He was shown the closely held Park Police report and some crime scene photos. It was a considerable journalistic coup, but at the same time there is something wrong when the police show their reports to one or two chosen allies in the press, while unjustifiably withholding it from anybody who actually knows the details of the case—in fact, it is a form of police corruption. It nevertheless formed the basis for McAlary's front-page blockbuster "Case Closed."

McAlary was tricked into writing that the Confidential Witness was a fiction created by a truant Park Service worker who had been drinking in Fort Marcy Park. Somebody had overplayed their hand.

It was this article that caused the Confidential Witness to come forward with his allegation that there was no gun in the hand. McAlary was wildly wrong. But you are forgiven for being wrong about the Foster case if you toe the line.

Being right is much more hazardous to your career. The door closed on Chris Ruddy at the end of a fast, furious week in early March 1994. He was "nailed" on the photos. Ruddy had written a story on March 7 reporting that the "crucial" crime scene pictures were missing and that there were no "relationship photos."

Documents released a year later showed that this was essentially true. All of the 35 mm photos were underexposed and most of the Polaroids had disappeared. All that remained were a few close-up shots. But it was a subtle point, one that ABC News chose to obscure when the network was leaked the surviving Polaroids—clearly with the purpose of discrediting Ruddy. ABC went on the air with the now famous photo of the gun in Foster's hand, leaving an impression in the mind of all but the most attentive viewers that Ruddy had claimed there were no crime scene photos at all.

Ruddy never wrote another story about Vincent Foster for *The New York Post*. "It didn't matter what I said after that, nobody wanted to listen. And in a way I don't really blame them," he said.

But the *coup de grace* was Ellen Joan Pollock's story in *The Wall Street Journal* on April 4 saying that Fiske had concluded that Foster's death was a suicide. Fiske had indeed come to this conclusion, but not for the right reasons. As we have seen, the record shows that he had not conducted the key witness interviews by then and the FBI crime labs had barely begun to examine the forensic evidence. But that was not known in the editorial offices of *The New York Post* or any other newspaper until much later.

"So that's it, case closed," said *The Post*'s editor, Ken Chandler.

Ruddy limped on through the early summer, but his career at the newspaper was finished. Chandler was graceful about it afterward. "The truth is, Chris Ruddy trod where others fear to tread. When you do that, you get criticism and scorn heaped upon you," he said. "When you're writing about something you can't get answers to, you have to keep pushing, and he did."

Ruddy, of course, refused to give up. He launched one of the most remarkable guerrilla campaigns in the history of American journalism. This has led to a good deal of tut-tutting at the gatherings of the guild. But what was the man supposed to do? Drop the story, knowing that a grievous abuse of power had taken place?

Not Ruddy. He waged war on the airwaves, broadcasting night after night across the country on the radio talk circuit where he soon became a folk hero. He gave speeches, endlessly. He lobbied on Capitol Hill. He lobbied at the Christian Roundtable meetings in Tennessee. He lobbied wherever people would listen. He built alliances: with Reed Irvine's Accuracy in Media in Washington; with Jim Davidson's *Strategic Investment*; with the Western Journalism Center in California; with Jeremiah Films (which made *The Clinton Chronicles*). He signed up with Richard Scaife, writing about the Foster case for *The Pittsburgh Tribune-Review*. It was a modest little brigade. But it was enough for insurgent warfare.

One of his coups was to persuade Joseph Farah, the Executive Director of the Western Journalism Center, to commission a team of forensic experts to do a two-month review of the Foster case. Farah, the former editor of *The Sacramento Union*, started the Center in 1991 to restore the forgotten mission of American journalism: rooting out government corruption and exposing abuse of power.

The forensic team was led by Vincent J. Scalice, a former homicide detective for the New York City Police Department. Scalice had worked with the FBI on the assassinations of John Kennedy and Martin Luther King. He had been a Consultant Member for the House Select Committee on Assassinations.

The so-called Scalice Report, released in April 1995, concluded that "a high probability exists that Foster's body was transported to Fort Marcy Park." It honed in on the fact that no traces of soil could be found on Foster's shoes, under a microscope, even though he had supposedly walked 700 feet through the overgrown park.[4] The investigation did two simulation walks to see what residue was left after walking to the crime scene. Both models had visible soil all over their shoes.

While Scalice did not conclude outright that the death was a homicide, he certainly suggested it: "[T]he lack of extraviated blood on the front of the body is inconsistent with death by intra-oral gunshot, which raises the likelihood that Foster's heart had already cessated and that death would have been caused by other means."

It was picked up by Reuters, Cox News Service, and *The Washington Times*, among others, and created a huge stir in the *Samizdat*. At the Office of the Independent Counsel copies were put in the pigeonholes of the prosecutors and FBI agents associated with the Foster case.[5] It had been a triumph. So Ruddy prepared a second strike.

"I wanted to pull away the pillars of the cover-up one by one, so they couldn't use them again," he said.

In the fall of 1995 he commissioned three handwriting experts to study the authenticity of the "suicide note" found in Foster's briefcase. This time it was funded by James Dale Davidson, a tall, slender, elegant man of dry humor and considerable wealth. He owns a beautiful Queen Anne estate in rural Maryland dating from the 1690s, a chateau in France, and a huge apartment in Buenos Aires—currently his favorite haunt.

Having been wined and dined by Davidson at many of the best restaurants in Washington (he considers them adequate, but below Argentine standards), I must confess a personal bias in his favor. Best known as President of the National Taxpayer's Union, he is also an accomplished author. He co-edits the *Strategic Investment* newsletter with William Rees-Mogg—or the Baron of Hintonblewitt to use his correct title—a member of the House of Lords and a former editor of *The Times* of London. *Strategic Investment* is tailored to those who want hard intelligence for investment purposes, long before it appears in the general press.

Davidson had the same tutor as Bill Clinton at Oxford, enjoyed Clinton's "charm and geniality," and contributed to his 1992 presidential campaign. "I knew he was a bounder, of course, but my hope was that he'd turn out to be the Carlos Menem of North America and slash entitlement spending," said Davidson.[6]

But questions of economic management were soon overtaken by the much greater issue of the rule of law. For Davidson the Foster cover-up is a marker of the declining integrity of the American democratic system. If the U.S. judicial system cannot summon the courage to deal with this case, if it behaves like the Mexican or the Indonesian or the Nigerian judiciaries, then there is no reason to pay a "rule of law" premium on U.S. stocks, bonds, and real assets.

He recommends investing in countries at a positive stage of the moral and cultural cycle, like Chile, where judges, prosecutors, and police cannot be bought so easily. A Chilean policeman in the 1990s, he asserts with contrarian mischief, is much more honest than a U.S. cabinet officer.

But at a deeper level Davidson is afraid that Foster's death, which he calls an "extra-judicial execution," is a sign of incipient fascism. He notes that the Clintons have mastered the art—described by Hannah Arendt in *The Origins of Totalitarianism*—"of turning all questions of fact into questions of motive." The Clintons do not try to rebut allegations. They use surrogates to muddy the waters and smear opponents, just as the National Socialists used to do. That they should be able to employ this practice to obscure the violent death of a top White House aide throws into doubt the durability of the republic.

"A government that winks at murder will wink at anything," he says, sniffing the aroma of a Corton Charlemagne, Premier Cru. "What's left after that? Cannibalism?"

So Davidson agreed to finance the first serious analysis that has ever been conducted of the "suicide note." Lisa Foster, of course, had authenticated the note. But that is meaningless. Family members do not have the training to spot forgeries. As for the official efforts, they were a humiliating glimpse at the practices of American law enforcement.

The Park Police had asked Sgt. Larry Lockhart of the Capitol Police to look at the note. He had no certification in handwriting analysis. Using a single sample of Foster's handwriting he authenticated the note in less than an hour.[7] He later repudiated his own findings.[8]

A year later, Agent Henry Mathis of the FBI crime labs had a look. This time the FBI added 18 samples of Foster's check signatures. The result was inconclusive. "A qualified opinion is rendered in this case as the known writings of Foster are limited in quantity.... It is suggested additional... writings by Foster be obtained for comparison."[9]

Good suggestion. But it was never done. The FBI never obtained further samples of Foster's handwriting. In the end Agent Mathis authenticated the note using the same single sample used by the Park Police. In Canada, Germany, or Britain, it is usual to use ten to fifteen samples. To rely on one sample alone is considered malpractice. I would be surprised if the FBI habitually adheres to inferior standards.

Properly speaking, it was not a suicide note at all. Lisa Foster told the FBI that it was written in his bedroom on or about July 11, nine days before his death, as the opening argument of his defense should he be called to testify before Congress about Travelgate.

"I made mistakes from ignorance, inexperience and overwork," it begins in a tone of mawkish self-pity, before ending plaintively: "I was not meant for the job or the spotlight of public life in Washington. Here ruining people is considered sport."

It presses all the right buttons—Travelgate, hostile editorials in *The Wall Street Journal*—the things that we can safely dwell on without causing a moment's lost sleep in the White House.

The note was found in Foster's leather briefcase by Associate White House Counsel Stephen Neuwirth six days after Foster's death. It was torn into 27 pieces—the 28th piece was missing.[10] The FBI's Louis Hupp used state of the art equipment to check for fingerprints—an argon ion laser florescence test, and a diazofluorine chemical test—but all he could find of any use was a single palm print. It did not belong to Foster. When asked in closed-door testimony if it was Bernie Nussbaum's print, he was instructed not to answer by a lawyer for the Starr investigation.[11]

The briefcase had been searched four days earlier by Bernie Nussbaum in the presence of a team from the Justice Department. He had removed some files, peered into the briefcase from about two feet, and declared it empty. Twice.

"It would have been impossible for him to miss that many torn scraps of yellow paper," said Sgt. Pete Markland, who was there representing the Park Police. By this stage Markland was convinced that Nussbaum was engaged in some sort of mischief. "It was absurd. I sat there shaking my head the whole time. I was disgusted."[12]

When Neuwirth picked up the briefcase the next week on Monday, July 26, the pieces of yellow legal paper that had been invisible before suddenly materialized. Neuwirth's behavior that afternoon was very odd. At one point he asked to have Vince Foster's typewriter uprooted and taken into Nussbaum's office.[13] One of the secretaries told him there were plenty of other typewriters. But no, Neuwirth wanted Foster's typewriter. Then he changed his mind.

When he found the note he came charging out of Foster's office, satchel in hand. He went into Bernie's office, banged the door, came charging back out again saying, "Where's Bernie? Get Bernie!" Then he charged back in again and slammed the door.[14] A "slapstick comedy" wrote the secretaries to one another in surreptitious e-mail exchanges.[15] Then the First Lady came over from her office next door to look at the note. "I can't deal with this thing, Bernie," she said. "You deal with it."

But did Neuwirth really find the note? Documents now lodged with the National Archives refer to a handwritten note by White House aide Bill Burton dated July 26, 1993. "Far happier if discovered [by] someone other than Bernie," it says. Burton was describing a meeting shortly after the discovery of the note that was attended by Neuwirth, Nussbaum, Burton himself, and Hillary Clinton. It is natural to infer that the Neuwirth story was concocted. If so, Neuwirth perjured himself in congressional testimony, and Hillary Clinton was party to the deception.

The Clinton circle was determined that no outsiders should get to see a copy of the original note. Webb Hubbell lobbied Phillip Heyman, the Deputy Attorney General, requesting that no photocopies of the note should be allowed to get out. Lisa Foster was "adamant" about this, he explained.[16] Since Hubbell was chief of the civil side of the Justice Department at the time—and widely viewed as the "real" Attorney General—Heyman was unlikely to rebuff him. The request was formalized by Lisa Foster's handler, White House "surrogate" James Hamilton, who asked "that a photo of the note not be released under FOIA."[17]

In a hand-delivered letter to the Attorney General dated August 25, 1993, Hamilton asked that the "original torn pieces of Vince's note be returned" and added in a faintly menacing tone: "Please do not underestimate the depth of Mrs. Foster's feelings about this matter."[18]

The text of the note was made available in printed form, of course. No problem with that. But a photo of the original? Absolutely not. *The Wall Street Journal* fought a FOIA lawsuit to shake it loose. Still no luck. The note could be reviewed with an appointment at the offices of Carl Stern, the Justice Department spokesman, but no photographs could be taken. Finally, in July 1995, a copy of the note was leaked to *The Wall Street Journal*.

Chris Ruddy pounced. He contacted the most distinguished handwriting experts in the world. One of them was Dr. Reginald Alton, emeritus fellow of St. Edmund Hall at Oxford University and former Chair of the English faculty, who had authenticated the C.S. Lewis diaries. A brave man—he was awarded the Military Cross for outstanding courage on the battlefield in the fight against fascism—he agreed to look at the note, although he did not want anything as squalid as payment for his services.

The note, he said, was a fake. It was the work of a "moderate forger, not necessarily a professional, somebody who could forge a cheque or a pass in a prison camp."

At a press conference in Washington he was self-effacing and begged Americans not to "mistake me for another interfering Brit." He went through the letters one by one on a screen, showing how Foster would write the letter "b," for instance, in a single "fluid, cursive motion" while the forger would need three or four strokes to replicate the general shape.

It was a big story in the British press, and it electrified the *Samizdat* in the United States. Otherwise, it was ignored. Even the Senate Whitewater Committee chose to overlook Dr. Alton and the congruent findings of his two American colleagues.

"I thought it would be explosive," said Joe Farah from the Western Journalism Center. "Here were people with technical expertise, looking at this coldly and coming to stunning conclusions. I thought it was just the thing to elevate it to the front pages, but it didn't get on the radar screen…. I have to wonder now: What will it take to make the press look at this thing? If somebody confessed to the crime, would that do it?"[19]

"Probably not," I replied.

The White House, however, was exhibiting the reflex twitches of panic. A good part of the "Communication Stream of Conspiracy Commerce" report targeted Chris Ruddy and the forged note.

Section VI is entitled "The Foster Forgery Note Example: How The Media Food Chain Transforms Fiction into Fact."

The report included the transcripts of CBS's *60 Minutes* special on Chris Ruddy, which historians may regard one day as a prime exhibit of state-sponsored propaganda. There is a world of difference between inaccurate reporting and the dissemination of deliberate lies. This particular effort, broadcast on October 8, 1995, included a generous mix of both.

Playing down the presence of unexplained white, tan, grey, blue, red, and green carpet fibers found all over Foster's clothes, correspondent Mike Wallace stated: "The FBI and the Park Police say the fibers are not significant. Anyone who walks on a carpet picks up fibers. And since all of Foster's clothes were put into one bag, all of his clothes would probably have fibers on them."

In fact, the case documents show that the Park Police did not put the clothes in one bag. Foster's suit jacket and his blue silk tie with swans were recovered from his Honda on the night of his death.[20] His shirt, shorts, trousers, belt, socks, and shoes were removed from the body the next day at the morgue and bagged separately.[21] Both sets were covered with the same multicolored fibers.

Let us give Wallace the benefit of the doubt on that one. Let us call it poor staff work. It happens all the time in journalism.

But then Wallace crossed the line.

"You know and I know that there was blood all over the back of [Foster's] shirt," he said to Chris Ruddy on camera.

"Dr. Haut, in his FBI report and his interview with me, said there was not a lot of blood behind the body," said Ruddy.

Cut to Dr. Donald Haut, the Fairfax County Medical Examiner who examined Foster's body at Fort Marcy Park.

"Was there a suspicious lack of blood at the scene?"

"Absolutely not."

"Did you tell a reporter by the name of Christopher Ruddy that there was an 'unusual lack of blood'?"

"No."

"Dr. Haut says that Ruddy simply got it wrong," narrated Wallace. "Here's another mistake...." And so it went on.

But Dr. Haut had changed his story. His statement to the FBI on April 14, 1994, confirmed everything that Ruddy had said. "Haut did not recall seeing blood on the decedent's shirt or face and no blood was recalled on the vegetation around the body.... Although the volume of blood was small, Haut did recall that the blood was matted and clotted under the head." Haut also expressed surprise that a .38 caliber revolver could have caused such little damage.[22]

This FBI statement was in the public record. Ruddy offered to provide *60 Minutes* with a copy of the document, as well as a taped interview in which Dr. Haut told Ruddy that "there was not a hell of a lot of blood on the ground"—which, by the way, is very similar to what he told me in an interview in 1994. After the filming, Ruddy sent Wallace a detailed memo that included Dr. Haut's FBI statement. He offered *60 Minutes* a copy of the tape, but they did not request it until after the segment had aired.

So instead of holding the public official to account, demanding to know why he was equivocating on national television, Mike Wallace decided to crush the beleaguered reporter who was telling the truth.

The broadcast caused a storm of protest. The phone lines to *60 Minutes* were flooded with calls from the *Samizdat* pointing out the errors in the piece, and a week later the network felt compelled to issue a partial correction. By this stage, Wallace must have known that he had committed a journalistic atrocity. So it is all the more astounding that *60 Minutes* should have decided to broadcast the original program a second time, with heavy promotion, in July 1996.

"It had a devastating effect. It chilled any further interest in the story," said Ruddy.

The worst sin a journalist can commit is serving as the instrument of coercive power, and too many in the American media seem content to do just that.

CHAPTER FIFTEEN

THE VERDICT OF DEPRESSION

VINCENT FOSTER WAS exhibiting symptoms of extreme suspicion bordering on paranoia during the final days before his death. He did not trust the telephones at the White House, or even the trash collection.[1] At night he kept waking with panic attacks, his heart pounding violently. Sometimes he would get up in the morning and tell Lisa that he had not slept a wink all night.[2]

"How did I get myself into all this?" he said to her.[3]

But he did not confide in Lisa about the full secrets of his work. He confided in no one.[4] Four days before his death, on Friday, July 16, he had his blood pressure checked at the White House infirmary. It was 132/84 (a normal reading for a man his age is 120/75). Part of the problem was that he had stopped his regular routine of jogging three or four times a week. He was no longer working off the adrenaline. But something was eating at him.

On Monday, July 19, he called his doctor in Little Rock, Dr. Larry Watkins, who prescribed Desyrel to help him battle insomnia. Dr. Watkins had suggested a sleeping pill called Restoril back in December, but now he decided that something stronger was needed.

Still, he considered the problem "mild and situational." He did not think that Foster was "significantly depressed."[5]

The White House would like us to think that Travelgate drove Foster to the brink. This is the authorized Beltway version. "The single greatest source of his distress was the criticism he and others within the Counsel's Office received following the firing of seven employees from the White House Travel Office," concluded the Fiske Report.

I do not find this to be a remotely convincing explanation for why he thought his telephones were bugged, or for anything else about his final days.

Foster certainly had grounds for remorse over Travelgate. The putsch, carried out at Hillary Clinton's behest on May 19, 1993, involved a nasty misuse of the criminal justice system to discredit the victims. But the crisis was subsiding by July 20. Foster had escaped without reprimand in the White House "Management Review."

On Capitol Hill the Democrats controlled the investigative apparatus of both chambers and seemed set to continue doing so *ad aeternum*. They were stonewalling on the issue with their usual aplomb. On July 14 they voted down a "House Resolution of Inquiry" that would have compelled the White House to turn over "all responsive documents and answer questionings concerning FBI and IRS actions related to the firings." On the Senate side things appeared to be equally well under control.

Foster's eldest son, Vincent III, who worked as an aide to Arkansas Senator Dale Bumpers, had attended the preliminary hearings of the Senate Judiciary Committee. He reported back "that he didn't think it was a big deal."[6] Travelgate wasn't going anywhere. It certainly cannot explain Foster's mounting paranoia.

The Fiske Report did not mention Foster's concerns about the deadly Waco assault, a much more serious abuse of power and one that cast the Justice Department and the FBI in a dreadful light. Why was this totally omitted from the report?

The Branch Davidian siege was clearly on Foster's mind. He was "drafting a letter involving Waco" on the day of his death, surely a point of some significance.[7] What was in this letter, may we ask? He kept a Waco file in the locked cabinet that was off limits to everybody, including his secretary.

His widow mentions Waco twice in her statement to the FBI. "Toward the end of his life, Foster had no sense of joy or elation at work. The Branch Davidian incident near Waco, Texas, was also causing him a great deal of stress. Lisa Foster believes that he was horrified when the Branch Davidian complex burned. Foster believed that everything was his fault."[8]

I am not trying to suggest that Waco was the true cause of Foster's demise, although that is possible. I merely wish to illustrate that Vincent Foster was involved in a lot of things besides Travelgate. What was he doing, for example, with files from the National Security Agency?

His executive assistant, Deborah Gorham, testified in a closed-door deposition to the Senate Whitewater Committee that Foster had handed her "two one-inch binders that were from the National Security Agency" to place in the encrypted safe in the Counsel's office. She spoke with great precision, choosing her words carefully. Asked again, she repeated "National Security Agency." One of the binders was white, but she could not remember the color of the other. This occurred in March or April 1993 and was the only time that Foster ever asked Gorham to put documents into the safe.[9]

This was a remarkable revelation. The NSA, of course, is the ultra-secret arm of the Defense Department, in charge of electronic eavesdropping and satellite intelligence around the world. It requires a Sensitive Compartmented Information clearance to handle NSA material, higher than Top Secret. Boyden Gray, the White House Counsel in the Bush administration, told me that he did not know of any occasion when the Counsel's Office handled NSA documents during his tenure.[10]

There may well be a mundane explanation for Foster's NSA ties, but the White House has not offered one. Instead, it tried to deflect the matter. Spin-control officer Mark Fabiani said the files had come from the National Security Council, a totally different outfit. The NSC, of course, is the President's personal team of foreign policy advisers at the White House. You do not require an SCI security clearance to handle internal White House documents.

Again, I am not asserting that there was—or was not—a national security dimension to this case. The point is that Foster was involved in activities that belie the carefully drawn portrait of a bemused country lawyer, and that have clearly been obscured on purpose.

For what it is worth, I doubt that espionage or any such exotica contributed to Foster's death. I suspect that it was something more intimate. Let it be noted that Foster was handling the Clintons' private legal affairs at the White House: preparing a blind trust, doing taxes, tying up the loose ends of the Whitewater Development Corporation, and who knows what else. It was so blatant that it raised a few eyebrows among the old-timers on the executive staff.

"He seemed to spend an inordinate amount of time being the President's and the First Lady's personal attorney as opposed to what I perceived to be the role had historically been," said Linda Tripp, one of the executive assistants in the Counsel's Office, rather garbledly.[11]

Whether or not this was illegal is a fine point, but there can be no question that Foster was behaving as the general factotum of the Clintons. He took care of things behind the scenes, just as he had been doing for years.[12] That is what interests me most of all.

*   *   *

Before they closed down his investigation, Miquel Rodriguez was planning to break the inner circle of the Clintons one by one before the grand jury. It was his suspicion that Foster was being lobbied intensely by the core group of Arkansans at the White House during the days before his death, as if he were being called to do something that put him in a very awkward position and was resisting.[13]

On Friday, July 16, 1993, the Fosters were scheduled to have dinner with their old friends from Little Rock, Webb and Susie Hubbell.[14] But the Fosters broke the engagement and instead drove to the gracious eighteenth century town of Easton on the Chesapeake Bay. Lisa Foster gave a brief description of the trip in her FBI statement on May 9, 1994, but the handwritten notes of the interview are either missing or redacted—always a sign that something is seriously amiss.

Hubbell, who was then *de facto* chief of the Justice Department, followed them to the Eastern Shore and tracked them down at the Tidewater Inn.[15] For the rest of the weekend the Fosters were corralled by Hubbell and his friends Harolyn and Mike Cardozo, who had an immense estate outside Easton.

Vince went boating, recounted Hubbell later. He hit some golf balls, and ate some crab. Lisa was given a tennis lesson by star coach Nick Bollettieri. They talked of old times, how things had changed. Vince remarked how much he missed the decompression of long summer vacations up at the family cabin in Michigan. It was a relaxing weekend.[16] Or at least, that is what Webster Hubbell said. Lisa Foster told the Park Police that "it had not gone particularly well."

The Arkansas Group—as the insiders called themselves at the White House—were very interested in the outcome of that weekend, as if something were riding on it.

Back at the office on Monday morning, Foster went through his papers and drawers. He was taking care of unfinished business, tying up loose ends. His secretary, Deborah Gorham, noticed a "major and uncharacteristic 'lull' in his work pace."[17] Hubbell came over from the Justice Department in person to say "hi," yet again. Bill Kennedy called, twice.

At one point Foster went off to see the White House Credit Union to sort out his overdraft problems. He was obviously strapped for cash. Instead of earning $295,000 a year as a litigation lawyer, he was drawing a government salary that was less than half that figure. Even so, something strange had been going on. Without telling Lisa, Foster had made several large withdrawals of $3,500 each from the account.[18]

In the afternoon he was visited by Marsha Scott, the White House Director of Correspondence. She had dropped in to find out how the weekend had gone.[19]

Scott used to come over from the Old Executive Office Building quite often to visit Vincent Foster. But their tête-à-tête the day before his death was different. It was a closed-door session that lasted for over an hour, possibly as long as two hours.[20]

Her last words to Vince Foster: "If I talk to Bill before you do, what do you want me to tell him?"

It would appear that she was an envoy from the President, sent to learn Foster's thoughts. In the handwritten notes of her FBI interview she admitted that she had been to see Clinton that afternoon. This was subtly changed in the FD-302 statement provided to the Senate. The FBI had tweaked her words to reduce the exposure of the President.[21]

She would be with the President the next night, too, after Foster's death. The Secret Service logged her into the living quarters of the White House at 00.50 on July 20, 1993, and she was not logged out again until the next morning.[22] The logs support a story that Eileen and David Watkins told Rebecca Borders of *The American Spectator*. They said that Marsha Scott talked openly about her affair with Bill Clinton and had bragged about her comforting labors on the night of Foster's death.

She was "pretty pumped up about the whole thing," said Eileen Watkins. "She told me 'I spent the night in his bed. I had my head in his lap, and we reminisced all night long.'"

Marsha Scott is one of the most enigmatic figures of the tight-knit Arkansas Group. Her mother was an Olympic hurdler in the

1950s; her father an American football star; and she was a true child of the 1960s. Before her sudden elevation to epistolary duties at the White House, she was saving trees in the eco-radical enclave of Santa Cruz, California.

But though outwardly hip and laid-back, she is clearly an operator of some talent. In 1994 she was in charge of the "Big Brother" database program at the White House. And we now know that she was the principal conduit between the Clintons and Webb Hubbell, after Hubbell was sent to prison for fraud.

Her memory failed her when she was interviewed by the FBI. She could not remember what they had talked about in Vince Foster's office on July 19, 1993. "It was an incredibly painful time and her way of dealing with matters such as that was to block it out. She remembers impressions, she does not remember specific conversations," reads her statement.[23]

She did recall however that Foster was a little chilly, failing to get up from his desk to greet her, as if she had interrupted his train of thought. Reflecting on it afterwards she concluded that he had "painted himself into a box with no windows," but at the same time "she got the sense that he had come to some sort of decision and was, if anything, relaxed as a result."[24]

Later that night, at about 8:00 PM, President Clinton himself called Foster at his home in Georgetown. He asked him to come back to the White House.

"I hadn't seen Vince in a while, and I hadn't had a chance to talk to him in a few weeks. So I decided I would call and invite him to the movie that night," said the President in a deposition.[25]

"That was *In the Line of Fire?*"

"Uh-huh."

"Who else was there?"

"Just a couple of us. I think Mr. Hubbell was there. I think Mr. Lindsey was there."

It was the inner core.

Foster refused the invitation. He chatted to the president for ten to fifteen minutes about "organizational issues" and the two men agreed to meet Wednesday morning at the White House.

"He was already home with Lisa, and he didn't think he should leave and come back to the White House. I understood that," said the President. "Then I asked him, you know, if he had a good time over the weekend, and he said they had a great time."

I strongly suspect that Foster's rebuff was read by the Arkansas Group as an indication that he was no longer on the team.

"No one can ever know why this happened. Even if you had a whole set of objective reasons, that wouldn't be why it happened," said President Clinton in an opaque address to his staff, the morning after Foster's death. "He had an extraordinary sense of propriety and loyalty, and I hope that when we remember him and this, we'll be a little more anxious to talk to each other and a little less anxious to talk outside of our family."[26]

*   *   *

I do not know whether Vincent Foster was depressed before his death. It is irrelevant anyway. The hard evidence indicates that the crime scene was staged, period. Even if Foster was depressed, somebody still put a gun in his hand, somebody still inflicted a perforating wound on his neck, his body still levitated 700 feet into Fort Marcy Park without leaving soil residue on his shoes, and he still managed to drive to Fort Marcy Park without any car keys.

That said, the dishonest manipulation of the facts about Foster's state of mind, and the anonymous leaks to the press that have subsequently been disproved by the official record, make for an interesting case study of a cover-up in progress. It is quite clear from the archive of documents that almost nobody realized that Foster was depressed at the time of his death. That story evolved later.

Foster had been in a filthy mood at the beginning of the year, flying off the handle at the slightest encroachment on his precious time.[27] When the family came up for the inaugural, Vince had left Lisa and the children on their own, and slipped away to his work. Lisa was so upset she boycotted the inaugural ball that night.[28] There had been ups and downs, obviously.

But by the early summer of 1993 things were looking up. Foster's children had arrived, putting an end to the deracinated bachelor life of those first miserable months in Washington. First came Laura, the daughter he adored.[29] "I have a distinct memory of him celebrating Laura's birthday and bringing her to one of our Friday night movies," said Hillary Clinton.[30] "He had his arm around her and they looked so happy. He seemed very happy that finally he was going to have his family back."

By July, Foster was making an effort to control his workaholic habits. He was planning weekend getaways outside Washington with Lisa, and was promising to come back earlier each night from the White House. On Monday, July 19, as the family were standing around the kitchen after supper, Foster suggested that it would be fun to buy a family boat.[31] He chatted warmly about different kinds of crafts with his youngest son, Brugh.

The next morning his "mood seemed better than it had in a while," Lisa Foster told the Park Police.[32] (Ten months later she told a dramatically different version to the FBI, but by then she was being advised by White House "surrogate" James Hamilton.)

He drove his children to work, chatting happily enough. Vincent III commented afterward that "his dad was in such a happy mood when he dropped us off."[33]

That afternoon Foster's sister, Sharon Bowman, arrived from Arkansas for a visit. Foster had arranged to take his niece, Mary, to lunch at the White House mess. He was back to his old courteous, thoughtful self.

Perhaps Foster's conduct during these last days and hours before his death could be construed as symptoms of depression. But it strikes me that the Fiske Report conflated the issue of clinical depression with symptoms of stress, insomnia, anxiety, and above all fear. I will leave it to psychiatrists to judge whether these two mental conditions are one and the same. These things can be subjective. But what we do know is that Fiske played fast and loose with the evidence.

The report said that it was "obvious to many that he had lost weight,"[34] but in fact he had gained weight in Washington.

On December 31, 1992, Dr. Watkins weighed him at 194 pounds in Little Rock.[35] At the autopsy, after some loss of blood, he weighed 197 pounds.

Fiske distorted the witness statements of those who disputed the assertion that Vincent Foster was depressed. Deborah Gorham, Foster's executive assistant at the Counsel's Office, told the FBI that she "did not see anything in Foster's behavior which would indicate a distressed state of mind" and that "he had not made any statements or comments indicating despondency and she had not noticed any physical changes in Foster from the time she started as his secretary to his death."[36]

The inventive Mr. Fiske somehow transformed this into "Gorham confirmed that Foster's productivity dropped significantly in the last few weeks of his life."[37] She makes no such assertion in the declassified portions of her FBI statement. But then seven pages of her 302 write-up are censored under a specious claim of national security. So we cannot be sure.

The Foster family was stunned when the Park Police first notified them of the death. "Mrs. Foster nor other relatives, or friends were able to provide any insight as to why Vincent Foster would take his life," wrote Park Police Detective John Rolla. "One of the last things I got from Mrs. Foster... I asked her, was he... did you see this coming, was there any signs of this, and of course everyone said no, no, no, no. He was fine. This is out of the blue."[38]

This was Lisa's spontaneous reaction on the night of the death. Once again, it bears no relation to the "Hamiltonized" version she elaborated for the FBI a year later. Without wishing to belabor the point, here is a sampling of testimony from those who saw the most of Foster in the weeks before his death:

* Betsy Pond, secretary in the Counsel's office: "There was nothing unusual about his emotional state. In fact over the last several weeks she did not notice any changes, either physically or emotionally. She noticed no weight loss.... She was not aware of any depression problems."[39]

* David Watkins, Director of Administration: "I saw him every day and I never picked up anything to suggest he was deteriorating.... It wasn't clear to me at all."[40]

* Webb Hubbell "did not notice Foster acting differently in the days or weeks before his death."[41]

* James Lyons, a Denver attorney working with the Arkansas Group. Foster telephoned him on July 18. They were due to have dinner three days later. "Lyons had seen no evidence of depression or psychiatric imbalance."[42]

* Nancy Hernreich, Deputy Assistant to the President and a member of the core Arkansas Group, recalled "seeing no changes in Vincent Foster's physical or psychological presence."[43]

* Beth Nolan, Associate White House Counsel under Foster, "did not recall anybody ever remarking about Foster holding up or not holding up, and she did not herself notice any weight loss."[44]

* Lorraine Cline, Foster's longtime secretary at the Rose Law Firm. Came up to see him in D.C. in late May. "He was reserved and quiet but not depressed. She was surprised to read in the media that he had been depressed."[45]

* Susan Thomases, intimate of Hillary Clinton, told the FBI: "She last saw Vincent Foster on Wednesday or Thursday before his death. She believes that they had lunch together with some other people in Washington.... She noted no change in his demeanor or physical appearance.... His death came as a complete shock to her and she can offer no reason or speculation as to why he may have taken his life."[46]

This is rather interesting because James Stewart, in his best-selling book *Blood Sport* quotes Thomases as saying that she met Foster furtively before his death at a boarding house on 2020 O Street. It was Wednesday night, July 14. She alleged that he bared his soul and confided that his marriage "had not been what he'd hoped for, and it hadn't been for years.... [Lisa] was completely dependent on him, and this had become a burden." Thomases was deeply concerned about the "change in his appearance and demeanor."

This statement is in glaring contradiction to what she told the FBI as a witness in a criminal investigation. This is not an academic question, for it was Thomases who talked Stewart into writing *Blood Sport* in the first place. What was her purpose?

The official documents indicate that the only member of Foster's family and close circle who said from the beginning that Foster was depressed was his sister, Sheila Anthony. She is a Clinton loyalist and a Washington power-broker in her own right. As a top official at the Justice Department, she was in charge of choosing U.S. attorneys, U.S. marshals, and U.S. federal judges. In other words, she picked the staff for the federal machinery of coercion. She was later appointed Assistant Attorney General.

At a dinner at the Cactus Cantina on July 9, which Foster paid for using his American Express Card, leaving a 20 percent tip as always, he mentioned that overwork and constant stress were grinding him down. He was thinking of resigning.[47]

A week later he telephoned to say that "he was battling depression for the first time in his life" but was reluctant to visit a psychiatrist because it might endanger his security clearance. He also wanted to be absolutely sure that everything revealed in therapy would be confidential and beyond the reach of subpoenas.[48] Sheila Anthony called Dr. Charles Hedaya in Chevy Chase and explained that her brother was handling "Top Secret" issues at the White House and "that his depression was directly related to highly sensitive and confidential matters."[49]

She left Dr. Hedaya with the impression that Vincent Foster was caught "in a bind." On Monday, after returning from the Eastern Shore, Foster told his sister that he was "feeling good" and had decided not to see a psychiatrist.

It is always possible that Ms. Anthony was seeing the matter through her own prism, pushing her brother toward treatment out of sibling bossiness. Foster himself never visited a psychiatrist. Be that as it may, the bigger point is that the U.S. judicial authorities have tried to convince us that Foster's depression was visible to everybody around him. That is simply not true. Clearly, this story was concocted to compensate for the paucity of forensic evidence at the crime scene.

I once asked a gathering of thirty Washington journalists what they considered to be the most compelling evidence that Vincent Foster committed suicide. There was a brief silence, then somebody said: "Well, he was depressed."

It was a very good answer. The depression is all they have, and by "they" I mean Fiske, Starr, the Justice Department, the White House, *The Washington Post*, the governing class. Take that away, and there is nothing left to sustain the ruling of suicide. Nothing.

CHAPTER SIXTEEN

THE PARKS MURDER

"I'M A DEAD MAN," whispered Jerry Parks, pale with shock, as he looked up at the television screen. It was a news bulletin on the local station in Little Rock. Vincent Foster, a childhood friend of the President, had been found dead in a park outside Washington. Apparent suicide.[1]

He never explained to his son Gary what he meant by that remark, but for the next two months the beefy 6′ 3″ security executive was in a state of permanent fear. He would pack a pistol to fetch the mail. On the way to his offices at American Contract Services in Little Rock he would double back or take strange routes to "dryclean" the cars that he thought were following him. At night he kept tearing anxiously at his eyebrows, and raiding the valium pills of his wife, Jane, who was battling multiple sclerosis. Once he muttered darkly that Bill Clinton's people were "cleaning house," and he was "next on the list."[2]

Two months later, in September 1993, Jerry and Jane went on a Caribbean cruise. He seemed calmer. At one of the islands he went to take care of some business at a bank. She believed it was Grand

Cayman. They returned to their home in the rural suburbs of Little Rock on September 25. The next day Jane was in one of her "down" periods, so Jerry went off on his own for the regular Sunday afternoon supper at El Chico Mexican Restaurant.

On the way back, at about 6:30 PM, a white Chevrolet Caprice pulled up beside him on the Chenal Parkway. Before Parks had time to reach for his .38 caliber "detective special" that he kept tucked between the seats, an assassin let off a volley of semi-automatic fire into his hulking 320 pound frame.

Parks skidded to a halt in the intersection of Highway 10. The stocky middle-aged killer jumped out and finished him off with a 9 mm handgun—two more shots into the chest at point blank range. Several witnesses watched with astonishment as the nonchalant gunman joined his accomplice in the waiting car and sped away.[3]

*   *   *

It was another three months before news of the murder of Jerry Luther Parks reached me in Washington. The U.S. national media were largely unaware of the story, which surprised me because Parks had been in charge of security at the 1992 Clinton-Gore campaign headquarters in Little Rock.[4]

On my next trip to the state I decided to drop by at the archives of *The Arkansas Democrat-Gazette* to see if they had covered the death. There were two routine homicide stories by reporter Ward Pincus, mostly focusing on disputes that Parks had had with a former partner.

I contacted the writer, who had since moved to New York. To my surprise he turned out to be the son of Walter Pincus, the intelligence correspondent for *The Washington Post* and a friend of Vincent Foster. In fact, Walter Pincus had lunched with Foster at the Federal City Club on July 9, eleven days before the death.[5] Afterward Pincus had written an "op-ed" piece in *The Post* saying that Foster was visibly cracking under the strain of Washington life.

It was a persuasive article, the suicide clincher. I remember reading it at the time and thinking: "Well, that's it, then, case closed."

What his son told me was astounding. When he spoke to Jane Parks the day after the death she said that her husband had been involved with Vince Foster and she seemed to think there was a political dimension to the murder. She was distraught, almost hysterical. Ward Pincus did not know what to make of it, so he consulted his editors at *The Democrat-Gazette*. Should he go out to visit the widow and try to find out what on earth she was talking about? No, they said, don't bother. Soon afterward, Jane Parks withdrew into her shell and refused to give any interviews to the press.

By asking around, I learned that her son Gary, then 23, might be willing to talk. He was half-underground, sleeping on the floor in different houses, afraid that he too could be the target of attack. Messages were passed back and forth through the informal network of civic opposition in Arkansas. He agreed to talk, given that I was a "foreigner," he said, and not part of the corrupt U.S. media cabal. It was a sentiment I encountered often in Arkansas.

We met for dinner at the Little Rock Hilton. His escort arrived first, "sweeping" the lobby, the bar, and even the bathrooms, before giving the all clear. It was like being back in El Salvador or Guatemala, where I had worked as a correspondent during *la violencia* of the early 1980s. I never imagined that I would witness such a spectacle in the United States.

A big strapping fellow like his father, Gary Parks was in constant pain from a wound he had suffered in the navy. A propeller had ripped through his right shoulder. He described his father as a harsh martinet, who once made him run miles in freezing cold weather, drenched and shirtless. But in the security business the name of Jerry Parks was good metal. Bill Clinton had appointed him to the board of Arkansas Private Investigators. He was a player. He knew how to keep his mouth shut, too.

Wolfing down a huge piece of steak—he seemed to be half-starved—Gary then said that his father had been collecting files on Bill Clinton. "Working on his infidelities," he said, grinning. "It had been going on for years. He had enough to impeach Bill Clinton on the spot."

At some point in 1988, when he was about 17, he had accompanied Jerry on four or five nocturnal missions. Armed with long-range surveillance cameras, they would stake out the haunts of the Governor until the early hours of the morning. Quapaw Towers was one of them, he remembered. That was where Gennifer Flowers lived.

It was a contract job, Gary believed, but he did not know who was paying for the product. Some of the material was kept in two files, stored in the bottom drawer of the dresser in his parents' bedroom. He had sneaked in one day, terrified that his father might catch him, and flicked through the papers just long enough to see photos of women coming and going with Governor Clinton, and pages of notes in his father's handwriting. In one of the photos Clinton was with Captain Raymond "Buddy" Young of the State Police.

In late July 1993 the family house on Barrett Road was burgled in a sophisticated operation that involved cutting the telephone lines and disarming the electronic alarm system. The files were stolen.[6] Gary suspected that this was somehow tied to his father's death two months later.

"I believe that Bill Clinton had my father killed to protect his political career," he told me that evening. "We're dealing with a secretive machine here in Arkansas that can shut anyone up in a moment."

It was a startling allegation. He was accusing the President of the United States of using a death squad to eliminate enemies. I knew at once that this was a news story that had to be pursued. It was an infinitely more serious issue than Whitewater, and Watergate, too, for that matter.

But why would a bimbo file cause such alarm? And how much did Gary Parks really know anyway? He had been away in the navy. His father had kept him in the dark.

It was imperative to interview his mother. It was she who knew the secrets.

*   *   *

At first Mrs. Parks would not talk to me, except to confirm in a general way that there were indeed files, that they had been stolen, and that Gary was telling the truth. The Little Rock Police had told her not to talk to the press until the case was solved, and she had agreed.

But by the spring of 1994 she was losing faith. The original detective, Tom James, had been pulled off the case. It was becoming apparent that the eyewitness accounts of the death were being ignored by the police. Witnesses had described two assassins: hefty men, with beer bellies and broad shoulders, greyish hair, in their late forties or early fifties.[7] Yet the police kept saying that there was only one killer in the car.

Jane Parks went to visit a top official from the State Police whom she knew well from her church network.[8] He told her outright that the murder was a conspiracy hatched in Hot Springs by five men who moved in the social circle of Buddy Young, the former chief of Governor Clinton's security detail and now the regional director of the Federal Emergency Management Agency for the south-central United States. She was given the names of the five men, and was told that they had flipped coins to decide which two would carry out the execution. And finally, she was told that nothing was ever going to be done about it.

Torn by conflicting impulses, afraid for the safety of her two sons, she agreed to meet me. It was the beginning of a three-year dialogue in which she slowly opened up, and slowly came to terms with her husband's life as an officer in the Dixie Cartel. With time, and new drugs that restored a degree of health, she began to recall the details that had been repressed and buried.

Her account confronted me with a journalistic dilemma of the first order. Certain episodes could be corroborated, which established a pattern of veracity, but the most shocking allegations were based on her word alone. I made an intuitive decision to publish. At times the moral imperatives of reportage require one to violate the Columbia School codex. Somebody has to give a voice to the little people. I offer readers her story for what it is: her word, sometimes supported by other evidence, sometimes not.

Jane Parks is a slender, elegant brunette, with high cheekbones and a Scots-Irish look about her. On her good days, one would never have known that she was suffering from multiple sclerosis. Tanned and carefully made up, with a soft southern voice, she is undoubtedly an attractive woman. Unaware of who she was, Kenneth Starr had onced chatted her up at the Little Rock Athletic Club. She, in turn, noted that he had a "gorgeous body" in his gym shorts.

But at the same time she is a fervent Pentecostal, a member of the Assembly of God Church. She had separated from Jerry Parks early in their marriage, during his brash, heavy-drinking days. The condition for reunion was that he give himself to the Lord and be born again, which he did. Although not everybody was convinced.

"Jerry professed to be a devout Christian. He was obsessed with that image, but he was one of the biggest hypocrites I've ever met in my life," said his former business partner, and enemy, John D. McIntire. "He was power-hungry, out to prove that he was a big shot."[9]

Jane Parks was not entirely convinced either. But going through the motions was a good deal better than the boorish behavior of the past. At least he had stopped drinking.

In the summer of 1984 Mrs. Parks was the manager of a mid-scale apartment complex called Vantage Point. She was informed by the real estate agents that a nonpaying guest would be coming to stay for a while. She was told to take care of him, no questions asked. The guest turned out to be Roger Clinton, college-dropout, rock-musician, consumate scoundrel, kid brother, or, to be more precise, half-brother, of the Governor—and a Clinton appointee to the Arkansas Crime Commission's Juvenile Advisory Board.

Mrs. Parks installed him in the corporate suite, room B107. The suite and her offices had originally been part of the same condominium, but they had been divided in two by a thin partition. For the next two months she and her assistant found themselves the reluctant audience of Roger Clinton's Bohemian recreations. Even during the quiet office hours of 9 to 5 the goings-on were wild. And sometimes the conduct was so *outré* that the two of them would have to leave their office and wait outside until the ecstasies had subsided.

The Kid Brother was going through a bad patch. At that time he was nearing the disastrous culmination of a five-year cocaine addiction. "By mid-1984, Roger spent virtually every waking hour getting high or trying to get high," wrote Arkansas commentator Meredith Oakley, in her book *On the Make*.

Roger was already the target of a sting operation by a joint state-federal narcotics task force. In April 1994 he had been filmed by hidden surveillance cameras at an apartment in Hot Springs disparaging "niggers," and cutting a rock of cocaine for sale.

"Boy, this is some good coke," says the undercover informant. "It's decent, it's decent," allows the Kid Brother. He knew he was under suspicion but cockily assumed that he was untouchable. "I've got four or five guys in uniform who keep an eye on the guys who keep an eye on me," he explained.[10]

The surveillance archive is a revealing set of tapes. At one point Roger reached for the telephone to order some merchandise from his Colombian friend Maurice Rodriguez, a man listed on FBI documents as an international trafficker with ties to the Colombian cartels.[11] This is not a mixed-up kid who crosses the line a couple of times and gets caught. This is a serious drug dealer who boasts of his technique for getting through airport security with bags of cocaine strapped to his body—once in the company of Big Brother. People are sent to prison for life for dealing cocaine on this scale.

He needed the money badly.

"I've been saving up for a Porsche," he says. "I want a Porsche so bad, I can spit."

The full uncensored set of tapes was first brought to light by free-lance journalist Scott Wheeler, who has spent four years digging into the organized crime world of Hot Springs and Mena—at great personal risk. They serve as a very raw exposure of the symbiotic corruption of the Clinton brothers.

At one point in the tapes, the undercover informant, Rodney Myers, asks Roger if he can take care of a sewer permit for a condominium project in Hot Springs. Construction had been held up by the Pollution Control Board. A $30,000 fee was negotiated, sweetened with the offer of a job for Roger.

Kid Brother says he thinks that he can "do something," having explained that "we're closer than any brothers you've ever known. See, I didn't have a father growing up, and he was like a father to me growing up, all my life, so that's why we've always been close. There isn't anything in the world he wouldn't do for me."

At their next meeting Roger comes back to the subject. "About your other thing, I talked to Big Brother, it's no problem." But there is a snag, warns Roger. Big Brother had made some calls and discovered that there was one hold-out on the Control Board.

Could the man be bribed, asks the informant?

No, says Roger, with disgust. The holdout is a decent, upstanding man. But the Board would do what Big Brother wanted in the end.

None of the truly damning dialogue on the tapes was made public in court proceedings, or brought to the attention of the Arkansas people. In his book *Partners in Power*, Roger Morris says that the segments implicating Governor Clinton were sent to the Public

Integrity Office of the Justice Department in Washington. "I guess they just got lost," one police officer told Morris, bitterly.

The Kid Brother was arraigned in U.S. federal court on August 14, 1984. He pled not guilty to six counts of drug dealing and conspiracy, but soon "rolled over" and became a snitch for the drug task force. The announcement of his plea agreement was delayed until after Governor Clinton was safely reelected in November. In January 1985, locked arm in arm with his devoted mother and brother, Roger was sentenced to two years in the federal penitentiary in Fort Worth. Judge Oren Harris said that he could not reasonably impose probation after learning that Roger had continued snorting cocaine after his arrest.

Bill Clinton, of course, handled it all with great sensitivity and *savoir faire*. "My brother has apparently become involved with drugs," he announced. "A curse which has reached epidemic proportions and plagued the lives of millions of families, including many in our state." His spokesmen insisted the Governor never knew his Kid Brother had tried drugs.

The spin must have been galling for Hot Springs Detective Travis Bunn. A highly decorated Army Special Forces sergeant-major, it was he who had mounted the original case against Roger Clinton. In the spring of 1984 Bunn had recorded Roger Clinton saying: "I've got to get some for my brother, he's got a nose like a Hoover vacuum cleaner."[12]

Bill Clinton later turned his brother's scandal to advantage. He intimated that he had "signed off" on the police investigation of his own brother, allowing the process of criminal justice to run its course without meddling. His trouble-shooter, Betsey Wright, claimed that Clinton had written a note to the Commander of the State Police stating that there would be no interference from the Governor's Mansion and that he wanted the matter handled in a routine fashion.

It was utterly bogus, the very opposite of the truth. In reality the Clinton machine had done everything it could to contain the case. Apparently, Detective Bunn felt he had enough evidence from the surveillance tapes to launch an investigation—in conjunction with federal authorities—of Governor Clinton himself. When he broached the question with the Arkansas State Police, they muscled in immediately and sabotaged his case.

Roger Clinton was arrested before he could provide any more damaging revelations on surveillance tapes, and was kept sequestered. In violation of usual police procedure, Bunn was denied access to the prisoner. He was told, tartly, that Roger "didn't know anything."

When Bunn complained to the head of the State Police Criminal Investigations Division he discovered that the arrest of Roger Clinton had not been authorized by the proper officials. It was outside the normal chain of command. Nothing could be done. "The whole thing was damage control, orchestrated by the Governor's Mansion," said a State Trooper close to the probe. "They had no right butting in on the Hot Springs police like that."[13]

The Governor was off the hook. But it was too late to save Roger.

This, then, was the shape of Roger Clinton's life when he moved into the corporate suite at B107 Vantage Point. The Kid Brother soon made himself at home. Lounging about in his shorts, showing off his gold accoutrements at the pool, he was a quick hit with the teenage girls at the complex.[14]

Women came by at all times of the day and night, sometimes delivered by uniformed State Troopers. Roger would have the door open, the "ghetto blaster" cranked up playing acid rock. Jane's assistant, who was in charge of tenant relations, had to inform the Kid Brother of the complaints that were pouring in from residents who paid $550 a month for the promise of tranquility at Vantage Point.

From time to time the Governor would appear, usually in the middle of the afternoon. The limousine would be parked along the side of "A" Block, somewhat obscured from view. Jane remembers seeing the driver sitting there listening to music. She soon learned to distinguish between the voices of the two brothers behind the thin partition.

"Roger was the filthy one. He was gross. That's how you could tell," she said. But if the language was different, the behavior of the two was much the same. They were sharing joints of marijuana. There could be no doubt about it. She could hear Roger saying what it was, where he got it from, what it was like. Then she could hear the Governor bleating his approval: "This is really good shit!"

It was not just marijuana either. Two or three times a week the Governor was buoying his spirits with a snort of Kid Brother's Colombian rock. The repartee was coming through the vents. She was as certain as if she had been in the suite herself. Sometimes the two brothers were alone. Sometimes young women were invited to join, and the little party was consummated with raucous orgasms. The bed was pressed up against the partition wall, just a few feet from the desk of Mrs. Parks. On two occasions she heard the Governor copulating on the bed. Who the visitors were, exactly, she did not know. But some of them appeared surprisingly young.

Jerry Parks was then head of the Little Rock branch of Guardsmark, a security firm based in Memphis. But he also did private detective work on the side, so when Jane alerted him to the goings on at B107, he began his own discrete surveillance. He wrote down names, dates, license plates; he snapped photos from the balcony of the Parks condo on the third floor of "B" block, across the yard. By the end of Roger's stay, Parks had collected a thick dossier on the comings and goings of Big Brother. Jane Parks believes that some of that material was in the files stolen from their house in July 1993.

Jane Parks's account of the goings on at Vantage Point is broadly corroborated by her assistant. Unlike Jane, who can be demure, even faintly stern, the assistant is a gregarious, voluble young woman who worshipped at the same church. We had lunch at a barbecue joint in North Little Rock. A chicken-wing sort of place, with faux leather booths. It was dark and largely empty. She was nervous, holding things back. But she did confirm the critical point. The incidents happened, Bill Clinton was present on frequent occasions, and drug use was rampant.

"Everything Jane Parks told you is true. That woman does not know how to tell a lie," she said. "Bill had his girlfriends in there. You could hear them through the walls. They looked to me very young girls, probably 17, 18 years old."

I pulled out some confidential files from the Arkansas State Police and started going through the names of young women to see if any of them rang a bell. Lost in concentration we did not notice that a large, corpulent, bearded, redneck wearing dark glasses had crept up on us. When I flicked my head around, I suddenly saw him sitting at the next table, staring pointedly at my guest. There was nobody else left in the restaurant.

"Do you know him?" I whispered.

"No, no, I don't," she said looking up with fright. The man did not take his eyes off her.

"Please, can we get out of here? Right now," she said.

We got up without finishing our food. The big bruiser got up, too, and followed us to the cash register. Outside, I waited to see which vehicle he got into so that I could trace the plates. But he just stood there waiting, and watching, with the hint of a smile flickering beneath his salt and pepper beard.

The Machine had left its calling card.

*   *   *

It was another two years before Jane Parks began to tell me the rest of the story. She had remarried and moved to Batesville, two hours' drive from Little Rock. Her new husband was an attorney named Harvey Bell, the former Arkansas Securities Commissioner. His life, too, had intersected with that of Vincent Foster. A colonel in the Arkansas National Guard, Bell told me that he had been the commander of Foster's reserve unit and had later crossed swords with him in court. "Vince liked to think of himself as a master chess player, moving all the pieces, controlling the game," he said. "He was always scheming in the shadows."[15]

Jane felt safer in Batesville. The threatening telephone calls that she had been receiving had stopped. Her illness was in remission. She had held back before, she explained, for fear of violent reprisals against her two sons and herself. But she was weary of bottling up her secrets, and she no longer felt the emotional compulsion to cover for her first husband. "I've been praying about it. I decided that if you tell the whole truth it'll set you free."

She revealed that Jerry Parks had carried out sensitive assignments for the Clinton circle for almost a decade, and the person who gave him his instructions was Vince Foster. It did not come as a total shock. I already knew that there was some kind of tie between the two men. Foster's brother-in-law, Lee Bowman, told me long ago that Vince had recommended Jerry Parks for security work in the mid-1980s. "I was struck by how insistent he was that Parks was a 'man who could be trusted,'" said Bowman, a wealthy Little Rock stockbroker.[16]

Jane thought that Jerry and Vince Foster had gotten to know each other when the Rose Law Firm represented Guardsmark in litigation. Vince had fed him little tasks during the 1980s, she believed, rewarding him along the way. In late 1989 he helped to secure Jerry a $47,959 loan from the Arkansas Teachers Retirement Fund, a huge piggy bank used by the Clinton Machine for political payoffs. As reported by James Ring Adams in *The American Spectator*, the loan went through the Twin City Bank of North Little Rock, a bank that had played a role in the Whitewater saga.

Jerry, in turn, "respected Vince Foster more than anybody else in the world."[17] It was a strange, clandestine relationship. Foster called the Parks home more than a hundred times, identifying himself with the code name, "The Congressman." Jane met him only once in person. It was at a "Roast and Toast" of the Governor. He walked over, graceful as always, and said: "Hello, you must be Jerry's wife. I'd heard he'd robbed the cradle."

By the late 1980s Vince trusted Parks enough to ask him to perform discreet surveillance on the Governor. "Jerry asked him why he needed this stuff on Clinton. He said he needed it for Hillary," recalled Jane. It appears that Hillary wanted to gauge exactly how vulnerable her husband would be to charges of philandering if he decided to launch a bid for the presidency.

Had he learned to be more cautious? How easily could he be caught? Was it bad enough to destroy a candidacy? These were things she needed to know before subjecting herself and her daughter to the media glare of a national campaign. This moral check-up was a very understandable precaution.[18]

Later, during the early stages of the presidential campaign, Parks made at least two trips to the town of Mena, in the Ouachita Mountains of western Arkansas. Mena had come up in conversations before. Jane told me that Parks had been a friend of Barry Seal, a legendary cocaine smuggler and undercover U.S. operative who had established a base of operations at Mena airport. Parks had even attended Seal's funeral in Baton Rouge after Seal was assassinated by Colombian pistoleros in February 1986.

One of the trips was in 1991, she thought, although it could have been 1992. The morning after Jerry got back from Mena she borrowed his Lincoln to go to the grocery store and discovered what must have been hundreds of thousands of dollars in the trunk. "It was all in $100 bills, wrapped in string, layer after layer. It was so full I had to sit on the trunk to get it shut again," she said.

"I took a handful of money and threw it in his lap and said, 'Are you running drugs?' Jerry said Vince had paid him $1,000 cash for each trip. He didn't know what they were doing, and he didn't want to know either, and nor should I. He told me to forget what I'd seen."

They had a bitter quarrel and barely spoke to each other for two weeks. They made up on Jerry's birthday on July 3. "The whole thing was becoming scary," she said of that time. "He was in over his head."

He told her that he would leave his Lincoln at a hangar at the Mena airport, go off for a coke, and by the time he came back they would have loaded the money into the trunk with a forklift truck. He never touched it. When he got back to Little Rock he would deliver the money to Vince Foster in the K-Mart parking lot on Rodney Parham boulevard, a little at a time. They used a routine of switching briefcases, a "flip-flop mail carrier" made of leather.

Foster and Parks had other operations running. The two of them had bugged the Clinton-Gore headquarters in Little Rock. "Vince knew that somebody was stealing money from the campaign, and he wanted to find out who was doing it," she said. If her memory is correct, it suggests that Foster was far more deeply involved in the 1992 campaign than previously thought. It raises extra questions about the bundles of cash coming through Mena. Was it campaign money? If so, how was it laundered? How could so much cash have been spread around without flagging the Federal Election Commission?

Contact with Foster was rare after he moved to the White House. But he telephoned in mid-July 1993, about a week before his death. He explained that Hillary had worked herself into a state about "the files," worried that there might be something in them that could cause real damage to Bill or herself. The conversation was brief and inconclusive. Jerry told Vince Foster that there was indeed "plenty to hurt both of them. But you can't give her those files, that was the agreement." Jerry did not seem too perturbed at the time.

A few days later Foster called again. Jane is sure that it was either Sunday, July 18, or Monday, July 19, the night before Foster's death. Jerry was in the living room with his feet up, watching the History

Channel on TV. Jane was puttering in and out of the kitchen. It was around 8:30 PM, central time.

"Vince was calling from a pay phone," said Jane, who overheard one side of the conversation and then learned the rest from Jerry afterward. "He kept feeding coins into the box, and then he told Jerry to hold on. He must have been near a mini-mart or something because he said he had to get more coins.[19] Then he called a second time, and they spoke for 30 minutes or more."

This time it was a heated exchange. Vince said that he had made up his mind. He was going to hand over the files and wanted to be sure that he had the complete set.

"You're not going to use those files!" said Jerry, angrily.

Foster tried to soothe him. He said he was going to meet Hillary at "the flat" and he was going to give her the files.

"You can't do that," said Parks. "My name's all over this stuff. You can't give Hillary those files. You can't! Remember what she did, what you told me she did. She's capable of doing anything!"

"We can trust Hil. Don't worry," said Foster.

Jane does not know exactly what files Foster wanted, but assumes he meant everything that Parks had done for him over more than a decade. Nor did she know what Foster meant by "the flat."

If the telephone call was made on Monday, July 19, it must have occurred an hour or so after President Clinton had called Foster at home and chatted to him for fifteen minutes about "staff problems." Clinton said that he called to invite Foster back to the White House to watch *In the Line of Fire* with Webb Hubbell and Bruce Lindsey. Foster had refused.[20]

But I suspect that Jane Parks has muddled the day. Foster was with his family that night. He was in a happy mood, chatting in the kitchen with his youngest son Brugh about buying a boat. It is more likely that the call was made on Sunday, July 18, after Vince and Lisa had returned from a weekend trip to the Eastern Shore.[21]

Vince was making calls late that night. Between 8:00 and 9:00 PM Foster telephoned James Lyons, a Denver attorney who had handled personal business for the Clintons.[22] This is an interesting call, too. Foster had spoken to Lyons earlier that week asking whether he would be able to come to Washington on short notice, if necessary.[23] Lyons did in fact agree to come. The two men had arranged to meet for dinner on Wednesday, July 21.

Whatever Foster said to Jerry Parks, he cannot possibly have met with Hillary Clinton at "the flat" or anywhere else. She was on the West Coast during the days preceding his death. On the afternoon of July 20 she was on an aircraft flying from Los Angeles to Little Rock. But that does not preclude the grim possibility that Foster thought he was going to a rendezvous with the First Lady on July 20, and met his death instead.

*   *   *

The rambler-style home of the Parks family was swarming with federal agents on the day after Jerry's assassination. Jane remembers men flashing credentials from the FBI, the Secret Service, the IRS, and, she thought, the CIA. Although the CIA made no sense. Nothing made any sense. The federal government had no jurisdiction over a homicide case, and to this day the FBI denies that it ever set foot in her house.

But the FBI was there, she insisted, with portable X-ray machines and other fancy devices. An IRS computer expert was flown in from Miami to go through Jerry's computers. Some of them stayed until 2:00 or 3:00 in the morning. The men never spoke to Jane or tried to comfort her. The only conversation was a peremptory request for coffee.

The FBI agent in charge was tall man of about fifty, with blue eyes. Tom somebody, she thought. He never left a card. Jane was under the impression that he was from the Hot Springs office, which didn't make any sense either. When she told him that the murder might have a political dimension because of Jerry's dealings with Vince Foster and Bill Clinton, the man cut her short. "He threw up his hands and said, 'I don't want to hear anything about that.'"

With the help of the Little Rock Police Department the FBI ransacked the place, confiscating files, records, and 130 tapes of telephone conversations—without giving a receipt. "I've asked them to give it all back, but the police refuse to relinquish anything. They told me there's nothing they can do about the case as long as Bill Clinton is in office."

Without access to the complete records, Jane has been unable to reconstruct her husband's activities in the months before his death. She knows that he was calling the White House in early 1993 demanding full payment for work performed by American Contract Services during the campaign.[24] The firm was owed $83,000, she believed.

When Jerry complained to his client contact, Dee Dee Myers, she insisted that the money had already been paid. "I have the company's signature on the back of the checks," Myers told him. The checks were drawn on the Worthen National Bank in the name of the "Clinton-Gore Presidential Transition Planning Foundation." Most of them were signed by David Watkins.[25]

"We don't sign our checks, we stamp them," Jerry replied.

Somebody inside the campaign had been embezzling the money, he was told, but he was promised full payment anyway. The check never arrived. In the end, the campaign said that it was only going to pay him thirty cents on the dollar. Parks was seething. He had been contracting workers at $5.00 an hour and billing the campaign at a rate of $7.23 an hour, a relatively modest mark-up.[26] A settlement on these terms would have been ruinous. That is when he began to play hardball with Betsey Wright and Webb Hubbell, calling them in Washington to express his wrath.[27] Whatever he said, it seemed to work. On July 22, 1993, two days after Foster's death, Jerry received his check for $83,000.

Was it possible that he had begun to make some hints about his confidential files, starting with the Vantage Point material but then perhaps escalating to matters of campaign finance? Could he have triggered a nuclear alert by alluding to documentation that was not supposed to exist?

"No, I don't think so," said Jane, loyally but without total conviction. "Jerry would never have been so stupid as to try to blackmail the President of the United States."

I do not pretend to understand why Jerry Parks was murdered. But the indications that the Parks case is somehow intertwined with the death of Vincent Foster is surely compelling enough to warrant a proper investigation. Instead, nobody cares to learn what Mrs. Parks has to say.

Why is it that every utterance from the lips of one widow—Lisa Foster—is treated with reverence, while the other widow, brushed aside by an arrogant FBI, offers a conflicting version of events that is totally ignored by the American press?

Is Lisa Foster an inherently more accurate witness of events than Jane Parks simply because she belongs to a higher social caste? Is that what American justice and journalism has come to?

"COME TO ARKANSAS.... YOU MIGHT EVEN LEARN A THING OR TWO"

—Bill Clinton, accepting the Democratic
nomination, July 1992

CHAPTER SEVENTEEN

DEATH SQUAD

THE TREMOR HIT on June 11, 1997, when a Little Rock jury convicted Dan Harmon on five counts of racketeering, extortion, and drug dealing. It meant nothing to the political classes in Washington, but those who understood the nexus of relationships in Arkansas saw it very differently. Harmon was one of the commissars who had enforced a politicized criminal justice system during the tenure of Governor Clinton. Now a jury of Arkansans had found him guilty of running his Seventh Judicial District prosecuting attorney's office "as a criminal enterprise for six years" and "demanding money in return for dropping charges."

Among those attending the trial at the U.S. District Court was Jean Duffey, one of his many victims. Years before she had told me, in one of her acerbic asides, that "if you freed all the prison convicts in Arkansas, and locked up all the judges and prosecutors, you would do wonders to raise the moral condition of the state."

Here, at last, were the first glimmerings of vindication. She listened tensely, with bittersweet emotions, as Dan Harmon was painted by one witness after another in unflattering colors. He was

255

a wife-beater; he took payoffs; he dealt drugs. A woman testified that she had delivered $10,000 in cash to Harmon's office as the bribe to drop a marijuana charge.

Fine as far as it went, thought Duffey, but the prosecution was holding back. She knew that Dan Harmon was much worse than that. His crimes were heinous. She suspected that the U.S. Attorney for the Eastern District of Arkansas was engaged in damage control. Experience had taught her to expect the absolute minimum from the U.S. Justice Department. But at least Harmon had now been exposed as a criminal, and that was something. At least he could not inflict any more judicial atrocities on the people of central Arkansas. That was no small victory.

A gaunt, fearless woman with piercing eyes, now aged 50, and an animal-rights vegan to boot, Duffey is the sort of American who reassures you that the founding character of the republic lives yet. When I met her, she was an algebra teacher at the Sam Rayburn High School in Pasadena, Texas, but that was a second career she had adopted in political exile, as a refugee from Arkansas. By metier, she is really a prosecutor.

In March 1990 she was appointed head of the Seventh Judicial District drug task force, a joint federal and tri-county probe into the epidemic of narcotics trafficking in central Arkansas. It started badly. Her supervisor, Gary Arnold, walked in and said: "Jean, you are not to use the drug task force to investigate any public official."[1]

But it was not her character to confine herself to the street "mules" while the managerial class carried on with impunity. With a team of seven undercover police officers it did not take long to establish what she already suspected: The local judiciary was up to its neck in corruption, behaving much like the *fiscalia* of a backward Mexican province.

"We heard right away that if you got busted you could buy your way out," said Duffey. "It was an extortion racket. You'd pay off the prosecutor, who'd share the profits with the judge, and the case would be dropped." Soon they learned that it was even worse: The clique not only protected the drug flow, they essentially operated the business. Dan Harmon, then 45, the former Saline County prosecutor, and soon to be the Seventh Judicial District prosecutor, was the enforcer for the local smuggling enterprise.

It was not easy to conduct the investigation. Dan Harmon, a mustachioed dandy of great personal charm with a concealed penchant for violence, soon found out that the task force was poking around in his affairs. He launched a smear campaign with the help of friends at *The Benton Courier* and *The Arkansas Democrat*, accusing Duffey of every sin from embezzling funds to child abuse.

Instead of fighting back in public, she took the findings of the task force to the U.S. Attorney's office in Little Rock, hoping that the federal government would have the gumption to confront the local narco-brotherhood. Assistant U.S. Attorney Robert Govar encouraged her to fight on. Dan Harmon would soon be indicted by a federal grand jury, he promised. She would be absolved.

But both of them underrated Harmon's reach. In November 1990 Duffey was fired by the Seventh Judicial District committee that had appointed her. Half of the task force resigned in sympathy.

The federal probe into Saline County corruption was still running, so Duffey was able to continue her crusade vicariously by offering her witnesses to the U.S. Attorney's Office. On the afternoon of December 10, 1990, her best informant, Sharlene Wilson, walked into the U.S. District Court in Little Rock and blurted out in front of an astonished grand jury that she had provided cocaine to Bill Clinton at Le Bistro nightclub during his first term as governor.

It had no criminal implications for Clinton because the statute of limitations had passed long before. But matters were clearly getting out of hand. Within days the federal investigation was closed down. U.S. Attorney Charles Banks went into full cover-up mode.[2] He was a Republican appointee but that meant nothing in Arkansas. What mattered were the interlocking relationships of power. Assistant U.S. Attorney Robert Govar was pulled off the case.[3]

A month later Sharlene Wilson contacted Duffey in a desperate panic and arranged a surreptitious meeting at Lake Catherine on January 7, 1991. It was then that she revealed what she had blurted out in a moment of misguided candor at the grand jury.

"She was terrified. She said her house was being watched and she'd made a big mistake," said Duffey. "That was when she told me she'd testified about seeing Bill Clinton get so high on cocaine he fell into a garbage can…. I have no doubt she was telling the truth." Duffey has provided me with her contemporaneous diaries recording the conversation.[4]

For both Sharlene Wilson and Jean Duffey matters took a drastic turn for the worse when Dan Harmon became prosecuting attorney for the Seventh Judicial District in January 1991. He immediately summoned a county grand jury and issued a subpoena for all the records of the task force, which included the incriminating files on his own activities. If Duffey had complied it would have exposed 30 witnesses and her confidential informants to violent retribution. She refused.

Harmon issued a felony warrant for "avoiding service." Harmon's ally, Circuit Court Judge John Cole announced publicly that once arrested she would be held without bail. "That is when I got really worried," said Duffey. "I got a message from one of the dispatchers that I would never get out of jail alive, and I didn't doubt it. Some of the cops had already been warning my family there was a $50,000 price on my head."

She went into hiding on a ranch in northern Arkansas. During the early months of 1991 she was on the move, emerging from time to time for a clandestine meeting with her husband and three children, but always one step ahead of Dan Harmon's men. *The Arkansas Democrat* called her a "felony fugitive" in blaring headlines. Finally she fled to Texas. The family followed.

"I was dragged through the mud, totally discredited and professionally destroyed, but I have no regrets," said Duffey. "We tried to do what was right; we did everything that we possibly could; all that was left was to get on with our lives.... I became a school teacher, and you know what? I just love it."

It took longer to deal with Sharlene. In the mid-1980s she had been one of Harmon's lovers, on and off, and an accessory in his illicit operations. That, of course, is why she had been so invaluable to Jean Duffey, guiding her through the underworld of organized drug trafficking in Arkansas. Sharlene, in essence, had served as paramour to the cartel.

She had bedded with most of the criminal fraternity, including Roger Clinton, in a decade-long career of vertiginous debauchery. She had even done a stint for three or four months unloading bags of cocaine at the Mena Airport in the mountains of Eastern Arkansas. If there was anybody who knew the business inside out— where the aircraft made their drops at night, who picked up the deliveries, who laundered the money, who ordered the hits—it was Sharlene Wilson. She was a dangerous woman. What's more, she had gone spiritual. She was trying to rectify her life, hoping to regain custody of her lost son. She posed a threat to the whole organization.

But Harmon had to be careful, bide his time. Sharlene had become an undercover informant for the U.S. Drug Enforcement Administration, and the DEA did not like it when their sources had fatal accidents.[5] So with a nice sense of irony he used the Seventh Judicial District task force, now completely under control, to set her up on drug charges.

His opportunity came when a close friend of Sharlene's, Joann Potts, was arrested and agreed to "roll over" to avoid prosecution. Potts was sent on repeated visits to Sharlene's house to arrange a drug deal. Sharlene succumbed.[6] She gave Potts a joint of marijuana, then made the fatal mistake of fetching her some methamphetamine. The woman was crying, saying her husband was cheating on her, that her car wouldn't start, that life was hell, and she "needed to get high really bad."[7]

"I'm not denying that I did it," Sharlene later told the court. "I'm saying that I've been pushed and pushed into this whole situation. The girl would not leave me alone, and I cared about her genuinely."

Sharlene was arrested by Dan Harmon in person. "He yelled, 'Bitch, I told you that if you ever breathed a word about me I'd take you down. You're going to prison, bitch,'" she said.

Harmon then prosecuted the case, neglecting to tell the jury that they had been lovers. He offered her a plea agreement of 116 years. A bit stiff, she felt, opting instead for a trial. She was convicted and sentenced to 31 years in prison for delivery of methamphetamine and marijuana. Still a bit stiff, for a first drug conviction.

"They couldn't silence her so they locked her up and threw away the key," said Duffey. "That's Arkansas for you."

But this time the powers that be in Arkansas did not have the last say. Represented by a talented, maverick lawyer, John Wesley Hall, Sharlene took her appeal all the way to the U.S. Supreme Court. In a unanimous opinion written by Justice Clarence Thomas on May 22, 1995, the Court found that Harmon's men had violated Sharlene's Fourth Amendment rights by failing to adhere to the "knock-and-announce principle" before entering her home.[8]

Citing English common law, Justice Thomas noted that a man's house is "his castle of defense and asylum" and that the King may not send his sheriff into a person's house, either to arrest or to do other execution of the King's process, without signifying the cause and requesting that the doors be opened. Harmon had forgotten to study his Blackstone *Commentaries*. So had the Arkansas courts.

"The judgment of the Arkansas Supreme Court is reversed and the case is remanded for further proceedings," concluded Thomas. It did not get her off the hook entirely. Other convictions still held. But it bolstered her claim that she had been a victim of legal foul play, and it occurred at a time when Harmon's vicious sway over the Seventh Judicial District was fast coming to an end.

*   *   *

"I don't know if I trust you. I don't know if I trust anybody any longer," said Margie Wilson, in the sing-song cadence of rural Arkansas, as she hobbled around her dusty, cluttered trailer.

I was trying to persuade her to take a message to her daughter, Sharlene, in the Arkansas penitentiary for women. I knew that Sharlene would refuse to talk to me without knowing what it was about, but I did not want to alert the wrong people by sending an explicit letter through the prison system. I had to get in by stealth and tape her story before the portcullis came crashing down. The weekend family visit was my best bet.

"Since you're a friend of Jean Duffey I'll do it," said Margie, wearily. "Though I don't see what good it'll do my daughter talking to you.... She knows too much stuff about the Clinton brothers, too much for her own good."[9]

The penitentiary protruded inelegantly from the flat, sweltering cotton fields near Pine Bluff. A team of male convicts was out in the midday sun, slowly pulling up grass with their hands. Uniformed guards watched on horseback, no doubt envious of the loose white clothes worn by their wards. It was deathly silent.

At the women's compound I was shown into the warden's board-room and told to wait while Sharlene was escorted from her cell in Barracks 9-B. She had borrowed some makeup from one of the other inmates in an effort to recapture lost allure. But it could not mask the desecrating effects of a life on drugs. Though still comely at age 38, it was hard to imagine that she had once been the blonde bombshell who made the rounds with Roger Clinton in the governor's limo. She had grown frumpy on prison food. Her light brown hair was untended. All that remained where the laughing eyes.

I made it clear to her that my newspaper could not offer any money for her story. Nor could I guarantee her safety in any way, although I believed that she was probably at less risk going public.

"Mr. Pritchard, sir, I'll tell you anything you want to know," she said. "I'm not proud of what I've done, but if I'm doing time for dope, they should be, too. They've persecuted me. They took my house, my family. They've done everything but kill me, and when the time is ripe they may do that."[10]

She had been the bartender at Le Bistro, a Little Rock nightclub where Roger Clinton used to play with his rock band Dealer's Choice. Big Brother would come by from time to time with one or two of his State Troopers.

"Roger had all the pretty girls and drugs and the fast life, and Bill was pretty envious of this," she said. On one occasion "Roger the Dodger" came back to the bar and said he needed two grams of cocaine right away. They carried out the deal near the ladies room. The Dodger then borrowed her "tooter," her "one-hitter" as she called it, and handed it to the governor.

"I watched Bill Clinton lean up against a brick wall. He must have had an adenoid problem because he casually stuck my tooter up his nose," she said. "He was so messed up that night, he slid down the wall into a garbage can and just sat there like a complete idiot."

Afterward they went back to the Governor's Mansion and partied into the early hours of the morning. "I thought it was the coolest thing in the world that we had a governor who got high."

That was not the only time she snorted cocaine with Bill Clinton. She claimed to have been present with him at a series of "toga parties" at the Coachman's Inn outside Little Rock between 1979 and 1981. "I was, you know, the hostess with the mostess, the lady with the snow," she said. "I'd serve drinks and lines of cocaine on a glass mirror."

People shared sexual partners in what amounted to a Babylonian orgy. They were elite gatherings of ten to twenty people, mostly public officials, lawyers, and local notables, cavorting in a labyrinth of interconnected rooms with women that included teenage girls. Bill Clinton was there at least twice, she said, snorting cocaine "quite avidly" with Dan Harmon. She gave a graphic description of the sexual activities that Bill Clinton preferred.

She remembered seeing a distinctive mole at the base of his stomach. "It's darned me that he's managed to get elected through all this," she said.

"It's 'darned' a lot of people," I concurred.

Sharlene was surprisingly frank about her job at the Mena Airport in the mid-1980s. The cocaine was flown in on twin-engine Cessnas, sometimes as often as every day. "I'd pick up the pallets and make the run down to Texas. The drop-off was at the Cowboys Stadium. I was told that nobody would ever bother me, and I was never bothered.... If there was a problem I was to call Dan Harmon."

A lot of the cocaine that came into Mena was taken up to Springdale in northwest Arkansas, she said, where it was stuffed into chickens for reshipment to the rest of the country.

But she had another job, which she revealed to me two years later when we were allowed to meet and talk in relative privacy at the prison library. This time she was trembling with emotion, giving free rein to the terrible remorse that had been eating at her for nine years. She used to pick up cocaine deliveries on the railway tracks near the little town of Alexander, thirty miles south of Little Rock.

"Every two weeks, for years, I'd go to the tracks, I'd pick up the package, and I'd deliver it to Dan Harmon, either straight to his office, or at my house.... Sometimes it was flown in by air, sometimes it would be kicked out of the train. A big bundle, two feet by one and a half feet, like a bale of hay, so heavy I'd have trouble lifting it.... Roger the Dodger picked it up a few times."

But in the summer of 1987 one of the drops disappeared. Furious, Harmon brought out some of his men to watch the delivery on the night of August 22. They were expecting a delivery of 3 to 4 pounds of cocaine and 5 pounds of "weed." Sharlene was supposed to make the pickup that night but she had been "high-balling" a mixture of cocaine and crystal and was totally "strung-out." They told her to wait in the car, which was parked off Quarry Road. It was around midnight.

"It was scary. I was high, very high. I was told to sit there and they'd be back. It seemed forever.... I heard two trains. Then I heard some screams, loud screams. It... it...," she stammered, breaking into uncontrollable tears. She never did finish that sentence.

"When Harmon came back, he jumped in the car and said, 'Let's go.' He was scared. It looked like there was blood all down his legs."

She later learned that a group of boys had been intercepted at the drop sight. According to Sharlene some of them had managed to get away, but Kevin Ives, 17, and Don Henry, 16, were captured. Harmon's men interrogated them as they were lying on the ground, face down, hands tied behind their backs. They were kicked and beaten, and finally executed. One of the boys was stabbed to death with a "survival knife." The bodies were wrapped in a tarpaulin, carried to a different spot on the line, and placed across the railway tracks so that the bodies would be mangled by the next train.

The following day Harmon told Sharlene that she would have to ditch her car. He gave her $500 in cash and told her to deliver a packet of cocaine to an address in Rockford, Illinois. She went to an auto auction and bought an Olds Cutlass Supreme for $450 in cash and drove to Rockford. From there she fled to the obscurity of Nebraska.

Sharlene is too candid for her own good. After telling me her harrowing story she made a collect call to my office in Washington, and said in a tone that was by turns pleading and peremptory: "Everything I told you is off the record." She then sent a letter with a notarized stamp, or so it appeared, commanding me to adhere to her First Amendment rights.

I thought about this a great deal. Technically, under American journalistic convention, a comment cannot be put off-the-record retroactively. But Sharlene Wilson is not a public official. She is not a potentate who knows how to play the game of media spin. She is a convict in dire straights who is afraid to eat the food on her tray when it is brought to the prison boiler-room where she works. People in her predicament have an excuse to go "off-the-record" after the event.

On the other hand, I owe greater loyalty to the feelings of Linda Ives who lost her son Kevin to the death squad of the Saline County judicial authorities. Besides, I have Sharlene's signed confession, which she gave to the narcotics detail of the Little Rock Police Department on May 28, 1993. The FBI has it, so does the U.S. Attorney for the Eastern District of Arkansas. The whole damn government has it.

*   *   *

Kevin Ives was spending the night at the home of his friend Don Henry. At about 12:30 AM the two boys had apparently gone out "spotlight" hunting for deer in a wooded area near the railway tracks.[11]

At 4:25 AM the three drivers of a Union Pacific train coming up from Shreveport caught sight of an obstruction on the line. They jammed on the breaks but there was no chance of stopping the immense freight train in time. As they got closer they could see two bodies lying across the tracks, heads inside the rails, partly covered with a tarpaulin.[12] Not even the deafening whistle of the train could make them stir.

The Arkansas medical examiner, Fahmy Malak, ruled the deaths an accident. He said the boys had smoked twenty marijuana joints and fallen into a trance on the railway tracks, side by side. How he reached this astounding conclusion was a mystery because the state crime labs never tested the concentration of marijuana in their blood.[13]

Malak, an Egyptian with poor command of English, did not inspire confidence. In his most creative ruling he concluded that a James "Dewey" Milam had died of an ulcer and then been decapitated by the family dog. According to Malak, the animal had eaten the entire head and then vomited, leaving traces of half-digested brain matter. To Malak's chagrin, however, the man's skull was later recovered. No bites were taken out of it. The man had been decapitated with a sharp knife.

"That Malak survived in Arkansas is a testament to Clinton's power," wrote Meredith Oakley in her dispassionate Clinton biography *On the Make*. "He repeatedly lied about his credentials, misconstrued his findings, and misrepresented autopsy procedures. In the lab, he misplaced bodies and destroyed evidence. On the witness stand, he was a prosecutor's dream."

As has now been amply explored—by *The Los Angeles Times*, NBC's *Dateline*, and others—he obscured the negligent role of Bill Clinton's mother, Virginia Kelley, as the nurse anesthetist in the death of 17-year-old Susie Deer in 1981. Deer had been hit by a rock that broke her jaw and nose, but she was not in serious danger. Indeed, she was sitting up and chatting before surgery at the Ouachita Memorial Hospital.

During the operation, however, Virginia Kelley fumbled the breathing tube with disastrous results. Deer died from lack of oxygen. It was a clear case of medical malpractice, but Fahmy Malak concluded that the patient had died of "blunt trauma" to the head. With the extra touch that so captured the character of justice in Bill Clinton's Arkansas, the lad who threw the rock was prosecuted and convicted of negligent homicide.

Over the years, outraged families had tried to expose Fahmy Malak for what he was, a pseudo-scientific servant of power. But the doctor finally met his match in the immovable American spirit of

Linda Ives. A buxom housewife with blue eyes and bushy blonde hair, aged 38 when her son was killed, she had never been involved in politics. Nor had her husband, Larry, an engineer on the Union Pacific. "Our lives were going to the ballpark, going out to the lake... until the 'machine' reached into our lives."[14]

Linda declared war on Fahmy Malak and created such a stir that a county grand jury was called to investigate the case. The bodies were exhumed. In April 1988 a second autopsy was conducted by the Atlanta medical examiner Dr. Joseph Burton.

He found a "v" shaped "penetrating wound" into the "thoracic and left lower chest cavity" of Don Henry. He showed an enhanced photograph of the wound to six other forensic investigators. They all concurred that it was "a stab wound... consistent with it having been inflicted by something such as a large cutting edge knife."[15]

He also found that Kevin Ives had been smashed in the head with a rifle butt, probably Don Henry's .22 caliber hunting rifle. There was "considerable reaction within the lungs of both boys" indicating that they had not died immediately. The level of marijuana in Kevin's blood was 97.9 nanograms per milliliter, consistent with having smoked two marijuana cigarettes over the previous few hours. Don Henry's level was slightly higher, but not nearly enough to induce collapse.

"The preponderance of evidence in this case indicates that Kevin Ives and Don Henry sustained injuries prior to impact with the train, that these injuries were inflicted on them by another individual or individuals, that their bodies were placed on the track."

It was at this stage that the Clinton administration in Little Rock began to exhibit the body language of alarm. In May 1988 Governor Clinton's chief of staff, Betsey Wright, deflected an attempt by the grand jury to subpoena two outside pathologists who had looked at the train deaths during a review of the Arkansas crime labs. Wright responded with an affidavit asserting that the doctors had not been contracted "to provide second opinions on specific cases."

It was gratuitous obstruction. The grand jury, highly irritated, then issued a subpoena for Betsey Wright herself. For weeks she defied the order.

Shortly afterward, a team of state police investigators assigned to help with the case—at the insistence of the Henry and Ives families—were reined in by the head of the Criminal Investigations Division. One of the investigators was Trooper L. D. Brown. "I was told it had something to do with Mena and I was to leave it alone."[16]

Meanwhile, with a panache that has to be admired, Dan Harmon had managed to take over the case, first as a concerned private attorney and then as a special deputy prosecutor appointed by his friend, Judge John Cole. He took command of the grand jury, promising to turn over every stone until the fiendish killers were caught and brought to justice. Linda Ives believed him.

"I thought he was our knight in shining armor. He was the only one helping us when nobody else would, it didn't make any sense that he'd do this if he'd been involved himself," she said. "I was so naive, back then."

"People had been telling me all along about his drug use, but he'd explain it all, and I was easy to pacify. Dan Harmon can make you believe anything, if you want to believe it," she said. "It makes me shudder to think that I was on the phone to him every day, pouring out my heart."[17]

In December 1988 the grand jury reached the end of its natural life and was disbanded. Sadly, explained Harmon, the investigation had failed to crack the case, but the capable officers of the Saline County Sheriff's Department would press on. It was only later that Linda Ives would be told by two frightened jurors that Harmon had prevented the grand jury from calling witnesses.

Already, people associated with the case were beginning to die in what amounted to a reign of terror among young people in Alexander, Arkansas.

Keith Coney, who told his mother he knew too much about the railway deaths and feared for his life, died in a motorcycle accident after a high-speed chase. Coney had been with the two boys a few hours before their deaths. Linda Ives now believes that they met up again at the tracks. "I'm sure now that there were three of them out there, at least, and he was one who got away," she said.[18]

Boonie Bearden, a friend of the boys, disappeared. His body was never found.

Jeff Rhodes, another friend, was killed with a gunshot to the head in April 1989.

And on it went. The killing fields.

There had always been rumors that the railway tracks were a drop-zone for drugs. It was assumed the deliveries were coming by train. But in June 1990 the undercover officers of Jean Duffey's Seventh Judicial District task force stumbled on evidence of a much bigger trafficking operation involving aerial drops.[19]

Aircraft with no lights were observed flying very low over the tracks at night. One informant staked out the area and observed a twin engine plane coming in at approximately 3:00 AM at least once a week. "It would fly in extremely low over the field, reduce speed, before throttling up again. By the field is a children's colony[20] that is lit up each night like a 'Christmas Tree.' That was the 'beacon.'"[21]

The deeper the undercover officers looked, the more certain they became that the operation was protected at the highest levels of law enforcement in Saline County, Pulaski County, and Little Rock.

Three years later, long after Duffey had been driven into exile, a Saline County detective named John Brown came to much the same conclusion. A brave, stubborn, emotional man, with rugged good looks, he ignored all warnings that it would be wiser to leave the case alone. It came to a head at a tense closed-door meeting with Robert Shepherd, the man appointed by Bill Clinton to be Arkansas's drug czar.

"Shepherd put on his overbearing cop manner and said 'Brown, those two kids are dead. There's nothing you do can bring them back. Your career will prosper a lot more if you'd concentrate your efforts somewhere else,'" recalled Brown. "I walked to the door, and just as I was leaving I turned and said, 'Guys, unless somebody wants to discuss the big secret with me, and tells me why everybody wants me to leave this alone, I've got two kids dead and I still consider that murder in Arkansas.' I walked out and thought, 'Oh shit, have I got problems.'"

Brown's career did not prosper. Forced out of the Saline County Sheriff's Department, he was reduced to digging ditches at $6 an hour to support his young wife Karen and two small children. But he never cracked. Once, when I visited him at his home in the country, there was a volunteer providing protection around-the-clock. The man was unarmed, but at least there would be a witness if anything happened. I have no doubt that it was this informal network of friends and supporters that kept him going, and perhaps kept him alive, through the worst months.[22]

It was John Brown who finally broke Sharlene Wilson and extracted her confession. He then discovered a fresh witness, a lad who had been out with two friends that night looking for a marijuana patch. The witness had been about sixty feet away, hidden below the bank, watching a group of men talking on the tracks. "One of them I definitely recognized as Dan Harmon. Then I noticed two more people, Kevin and Don, walking down the railroad tracks."

At first it looked as if Harmon was just talking to the boys, but then a shot rang out. The witness turned and ran.[23]

At this point the FBI took charge. Phyllis Cournan, an athletic, single-minded agent from Philadelphia, had recently arrived in Little Rock on a routine assignment. An idealist at heart, eager to see the best in people, she was discovering to her shock and disgust that the rampant drug trafficking in Arkansas was being protected by the highest levels of the political machine. The most offensive abuse was the murder of Don and Kevin. If she could break that case open, she believed she could shake things loose in Arkansas.[24]

Cournan immediately gave the boy a polygraph test, which he passed, and placed him in the witness protection program. It was the beginning of a lonely FBI probe into the blackest narco-corruption of Bill Clinton's Arkansas. Cournan contacted Jean Duffey in Texas, persuading her to open the files of the drug task force. She went to see Sharlene in the penitentiary.

"She asked me if Roger Clinton had been on the railway tracks that night," said Sharlene. "And she asked me about Bill Clinton and whether he was into cocaine."[25]

Cournan was now being accompanied by an FBI agent from the Hot Springs office, Floyd Hayes. As the investigation progressed— that is to say, as she established with near certainty who had murdered the two boys—Hayes was assigned to be her partner. She also began to feel the presence of "The Machine," day and night. Her telephones were no longer secure. She had bouts of insomnia. Being a federal agent, she discovered, was no protection. Not in Arkansas.

Then, after eighteen months, the probe suddenly collapsed. In November 1995 Linda and Larry Ives went to see Special Agent Bill Temple, the number two man in the FBI office in Little Rock, and were given a taste of the bullying insolence of the FBI.

"He was so arrogant and smug," said Linda. "He said, 'Maybe in light of the fact that there was no physical evidence, maybe it's time for you all to realize that no crime occurred.' I slammed down my notebook and said, 'I don't have to listen to this bullshit' and walked out."[26]

"I think he intended to make me mad. I was crying throughout the entire meeting, and I cried for days afterward."

She went public, accusing the FBI of working to cover-up the murder of her son. The chief of the FBI's Little Rock office, I. C. Smith, countered in the local newspaper, *The Benton Courier*, saying that the Bureau had a "very real problem" establishing federal juris-diction in the case, and anyway it was not clear that the boys had been murdered.[27] He said that Linda Ives had "badly misquoted" Agent Temple's remarks.

"He never even asked me or Larry what had happened," said Linda. "He just came out and called me a liar."

For Linda Ives it was the last straw. She telephoned Phyllis Cournan, who had been present at the meeting. With the tape-recorder running, Linda Ives extracted from Cournan an acknowl-edgment that Temple had been quoted "verbatim."

Armed with evidence of FBI mendacity, Linda took her campaign to the airwaves. It was a harsh way to treat Phyllis Cournan, a dedi-cated agent Linda Ives admired in many ways. But Linda had learned that there was no use giving quarter to Louis Freeh's FBI. "I'm fighting a war, and I'll fight it any way I can," she said.

A few months later I had a final dinner with Agent Phyllis Cournan and her husband, a Secret Service Agent from Minnesota. Charming, educated, with a strong sense of duty, they were every-thing that one could hope for in the rising generation of federal agents. But priorities were changing. They had a baby now, the cen-ter of their lives.

We went to an Italian restaurant in Little Rock—at their expense, they would not let me bill it to my newspaper—and talked about the amazing *mores* of Arkansas. None of us wanted to poison the evening by mentioning the train deaths, but the issue had to be confronted.

The boys were murdered, said Phyllis, and the FBI knew who did it. But the forensic evidence was contaminated. "We couldn't get anything out of the DNA," she said. "All we had were witnesses with huge credibility problems; we couldn't go to trial with that.... What were we supposed to do?"

She was putting the best face on it, trying to convince herself. I could sense her slipping away into the embrace of the Bureau. She had poured her heart and soul into the case, but when it came to the crunch she was going to be a team player.

Linda Ives now shifted her campaign into high gear. Incensed by the conduct of I. C. Smith, she joined up with a California film producer named Pat Matrisciana to make a documentary on the deaths. It was called *Obstruction of Justice*. The video, tightly documented, was a heart-wrenching exposé of "The Machine."

Journalist Micah Morrison then took up the cause on the editorial pages of *The Wall Street Journal*. (The rest of the media stayed away, with the exception of Phil Weiss in *The New York Observer*.) In one article, Morrison put in a plug for the "Train Deaths" web site that Linda Ives and Jean Duffy had constructed on the Internet. The site received 32,000 hits the next day. Angry letters poured into the offices of I. C. Smith in Little Rock.

The FBI was losing control. The nasty methods that the Bureau had been using for years, and getting away with, were suddenly being exposed for all to see on the Internet. Of course, the political Left had always understood that the Bureau could be abusive, with the mindset of a deformed cult. Now the Right was finding out, too.

Special Agent I. C. Smith was badly shaken. Once billed as a star agent picked by Louis Freeh to clean up the Bureau's operations in Arkansas, he suddenly found himself being recast as the new villain. Scrambling to recover, he shifted the investigation into Saline County corruption into higher gear. Nobody was going to be able to say that I. C. Smith was prostituting himself for Dan Harmon and his miserable accomplices.

Linda Ives, the housewife from Benton, had outmaneuvered the Bureau. But she still did not understand what it was about her son's death that had caused a federal grand jury probe to be shut down in early 1991, or why the FBI had backed away in November 1995, or indeed why the Justice Department's prosecution of Dan Harmon in June 1997 was confined to racketeering, when they knew perfectly well—or so she had to assume—that he had murdered her son.

Linda Ives, Jean Duffey, and John Brown all came to the same conclusion. They were pitted against Dan Lasater—the Dixie Godfather, and the friend of and provider for the Clinton brothers.

CHAPTER EIGHTEEN

THE DIXIE MAFIA

BANNED BY EDICT from smuggling drugs, the Italian
American Mafia missed out on the most lucrative crime wave
of the twentieth century. It was left to others to profit from the $100
billion a year market in cocaine, marijuana, and methamphetamines.
Those best placed, by geography and criminal tradition, were the
loose-knit groupings of the South, known to law enforcement as the
"Dixie Mafia."

The term was first coined by Rex Armistead, the Director of the
Organized Crime Strike Force in New Orleans in the 1970s.[1] Less
famous than the Cosa Nostra, the Dixie Mafia was, and still is, far
more dangerous. During a ten year period from 1968 to 1978 when
the Italian Americans were in the headlines for a spree of thirty
murders, their redneck counterparts quietly dispatched 156 victims.

"There wasn't a well from Mississippi to West Texas that didn't
have a dead body floating in it," said Armistead. "The big difference
was the lack of ceremony. It was just 'I'm going to get rid of
Ambrose today; I don't need permission; and I go out and do it.' As

simple as that. And that's the end of Ambrose. It hasn't changed much either."

"I see."

The Dixie Mafia formed a ring of interlocking interests that covered Louisiana, Texas, Oklahoma, Kentucky, Tennessee, and above all Arkansas. Their spiritual capital was Bill Clinton's hometown of Hot Springs, famous for its racetrack, its ornate bathhouses, its casinos, its prostitution, and its epic defiance of Prohibition.

The coat-and-tie yuppies of the modern Dixie Mafia are the children and grandchildren of bootleggers, a provenance they share with Bill Clinton. The trade has evolved. Clinton's grandfather used to serve moonshine from behind the counter of his store in Hope. Now the business is a high-tech operation involving fleets of aircraft, off-shore banking, and deep reach into the U.S. federal government.

Armistead warned me not to push my luck anywhere in the old Confederacy, but especially not in Arkansas. That counsel was on my mind as I drove through the backroads of the state with a box of documents slipped to me by dissidents in law enforcement. I had been given comprehensive intelligence files from the Criminal Investigations Division of the Arkansas State Police, going back as far as the early 1970s. I was told to copy what I needed, check that I was not being followed, and return the archive within 24 hours. I did exactly that, and as I fed the stack of papers into a photocopy machine at a Kinko's in Little Rock, I was scarcely able to believe what I was seeing. Among the famous names of the Arkansas oligarchy that jumped out from page after page of criminal intelligence files was Don Tyson, the billionaire president of Tyson Foods and the avuncular patron of Bill Clinton and Hillary Clinton.

A gruff barrel-chested man with a cropped beard and a reputation for ruthless business practice, Don Tyson is one of the great characters of Arkansas. He presides over the biggest chicken processing operation in the world from his "Oval Office"—a replica of the real one—with door handles in the shape of eggs. He usually wears khaki overalls with "Don" stitched on his breast pocket, and gets his hands dirty working side by side with his 54,000 employees. It is said that half of all American people eat a piece of Tyson chicken every week. The family business, based in Springdale, has grown at an explosive rate since the 1960s, swallowing up rival companies in a relentless quest for market share. "There's no second place. First place is the only place in the world," says Tyson.

But it was a high-wire act getting there. By 1979 the company's debt-to-equity ratio had soared to 1.3 at a time when interest rates were soaring. Already faced with a mushrooming debt service cost, Tyson was then hit by a severe cyclical downturn in the poultry industry. "It's like an airplane running out of gas," said Tyson at the time. "I can feel it. The engines are getting rough." But somehow he managed to prosper. Over the next five years Tyson foods was one of the fastest-growing Fortune 500 companies in the country. The turnaround was a feat of magic, a testimony to his inventive spirit.

The documents I was looking at made me wonder about the origins of his liquidity. Here were files from the U.S. Drug Enforcement Agency, marked DEA SENSITIVE, under the rubric of the "Donald TYSON Drug Trafficking Organization."

One was from the DEA office in Oklahoma City, dated December 14, 1982. It cited a confidential informant alleging that "TYSON smuggles cocaine from Colombia, South America inside race horses to Hot Springs, Arkansas." It cited the investigation tracking number for Don J. Tyson, a/k/a "Chicken Man," as Naddis 470067. A second document from the DEA office in Tucson, dated July 9, 1984, stated that "the Cooperating Individual had information concerning heroin, cocaine and marijuana trafficking in the States of Arkansas, Texas, and Missouri by the TYSON Organization." The informant described a place called "THE BARN" which TYSON used as a "stash" location for large quantities of marijuana and cocaine. "'THE BARN' area is located between Springdale and Fayetteville, Arkansas, and from the outside the appearance of 'THE BARN' looks run down. On the inside of 'THE BARN' it is quite plush."

The files contain raw police intelligence. Such allegations have to be treated with great caution. But these DEA informant reports are buttressed by a much bigger collection of state intelligence documents. Files marked "Very Confidential" trace allegations about Tyson and drug trafficking as far back as 1973.

A memo by the Criminal Investigative Section, dated March 22, 1976, states that Don Tyson "is an extremely wealthy man with much political influence and seems to be involved in most every kind of shady operation, especially narcotics, however, has to date gone without implication in any specific crime. TYSON likes to think of himself as the 'King of the Hill' in northwest Arkansas, and quite possibly this might not be erroneous." The memo was triggered by a dispute between Tyson and the Teamsters Union over allegations of drug dealing and prostitution at a Teamsters'-owned hotel leased by Tyson.[2] Two sets of documents refer to alleged hit men employed by Tyson to kill drug dealers who owed him money. Another report alleged that Tyson was using his business plane to smuggle quart jars of methamphetamine. All told, it was a staggering portrait of a drug baron.[3]

None of the allegations led to criminal charges, and it would soon become clear why. Police officers who tried to mount a case against Tyson were destroyed by their superiors in the State Police. The first to try was Beverly "B. J." Weaver, then an undercover narcotics officer in Springdale. Working the streets and bars of northwest Arkansas, disguised as a deaf woman, she collected detailed intelligence on Tyson's alleged smuggling network.

"There were loads going out with the chickens," she explained.[4] "They'd put the coke in the rectums of the chickens, live chickens. That's how they'd move it."

As the allegations from her informants mounted, she requested the intelligence files on Don Tyson. That is when her problems began. Her colleagues in the Springdale office—who she now believes were "on the take" from the Tyson machine—put out the word that she was "not stable," that she had "flipped out." Then it got rough. "They started passing out my photo on the streets, which put my life in danger. I became paranoid. I didn't trust my phone line. There was nobody I could really trust."

She drove to Little Rock to seek the support Colonel Tommy Goodwin, the commander of the State Police. He brushed her off. "You narcs are all paranoid," he said. "You see too many shadows in the dark."[5]

By 1987 her position was untenable. Her career in ruins, she resigned from the police and found a job as a security guard in the Bahamas. "I went as far away as I could go, just to fade into nothing," she told me.

After she left, the State Police drove the knife in even further, accusing her of making off with police funds, a charge she vehemently denies. She felt so ashamed she could not face her own family. "For seven years I haven't been home again," she said, weeping.

When I visited her in 1994 she was working at the cosmetics counter of a department store in Florida. Brittle, highly emotional, she had not come to terms with her ordeal. "I believed in what I did, and I was proud of what I did," she kept saying, plaintively. But they had broken her spirit.

The next to take up the challenge was Trooper J. N. "Doc" Delaughter, then 38, who drew on Weaver's work to launch a second investigation of Don Tyson in 1988. A soft-spoken man, with a cherubic face and golden hair, he had been elected Sheriff of Arkansas's Nevada County four times before joining the State Police. He came from a wealthier background than most officers in the force. With a modest inheritance from his father, and an extra stipend from his duties as a captain in the Arkansas National Guard, he enjoyed a degree of independence that was extremely threatening to the old-boy network. He also had ties to federal officials through his service in the National Guard. In July 1988 friends in the Guard set up a meeting with Michael Fitzhugh, the U.S. Attorney for the Western District of Arkansas, who agreed that the allegations against Tyson were serious enough to warrant a full-scale investigation.[6]

The next day Delaughter fired off a memo to the chief of Criminal Investigations at the State Police. "The conversation was centered around Don Tyson's illegal use and distribution of cocaine. Mr. Fitzhugh told this investigator that he was interested in prosecuting a criminal conspiracy to process or distribute a controlled substance. Mr. Fitzhugh went on to say that he wanted a combined investigation team of the FBI, DEA, IRS, and the State Police."[7]

The memo set off alarm bells at the headquarters of the State Police. Sergeant Larry Gleghorn warned Delaughter that he would be hammering "the nails in his own coffin with this department" if he persisted.[8] Delaughter was pulled off the case soon afterward. The Tyson matter would be transferred to the Springdale office, he was told by Major Doug Stevens, the head of criminal investigations. That was the end of it. The U.S. Attorney said that he did not know why the probe fizzled out, when I interviewed him years later. "The ball was in their court. For whatever reason I never heard another word from them about the thing," he said.[9]

The State Police commander, Colonel Goodwin, said that "there was not enough information to start an investigation." Asked about the DEA intelligence documents, he told me that "they weren't in the Tyson file back then."[10] This was not true. The DEA files were already available to State Police investigators.

For Delaughter it was the end of his career in law enforcement. He was transferred to highway patrol, and his department began a nitpicking scrutiny of everything he did. When that did not provoke his resignation, they sent him off for a mental evaluation. It was the

B. J. Weaver treatment, tainting him with comments about his mental stability. The police psychologist deemed him a "danger to society" on the grounds that he had "built up a lot of anger" and was confrontational.[11] It was recommended that Delaughter be suspended from service. An evaluation by a private psychologist disputed these findings, but by then Delaughter knew that he was beaten. He resigned in 1990 and went into the lumber business.

"Trying to bring these guys down is not conducive to a good career," he said, with a wry smile as we sat drinking beer on the veranda of his remote lakeside cabin. "You develop leprosy. Fast."

But the past is beginning to catch up with Don Tyson. He has been named as an official target in a criminal probe by Independent Counsel Donald Smaltz, who was appointed to investigate bribery allegations against Agriculture Secretary Mike Espy, who was later indicted. His chief lobbyist, Robert Greene, has been indicted for lying to investigators in the case. From small beginnings, the Smaltz investigation has widened into a full-scale probe of the Tyson business empire, provoking vehement accusations that it is a "politically motivated witch hunt."

The Espy affair is a textbook case of Arkansas *mores* penetrating the U.S. federal government. CBS News's *60 Minutes* reported that Espy was flown to Arkansas to seek the blessing of Don Tyson before he was nominated to his cabinet post. Once installed at the Agriculture Department, Espy proved to be a friend of the chicken industry. The department scuttled a plan for tougher standards on poultry fecal contamination. This required shifting the bureaucratic machinery into reverse gear. The plan had already been drawn up, approved, and was set for implementation. The effect was to reduce the likelihood that Tyson products would face random inspection.

The Smaltz probe has produced a surprising spin-off. In December 1994 *Time* magazine reported that Joseph Henrickson, 43, the number two pilot of the company's aviation division, had been interviewed for three days by Smaltz and a team of FBI agents about alleged deliveries of cash to the Governor's Mansion. Henrickson said that he carried sealed white envelopes containing a quarter-inch wad of $100 bills, on six occasions, from Tyson's headquarters to Little Rock. He was led to understand that the envelopes were going to Bill Clinton. In one case, a Tyson executive handed him an envelope of cash in the company's aircraft hangar in Fayetteville and said, "This is for Governor Clinton."

"I nearly fell off my chair when I heard Joe make the allegation. I took over the questioning," Smaltz told *Time*. But Smaltz did not have the mandate to investigate Bill Clinton. His probe was confined to the alleged "gratuity giver," Tyson Foods. After Henrickson was called to testify before a federal grand jury in Washington in early 1995, Smaltz made a formal request to the Justice Department for broader jurisdiction. Attorney General Janet Reno refused, ordering Smaltz to stick more closely to his original brief.

In light of the Henrickson allegations, and the fact that two investigations into Tyson's alleged drug activities were shut down by the upper echelons of the Arkansas State Police, any commerce that ties Don Tyson to Bill and Hillary Clinton demands close scrutiny. This includes the brokerage account in Hillary Clinton's name that turned $1,000 into $99,537 between October 1978 and July 1979. This speculative venture was the initiative of James Blair, the general counsel of Tyson Foods.

Having done a fair amount of trading myself on exotic markets, often with high leverage, the ratios in themselves do not surprise me. These sorts of profits can be made. But they are not made in the way that Hillary Clinton made them. The trades began three weeks before the 1978 elections, when Bill Clinton was riding high in the polls and seemed set to win his first term as Governor of Arkansas. It was shortly after the Clintons had signed up with Jim McDougal in a sweetheart land deal called Whitewater. Perhaps this was coincidence, but I doubt it.

The first transaction was a bet that rising cattle prices were due for a snap correction, a temporary fall in a buoyant market. That is exactly what happened. By the end of the day, October 11, 1978, cattle prices had fallen one and a half cents a pound. Mrs. Clinton netted an instant profit of $5,300. Within a couple of weeks she felt confident enough to start making large cash withdrawals from her account: $5,000 on October 23; another $15,000 for Christmas. The money was rolling in.

When *New York Times* reporter Jeff Gerth first broke the story in 1994, Hillary Clinton claimed that she had conducted the transactions herself after studying the market pages of *The Wall Street Journal*. This caused a good deal of mirth on the Chicago Mercantile Exchange. "Buying iceskates one day, and entering the Olympics a day later," wrote Mark Powers, editor of *The Journal of Futures Markets*. The White House subsequently retreated step by step until it was acknowledged that Hillary Clinton's broker had exercised complete discretion in handling the day-to-day trades.

His name was Robert "Red" Bone, a former truck driver and personal bodyguard for Don Tyson. Bone rose to become vice-president of Tyson Foods, where he was in charge of the egg division. It was a position he used for lucrative insider trading—both for himself and for the Tyson operation—until regulators suspended him for a year in 1977 for allegedly trying to corner the eggshells futures market. He was later sanctioned by the Chicago Mercantile Exchange for "repeated and serious violations of record-keeping functions." When he regained his broker's license he joined the commodity brokerage firm REFCO, which had privileged information about daily movements in cattle prices. Indeed, REFCO chairman Thomas Dittmer had such vast cattle holdings himself that he could flood the market and cause snap changes in futures prices.

In his book *Blood Sport*, James Stewart offers a detailed account of Bone's *modus operandi* at REFCO's offices in Springdale. It describes how Bone gleaned his inside tips each day on the hotline to REFCO's headquarters in Chicago. Stewart implies that although Bone was engaging in shady practices, Hillary Clinton's transactions were clean. But in the lightly regulated commodities markets of the late 1970s it was easy to "cherry pick" trades at the end of the day, allocating gains to one account and losses to another. This loophole was well-known in financial circles. It was part of market folklore that the most effective way to carry out the illicit transfer of money from one party to another was through a "straddle." By placing one bet that the market would go up, and an off-setting bet that it would go down, the profitable trade could be allocated to the beneficiary, while the "donor" swallowed the loss. It was absolutely foolproof. "During the late 1970s and early 1980s, straddles were used for all kinds of illegal activities, ranging from tax evasion to money-laundering and bribes," wrote David L. Brandon, former chief of the commodities section of the IRS, in an article in *The Wall Street Journal.*

To make it look plausible, the beneficiary would have to have a few losing trades mixed in with the gains, but in reality there was no risk at all. An investigation by the Chicago Mercantile Exchange in 1978 suspected that REFCO was doing precisely this. One of REFCO's Springdale brokers in fact admitted under oath that the office had been manipulating the futures contracts by "allocating them to customers after the market closed."

Stewart reports that Hillary found the experience nerve-racking and decided to retire from the market after a fresh windfall of $40,000 in July 1979, which brought her total profits to almost $100,000. But three months later, she was plunging back into the commodities market, this time with a broker at Stephens Inc., in Little Rock. When CBS News's *60 Minutes* asked Don Tyson if Hillary Clinton's cattle trades were a "payoff" from him, he vehemently denied it.

If Tyson was funneling money to the Clintons, it is possible that the Clintons were not entirely aware of what was being done. This is the notoriously grey zone of *mens rea*, but it would not be the first time that a political family was suborned by degrees like a lobster being cooked slowly in the pot. The thought occurred to me after I was told an anecdote by Larry Patterson, an Arkansas State Trooper assigned to the Governor's detail in the mid to late 1980s.

He remembers standing in the foyer of Tyson's house one evening, waiting for Clinton to finish dinner. Tyson appeared, struck up a conversation and invited him to take a trip on his 63´ yacht in Baja California. "Bring your friends along," Tyson added, offering his corporate aircraft as transport. Tyson put his arm around Patterson, pressing the invitation, just as the Governor appeared.

"What was all that about?" Clinton said, as they got into the limo.

"He asked me out on the yacht."

"Listen to me," said Clinton sternly. "Don't go. If Don Tyson gives you something, it's because he wants something back. You'll never shake him off."[12]

CHAPTER NINETEEN

THE DAN LASATER DRUG TRAFFICKING ORGANIZATION

PATTY-ANNE SMITH was sixteen years old when she fell under the ruinous influence of Dan Lasater, friend and patron of the Clinton brothers. She was a cheerful, gregarious girl, a cheerleader at the North Little Rock "Ole Main" High School. Her nicknames were Muffin and Precious. She was still a child, but not for long.

"I was a virgin until two months after I met Dan Lasater. He plied me with cocaine and gifts for sexual favors and I finally gave in and slept with him," she said in a police statement at the offices of the U.S. Attorney in Little Rock.[1] At the time Lasater was 40, more than twice her age. Under his tutelage she soon became addicted to hard drugs. She would help herself to the limitless store of cocaine in the kitchen wall-safe at Lasater's apartment at 12B Quapaw Towers. "I could get an eight-ball whenever I wanted it. I carried a vial of it around at school."[2]

Lasater arranged for a corrupt doctor to give her "a pelvic examination and prescribe birth control pills." Once on contraceptives, she was made available to Lasater's business colleagues, including

Arkansas State Senator George Locke.[3] In the end Patty-Anne fled Arkansas after it was explained to her that he planned to use her "as a semi-prostitute to 'entertain.'"

Patty-Anne was not the only victim. Michelle Cochran, then 19, had much the same experience. "He used drugs and money eventually to seduce me. As a result of the relationship I became addicted to cocaine," she told the State Police.[4] So did Gina Hartsell. Lasater flew her to Las Vegas in one of his private jets, enticed her with cocaine, and seduced her that night at the Bob Hope Suite of the Riviera Hotel. Before long she was so addicted that she "would sometimes get up and snort cocaine in order to start my day."[5]

But it was Patty-Anne Smith who suffered the most traumatic loss of innocence. The feds tracked her down in 1986 as a witness in a joint state-federal probe of the Lasater cocaine ring. When they found her she was a "basket case," in the words of one investigator, working as a "drugged-out party girl" at the Tahoe Beach and Ski Club in California.[6]

As I read through her statement in the narcotics files of the Arkansas State Police eight years later, I wondered what had become of her. By all accounts she had simply vanished, and for good reason. She had been threatened by Lasater's enforcer. "Chuck Berry told me that I was one of Dan Lasater's most trusted people and knew a lot about cocaine and his personal life," she told the Arkansas State Police. "If I ever betrayed his personal trust and hurt Lasater in any way I would not 'see daylight' to tell about it anymore."[7]

She was not easy to find. First I had to track down her mother, who then passed messages back and forth thinking that I was one of her daughter's numerous suitors. Apparently, she approved of my Oxford accent, which generally seemed to go down well in Arkansas. I eventually met up with Patty-Anne in Florida. She was still beautiful, making a living as best she could on the margins of the jet set.

Blessed with the beautiful lithe body of a fashion model, she had green eyes, long blonde hair, and a slight rasp in her voice.

How did it all start? I asked her as we sat on the terrace of an Art Deco café, looking out over the Atlantic.

"I was working at Busters, as a seating hostess. It was a Friday night. He came in with a large entourage and wanted a table. The place was packed, but I somehow managed get them seated and he gave me a hefty tip. I'd never seen a $100 bill before.... A few hours later he called me up, wanted me to come over to a party. He said the chauffeur was waiting for me outside with a limo. I thought it was kind of neat."[8]

"I was the youngest of all the girls. We were like hens in the roost, with the rooster," she explained. "We girls got along in a bitchy kind of way because we didn't want to be expelled from the roost.... He bought us all."

"I'll never be the same sweet Patty I was, I'll never trust people again. It's made me the cynical bitch I am now." Her mother knew that something awful had happened, but Patty-Anne was too ashamed to confess her story. The shame lingers. "How can I marry now, or have children? I have too much explaining to do."

She had moved fifteen times, tormented by her nightmares, too frightened to venture near Little Rock. "I knew a lot more than I should have known. I was there in the apartment at 12B when Dan did his business dealings. I'd be coming and going with champagne, and I'd hear the conversations," she said. That was how she learned that Lasater was mixed up with the Contra supply operation in Nicaragua. "I didn't think anything of it at the time. Then all that stuff broke in the news years later, and I thought 'wow.'"

The Clinton brothers were part of the scene. "I met Bill Clinton several times, he'd know my name and I thought he was a wonderful person, but I can tell you that he was never acting like a governor when I saw him." She claims to have witnessed him taking cocaine on two or three occasions, although only one of them stands out in her memory. It was late at night, around one in the morning, in a room off the kitchen in Lasater's residence. The only people present were Patty-Anne, Lasater, and Bill Clinton. "He was doing a line. It was just there on the table."

Given the circumstances, that allegation is, obviously, impossible to verify, but Patty-Anne's general testimony was used in 1986 by federal authorities to help convict Dan Lasater of "social distribution of cocaine."

What is possible to verify is that Bill Clinton and Dan Lasater are rewriting history when they now claim they hardly knew each other.[9] The reality was spelled out in the sworn deposition of Corporal Barry Spivey, a State Trooper who served on Governor Clinton's security detail from 1979 to 1984. Spivey is not one of the troopers who came out publicly against Clinton. He gave this interview because he was compelled under subpoena.

Spivey: "I can recall flying on Dan Lasater's Lear jet. It was nice. It impressed me, I recall.... I flew from Little Rock to Lexington, to the Kentucky Derby, the Governor and I and Dan.... There was other times that Governor Clinton took flights with Dan personally or in Dan's plane. But that was the only time I was with him."

Q: "Do you remember Dan Lasater coming to the Mansion?"

Spivey: "Well, he dropped in. Just kind of off-the-cuff, drop-in things.... Day and night, weekends, all day. He just came when he wanted to. I wouldn't log Dan in because I knew that he and Bill were friends.... Dan was never shown in through the front door. Dan went in through the kitchen....You just didn't go through Miss Liza's kitchen unless you were part of the kitchen circle."

Q: "How many times would you say you took Governor Clinton down to Dan Lasater's?"

Spivey: "Six, eight, ten times. A lot of times he'd say stop and he'd jump out and run in and I'd circle the block and he'd jump back in. Sometimes I might park and sit there for an hour.... I know he went a lot more times than when I was with him, when the other guys were driving.... He went by there a lot."[10]

*   *   *

Dan Lasater is a talented entrepreneur. Born poor in rural Arkansas, he started a chain of hamburger restaurants called Scotty's at the age of 19 and succeeded in undercutting McDonald's by selling burgers at 12 cents instead of 15 cents—and making up the profits with a higher price for french fries, a formula that apparently made him a millionaire by his mid-twenties.[11] By the time he was 30 he was the owner of the Ponderosa steakhouse chain in Ohio and Indiana, with annual sales of more than $300 million. Cashing in his equity for around $15 million,[12] he turned to horse racing and soon became the most successful breeder and racer of thoroughbreds in the world. With stables of 80 horses in Florida and Kentucky, he was the leading money winner three years in succession—1974, 1975, and 1976—netting a total of $10 million in prizes, and winning the Eclipse Award of the racing industry. But according to a police statement by one of his employees, Lasater's success with the horses was achieved by "putting in the boot"—fixing the races.[13]

It was at the Oaklawn Race Track in Hot Springs that Lasater first befriended Virginia Kelley, the mother of Governor Clinton, and began to close his vice around the First Family of Arkansas. Collecting governors was one of his business specialties. In early 1983 he bailed out Governor John Y. Brown of Kentucky with $300,000 cash in a paper sack at the Lexington airport. At the time Brown was desperately trying to stay one step ahead of the IRS. He had withdrawn $1 million out of a Florida bank without a "cash transient" report.[14] "I just took care of John Y.'s money problems," Lasater told his colleague Michael Drake.[15]

Lasater also tried to befriend Governor Tony Anaya of New Mexico, offering him a consulting job at the end of his term. Anaya never took up the offer, but he did use taxpayer funds to construct an 8,900-foot runway at the Angel Fire Ski Resort owned by Dan Lasater.

The governor was viewed by his opponents as naive but honest. However, the Attorney General's Office in Santa Fe was later to investigate Lasater for suspected "narcotics trafficking via aircraft with possible Organized Crime ties" operating out of Angel Fire.[16] At the time of the alleged drug trafficking, Angel Fire was managed by Patsy Thomasson, later to become Director of the Office of Administration at the White House. "I put Patsy in as the assistant chairman, and she pretty well ran that project for me," said Lasater.[17]

But the show trophy of his collection was undoubtedly Governor Clinton, who seemed to require more favors than most. When Clinton needed a safe house for his delinquent half-brother Roger, it was Lasater who spirited him out of Arkansas and gave him a sinecure job as a "stable hand" in Ocala, Florida. And when Roger fell behind in payments to his Medellin contact—a stash of cocaine had been stolen from his convertible, which his mother had just given him—it was Lasater who paid the debt, or perhaps a better word is ransom.[18] The Colombians, apparently, were hinting that there could be violent reprisals against the Governor himself.[19]

Always restless, Lasater moved into the bond business in 1980. A brief business partnership with Senator George Locke was dissolved, because of enveloping SEC violations, before Lasater embarked on his own as Lasater & Company. One former broker told me that he never witnessed enough authentic business to justify the existence of Lasater's office at 312 Louisiana Street. He suspected that Lasater was "shuffling money."[20] By the mid-1980s Little Rock was a hub of petty racketeering and fly-by-night securities trading. The target: small, deregulated thrifts that had been neglected by the big firms on Wall Street. "You have no idea how crazy it was here in the mid-eighties," said Ron Davis, a former Lasater broker. "At one point there were 54 investment houses in

Little Rock. There were 4,000 brokers working in this city. In 1987 we did more institutional sales than any other city in the world, and that includes New York, London, and Tokyo. You had used car dealers signing up making a $1 million a year in commissions."[21]

For investigators attuned to the methods of organized crime, the Lasater empire looked suspiciously like a laundromat for tens of millions of dollars of drug profits. Nor was this an idle hunch. In 1977 Lasater had lost a Lear jet in Santa Marta, Colombia, after it was confiscated by the Colombian authorities on suspicion of narcotics trafficking. The aircraft was insured at Lloyds of London, so he was not too bothered by the event, but the FBI took note.[22] The jet had been leased to a Las Vegas outfit called Jet Avia, which was under investigation for Mafia ties. It had been flown to Colombia to evacuate a badly burned pilot who had crashed a DC-6 loaded with marijuana in the jungle.[23] Among the passengers on the jet was Jamiel "Jimmy" Chagra, viewed as one of the most dangerous mob bosses in the United States. In 1982 he was prosecuted for conspiring to murder Judge John H. Woods, the first U.S. federal judge to be assassinated this century. He was acquitted on that charge, but was ultimately convicted on charges of cocaine smuggling.

Lasater was a player in the cocaine trafficking network of the Dixie Mafia as early as the mid-1970s. Intelligence reports show that the DEA had opened a file on Lasater in 1983 and had assigned him a tracking number of 141475.[24] Lasater was tipped off at once. A source called him in 1983 to inform him that he was listed in the computer as the subject of a DEA probe.[25]

In February 1984 Lasater, accompanied by Patsy Thomasson, flew to Belize in his private jet to negotiate the purchase of a 24,000-acre ranch.[26] The deal fell through because of a dispute with the "governor of Belize who was hard to deal with." One member of the Lasater party boorishly proposed "that the governor should be wasted."[27] This caused some heartburn for the U.S. Ambassador who was present during these interesting negotiations. Also present was a lawyer from Washington, D.C., named Ed Cummings, who had flown down with Lasater.[28]

Ostensibly, Lasater was looking for a horse farm. But the property, known as the Carver Ranch, was in fact a refueling stop for smugglers coming up from Colombia. Located near the border with the Yucatan, it has cropped up in a number of investigations. One of them was the "Mena" probe of Arkansas State Trooper Russell Welch, which focused on the smuggling empire of Barry Seal. This is what Welch wrote in his notebook during a debriefing of one of Seal's pilots: "With orders from Seal he would fly to a place in Southern Colombia, bordering Peru, and pickup 200 kilos of cocaine. This operation was to be staged from 'Carver Ranch'... operated by Chester Cotter. Seal met Cotter through Roger Reeves. [Roger Reeves was the intermediary who introduced Barry Seal to the Medellin Cartel.] Seal used this ranch frequently."[29] So, apparently, this ranch was no horse farm. It was part of the Medellin trafficking empire.

It was certainly well known among the drug pilots. Basil Abbott, a convicted smuggler, told me that he used it frequently when he operated from Belize in the early 1980s. He remembers Cotter, the manager, as a man with legendary sway over the local "peons." He would have the fuel supplies ready at the landing strip. The usual route to the United States, explained Abbott, was through a blind spot in the mountains of Mexico, near Monterrey, crossing the border five miles east of the McAllen control tower. "There were about seven or eight of us doing it, and none of us ever got caught," he said. On one occasion in early 1982 he flew a Cessna 210 full of cocaine into Marianna, in the rice delta of eastern Arkansas. The aircraft was met by an Arkansas State Trooper in a marked police car. "Arkansas was a very good place to load and unload," he said.[30]

Lasater had his own agents in the State Police. One of them was a narcotics investigator named Mike Mahone, whom he had befriended at the Oaklawn Race Track in the box of Virginia

Kelley—Governor Clinton's mother.[31] Lasater spotted easy prey. The subsequent courtship offers a revealing insight into his methods of corrupting law enforcement. First he invited Mahone to spend the July 4th weekend, 1985, in one of his condominiums at the Angel Fire Ski Resort.[32] Having broken the ice, the bribery began. It was disguised, of course. What Lasater did was to instruct one of his subordinates to buy a run-down property belonging to Mahone. The price was inflated, netting the State Trooper a windfall profit.[33] Lasater also paid off $7,500 of a delinquent loan that Mahone had taken out in his sister's name.

In return for these little favors, Mahone was generous with police intelligence. In the early summer of 1986 he met with Lasater and Senator Locke at a hotel in Chicago to brief them on the status of the investigation into their drug activities.[34] He warned them to be careful of their telephones and told them that the two State Troopers on the case—Doc Delaughter and Larry Gleghorn—had a "hard on" for Lasater. The two officers could be found at "Spanky's" restaurant, he added, as if tempting Lasater to take drastic action.

Trooper Mahone advised Lasater to freshen up his image by donating money to the Gyst House for Drug Abuse. So, with a nice sense of the absurd, Lasater launched a philanthropic *Blitzkrieg* that included funding for the Florence Crittenden Home for Unwed Mothers. This caused huge amusement at Lasater & Company, where the running joke was guessing which of the unwed mothers Lasater had sent there in the first place.[35] (Years later, Lasater was profiled by CNN's investigative reporter John Camp as a humble born-again Christian, trying to redeem his soul by helping in a soup kitchen.)

It was chilling for Doc Delaughter to discover that he was being betrayed by criminal elements within his own police department. But nothing about this case was normal, least of all the two status reports he gave to Colonel Tommy Goodwin, the commander of the State Police. They were strictly verbal, conducted on the telephone, and both times the calls were patched through to the personal offices of Governor Clinton.

"I don't know if Bill Clinton was listening on the line," said Delaughter. "I wasn't in the room. But he had no business being in the loop."[36]

Delaughter believed that he had sufficient evidence to pursue a full-fledged investigation of Lasater for drug trafficking. At the very least there were grounds for probing his transportation of cocaine on private jets. But Delaughter was squeezed out of the investigation, prevented from attending the critical interviews of Lasater, Senator George Locke, and Roger Clinton. In the end, U.S. Attorney George Proctor offered Lasater a plea agreement that charged Lasater with a conspiracy to distribute cocaine for "recreational use." It was a slap on the wrists. Lasater was paroled after one year, most of it spent at a halfway house in Little Rock. The prosecutor was later appointed to be head of the Justice Department's Office of International Affairs by President Clinton.

At the sentencing U.S. Federal Judge Thomas Eisele said: "There are a lot of people who would like to believe that your financial success was derived, because it was so spectacular, from nothing less than being in the drug business. But I have to rely on the evidence, and there is absolutely no evidence to suggest that you were making money in the drug business," he intoned before falling into tabloid cliché: "I think we are dealing with essentially an American tragedy, a case where the American dream turned into the American nightmare."

Others in law enforcement were less inclined to regard Lasater as a victim. According to *The Albuquerque Journal*, the FBI and U.S. Customs in New Mexico opened a fresh probe in 1988 under the auspices of the Organized Crime Drug Enforcement Task Force, naming Dan Lasater as the chief target. But it fell apart in early 1989 due to jurisdictional bickering between the FBI and Customs on one side, and the DEA on the other.[37]

Governor Clinton gave Lasater a state pardon in 1990, purportedly so that he could regain his hunting license. The pardon was of dubious validity, because Lasater had been sentenced by a U.S. federal court, not a state court. But it sent a signal to the Arkansas authorities that Lasater should be allowed to resume his financial and broking activities without hindrance.

Lasater retreated to a 7,400-acre heavily guarded estate in the Cockspur Mountains of Saline County. (Complaints by neighbors about low-flying aircraft had been passed on to the DEA, according to Captain Gene Donham of the Saline County Sheriff's Department.) But Lasater's influence lives on through the tenacious Patsy Thomasson, his adjutant and partner in adventures at the Carver Ranch. Her rise to prominence in Washington is remarkable, given that she worked so closely with Lasater—a convicted drug distributor—continuously from June 1983 until July 1992. "I was his eyes and ears. Whatever needed to be done I did," she explained.[38]

The Albuquerque Journal reported that Thomasson was still listed as the registered agent of Lasater's Phoenix Mortgage Company after she went to work at the White House. She was executive vice president of Lasater & Company, and president of Angel Fire Corporation and the Phoenix Group Incorporated. She was the signing officer for Agency del Sol, Portfolio Services Incorporated, Emerald Isle condominium development, and Starfire Resorts Incorporated.

When Lasater was sent to prison, she was given "durable power of attorney" to manage his business empire. This included everything from signing checks, to selling off his properties, and filing lawsuits in his name.

A self-styled "yellow-dog Democrat" with short black hair and a brusque no-nonsense manner, she had once served on the staff of

Arkansas Congressman Wilbur Mills. At Lasater's, she was viewed as the link to the Democratic Party by the firm's employees. "We'd all have to make contributions to the Clinton campaign funds, any-where from $500 on up, scaled on earnings," said one bond sales-man, describing the obligatory tithing system at the firm. "Patsy was the one who handled the money."[39]

Feared and disliked by many members of the firm, she was clearly a favorite with Bill Clinton. He installed her as executive secretary of the Arkansas Democratic Party to help build the foundations for his presidential bid. After the 1992 elections, she was catapulted into one of the most powerful positions in Washington—Director of the White House Office of Administration, in charge of personnel, computers, security, and drug testing—where she continued to make her presence felt in the successive scandals that have beset the Clinton presidency.

She participated in a six-hour meeting on May 15, 1994, with the FBI that eventually led to the investigation and firing of the Travel Office staff. And it was, of course, Patsy Thomasson who was found sitting in Vincent Foster's office on the night of his death, rifling through his drawers. All this without benefit of a White House secu-rity clearance. For reasons that have never been explained, the Secret Service refused to give Patsy Thomasson a White House security clearance until March 5, 1994.[40]

*　　　*　　　*

Nobody was more astonished by the vaulting ascent of Patsy Thomasson than Dennis Patrick, a truck driver in Florida. He was listening to the Rush Limbaugh radio show just before Christmas 1993 when suddenly her name cropped up in the midday commen-tary. "Rush made some comments about Patsy Thomasson remov-ing some documents from Vince Foster's office," he said. "Then he started talking about Dan Lasater, and I thought 'My God.'"[41]

The names brought back a flood of confused memories. Dennis went rummaging through boxes of documents at home and unearthed a wad of trading receipts from a brokerage account in his name at Lasater & Company. He had looked at them years before but the documents were hard to interpret, and anyway his life had been in such a shambles that he had somehow missed their full significance. This time he looked closer.

The trading tickets showed that "his" account had been buying bonds worth tens of millions of dollars in late 1985 and early 1986. In a single trade on July 31, 1985, Patrick & Associates bought a block of Federal Home Loan Mortgage Corporation bonds for $6,763,373. On September 18 it bought a block for $9,492,216. It was constantly buying and selling Treasury Bills in blocks of $1 million or $2 million at a time, and GNMA pools for $5 million.[42]

Dennis took the slips to a friend from church, a stockbroker, who told him that these trades were not options trades—where a small sum of money can control large amounts of stock. These were actual buys and sells, face-value transactions by a man who could write a check for $10 million. Lasater & Company had been running huge sums of money through a "straw" account in his name.

Dennis was living in hiding with his wife and two young children in Coral Gables, Florida, when I first went to see him in early 1994. A gentle man with a tense, quivering voice and tired eyes, he seemed older than 42, but then he had a good excuse for premature aging. If a Hollywood screenwriter concocted his story, it would fail the test of plausibility.

He had once been a rising star in the Appalachian coal town of Williamsburg, Kentucky. He came from a respected local family. His father had been Sheriff of Whitley County. His mother had been Circuit Court Clerk, and he stepped in to succeed her after her death. The youngest Circuit Court Clerk in the country, aged 24, he did a good job. "He had integrity," said Marlyn Arnold, chief deputy clerk. "He saw that everything was run right. It seemed like every-body loved him."

"I was asked to run for state office by the Kentucky State Republican Committee," recalled Dennis, shaking his head with melancholy regret. "My goal was to be governor. I thought that one day I might really lead the state of Kentucky."

But if Dennis had a failing, it was a willingness to go along to get along. In the summer of 1985 he was contacted by an old college friend, Steve Love, who was making a fortune trading bonds at Lasater & Company in Little Rock. Love drove up in his Lamborghini, flush and exuberant, and began to lure Dennis into Lasater's flashy, vulgar world. In July 1985 he invited Dennis to stay at one of Lasater's luxurious beachfront condominiums in Destin, on the Gulf of Mexico. Out fishing, Dennis caught a Wahu, which Lasater & Company mounted at exorbitant expense and shipped back to Kentucky.

"When I look back now I realize that I was just a clay pigeon. I was being set up from the beginning," said Dennis. "We were out on a fishing boat and Steve turned and said 'I've got the inside on this. I can make you a great deal of money, Dennis, and it won't cost you anything.'" It wasn't something that Dennis wanted to get mixed up in. His income as Circuit Court Clerk was less than $25,000. His total assets were only $60,000, including the value of his house. He was in no position to play with the big boys on the bond market. "I should have just said no, but they were being so generous I felt obligated. I told Steve to send me something so I could read up and see what I was getting into. He changed the subject."

A few days later Steve Love called up and said: "I've just earned you $20,000, but I need you to come down to Little Rock and open an account." Dennis was ecstatic. He jumped into his pickup truck and raced to Arkansas. "My God, I would have ridden rollerblades to Little Rock for $20,000 dollars." At the Capitol Hotel he was treated like royalty and given the best suite. He was escorted to the

First American Bank and $21,932 was deposited in his newly opened account.[43] The money went through Dennis's fingers like water. "I spent the lot," he said, sheepishly. "My fear was that they were going to ask for it back."

Years later Dennis was interrogated about this by FBI agents working for the Whitewater investigation. Why did he take the money? "Hell," he replied. "Hillary Clinton took a hundred thousand dollars without asking any questions, didn't she? And she's supposed to be one of the best lawyers in America." This caused considerable mirth at the Office of the Independent Counsel. Indeed, the FBI agents interviewing him had to leave the room until they could control their laughter.

After a grueling cross-examination, FBI Agent Mike Smith told Dennis that he was "a vital witness in the overall investigation of Whitewater." But Dennis was never contacted again.

Dennis's trip to Little Rock was a whirl of high-life extravagance, ending at a nightclub where Roger Clinton was playing in the band. "Good to have you aboard," said Lasater, patting Dennis on the back and promising him that the firm would make him a rich man. Lasater's senior vice president, Billy McCord, told Dennis that $20,000 was nothing. Dennis was going to make that much every week.

"I was already thinking of buying farms up in Kentucky," confessed Dennis. He was hooked. When the firm offered to send a Lear jet to London, Kentucky, to fly him to Angel Fire for an elk hunt, he accepted eagerly. He asked whether he could invite his girlfriend Karen (later his wife), who was in the little town of Paducah. The aircraft was put completely at his disposal. So he called Karen from the air phone, and the Lear jet collected her off the tarmac.

During the flight Steve Love repeatedly tried to get Dennis to sign a set of papers that would formalize his relationship as a client of Lasater & Company, and Dennis kept trying to put it off. "I began to get a queasy feeling in my stomach, even then. I don't know why," said Dennis.

Then the music stopped, as abruptly as it had begun. After the trip to Angel Fire, Dennis never heard another word from Lasater & Company.

His life began to fall apart a few weeks later. In October 1985 the ATF contacted Dennis and told him that an armed criminal by the name of Patrick Henry Talley, who had recently been granted early parole from a federal penitentiary in Oklahoma, had been apprehended in Alabama. "They told me that Talley had been 'dispatched to murder' me." Apparently Tally had been arrested after a fight in a bar. Among Talley's possessions police discovered a picture of Dennis, a hand-drawn map of his house, a picture of his Blazer jeep and its license tags, as well as $30,000 in cash and an Uzi submachine gun with a silencer. Talley was driving a motorbike with no serial numbers on it—a classic "drop bike." Though Talley confessed to the ATF that his intent was to murder Dennis Patrick, the U.S. Attorney's Office in Alabama declined to investigate the apparent contract hit and allowed Talley to plead guilty to a minor firearms violation.[44]

When Dennis met with an ATF officer, he found himself accused of high level involvement in narcotics smuggling. "You'd better start talking because those bastards are going to kill you, and we're going to hang you out to dry," warned the officer.[45]

If that was shocking, what happened next was bizarre. Sex ads with his name and address were published in magazines. "White, Bi, male seeks satisfaction, Anytime, Anywhere, with Anyone. Nothing too kinky for me to enjoy," was one that appeared in *Modern Publications*. Rolls of film with pornographic pictures were dropped off at the photo shop. Dennis's name and address were on the cover envelopes. "I wouldn't pick up the pictures, but it didn't make any difference, it started spreading like wildfire," he said. The mystery of who placed the sex ads and pictures was eventually solved—as we shall see—but not before even more harmful rumors spread.

A woman he had chosen to work in his office as a deputy clerk came to him, highly distraught, to say that she could not take the job. The minister of the First Baptist Church, Dennis's own church, had told her to stay away from him, because he was "heavily into drugs."

"That just busted my chops," said Dennis. "For a while people stick with you, but when it keeps coming they pull away, and you're all alone…. It reached a point where people would walk out of the barber shop when I came in…. And I still didn't know why it was happening."

"It was all out war. I was getting sued left, right, and center, fictitious lawsuits, draining me of every penny I had." Then his house was firebombed. On October 15, 1985, a gas grenade canister was hurled through the window, setting the curtains and walls on fire. Dennis was not there. After the ATF warned him about the attempted contract hit on his life he had been sleeping in barns, or in his jeep, always watching his back.

Terrified, he now began to take exceptional precautions. He bought a bullet-proof vest, and turned his house into an electrified fortress with live wires activated at night. Inside he had seven guns carefully placed in different spots. One was a shotgun mounted in the kitchen with a triggering mechanism attached by string to the kitchen door. He even linked a copper wire from his Chevy Blazer to an electric cable under the ground so that anybody trying to plant a detonating device in his car would be blown up in the process.

"There are a lot of animal instincts in a human being that you don't know about until something like this happens," he said. Perhaps it was animal instinct that led him back to his house on Friday, December 13, 1985. He was standing by the kitchen window getting a drink of water when an old Bonneville with Tennessee tags drove up. "I knew at once that this was it…. A man got out with a package and started walking up toward the door. The next thing I know he'd hurled a bomb at the window, but it hit the corner and exploded outside. It was a military CS gas grenade that he'd covered with candle wax and shotgun pellets."

What happened next was something straight out of a Charles Bronson movie—with this difference, it is attested to in sworn depositions before the U.S. District Court of the Eastern District of Tennessee.

The would-be assassin sprinted back to his car with Dennis, barefoot, running after him in the snow. His assailant raced off the wrong way up a blind alley, giving Dennis enough time to jump into his Blazer and go careening down I-75 in hot pursuit. As they wove through the mountains at 100 mph, dodging in and out of heavy trucks, the assailant fired a .38 Smith & Wesson out his window. Dennis rammed the assailant's truck, but the impact sent Dennis's own Blazer spinning out of control, finally bouncing back on the tarmac.

When the assassin pulled off the freeway, Dennis fired a Belgian Browning 270 deer rifle with an eight power scope at the assassin's car. "I shot his tire out, and then just started to dismantle the car shot by shot…. I blew out the windscreen, the gas tank…. I was going to make sure that this one never got away."

The Jellicoe Police arrived, followed in quick succession by the Tennessee State Police and the ATF. The assassin was arrested. He was a Texan named Danny Starr Burson. In a deposition given a year later he admitted that he had been contracted for "$20,000 plus expenses" to kill Dennis Patrick and his wife with a KG-9 machine gun.[46] He described how he bought a "drop car" under a false name, how he found a spot in some foliage where he sat at night, wearing camouflage, his face painted, and watched Dennis's house with a set of night binoculars.

"Was it your instructions at the time to kill Mr. Patrick and his wife, or to only put him under surveillance?"

"No, it was to kill 'em."

"Why didn't you do it?"

"Couldn't find him."

He admitted that he had put Dennis on a pornographic mailing list. It was one of the tricks in a harassment manual he had picked up at a gunshow. He referred in opaque terms to the organization that contracted him as a multi-million dollar outfit with military ties. As a case of conspiracy to murder that crossed state lines, the federal authorities had jurisdiction, but the ATF left it to the local authorities. Burson pleaded guilty to "wanton endangerment" and "criminal mischief." He was sentenced to five years, but was immediately released on probation. Omitted from the deposition was a crucial piece of testimony. In an examination under oath shortly after the attack he had said:

"This guy called me named Steve… and I met him in Little Rock, at a McDonald's near downtown… and he told me he wanted to harass this guy Patrick."

"Steve who? Do you know?"

"No, sir."[47]

There was one last plot to murder Dennis Patrick. A group in Texas—penetrated by an ATF informant wearing a body microphone—planned to blow up his Chevy Blazer, and if that failed to kill him, to attack his house with an "M-72 anti-tank weapon" (sic). Thanks to the informant, the group was charged with conspiracy to commit murder, and sent to prison. But the ATF investigator in charge of the case, John Simms, could not fathom why anybody would go to such lengths to eliminate a Circuit Court Clerk of modest means in Williamsburg, Kentucky. "Somebody, somewhere, was really determined to kill this guy," he said. "But I never was able to get to the bottom of it."[48]

"I think John Simms felt sorry for me," said Dennis. "He came to my house one day and sat down in the kitchen. My wife was there, six months pregnant, and he looked up and said 'Dennis, I don't know what I can do for you…. This thing is too big.'"

The local newspapers attributed the attacks to a dispute between Dennis and his business partners in a wildcat drilling venture in Kentucky. One of the conspirators from Texas, James Josey, was involved with civil litigation against Dennis over some marginal oil and gas leases.

"If you added up the whole company I was involved in it wasn't worth $25,000," said Dennis. James Josey later phoned Dennis from prison to confess that the conspiracy was much bigger than he imagined. "There are a whole lot of people who want you dead," he said, in a taped exchange. "There are a lot of things I can't disclose right now.... We're in very thin shoes." Josey intimated that he had been exploited by a powerful organization and used as a patsy. The murder attempts, he said, had nothing to do with the oil leases.[49]

Dennis had been warned long before by a disenchanted broker at Lasater & Company called Linda Nesheim that people with ties to the firm were trying to kill him. "Linda kept talking about Patsy Thomasson," recalled Dennis. "She told me that Patsy was the one in charge, that she was the one who could put an end to my whole nightmare."[50]

But at the time it didn't make much sense to him. "I couldn't figure out why Lasater would do this to me. I didn't know back then that he'd run $100 million, or $150 million, or whatever it was, through my account."

Eight years later, Dennis managed to speak to Nesheim again, if only for a few minutes. This time she was more circumspect. "They're bigger than we are, they're larger than you can imagine. I know you have a son, and I know you love him. I have a daughter, and I love her too," said Nesheim. "Just leave this alone, Dennis."[51]

Dennis limped through to the end of his term as Circuit Court Clerk, then left town with his pregnant wife, Karen, and his infant child, Robert.

"We drove, and drove, and drove, always going South, to get as far as possible from Kentucky," he said. "We ended up here in Florida, living in a motel with roaches. Here I was with a college degree, working a dump truck... but that's all I was fit for. I couldn't think, I couldn't focus, I was a burned out husk of a man.... I still am."

His friends did not know whether he was dead or alive. "How could I face them when I'd been stripped of my whole life, my name, my integrity, everything I had?" Too proud to return to Williamsburg in disgrace, he preferred to build a new identity as a working man in Coral Gables, Florida. And that is how he was living when two British reporters, Chris Wood from *The Economist* and I from *The Sunday Telegraph*, invaded his refuge in the spring of 1994.

It was only after we started writing about Dennis that the worst details came to light. *The Economist* was leaked a confidential document dated March 15, 1989, entitled "REPORT FLINTLOCK SCORPIO 000289." It profiled Dennis Patrick as "an associate of the Lamida Family of Long Island, New York.... Subject allegedly has been under suspicion of trafficking in cocaine with the Lamida Family. He has hidden all assets... under the drug cartel in Florida."[52]

The report called for an urgent investigation. "Need two operatives to proceed immediately for additional information to Cape Coral and Williamsburg, Kentucky." In a supplementary page it stated that "subject is known to carry a 9 mm UZI in his vehicle while traveling. He must be considered armed and dangerous at all times."

The documents included a printout of telephone calls from Dennis's house made between August and September 1988. According to the printout six calls were made to a place called Lehigh Acres, "a swamp with small landing and drop zones." There was a trading receipt from Lasater & Company for a Federal Home Loan Mortgage Corporation bond sale worth $9,492,216 and an asset statement, dated December 13, 1985, that was drawn up by a

Memphis accountant named Ron Moore. It listed the net worth of Patrick & Associates (the associate had been Dennis's first wife) as $12,339,850.

The FLINTLOCK SCORPIO document portrays Dennis as a wealthy drug smuggler capable of trading $9,492,216 in bonds in a single block. The question is, who was behind FLINTLOCK SCORPIO? Who had a motive to give a dump truck driver the false identity of a man with this kind of money? The report carries no government identification or letterhead. Its style and lettering look like an amateurish rendition of an FBI document. But similar charges were appearing elsewhere. Dennis was informed that his name appeared on Florida police computers as an associate of Colombian cartels.[53] Moreover, in 1989 an FBI agent in Louisville went to Williamsburg, Kentucky, to inform the Police Department that Dennis Patrick was involved in a Florida drug cartel.[54] Whoever was behind this effort had deep reach into U.S. law enforcement.

For Dennis's erstwhile "broker," Steve Love, life has had its up and downs, too. When I tracked him down in a small town in Pennsylvania, he was a different man. The Lamborghinis were gone. He, too, had been living half-underground for years, frightened that the past would catch up with him. "I find it extremely painful to think of what happened at that time," he said. "I was just a scapegoat. I was used by Lasater, and flushed away, my whole life destroyed.... I finished up sleeping on park benches."[55]

He professed remorse. "Dennis never did anything wrong, and I'm deeply sorry that I got him mixed up in it. The fellow was like a brother to me."

Love swore that he was not responsible for the monster trades of $9 million at a time in the account of Patrick & Associates. His "broker number" was on the transaction slips, he admitted, but the orders had been given by the higher-ups who ran Lasater & Company. "There was an awful lot of money going through that business, that's all I can say, and most of us didn't really know what was going on," he said.

Did Lasater & Company order his murder? I asked outright.

"They certainly didn't want anybody to blow the whistle," he replied.

*   *   *

In 1989 the Arkansas Committee, a group of left-wing students at the University of Arkansas, started investigating the alleged nexus of drug-running, money-laundering, and covert activities linked to Mena Airport. The Arkansas Committee's lead advocate, Mark Swaney, came to suspect that Lasater and others were laundering funds through the Arkansas Development and Finance Administration (ADFA), a state-controlled investment bank created by Governor Clinton in 1985 to provide "low interest finance for economic development."[56]

There was no need for Clinton to create ADFA. The state already had the Arkansas Housing Development Agency and the Arkansas Industrial Development Corporation (later made famous by a clerk named Paula Corbin Jones). But these two bodies had semi-independent boards. ADFA gave Clinton a patronage machine that answered to the Governor alone. It was a versatile instrument. As James Ring Adams reported in *The American Spectator*, it was designed with the help of a Boston consultant named Belden Daniels and allowed Clinton to tap into the huge reserves of the Arkansas Teachers Retirement System. At the same time, Clinton steered bond business to Lasater, and low interest industrial loans to the others in the Arkansas group—Seth Ward, for instance, the father-in-law of Webster Hubbell—frequently without due diligence and over the objections of the agency staff.[57] "They were giving money away like candy to the insiders," said Mark Swaney.[58]

Believing that ADFA's records would reveal the story of a national security operation run amok in his home state, Swaney tried to pry open the books. His FOIA requests were stonewalled. He fought a protracted lawsuit that eventually compelled ADFA to let him review some of the archive. It was not exactly full disclosure, but what he found was enough to confirm his suspicion that the agency was engaged in practices that were far outside the scope of a state development agency.

Funds had been flowing offshore. ADFA had done at least $250 million worth of business with the Fuji Bank of Japan. In December 1988, for instance, ADFA raised $50 million for the purpose of building and buying houses for the needy of Arkansas, but instead, ADFA wired the $50 million to the Fuji Bank, Grand Cayman Branch, account number 63119808.[59] It was a nice piece of arbitrage profiteering. ADFA raised the money at 7 percent interest with tax exempt status, and loaned the money to Fuji at an interest rate of 9.37 percent, generating a profit of about $1 million on a ten-month investment. Whether the money—all of it, plus interest—came back from Grand Cayman is anybody's guess. ADFA has not provided the wiring documents. When the bonds were remarketed in October 1989 the principal had fallen to $47,915,000.[60]

In 1987 ADFA borrowed $5.04 million from Japan's Sanwa Bank to buy stock in a Barbados company called Coral Reinsurance.[61] With 84 of the 1,000 shares issued, ADFA was in fact the biggest single shareholder. The activities of Coral Reinsurance triggered an investigation by the Delaware Insurance Department in 1992, which cause panic at ADFA.[62] Among the documents obtained by Mark Swaney were a series of memos by Bob Nash, who had taken over as director of ADFA (he is now White House chief of personnel). "Why are they asking about this??!!" scribbled Nash. "Why no other states, only private people? Who was the mover and shaker on this?... CALL ME."

Swaney believes that ADFA was created by Clinton as an instrument for Dan Lasater. What we know is that Lasater wrote at least eight letters to Bill Clinton recommending people for the board of

ADFA. Most of them were appointed. The letter and telephone traffic between Lasater and the Governor's Mansion suggest that ADFA was essentially answering to his instructions.[63]

In 1984 and 1985 there was an explosion of housing bond issues. They spiked to $300 million a year, way above their usual level of between $50 and $100 million. It is exceedingly hard to find an actual bricks-and-mortar house built with all this money. As an experiment, I tried auditing ADFA's $175 million housing issue from July 1985, but the money is impossible to trace.[64] "It just disappears on you, it goes into night and fog," said Mark Swaney.

The finance director, Bill Wilson, admitted to me that ADFA "had trouble getting enough house buyers."[65] If that was the case, why raise the money in the first place? It was a confession that the purpose of the bond issue was to generate commissions—or soak up money. Wilson was soft-spoken and charming when I paid a visit, but one of his aides destroyed the effect by switching on a tape-recorder as soon as we started chatting about the exploits of Dan Lasater.[66]

Lasater & Company was deeply involved in the demise of thrifts in Illinois. One of them, First American Savings and Loan of Oak Brook, Illinois, fired back with a lawsuit against the firm in October 1985, alleging that Lasater had transferred "unprofitable investments from his personal account to the account of the Plaintiff" after trading was closed.[67] The suit was taken over by the government's Federal Savings and Loan Insurance Corporation in April 1986, after First American was seized by regulators. It hired the Rose Law Firm to handle the case. The attorneys were Hillary Clinton and Vincent Foster. They settled for a modest $200,000 in a sealed agreement that drew a veil over the reasons for the collapse of the S&L. *The Chicago Tribune* ran a blistering series on Hillary Clinton's role. It accused her of a "glaring conflict of interest" for negotiating "a secret, out-of-court settlement" that ended a suit "against a family friend and an influential benefactor of her husband."

Patsy Thomasson handled the case for Lasater, who was by then in prison. She was more than just an executive vice-president. She was also a "financial and operations principal" of the brokerage firm, with direct liability for criminal misuse of client accounts. According to the Arkansas Securities Commission, she held the key 24, 27, and 53 series brokerage licenses (as well as a Masters in Economics from the University of Missouri), making her one of the most highly qualified broking principals in the country. "She's as smart as a whip with these licenses, a very rare find," said a spokesman for the National Association of Securities Dealers. "But she was sitting in front of a howitzer. If any of the brokers had got in trouble, she would have been responsible."

She must have been fully cognizant of the transactions in the account of Patrick & Associates, if not involved herself. Her role was certainly something that seemed to interest the Republicans in the early summer of 1994. After Dennis Patrick went public with his amazing story, he was summoned to Washington and ushered from one office to another on Capitol Hill. Senator D'Amato (R-N.Y.), for one, was in high dudgeon. "This man should be sworn in, he should be deposed. We should have a right and the people should have a right to hear his testimony, and to judge," he thundered on the floor of the Senate. "There are substantial documents to show tens and tens and tens of millions of dollars being funneled through this fellow's account, a person who has absolutely no wealth, and the question is how? And the question is why?"

But it was all bluster. "D'Amato's office never called me. When he got into the majority he didn't do anything about it," said Dennis. A year and a half later Dan Lasater was called to testify before the Whitewater Committee. He was not asked a single question about the trading in the Patrick account. (D'Amato told *The Wall Street Journal* that it was outside the scope of his investigation.) "I think all these investigations of Clinton are red herrings, just trying to divert attention from what really went on," said Dennis in disgust.

"One day I want to go back to the mountains and woods of Kentucky and go squirrel hunting again like I once did. I want my kids to come back with me to a town where nobody questions my integrity," he said one evening, sitting in the garden of my house in Washington.

"When I think what these people have done to me, the living nightmare they've put me through, I don't think death could have been worse. I would never have believed that what happened to me could happen to anybody in the United States of America. I've never been a militant, but you look at the Red, White, and Blue, and you think of the renegades running everything, and it makes you wonder whether we'll have to fight to get our country back."

CHAPTER TWENTY

BARRY SEAL, AIR CONTRA, AND MENA AIRPORT

I T IS AN UNDISTINGUISHED place, tucked away in the remote Ouachita Mountains of western Arkansas. The architecture is plain, and the food even plainer. But the town of Mena boasts a regional airport with a cluster of first-class retrofitting stations for small and medium-sized aircraft. This is how it became the site of one of the most enduring conspiracy theories of the late twentieth century.

The Mena scandal has been running for ten years now, kept alive by an accretion of new evidence. There is nothing complicated about it. The core allegation is that the airport was used to transport weapons to the Nicaraguan Contras in the early phase of U.S. intervention in Central America.

In late 1983 and early 1984 this may have been perfectly legal, but it crossed into the grey zone once Congress passed the second Boland Amendment restricting the Contra support activities of the CIA and the Defense Department. It is no secret, of course, that the Reagan administration was carrying out a covert operation against Nicaragua in defiance of the will of Congress. But Mena went beyond anything that was revealed by the various noisy investigations into the Iran-Contra affair.

What makes it so fascinating today is evidence that the CIA's base of operations was in Arkansas, and that Governor Bill Clinton was actively involved. The idea that an outwardly liberal and progressive Democrat like Bill Clinton was secretly assisting Oliver North's crusade against the *Revolucion Sandinista* is so shocking that the American press has dismissed it out of hand. But it is precisely because Mena turns the world upside down that it matters so much. If true, it validates an inchoate suspicion felt by many Americans that things are not what they seem. It suggests that the political rhetoric of the two parties in Washington is mere window dressing, while the real decisions are made in secret collusion without democratic accountability. To examine Mena is to examine the institutional condition of the United States. As for the president, it exposes him as a remarkable counterfeit, willing to betray his liberal principles for self-advancement.

It was the political Left that first became exercised about Mena. They were alerted when a Fairchild C-123 military transport was shot down in Nicaragua on October 5, 1986. The plane had been used earlier by cocaine smuggler Berriman Adler Seal, who based his fleet of aircraft at Mena. Arkansas Congressman Bill Alexander, the Democratic Deputy Whip in the House, made it his lonely crusade in the late 1980s to find out whether drug smuggling had somehow become intertwined with rogue operations by the CIA at Mena. The left-wing press, *The Nation* and *The Village Voice*, doggedly pursued the story, led by an Irish radical named Alexander Cockburn. He passed the baton to two liberal authors, Roger Morris, author of the Clinton biography *Partners in Power*, and Sally Denton. They wrote a long exposé called the "Crimes of Mena" for the "Outlook" section of *The Washington Post* in 1994, only to see it spiked at the last moment.[1]

Until now, no one has provided documentary evidence that Barry Seal's Mena-based air fleet was part of the "Air Contra" supply operation, or that Seal was actually running guns to Nicaragua under the cover of drug smuggling. With due acknowledgment to my colleagues on the Left, I beg to offer the elusive proof.

*   *   *

For Deborah Seal it has been a strange experience to see her late husband transformed into a figure of colossal dimensions, a man who single-handedly defeated Sandinismo in Nicaragua while supplying most of America's cocaine needs in his spare time.[2]

Deborah was a ravishing country girl working the cash register at a little restaurant outside Baton Rouge when she met Barry Seal in 1972. She was twenty. He was a great laughing bear of a man, a 747 pilot who knew the world and offered to take her flying. By then, he was already in trouble. In 1972 he had been caught trying to smuggle plastic explosives to Cuba in a DC-3, and had lost his job with TWA. The smuggling charges against him were eventually thrown out by the judge on technical grounds, an outcome that led congressional investigators to suspect that he was involved in "national security" activities even then.[3] He tried his hand at a variety of small businesses, but by 1977 was smuggling again.

He cut quite a figure in the narco-culture of the Deep South, always back-slapping in his jocular way, always armed with a sack of $50 in quarters to use at public telephones.[4] "I really didn't know what was happening at first," said Debbie Seal. "He'd be traveling, you know, and I was at home with the babies. We had a nice house, but nothing special."

Then it started becoming obvious. He was charged with cocaine trafficking in Honduras. It took him nine months to get out of prison. "Barry had bribed the government to get out, but then there was an election in the middle of it, and he had to pay off a whole new set of officials," she said. In the meantime, he made himself comfortable. "He built himself an air-conditioned house inside the prison with a movie screen and a projector, and the jailer sent these couriers out to fetch his meals from the best restaurants." Debbie would fly down every weekend from New Orleans. The staff would treat her like royalty, throwing her a birthday party, making little gifts. "They liked Barry. He raised the standard of living of everybody in that prison."

At times Barry would make cryptic comments about his work for "the Company" without telling her outright whether he had ever worked for the CIA. He would spin yarns about the Bay of Pigs, and talk of his time in Special Forces, yet his discharge papers list him as an E-2 Private with parachute training in the Louisiana National Guard. "I always had the sense that he was working for the government," his widow says, "but I don't have anything on paper to prove it... and I don't suppose I ever will."

In June 1984 Barry flew his family—on his private Lear jet—to the Wright-Patterson Air Force Base in Ohio. Debbie took the children swimming every day while Barry inspected aircraft and schmoozed with the military. He was hobnobbing with some general, which impressed her at the time. She does not remember much about visits to the base, except for seeing a big military cargo plane with a ramp at the back that Barry seemed to be interested in.[5]

By late 1981 Barry Seal had made direct contact with the Colombian cocaine cartels. Over the next three years his fleet of aircraft would become the dominant smuggling conduit for the Medellin Cartel, which reportedly controlled 75 percent of all the cocaine exported from Colombia. The Colombians learned to respect him. They were losing loads of cocaine at a fearful rate as the Reagan administration cranked up its war on drugs in the Caribbean. Seal knew how to get through the defenses. He had never lost a single shipment for the Cartel.[6]

He needed a sophisticated base of operations, far enough inland to evade the stringent patrolling of the coastal states. He chose Mena. "We had gotten so high-tech at that time. Rather than use barnyard mechanics, hiding in the back of hangars... [we needed] a

professional shop. That whole airfield is one of the most professional aviation retrofit places in the country, and that's why we went
up there," explained Billy Bottoms, a pilot in the organization.[7]

Seal took over a ragged outfit called Rich Mountain Aviation and
turned it into a command center with two hangars large enough to
hide his aircraft. His fleet had secret fuel "bladders" installed in the
floor of the aircraft to extend their flight range. The work was done
so professionally that inspectors from the DEA and U.S. Customs
invariably failed to detect it. Trap doors were fitted so that he could
drop duffel bags of cocaine in mid-flight before landing empty. The
police never knew where to look because he did not decide where to
make the drop until the last moment, using his state-of-the art gear
to give immediate "Loran" coordinates to his helicopter crews.[8]

"I made it a rule to keep my smuggling aircraft out of sight at all
times and fly through U.S. airspace only at night," Seal later
explained to the President's commission on organized crime.[9] He
liked to keep two models of each aircraft.[10] It was a trick that would
fool almost everybody who tried to investigate him. He had identical orange-striped Chieftain Navahos with Panther conversions,
N7409L and N62856; two Piper Senecas, N80482 and N80492;[11]
and most significantly two identical Fairchild C-123 twin engine
military transports, restricted aircraft that are officially designated
"weapons of war." Sometimes he would fly planes in formation—
one aircraft following in the radar shadow of the other—before having them separate for landing. His equipment was the envy of the
DEA. "All of his aircraft were equipped with the most expensive
cryptic radio communications we have ever seen," said DEA Agent
Ernest Jacobsen.[12]

The business was run like a covert operation, each component
insulated from the other. The contractors at Rich Mountain
Aviation did not fraternize with the pilots, and Barry Seal's other
business—money laundering—was done in faraway places: mostly
in the Cayman Islands, Panama, and Honduras.[13] Seal's pilots

operated under anonymous code numbers. Billy Earle, Jr., for instance, was assigned number 49. His father, Billy Earle, Sr., was number 33.[14] It ensured secrecy. Only Seal himself knew how all the pieces fit together, which is why journalists have found it so difficult to reconstruct.

"I don't believe there's any paramilitary group better equipped than my former associates," Seal told the President's commission. "The narcotics cartel I associated with was as professional as any Fortune 500 company."[15] Revealing some of his tricks—but not the best ones—to an open-jawed gathering of Pentagon top brass and federal officials, he explained that he "used pocket-sized digital encryption devices to send coded telephone messages; I also fitted my smuggling aircraft with Loran-C radar altimeters, beacon inter-rogating digital radar, communication scramblers..." and on it went. He said that he had made "about one hundred smuggling flights without ever being intercepted by U.S. interdiction authorities. His average load was 300 kilograms, with a top smuggling rate of $5,000 a kilo. On one flight alone he earned a transport fee of $1.5 million. Using wholesale prices, he must have smuggled anywhere from $3 billion to $5 billion worth of drugs into the United States.[16]

Putatively, Barry Seal became a "snitch" for the DEA after he was caught in "Operation Screamer," conspiring to smuggle quaaludes into Florida. Facing the likelihood of a long prison sentence—the federal judge in Florida called him a "heinous criminal"—he made overtures to the Florida office of the DEA. When that failed he went over their heads to Washington. He was helped out by his lawyer, the ubiquitous Richard Ben-Veniste, who later happened to be the chief counsel for the Democrats in the Senate Whitewater investi-gation. "I did my part by launching him into the arms of Vice President Bush, who embraced him as an undercover operative," Ben-Veniste later told *The Wall Street Journal*.

The DEA jumped to attention. Instructions came down to the Miami office from DEA headquarters in April 1984 to "work him."

Agent Ernest Jacobsen volunteered to take the assignment. He was known for his skill at cracking the hard nuts. "I knew if we could work a deal out, Barry Seal would be one of the best informants DEA ever had," he said. "I mean, every major trafficker in the world was talking to this guy."[17]

Seal immediately offered to help break the Medellin Cartel. He was working on a shipment of 3,000 kilos of cocaine. If he could pull off a sting, it could be the biggest cocaine seizure in history. But it was not easy work. Seal flew to Colombia to meet with the mercurial Carlos Lehder. Lehder had a machine-gun–waving tantrum at the airstrip and forced Seal to take off with too much cargo on a muddy strip. The "Lode Star" Howard 350 crashed. Mr. Lehder's Indian peons salvaged the merchandise. The Lode Star was burned and buried.

Seal survived. The Colombians found him a smaller Cessna Titan 404. It was not equipped to reach the U.S. without stopping, so Lehder told Seal to refuel at a 6,000-foot military landing strip used by the Cartel in Nicaragua, a country that was then governed by the Sandinista Front. Seal did as he was told, arriving on June 3, 1984. But nobody told him there was a flight curfew after 6:00 PM in Nicaragua. His left engine was shot out by Sandinista anti-aircraft fire. The plane made it to the Sandino International Airport in Managua, where Seal suffered his second crash landing in less than a week. He was promptly escorted to a Nicaraguan prison. The Cartel got him out the next morning. For the next three days he found himself a guest of the Colombians at the former mansion of Anastasio Somoza, the fallen dictator. They seemed to have the run of the place. It was there that he managed to snap pictures of the most wanted drug trafficker in the world: Pablo Escobar. "This guy had guts," said Seal's DEA handler. "This guy had more guts than you could know. He took pictures of everything, something I wouldn't have done."[18]

There was consternation in Washington when the pictures arrived. Pablo Escobar in Managua? Hobnobbing with the Sandinistas in Somoza's mansion? If it could be established that the Sandinista security forces were colluding with the Medellin Cartel, it would be a propaganda coup of the first order. Needless to say, it would also be a stick in the eye for the Democrats in Congress, who were mounting a campaign to cut off aid to the Contra rebels.

Meanwhile, Barry Seal still had to fetch Carlos Lehder's ill-fated load of cocaine. Seal told the DEA that he needed a big military transport aircraft. The Cartel were asking him to ferry 18,000-pound loads of coca paste once a week from Peru to three processing labs in Nicaragua, and from there to a 40,000-acre ranch in the Yucatan Peninsula of Mexico. I find this story impossible to believe. There is no reason to process coca paste in Nicaragua. It is far too bulky to transport long distances. The processing phase is carried out in the upper Amazon, close to coca fields in the Ceja de Selva foothills of the Bolivian and Peruvian Andes.

I visited that area with an American colleague in the mid-1980s and reached a cocaine processing settlement along the Rio Apurimac, where we were detained at gunpoint and interrogated. I was able to allay suspicions that we worked for the U.S. DEA by showing a British passport. Before letting us go they laughingly noted that there was nothing to stop them having us drowned in the Apurimac. Two gringos less in the world, who would give a damn? All in jest, mind you. We were loaded onto a motorized canoe loaded with coca. The smugglers nonchalantly picked up a unit of the Peruvian anti-drug police on the way and gave them a ride down to the next settlement. The troops actually sat on the coca sacks. I did not get the impression that the Cartel was suffering serious constraints in Amazonian Peru.

Be that as it may, Barry Seal supposedly convinced the DEA that he needed a Fairchild C-123K ex-military transport to maintain his relationship with the Medellin Cartel. He immediately found one for sale in a magazine called *Trader Plane*—as we shall see, this was a "cover story." The plane had already been activated by the Defense Department a year earlier. According to the DEA this C-123K, nicknamed the "Fat Lady," was sent off to Rickenbacker Air Force Base in Ohio[19] where a Pentagon team of 20 to 30 men worked round the clock for a week putting in new "vertical fins," long range tanks, and such like. Then the CIA took over. It fitted cameras covering the cargo ramp at the back of the aircraft. The CIA also installed a satellite tracking device.[20]

Seal and two crew flew directly from Homestead Air Force Base in Florida to the Cartel landing strip in Nicaragua. Pablo Escobar was waiting. A team of men identified as members of the Sandinista Interior Ministry were on hand to load the cocaine and fill the 20,000 gallon fuel tank, a bucket at a time, with Soviet aviation fuel.[21] But the CIA's cameras were not working properly. The remote control triggering device strapped on Seal's leg failed, so he had to reach up and start the cameras manually. "The cameras were a joke," said Ernest Jacobsen. "You can hear the motor that is supposed to be silent zinging inside the airplane…. Here you've got the Sandinistas with machine guns all around you and you've got a camera going off." It was a close run thing, but Seal managed to cover the noise by switching on some generators. He returned safely on June 25, 1984, with pictures that purported to show that the Medellin Cartel had a protected base of operations in Nicaragua.[22]

The White House was ecstatic. Lt. Col. Oliver North called a meeting at his office in the Old Executive Building. There was a congressional vote on Contra aid coming up. North wanted to go public with the DEA's information.[23] But the DEA was horrified, saying that to go public now would be to risk the biggest sting in the history of U.S. drug enforcement.

Word of Seal's spectacular sting leaked to *The Washington Times*. Showing great restraint, the newspaper agreed to delay publication for two weeks. Seal set off on the second leg of his kamikaze mission after having loaded the "Fat Lady" with a Cartel "wish list" of Trix breakfast cereal, water skis, bicycles, outboard motors, VCRs, pantyhose, and other goodies that were hard to come by in the arid supermarkets of *Nicaragua Libre*. He also had $1.5 million in cash to deliver to the Cartel from their American buyers. The DEA told Seal to deliver the money as he normally would. Oliver North, however, suggested that the cash be slipped to the Contras instead, an indication that he was quite willing to use drug profits to fund the Contra movement.[24]

While Seal was en route to Managua, General Paul Gorman, Commander of U.S. forces in Latin America, told an excited crowd at the San Salvador Chamber of Commerce that he "now had firm proof that the Sandinistas were actively and recently involved in drug trafficking, and the world would soon be given proof."[25] It was a good thing the Colombians weren't reading *El Diario de Hoy* in San Salvador the next day. By the time the Colombians found out, Seal had escaped. The DEA sting was cut short, but it was already enough to indict Pablo Escobar, Carlos Lehder, and Jorge Ochoa, the leadership roster of the "untouchable" Medellin Cartel.

This then is the "authorized" version of Seal's exploits for the U.S. government. In reality it is only half the story. Crucial details have been distorted or fabricated to disguise the second operation that Seal was conducting in utmost secrecy for the White House. What I have discovered is that Seal had a second C-123K. The serial number was 54-674. (The serial number of its sister ship, the "Fat Lady," was 54-679, tail number N4410F.) The second plane first appears in the records of Rich Mountain Aviation on December 26, 1983, long before Seal was contracted to work for the DEA. The first entry is a work order by mechanic Cecil Rice for a propeller. The C-123 was undergoing constant work. In March 1984 Rich Mountain Aviation billed Barry Seal $35,000 for work on the aircraft. In July 1984 the bill was $138,067 for total labor, parts, and gas.

Altogether this C-123 appears 15 times in the service log books of Cecil Rice after December 1983. The second plane flew only at night, and was kept hidden inside a hangar that was strictly off limits to normal employees of the company.

For two years it flew without being registered, a phantom ship with no legal tail number. According to the microfiche records at the Aircraft Owners and Pilots Association in Oklahoma City, it first appeared in July 1986 when Corporate Air Service put in a request for a tail number. This was the company that provided the air crews for the Contra resupply operation of Oliver North and General Richard Secord, known as "the Enterprise." It was managed by William Cooper, who was later killed when the "Fat Lady" was shot down by the Sandinistas.[26] Registering the aircraft was a careless slip. The motive, clearly, was to provide the aircraft with proper documentation—and a tail number—so that it could be sold as the Enterprise wound down in late 1986.[27]

The phantom C-123K, nicknamed "No Problema," is now owned by Joe Cadiz, a former operative in Barry Seal's Air Contra. He bought it in 1989 as a souvenir from the Cold War. His name was still etched on the tail, just as he had left it when he was working in Tegucigalpa, Honduras, providing forward maintenance for the Enterprise. The plane was supposed to be destroyed after the "Fat Lady" was shot down on October 5, 1986, and an American crewman, Eugene Hasenfus was captured. "Once Hasenfus started talking, Oliver North gave the order to get rid of all the airplanes," said Cadiz. "We didn't want to get caught with our pants down. The planes were flown to an airstrip in Honduras, where they were burned up in a ditch. They just bulldozed earth over the top."[28]

But in the mad scramble to leave Tegucigalpa the right engine of "No Problema" caught fire, so it was abandoned at the airport. For several years it sat there on a ramp in the custody of the Honduran Air Force, until Cadiz finally got it back again.

He had a special affection for C-123Ks. He had been a maintenance chief for the Fairchild transports in Vietnam, which was why he was drawn into the Air Contra operation. In the fall of 1983 a CIA contractor called Harry Doan asked him to do some maintenance work on a C-123K that he had bought that August. It was the other C-123, the "Fat Lady" (serial 54-679). The paper trail shows that the "Fat Lady" was brought out of storage by the director of the aerospace museum at Wright-Patterson Air Force Base in Ohio, Colonel Richard L. Uppstrom USAF. He sold it to a Roy L. Stafford to June 17, 1983,[29] who promptly resold it to Harry Doan, of Doan Helicopter on August 18, 1983.[30]

The "Fat Lady" was clearly being activated a year before the DEA sting in Nicaragua. Cadiz recalls that Seal came to view the plane in November 1983, although he says the chronology is hazy a decade later. In January 1984, just after the New Year holiday, Cadiz was invited to a dinner with Seal at Harry Doan's house. "Seal wanted to know everything about the aircraft: how much it would carry, how far it would go…. He said it was a clandestine operation and that he was working for the "State Department," but I figured that was just code for the CIA. I'd already heard things on the grapevine. Harry filled me in on the details afterwards."

Over the early months of 1984, Seal came down to test the "Fat Lady" and learn how to fly it. He was pressing Joe Cadiz to join the operation. "He wanted me to 'go down South' as crew chief for the aircraft. I kind of knew what it was about. At first I told him 'No.'" But in mid-1984 Cadiz finally agreed to help, once he was assured that it was a legitimate covert operation. The money was good. He was paid up to $3,000 a week for stints down in Honduras in 1985 teaching the "locals" how to maintain C-123s. By then he had begun to maintain the second aircraft "No Problema," which Seal had been servicing before at Rich Mountain Aviation in Mena.

Cadiz did not like to ask too many questions about the activities of Air Contra. His job was to keep the C-123s in the air. He did not need to know anything else. But along the way he learned that Seal was shipping crates of M-16 rifles from Mena. Cadiz said they were composite weapons drawn from Defense Department stocks with special parts manufactured by a firm called Brodix in Mena. "Harry Doan showed me a couple of these M-16s he had at his house. They had no serial numbers on them, you know, so they couldn't be traced."

It was Cadiz's belief that Seal was "coerced" into bringing cocaine back into the United States in order to generate profits for the Contra operation. "I really think that the government was behind the dope, I really do. They hung Seal out to dry. It wasn't fair what they did to that man."

Seal's two C-123s looked identical from the outside, both painted in black, green, and tan camouflage. Inside they had different radio systems and instrument panels. "No Problema" was the more sophisticated of the two. After the Nicaraguan sting operation, the "Fat Lady" was parked in full view at Mena airport. It did not raise eyebrows because it was now recognized as part of a legitimate DEA operation. The plane stayed there until June 1985, and was rarely flown again. Indeed it was slowly picked to pieces to provide spare parts for "No Problema," which was kept hidden in one of Seal's hangars.

With hindsight, it is clear what Seal was doing. He was using a real DEA operation as a front to obscure an even more sensitive assignment shipping weapons. The cover was masterful. It has caused confusion ever since, sending journalists and investigators on a false trail.

It is frequently asserted that Seal could not have been working for the Contra operation because he was strictly monitored by the DEA in 1984 and 1985. After the Medellin bust Seal worked on two major stings for the DEA, a considerable feat. "Here he is on the front page of *The New York Times* and all over, and President Reagan has him on TV.... It's amazing that the guy could actually buy an aspirin... after that," quipped his handler.[31]

The DEA insists that it had Seal under tight control. To do otherwise would be an admission of negligence since Seal was on bond restrictions. But when pressed in questioning by the House Subcommittee on Crime, Ernest Jacobsen acknowledged that Seal made "a lot of trips" and control was broken for days at a time.[32]

"Were you able to be in touch with Barry when he was off on trips.... Did he call in, for example?"

"No, for the simple reason that all the phones down there are tapped.... Even when he talked on the phone to me from Louisiana, he would talk in code and talk on pay phones.... I think it was probably from being in the dope business as long as he was. But he wouldn't call us. If he did, he would just call and say, 'I'm here, I'll be a couple more days,' and that would be it."

Asked if Seal could have been moonlighting, Jacobsen replied. "I don't think there's much time that I didn't know where Barry Seal was. I'm sure on weekends he could have done what he wanted to...."

Jacobsen concedes that his supervision of Seal was far more relaxed after the Medellin sting. "It was more sporadic, you know. We would talk to him every day, but you know, he was in Louisiana and we were in Miami."

Off the record, the DEA was much more candid. Take this entry from the handwritten diary of Russell Welch, the Arkansas State Trooper trying to investigate the crimes of Mena. "On June 4, 1985, agent Steve Lowrey (DEA) informed me in strictest confidence that it was believed, within his department, that Barry Seal was flying weapons to central and south America in violation of U.S. foreign policy.... In return he is allowed to smuggle what he wanted back into the United States."

Clearly, the DEA knew that Seal was not under control. It is also an open question whether Seal's DEA handler, Ernest Jacobsen, was in fact a CIA asset, as suspected by investigators for the Mena probe of the House Banking Committee.[33]

Seal did not live long enough to become a liability to the CIA. A federal judge in Louisiana sentenced him to a halfway house in Baton Rouge on earlier drug charges, even though the Medellin Cartel had put a $1 million contract on his head.[34] He was a sitting duck.

"We were at a Waffle House. That's when I saw them standing there, neat-looking, with Spanish complexions, dressed as salesmen," said Debbie Seal. "They had the trunk up, and Barry was looking at them. They exchanged glances but he didn't show any signs of fear."

The next day, February 19, 1986, two Colombian gunmen opened fire with a Mac-10 machine gun as Seal parked his car in front of the Salvation Army Center where he was confined. They were part of a six man team of Colombians. Three of them were caught, three got away.

After Seal's murder, the IRS seized everything from Debbie Seal. They froze her checking account, and sold the house from under her feet. She fled to Boston with three young children. But the IRS pursued her. She owed $29 million in back taxes from the estate of Barry Seal, they said. She had no money. All she had was a modest annuity from a life insurance policy. The IRS tried to take that away, too. After eight years, an appeals court finally ruled in her favor, accepting that she was an innocent spouse. To this day she believes that the CIA abandoned her family, leaving her to fend off the IRS as best she could rather than admit that Barry was one of theirs.

But life moves on. When the children were old enough, she embarked on a career in nursing. A good, honest profession.

Remarriage was out of the question. "I didn't date for eight years; there was no room in my heart for another man," she said. Besides, after Barry Seal the rest were all too boring.

Her husband had already written his own epitaph for inscription on his tombstone. "A rebel adventurer the likes of whom in previous days made America great."

CHAPTER TWENTY-ONE

THE MENA TWINS

IN NOVEMBER 1996 the CIA released a terse statement admitting that the agency had conducted "a joint training operation with another federal agency at Mena Intermountain Airport." It acknowledged for the first time that the CIA had used Mena for "routine aviation related services."

The short release was thin gruel, as one would expect from a declassified summary of a report from the Inspector General's office of the CIA. It absolved the agency of any wrongdoing. No evidence had come to light of CIA involvement in "money laundering, narcotics trafficking, arms smuggling, or other illegal activities at or around Mena."

The summary contained one demonstrable evasion. It stated that while the CIA had provided "technical support" in fitting the cameras to the "Fat Lady" for the trip to Nicaragua, that was the full extent of the agency's involvement in the Seal operation. In fact, the CIA had also fitted satellite equipment.

We know, at a minimum, that the CIA had more devices than cameras attached to the plane. In closed door congressional testimony given by Seal's DEA handler, Ernest Jacobsen, the following exchange took place:

"We put a SATNAV on it," said Seal's DEA handler, Ernest Jacobsen in closed door congressional testimony that is still classified.[1]

"What does that mean?" asked Associate Counsel Paul McNulty.

"Satellite tracking device."

"Did DEA put a SATNAV on it?"

"CIA."

"Are you certain of that?"

"Yes."

The CIA report also acknowledged that Governor Clinton's "fair-haired boy," Arkansas State Trooper L. D. Brown, was under review for recruitment in 1984. This was a major vindication for R. Emmett Tyrrell, Jr., the editor of *The American Spectator*, who described the astonishing misadventures of L. D. Brown in his biography *Boy Clinton*. The tale of L. D. Brown is so central to any understanding of Bill Clinton—and the Faustian pact the young governor was willing to make to advance his ambitions—that I would like to flesh out the details by quoting directly from 190 pages of sworn testimony that Brown gave under subpoena.[2]

I first met Larry Douglass Brown at a dinner given by Tyrrell at the Cosmos club in Washington. Something of a sophisticate, wearing a light grey Ralph Lauren suit, he was quite at home in the upper echelons of capital society. Later, we adjourned to the Jockey Club, one of President Clinton's haunts. L. D. considered the Armagnac quite satisfactory, if I remember, and talked about Russian literature. He has always been an intellectual. Now studying for a doctorate in political science at the University of Leicester in England, he was once a radical activist working on an off-campus magazine at the University of Arkansas called the "Grapevine," though Brown later, to Clinton's amusement, became an admirer of President George Bush.

He was, obviously, a different caste from the hot dog and ball game types who gravitated toward the Arkansas State Police. For Governor Clinton he was a soulmate, a refreshing break from the stultifying philistinism of Arkansas state politics. When Brown was assigned to the security detail at the Governor's Mansion between 1982 and 1985 he and Clinton became close friends. So close, he now admits sheepishly, that he propositioned more than a hundred women for the governor, and enjoyed the "residuals" himself. "I was no saint."

He was close to Hillary, too. She passed him her copy of *The New York Times*, quite a *recherché* newspaper in Little Rock in the early 1980s. His fiancée and future wife, Becky McCoy, was Chelsea Clinton's babysitter. It was a tight little group. At times Hillary would talk about Vince Foster, confiding the ups and downs of that tangled affair. They were in love, Brown says, but it was an affair of the mind more than anything else. Foster was devoted. He would do anything for her. And she took advantage of that. There was no one else on earth that she would trust like Vince Foster.[3]

Brown's specialty at the State Police was undercover narcotics. He had been trained at the DEA school in Miami, learning about air smuggling, conspiracy, and such like. He was already angling for a better job at one of the elite federal agencies. So he took note when he saw an ad for employment at the CIA in *The New York Times* on April Fool's Day 1984. "I was reading it when Bill walked in.... I showed him this ad and, you know, he read spy novels and things of that nature and he said, 'L. D. I've always told you you'd make a good spy. You need to fire off a letter to them'.... I sat down either that day or very soon thereafter and actually wrote a letter to this guy."[4]

"I started receiving correspondence from the agency.... They wrote to me from the Southwest office in Dallas." He was told to take a test at the University of Arkansas. "It's an eight hour test, no books. You do a psychological part, you do a language thing... the whole nine yards." Clinton gave him advice. "He told me I would probably have to write an essay.... I wrote an essay on Beirut.... That was May 5th, 1984."

"Did you receive any other communication from the CIA?" he was asked.

"I did. They would send me a letter to call them collect."

Brown was very careful in his diary. He wrote in Cyrillic script, often using Spanish words. He would refer to the CIA as "the Company." "I got this from Bill Clinton. He was a big John LeCarré guy.... So I would put 'May 25th, call Company.'"

Clinton was very encouraging. "I would tell him what it was I got in the mail and show him, and we would talk back and forth about each step that I would go through.... I had to write another essay, so I went back to Governor Clinton. We talked, I don't know if we were in the car or at the Mansion; usually we'd talk more in the car.... At that time there was a big discussion on funding for Central American rebels and I didn't know much about it. He knew everything about it.... We decided that I would write a paper on Marxism in Central America.... The domino theory and all that."

"You say *we* decided?"

"Governor Clinton and I.... I typed up what I thought was a pretty decent essay.... He started mashing in on it and changing and putting insertions, and telling me to expound on this." Brown kept the original, covered with Clinton's annotations. He also kept all of the letters that he exchanged with the CIA.

As the process moved along, Clinton made a call to Langley. "He said he was going to make a phone call for me.... I don't know who he called within the Agency.... He told me he had made the call. Now, I didn't press it or pry, but I appreciated it."

On August 30, 1984, Brown went to the Hilton Hotel in Dallas for his first interview. A man called Dan Magruder was waiting for him. After watching the Iran-Contra hearings, Brown identified "Dan Magruder" as Donald Gregg, the National Security Adviser of

Vice President George Bush from 1982 to 1989. Gregg was a career veteran of the CIA. His last posting for the Agency was at the White House, where he was directly involved in shaping American policy toward Nicaragua as head of the Intelligence Directorate of the National Security Counsel.[5] He left the CIA in 1982 to join Vice President Bush's staff, where he continued to help coordinate Contra policy behind the scenes.

"I went up and met the guy.... He told me that he had just gotten back from South Korea, that he was an Asia specialist.... He told me he was an operations officer which is what I wanted to do from talking to Governor Clinton about what the Agency actually did."

"What did Governor Clinton tell you about the Agency?"

"First thing, you don't call them 'agents.' They have an 'operations officer'.... You'd be stationed around the world. Ostensibly you'd be working for the State Department, or whatever."[6]

The meeting went well. Brown was told to expect a call. Instead, on September 5, he received a formal nomination letter from the CIA. "Your application papers for employment with the Central Intelligence Agency have been forwarded to our Headquarters in Washington D.C.... If you receive a tentative job offer, you may expect a lengthy period of processing before a firm offer will be made."

A month later, the expected call came through at Brown's unlisted home telephone. The caller identified himself as Barry Seal. "He knew everything there was to know about me: the application, the test, the interview, that I had been to Dallas."

They arranged to meet at the Cajun's Wharf in Little Rock. "He knew me on sight. I didn't know him, so he greeted me.... Big guy." They talked about the Governor. "How's the Gov? Called him 'the Gov'.... He knew about the essay and everything I had done."

Seal explained that he "had been flying for the Agency.... He asked me if I wanted to go on a trip. Of course, I worked a crazy shift back then.... He told me we wouldn't be gone overnight." Brown reported to Clinton. "I told him I met this guy and he wasn't at all what I expected. Kind of devil-may-care. His response was: 'You can handle it, don't sweat it; you'll have fun.'"

Brown met Seal several times, either at the Cajun's Wharf or at a Chinese restaurant near the Capitol—Fu Lin's, owned by Charlie Trie who was later implicated in the 1996 fundraising scandal, trying to funnel more than 600,000 laundered dollars into the Clinton Defense Fund.

Seal told Brown they were to take a trip from Mena. "It was real early in the morning that I had to be there.... I wrote in my book 'October 23rd.' It's either the day we went, or the day he first wanted to go." By this stage, Brown was extremely cautious about the entries in his diary. The notation for October 23 is the single word "ØПEOT" in Cyrillic script, meaning "Flight." Underneath was the letter "C," Russian for "S." It was code for Barry Seal. There are no other entries for the whole week. It stands there in isolation, making it hard for Brown to reconstruct events ten years later.

The details are of some significance because a CNN reporter named John Camp—the *eminence grise* of the Mena debunkers—claims that he was on the "Fat Lady" with Barry Seal the entire day of October 23, 1984. At the time, Camp was making a documentary about Seal for WBRZ-TV in Baton Rouge. So far he has failed to produce the filming schedules to support his claim. He certainly failed to impress the House Banking Committee when they interviewed him about the matter. "Camp was so evasive; we just concluded the guy was not credible at all," said one aide.[7]

Brown was surprised when he arrived at Mena Airport. "He hadn't told me it was going to be this huge airplane. It reminded me of the C-130s in the Little Rock Air Force base, but it wasn't four engines." Seal told him to leave everything behind, even his car keys. The crew was already waiting. "There was a white guy, probably 35 years old in the copilot's seat, and two Hispanic guys, they never said anything to me at all. They had little baseball hats on, like a military kind of hat."

"We flew for an hour or something like that and landed to get some gas. I was later told it was New Orleans, but I don't know that. We took off normally, but then he told me, 'Hang on, we're going down low.' We were over water and flying pretty low. I thought it was pretty dangerous to be flying like that."

They went up over land, then plunged again. "The back of the airplane opens up, I mean opens while we're flying. I could see out, it was mountainous, like tropical, jungle kind of stuff. They run this thing out the back door—a big pallet, about four feet wide and eight feet long, covered by a tarp thing. I didn't know what was going on, but I hung onto my seat."

They turned and landed at an airport. Brown was told later that it was Tegucigalpa in Honduras. "The two Hispanic guys got off. They came back with some duffel bags, like Army duffel bags, I guess you'd call it, with a green strap."

Seal did not say much when they returned to Mena. He gave Brown a manila envelope with $2,500 in cash and said he would be in touch. "The first person I told was the governor when I went back to work. I was anxious to let him know how everything was going. He was coming out of the kitchen, and we met on the walkway there and, you know, I had a big smile on my face. He said, 'Well, are you having any fun yet?' I said, 'Yeah, but this is some scary stuff.' He said 'Oh, you can handle it,' and pats me on the back…. He knew before I even said anything. He knew."

Seal was more expansive when they met a few days later at the Cajun's Wharf. He told Brown, "That was M-16s. They're going to the Contras in Nicaragua."

In his deposition, Brown was asked: "Did you believe that the trip was part of an operation sanctioned by the U.S. government and the CIA?"

Brown answered: "Absolutely."

Half of Mena knew that the gun-running was sanctioned. Note the rather cheeky testimony of Ken Maddox, an undercover contractor for the State Police, the FBI, and the drug task force in the Mena area.[8]

Maddox: "It's common knowledge it's a federal operation down there—you know, a CIA operation. They transport guns to foreign countries, they bring dope back, you know…. I mean, it's something that's common knowledge."

Q: "Can you tell me what information you have regarding guns being shipped out of Mena?"

Maddox: "I'd just as soon not disclose it at this time."

Q: "Because of your work you're doing with the federal government, you just don't feel like you can disclose that?"

Maddox: "Correct."

Q: "Did you personally see weapons that were either loaded or being shipped out of Mena?"

Maddox: "Yes, sir, I have."

Q: "On how many occasions?"

Maddox: "Several."

Q: "What kind of plane were they being shipped out on?"

Maddox: "Two different types. One of them was a big camouflaged plane, and one of them was a big black plane."

Q: "Was it a C-123?"

Maddox: "C-123s and C-130s."

Q: "Who was responsible for shipping those weapons?"

Maddox: "Other than our federal government, bless their hearts?"

Q: "It was your understanding that it was a federal government operation."

Maddox: "Correct. Uh-huh."

Q: "Did you have any reason to believe it was a CIA operation?"

Maddox: "To my knowledge, that is what it was."

Critics have tried to impugn Brown's credibility by asserting that the Contras had already shifted from U.S.-made M-16s to Soviet block AK-47s by late 1984. They are mistaken, however. The record shows that Contra leader Adolfo Calero was still contracting for M-16 ammunition as late as May 1985.[9] In any case the Contras balked at switching wholesale to Soviet gear, as General Richard Secord recounted in his memoirs, *Honored and Betrayed*. "With each successive arms deal, we tried to work Calero closer to standardizing his weapons. I often told him 'Look Adolfo, you've got all this crap—why not stick with one weapon, say, the Russian AK-47.' He'd only reply 'No, no, we like the G3 because of this, and the M-16 because of that,' as if he were on Safari…. The whole principle of standardization seemed to escape the Contras."

The North-Secord Enterprise was only just getting off the ground in October 1984, when L. D. Brown flew with Barry Seal. Secord had arranged for a $2.3 million purchase of weapons from Communist China through a Lisbon dealer called Defex Portugal. The shipment, however, was delayed. It did not arrive until April 1985.[10] In the meantime, Defex found arms elsewhere. It delivered the first load in January 1985. But the Contras could not wait that long. Their supply lines were dangerously stretched after a rebel offensive that had penetrated deep into Nicaragua. I was covering Nicaragua during that period and traveled extensively in the conflict zones around Jinotega and Matagalpa. I can remember hearing the gunfire in the hills around the provincial capital of Esteli. For the first time since the war began, the Contras were causing real psychological and military disruption to the *Revolucion Sandinista*. Oliver North, schooled in Vietnam, had vowed that this time the United States would not abandon its ally in the field.

The CIA had already spent the $24 million cap in Contra funding allowed under the first Boland Amendment. A second version of the Amendment, banning all assistance to the Contras, was already in the works, and would come into force on October 11, 1984.[11] There was a desperate need for a bridging operation as the CIA pulled back and the North-Secord Enterprise moved in. Barry Seal was the bridge. His organization equipped the rebel forces during the critical months of late 1984.

At the time the Contras were flat broke, although the first trickle of money was coming in from the $1 million a month that Saudi Arabia was paying into a secret fund controlled by Contra leader Adolfo Calero. The pallet of guns that L. D. Brown observed being pushed out of the back of the C-123 was probably surplus inventory that the CIA had stockpiled in advance. There is no doubt that the CIA tried to do this. Page 34 of the Congressional Iran-Contra Report has a section entitled *The CIA Tries to Stockpile*. It describes how the Agency was trying to get $28 million of weapons "free-of-charge" from the Defense Department in order to stay below its cap on Contra spending. The Department of Defense balked, but not entirely. "The project was finally terminated on February 12, 1985, after the CIA had obtained, without cost, 3 surplus Cessna aircraft, 10 night vision goggles, and a Bushmaster cannon."[12] If the CIA was able to get three aircraft in this manner, it would not have been hard to obtain Vietnam-era M-16s from the surplus inventory of the National Guard.

The second flight Brown took with Seal was on or around December 24, 1984. It was the same routine. Seal told him to leave behind any rings, keys, or papers that could identify him. "In case something happens, we're on our own."

Seal explained that they were essentially carrying out a covert operation in defiance of the U.S. Congress, one that was crafted with the specific intent of hoodwinking the Democratic leadership. He told Brown that Congress "didn't want to give money to these people down there, the guns... and what we were doing was circumventing this.... I wasn't going to ask any questions. He obviously knew what he was doing."

At the airport in Honduras Barry Seal picked up two duffel bags. Back at Mena Seal opened one of the bags as they were getting into Brown's Datsun 310 hatchback. "He reaches down and he pulls out a little wrapped package like I've seen kilos of coke packaged over the years and it had a number on it, number 2. Then I kind of reacted, it was obvious to him that I was very upset. I wanted to get out of there. First thing I started doing is looking around. Who's watching us? I got pretty panicky about it and that's when he says, 'Settle down, everything is going to be alright.' I drive back to Little Rock. I'm thinking, well, this is some kind of sting that they're working, maybe they're trying to nail somebody down there who is dealing drugs. But I thought the worst, you know, is this guy making some bucks on the side? Is he dealing dope? I'm trying to settle myself down. I'm thinking, well, this is an official operation. Clinton got me into this, the Governor did, it can't be as sinister as I think it is."

But his next encounter with Clinton was far from reassuring. "When I said they were bringing back coke he throws up his hands and said, 'Oh no, that's Lasater's deal.' I wanted him to tell me, oh, that's terrible. We've got to report this. I wanted him to deny knowing anything about it or to explain it away to me. But no, it was no surprise to him. He was surprised only that I had found out about it, that Seal showed it to me. I honestly don't think he ever thought I was going to see any of that stuff."

"'That's Lasater's deal,' and it hit me then that this was not a sting. This was actually a bad thing. I didn't think that we had Lasater working undercover for us. I was mad. I said, 'I'm out of it. Stick a fork in me, I'm done.'"

In his deposition Brown was asked: "When he said 'Lasater's deal,' did you know who he was talking about?"

Brown replied: "Oh, absolutely. I had met him a lot through the Governor. He came to the Mansion several times. There are not many people that can just drive through the back gate and go in the kitchen door. We've been to his racing box at the races. We flew on his airplane. He was a fixture. I knew that he was involved in cocaine. I had been at Lasater's house one time where there was a silver platter of what I thought was cocaine and I got the Governor out of there. I said, 'We need to go. Let's get out of here.' There were a lot of people there, a lot of girls there. He had to have seen it; I mean, it was obvious."

Feeling profoundly betrayed, Brown withdrew his application to the CIA and began agitating for a transfer from the Governor's security detail. But it was not so easy to escape. Once in, always in— like the Mafia. In January 1985 he was visited at the Governor's Mansion by an emissary from the CIA, sent to placate him. The man seemed to know his way about the place. He came in through the little-known Spring Street access, and nonchalantly pulled up next to Hillary Clinton's parking spot. He was Felix Rodriguez, the legendary Cuban emigré who had tracked down Che Guevara in the mountains of Bolivia.

Rodriguez had served as a CIA officer under Donald Gregg in Vietnam. It was Gregg who brought him into the Central American operation. Working under the code name of Max Gomez, he served as an adviser on aerial counterinsurgency against the FMLN guerrillas in El Salvador.[13] At a meeting in Washington, on December 21, 1984, Oliver North recruited Rodriguez for the North-Secord Enterprise. North later received a memo discussing "FR's Project" and "those who will be put under FR's care."[14]

Clearly, L. D. Brown was a designated member of this new White House venture know as "FR's Project." Rodriguez could be immensely charming, and he succeeded in reassuring Brown that "no more monkeying around with Seal would be involved. Don't worry about Barry," he said. "We're going to take care of that." Brown's next assignment was to guard the shipments of short-stock AK-47 rifles and other weapons that were arriving in metal canisters on a boat in the Bahamas, on their way to the Contras in Central America.[15] He made three trips to Freeport in the Bahamas on a twin engine Seneca in the spring, summer, and fall of 1985.

Brown must have proved himself a reliable operative. In May 1986 Felix Rodriguez upped the ante dramatically. He assigned Brown the task of carrying out a political assassination. Barry Seal had been gunned down three months earlier, ostensibly by Colombian gunmen, but Brown suspected that Rodriguez was eliminating anyone who knew too much about Mena. Brown did not want to be on the wrong side of a house-cleaning operation by the CIA, so he accepted the mission. But first he consulted Governor Clinton. "I'm going to take care of that problem in Mexico." he told Clinton. "Oh, that's good, L. D., that's good," replied the governor.

The target was the copilot Brown had seen on Seal's C-123. Brown took an American Airlines flight to Puerto Vallarta, Mexico, on June 18, 1986. A disassembled FAL 7.62 mm rifle was waiting for him in a straw bag at the guard house of the port. On the morning of June 21, he went to the Hotel Playa Conchas Chinas and was directed to his victim by the hotel desk clerk. He looked across and saw an American in his mid-thirties, playing with his children by the fountain. He shuddered and walked out. It was the end of his adventure with the CIA, or the Enterprise, or whatever it was that he had joined. The challenge now was staying alive.

As for the prospective victim, Brown had never seen him before.

*   *   *

The prospective victim was Terry Reed, another of the pilots who had worked for *Air Contra*.

He still has the hotel receipts from the Playa Conchas Chinas. It cost 15,250 old pesos a night, a lot for Mexico. He had driven down from Arkansas with his family on the instructions of Felix Rodriguez, his contact in the Enterprise. Felix had told him be at the hotel for a rendezvous with his new "handler" on June 21, 1986.

It was another ten years before Reed learned that an assassin had been waiting for him in the lobby of the hotel. It did not surprise him. Nor did it surprise him that the gunman should prove to be an

Arkansas State Trooper and a close aide of Governor Bill Clinton. Nothing surprised Reed any longer.

Reed told his Byzantine tale in *Compromised*, an underground classic that has sold 200,000 copies. In his book, Reed alleges that Governor Clinton was a willing participant in Oliver North's clandestine crusade against the *Frente Sandinista*.

After the book came out in the spring of 1994, I flew to Kansas City with a retired U.S. intelligence officer to ascertain Reed's credibility. I listened for five hours as the officer—who was himself involved in parts procurement for *Air Contra*, and who later gave classified testimony to the Iran-Contra Committee—questioned Reed about everything from the bombing of Cambodia to the nuts and bolts of clandestine CIA activity in Arkansas. They had many friends in common. Both had dealt with a Japanese American described in *Compromised* as the CIA's station chief in Little Rock. His code name was Aki Sawahata.

"There's no question he's telling the truth. He may have mixed a few things up, but that's inadvertent," the source concluded. "Hell, I was involved in Mena, and I didn't know what was going on either."

In subsequent years, more and more of Reed's story has been corroborated. L. D. Brown provides a big piece of the jigsaw puzzle, and sworn testimony in civil litigation has flushed out more. The Commander of the State Police, Colonel Tommy Goodwin admitted that during the mid-1980s he receiving briefings on a "CIA operation at the Mena Airport. The gist of what we were getting was that they were flying arms into Central America," he said.[16]

*   *   *

Reed is one of life's wounded souls. You can sense the grief of the man. So much patriotic expectation, so much disappointment. One institution after another has let him down. He is a walking indictment of the whole American system. If it had not been for the unshakable faith of Janis, his wife of sixteen years, he probably would have cracked.

Terry came from Norman Rockwell's America: Carthage, Missouri. He served in Vietnam. One of his jobs in Air Force intelligence was selecting drop zones for C-130 transports carrying out aerial resupply in Cambodia. He was a photo-intelligence analyst for Task Force Alpha, providing backup for Air America. In 1976 he was honorably discharged as a staff sergeant, after eight years service. He went into the machine tool business, but was soon recruited by the FBI's counterintelligence division to help fight industrial espionage by the Soviet block.

One thing led to another. In February 1982 he was called to the FBI offices in Oklahoma City to meet Oliver North, who was using the alias of John Cathey. North allegedly flashed CIA credentials— "The photo, the eagle, the whole nine yards"—although he was actually a Marine lieutenant colonel working for the National Security Counsel at the Reagan White House.[17] This may sound surprising, but note this little aside in Richard Secord's memoirs: "We used fake identities. Ollie's name was 'Goode,' for which he had a set of complete CIA-furnished dummy documentation."

North recruited Reed to assist a joint CIA-FBI investigation of Toshiba Machine Tools which was selling restricted U.S. defense technology to the Soviet Union. He would drop in at Reed's office in Oklahoma City from time to time, and he was close enough to the Reeds that he visited Oklahoma City's Mercy Hospital to give Janis Reed flowers to celebrate the birth of the Reeds' first child.

Reed's secretary, Anne Ellet, remembers North's office visits well. He would sit on the corner of her desk and try out his flirtatious banter.[18] She was stunned when he resurfaced four years later as Lt. Col. Oliver North, the star of the Iran-Contra hearings.

The Arkansas State Police went to great lengths to destroy evidence that linked Terry Reed and Oliver North to each other and to the Contra operation at Mena. In a sworn deposition, Michelle

Tudor, a secretary at the intelligence unit of the state police, testified about "shredding parties" that took place in 1988.[19]

Question: "Did you see references to Oliver North and Mena?"

"Yes, sir, there was one document in particular that I do distinctly
recall. There were certain areas blacked out as classified. It was by
Oliver North."

"In respect to these records, relating to Mena, did you see the
name Terry Reed?"

"Yes, sir."

"Was that on more than one occasion?"

"Yes, sir. It was repetitious."

"Was there anything unusual about the [shredding]?"

"Yes, sir, because it was so massive…. It began to bother me later
because the more I thought about it, the less sense it made to me."

When Oliver North was assigned the task of "holding the
Contras together in body and soul" by National Security Adviser
Robert McFarlane it was natural that he would turn to Terry Reed.
The two had struck up a friendship, of sorts. It was a Vietnam thing.
What North needed was a team of operatives like Terry Reed to
form a *Freikorps*. Terry says this happened in the fall of 1983. Critics
claim that this is impossible: Oliver North did not get involved until
1984. But again, they have not studied the official record. The Iran-
Contra committee found a note dated November 7, 1983, revealing
that North was already in contact with John Hull, an American
rancher who provided the Contras with an air strip in Costa Rica. It
also discovered White House memos from November 1983 in
which North was discussing the minutiae of weapons shipments to
the Contras.[20]

Terry Reed was activated that same month. A big, gregarious
man, who turned out to be Barry Seal, arrived unannounced at the
ultra-light aircraft plant that Terry had built in Little Rock. He was
accompanied by none other than Dan Lasater, whom he described
as his "investment banker." He took Terry aside and explained that

he was part of the John Cathey/Oliver North operation. Seal arranged to meet Terry at Fu Lin's, Charlie Trie's place. It was the insider's haunt for the staff of Governor Clinton. One of Trie's close friends was Bob Nash, then economic adviser to the Governor and now chief of personnel at the White House.

Seal explained that the mission was to create a "deniable" airlift to resupply Contra forces in the field. A few weeks later Seal's first C-123K would arrive at Rich Mountain Aviation at Mena. The chronology indicates that the White House was already making plans to "go private" with *Air Contra* a year before the Second Boland Amendment actually came into force. Barry Seal was the principal subcontractor. By law, he could continue working under CIA auspices until the cut-off date on October 11, 1984, then he would have to peel away and go private. It made sense for the CIA to use Seal. The best way to disguise a clandestine airlift in Latin America—where there was widespread sympathy for the Sandinistas—was to co-opt a narcotics smuggling fleet. It was also a good way to deceive the press and the Democrats in Congress. Smugglers had excellent "cover."

Terry Reed's job was to create a remote Arkansas air base to upgrade the skills of Contra pilots and teach them techniques for aerial resupply inside Nicaragua. It was reminiscent of the training given to Cuban exiles before the Bay of Pigs, except that this was an operation in the twilight zone, evading congressional oversight.

Reed chose a spot called Nella in the Ouachita National Forest, twelve miles north of Mena.[21] There were four flight instructors. One was Emile Camp, who had accompanied Seal on the Medellin sting in Managua. He died in a plane crash in 1985. Another, code named "Nebraska," was Seal's ex-brother-in-law, Billy Bottoms.[22]

It was not long before the State Police started getting reports of paramilitary activity.

"They were conducting military training at a small airport, dirt ramp just north of Mena. I forgot the name," said the police commander, Colonel Tommy Goodwin, in a sworn deposition

"Nella?" he was asked.

"Nella, that's correct, yes."

Reed's critics say that the Nella story cannot be true because the Contras did not have an air force. But this is to misunderstand the purpose of the training. What North and Secord needed were Nicaraguan-born crews to fly the C-123 and C-7 Caribou transport aircraft into the combat zone. It became clear why this should be a top priority when the "Fat Lady" was shot down by the Sandinistas in October 1986 with three Americans on board. But it was not easy to find Contra pilots. Most of them had no skills beyond single-propeller crop dusters. The flight instructors at Nella, including Terry, taught the teams to fly twin engine Cessna 404s. Barry Seal later upgraded five of the pilots to C-123 military transports. But the instructors were never able to train enough Nicaraguans to take over the whole fleet.

If Terry Reed's role had been confined to flight training at Nella, he might not have become a liability to Governor Clinton. But Barry Seal needed his machine tool expertise to help with the clandestine production of weapons parts at a series of plants scattered around Arkansas. Most of the M-16 components were surplus inventory from National Guard stockpiles, according to Reed. They could not be traced with any precision. But the parts that were required to make the M-16 fully automatic came under much more restrictive ATF tracking controls, so it was necessary to manufacture untraceable substitutes—bolt assembly, lower receiver housing, etc.—before assembling the M-16s for shipment to the Contras. Interestingly, the Iran-Contra Committee found a document from Secord's files discussing an outfit called American Arms Project, along with plans to purchase a manufacturing plant for gun parts. It specifically mentioned building "lower receiver housing."

It was this side of the operation that drew Terry into the vortex of the conspiracy, where he would witness meetings with the Governor of Arkansas. He paints a colorful scene in the book. Oliver North, Felix Rodriguez, and Bill Clinton holed up together in an ammunition storage bunker at Camp Robinson while an envoy from the CIA reads the riot act. "We didn't plan on Arkansas becoming more difficult to deal with than most banana republics," says the man from the CIA, dripping with contempt. "Our deal with you was to launder our money. This has turned into a feeding frenzy by your 'good ole boy' sharks, and you've had a hand in it, too, Mr. Clinton."

Reed was flabbergasted by what he heard. Nobody had told him that the Governor himself was mixed up with the operation. As it happened, Clinton had gate-crashed the meeting. He had heard that the Enterprise was shutting down in Arkansas—where endemic corruption had become a security risk—and he had come demanding an assurance that the White House would take care of all the loose ends stemming from Mena. It was a foolhardy thing to do. He had now exposed himself to Reed.

Far-fetched? Yes, but as we shall see, it was Terry and Janis Reed who invested five years building a federal lawsuit to prove this happened—and much else besides—and it was the White House that prevented them having their day in court.

For years Clinton denied all knowledge of trouble at Mena. He is contradicted by a mass of sworn testimony. For example, Trooper Larry Patterson was present when Governor Clinton was told that there were "large quantities of drugs coming into the Mena airport, large quantities of money, large quantities of guns, that there was an operation training foreign nationals.... [Clinton] had very little comment to make. He was just listening to what was being said."[23]

Clinton's position evolved at a televised press conference in 1994. Blindsided with a question about Mena by Sarah McClendon, the indefatigable doyenne of the White House press corps, he said,

"The state really had nothing to do with it. We had nothing, zero, to do with it, and everybody who's ever looked into it knows that."[24]

Really?

It would be more accurate to say that every attempt to investigate Mena was shut down before it could reach any conclusion. The first, and most heroic, was a joint IRS and State Police probe into narco-money laundering by Barry Seal's associates at Rich Mountain Aviation.

"The evidence was never presented to the grand jury," said IRS investigator Bill Duncan in a deposition. "There was a cover-up."

Q: "Are you stating under oath that the investigation in and around the Mena airport, of money laundering, was covered up by the U.S. Attorney in Arkansas?"

Duncan: "It was covered up."[25]

As for the State Police investigator, Russell Welch, he is lucky to be alive after a near fatal bout of poisoning. He would later discover that the commander of the State Police was helping the other side, slipping highly sensitive information to the targets of the probe. An internal State Police memorandum reveals Colonel Goodwin allowed an employee of Rich Mountain Aviation, Rudy Furr, to spend a day at the State Capitol going through the current investigation files of Russell Welch. "He could sit down with the records and make notes from them. Colonel Goodwin had been advised of his being there and periodically checked back to see if he was still there."[26] What sickened Russell Welch most of all was that Colonel Goodwin gave the man his telephone records, putting Welch's sources and informants in grave danger.

"It was a very disappointing, humiliating experience. I've got a lot of feelings, bitterness is certainly one of them," said Welch.[27] His handwritten diaries capture his mood of despair. "I feel like I live in Russia, waiting for the secret police to pounce down. A government has gotten out of control. Men find themselves in positions of power and suddenly crimes become legal. National Security?!"[28]

Bill Clinton was eager to see Terry Reed move away from Arkansas. In April 1986 he chatted with Reed outside Juanita's restaurant in Little Rock and strongly encouraged him to take up a new venture being offered to him in Mexico. Terry agreed. A month later Trooper L. D. Brown was sent to Puerto Vallarta to carry out the assassination.

When that failed, the State Police resorted to a different method. In October 1987 Captain Raymond "Buddy" Young, the commander of the Governor's security detail, planted a false profile of Terry Reed in the federal data bank. "Buddy Young has advised that he has received information which indicates Terry Reed may be involved in Mexican and/or South American drug trafficking."[29] Young claimed that the information came from the DEA via the El Paso Intelligence Center (EPIC). It was not true.[30] In collusion with the FBI office in Hot Springs an alert was put out asserting that both Terry and Janis Reed were "armed and dangerous."[31]

In June 1988 Terry and Janis were indicted on federal wire fraud charges in U.S. federal court in Kansas. The details of this case are exceedingly complex. Suffice it to say, it was later shown that Buddy Young had fabricated the physical evidence of a crime and back-dated his police reports. After two and a half years of purgatory in the criminal justice system, the Reeds were absolved of all wrongdoing. This was something of a miracle, given that the Arkansas State Police had ignored an order by the judge to release critical documents that the defense had requested—many of them had been shredded, as Melanie Tudor testified, but not all. The irate judge accused Buddy Young of demonstrating "a reckless disregard for the truth."

Buddy Young continued to provide services for Bill Clinton. As the presidential campaign got under way he warned the troopers who had served on the security detail not to reveal secrets. "It was pretty blunt. If I wanted to keep my job, I would keep my mouth shut," said Corporal Barry Spivey, in sworn testimony.[32] "If you don't want to get fired, you need to forget what you heard."

President Clinton rewarded Buddy Young by appointing him director of the Federal Emergency Management Agency for the south central United States, a powerful position with access to most of the federal machinery of coercion. Ensconced in his offices at FEMA headquarters in Denton, Texas, he resorted to more naked threats.

"I hear you're thinking of coming forward [with Troopergate]," he told Trooper Roger Perry in the late summer of 1993.

"We're thinking about it," said Perry.

"I represent the President of the United States," warned Young. "If you and whoever do that, your reputations will be destroyed, and you will be destroyed."

The Justice Department did not distinguish itself in the case against the Reeds. On June 5, 1990, the Assistant U.S. Attorney in charge of the case, Robin Fowler, gave the game away in a memo to his boss. "For some time I was prepared to dismiss the defendant's story as too incredible for any jury to believe, and I myself gave it little serious thought. Last week, however, I learned that the defendant was involved in classified FBI operations in 1981–1982 (at least part of which involved missions in Eastern Europe). This information, at the least, gives the defendant an aura of credibility that will take further investigation to dispel."[33]

During the criminal trial Terry and Janis had flown to Washington to meet with investigators for the Kerry Committee, which was looking into drug smuggling by the Contras. They were debriefed by Kerry's counsel, Jack Blum, over a period of three days in September 1988. At first Blum seemed excited. He already knew a covert operation had been based at Mena-Nella. In 1988 he had visited the area, confiding his thoughts to IRS investigator Bill Duncan at a meeting at the Lime Tree Inn in Mena. "Jack Blum... told Russell Welch and myself that PDF (Panamanian Defense

Forces) were being trained at Nella.... The information that I received from Blum indicated to me it was sanctioned at high levels of the U.S. government."[34]

Reed's information was exactly what the Democrats were looking for. He could provide details of the conspiracy to violate the Boland Amendment and subvert the will of Congress. But Terry and Janis never heard from Blum again. The final Kerry Report was a useful document, though the authors were clearly bent on scoring partisan points. The Reagan administration was fair game; Governor Clinton was not. The report did not contain a word about weapons being shipped from Mena, or about *Air Contra* training at Nella.

Terry and Janis launched their counterattack against Buddy Young on July 5, 1991, filing a federal lawsuit that charged him with violating their civil rights and planting false evidence. Their purpose was to discover why the chief bodyguard of Governor Bill Clinton had conspired to cause them so much injury. They had no prior quarrel with the man, so why had he done it? Who was behind it? The lawsuit worked its way slowly through the court system, ignored by the press but followed avidly by a large block of the American people in the alternative media. By the end of 1996 Reed's legal team were confident that they could prove their case in court.

"We were very close to cracking this. If we had been able to go to trial, we would have forced a lot of information to the surface in the legitimate venue of a courtroom," said Michael Dowd, the lead attorney for the legal team. But it never did go to trial.

On March 8, 1996, U.S. Federal Judge George Howard, Jr., ruled that Terry Reed could not introduce any evidence related to his "participation in missions sponsored by the FBI, the CIA or any other agency of the United States government... as well as any operations conducted in Southwest Arkansas regarding the training of Nicaraguan nationals... any reference to President or Governor Bill Clinton and/or Hillary Clinton and the Mena or Nella airports. Further, any reference to Dan Lasater... any reference to a business relationship of Barry Seal and Dan Lasater... and the Arkansas Development and Finance Authority."[35]

"It was a crippling blow. It meant we couldn't get in the question of motive, which was the whole point of the case," said Dowd. "The whole thing made me physically ill.... Now I know what it is to play hardball."

CHAPTER TWENTY-TWO

PAULA JONES: PERVERSE JUSTICE

I BECAME EMBROILED IN the Paula Jones affair by accident, on a houseboat in the Arkansas River. I was visiting two grizzled veterans of the fight against the political machine: Everett Ham, a top aide to Governor Winthrop Rockefeller in the 1960s; and Gene Wirgess, a former newspaper editor who had become something of a legend thirty years ago when he was sentenced to hard labor after all else failed to silence him. It was bad back then in Arkansas, explained Wirgess, who had had his teeth knocked out, and it was not much better now.[1]

I told them that I was having no luck persuading Paula's lawyer, Danny Traylor, to give me her unlisted telephone number in California. *The Washington Post* had been given an exclusive in the hope that a big liberal newspaper would give credibility to her story. Fine in theory, I told my companions, but the chances that *The Post* would ever publish such an article were close to zero.

Everett Ham agreed. It so happened that he knew the Traylor family. He picked up the telephone and bellowed: "Danny, get your ass over here right away."

Ten minutes later, Traylor came hurrying up the gangplank onto the boat. A pudgy, amiable young man with a taste for the good life, he happily accepted Everett Ham's tumblers of whiskey. We all did, even though it was the middle of the day, and it was not long before we were saying things that perhaps should not have been said.

Danny Traylor calls himself a "yellow-dog Democrat," but he is not very political by temperament. He must have felt slighted in some way, however, for he was cursing the White House. "My great grandfather didn't take a minié ball in the forehead at Shiloh to see the country finish up like this," he said, suddenly, a little taken aback by his own flourish.[2]

He started fulminating against the feminists who had refused to give Paula the time of day. Then he let rip against *The Washington Post*. He had handed them everything on a platter. A team led by Michael Isikoff had spent weeks investigating. They knew her allegations were true, said Traylor, but there was trouble higher up at the editorial level.

"They can't find it within themselves to hurt their boy. They just don't have the backbone or the gumption to run the piece," he said. "It sure does make them look bad, when you think of the way they went after Clarence Thomas."

Then he dropped his bombshell. Paula was so disgusted with the antics of the newspaper—although she liked Isikoff, personally—that she was thinking of filing a "Tort of Outrage" lawsuit against the president. That would make the press stand up and pay attention.

"Do you think it would be piling on, what with all of Bill's other problems?" asked Traylor, grinning a little sheepishly.

Nobody had ever filed a lawsuit involving private actions against a sitting president of the United States, let alone a country girl from Lonoke, Arkansas, with an attorney who was by trade a real estate conveyancer. Traylor was the first to admit that he was hopelessly out of his depth, but he did not know where to turn for a co-counsel of national stature.

In the banter that followed, I suggested that he talk to Gerry Spence, a Wyoming lawyer with a track record of confronting abuse of power. For a few minutes, I suppose, it could be said that I had become a consultant to the embryonic legal team of Paula Jones. Traylor did in fact contact Spence afterward, sending him an outline of the complaint. But nothing came of it. I mention this because James Carville has more or less accused me of orchestrating the lawsuit, and as a result I have been fielding calls from reporters about my putative role in "instigating" the case.

As the whisky flowed, Traylor admitted that he had already made overtures to the White House, passing messages through an intermediary with ties to Clinton. I later learned that this go-between was a Little Rock businessman named George Cook. Without telling Paula Jones, Traylor had explored the possibility of a quiet settlement. ("I found out about it the day before we filed in court," she told me later, in tears. "I couldn't believe Danny had done that to me.") But the damage was done. When the story came out in the press it looked as if she had been trying to extort money from the White House.

According to Traylor, the White House had sent a message back that there was a slush fund for the skirt problem, but before making an offer they wanted to gauge the final fall-out from the Troopergate scandal that had broken in *The American Spectator* a few weeks earlier, just before Christmas 1993. To their relief, the polls showed Clinton's approval rating actually rising. In early January it topped 60 percent, reaching the highest level of the Clinton presidency. Not even the gender gap was closing.

"The public ain't biting, Danny Boy. Take your girl and go on home," said the contact.

By the end of the afternoon, I had obtained what I wanted: Paula's telephone number. It was the beginning of a conversation that would stretch over three years. I made one trip to Long Beach to see her. Otherwise it was all conducted on the telephone. Over time, she pulled back on the instructions of her lawyers, handing me over to her husband Steve. An aspiring actor, who works as a ticket agent for Northwest Airlines, he is a greatly underrated figure in the Jones saga.

Paula went through the details of the story that are now known to the world. On May 8, 1991, then 24 years old, she was working the registration desk for a conference given by the Arkansas Industrial Development Commission at the Excelsior Hotel in Little Rock. At about 2:30 PM Governor Clinton appeared in the lobby and gave her a long look. A little later, State Trooper Danny Ferguson came over to fetch her, saying the governor wanted to talk to her upstairs. He added that "she made the governor's knees knock," which should have given her pause for thought. But Paula was a vivacious extrovert who sought to please. Besides, if Clinton had taken a shine to her, perhaps he would offer her a job at the governor's office.[3]

She accompanied Trooper Ferguson in the hotel elevator and was escorted to a suite where Bill Clinton was waiting. It soon became clear that his intentions were carnal. He praised her "curves" and started to run his hand up her legs.

"His face was red, beet red. I'll never forget that look," Paula said. "I tried to move away. I thought if I started asking about his wife he'd get the message."

He didn't.

"He pulled his pants down to his knees; he had an erection, and he asked me to kiss it. Then he just stood their holding it." At this point she jumped up from the sofa and said "I'm not that kind of girl."

Paula never mentioned noticing the "distinguishing characteristic," which she now says will buttress her claims against him. The subject never came up, and I never revealed what I had learned from two other women with apparent knowledge of Clinton's middle anatomy.

I suspect that it is a distinctive mole at the base of Clinton's stomach. Sharlene Wilson mentioned it to me during an interview at the Women's Penitentiary in Tucker, Arkansas, in May 1994. She had seen it years before during those toga *soirées* at the Coachman's Inn. It was not a subject she chose to dwell on. The detail came out in passing, offered spontaneously and without comment.

I was told exactly the same thing by Sally Miller Perdue, who was working in a home for the disabled in St. Louis when we discussed it in the spring of 1994. (She later went to China, her great passion in life, and took a job teaching English.) The two women moved in different worlds. It was highly unlikely that there had been any cross-contamination of the story. Perdue was a little more specific. She noted that the mole was a half-inch wide, but otherwise the descriptions were identical.[4]

A former Miss Arkansas, Perdue says that she had a three month affair with Clinton in the fall of 1983 when she was a radio host in Little Rock. He used to drop by her place at Anderson Square to smoke a "joint" of marijuana and play old songs from the 1950s on the saxophone, while she accompanied him on her Steinway grand piano. Clinton, she remembers, liked to cavort around wearing her black nightdress. Years later, during the 1992 presidential campaign, she was promised a federal job if she remained silent about the affair. The offer was overheard by a witness, who also heard the accompanying threat that "we can't guarantee what will happen to your pretty legs" if she declined the offer.[5]

As I looked into Paula Jones's story it became obvious to me—just as it had to Michael Isikoff—that there was substance to the allegation. It was more than a case of "he-said-she-said." Pamela Blackard, who was stationed with Paula at the registration desk, had signed an affidavit describing the approach by Trooper Ferguson, and then Paula's reappearance in a state of "embarrassment, horror, grief, shame, fright, worry, and humiliation."[6] Paula told her everything in graphic detail within minutes of her return.

An hour later she recounted the tale to her best friend, Debra Ballantine. "She came over to my office at about four in the afternoon. I could tell right away by her demeanor that she was upset," Ballantine told me. "Then she said 'You're not going to believe what just happened to me, Debbie, he pulled his pants down right there.' It was out of the blue. She didn't know anything about Clinton's reputation. She had the highest regard for him."[7]

I went to visit Paula's mother, Delmar Corbin, in a house full of religious artifacts. She had been married to a Bible missionary from the "Old Nazarenes," and the family had not allowed a television in their home until Paula, the youngest of three girls, was eighteen. An overweight, other-worldly woman, Mrs. Corbin told me how Paula came to see her two days after the incident. "Paula was afraid after it happened; it was on her mind night and day, that she was going to lose her job," she said. "She's a good girl. She doesn't know how to tell a lie."[8]

The list of witnesses went on. Paula's middle sister, Lydia, told me that Paula had come to see her, "trembling," afraid that she was going to lose her job.[9] It was simply inconceivable to me that this whole story had been fabricated three years later. Yet the American media had made a collective decision to dismiss her claim as "tabloid trash" to use the phrase of Clinton's $475-an-hour power lawyer, Robert Bennett. Why didn't she report the harassment immediately, they demanded? Why did she wait three years before coming forward? The questions displayed great naiveté about the prospects for a 24-year-old secretary, working at an annual salary of $10,270 for the State of Arkansas, if she confronted the political machine.

"Who was I supposed to report it to? It was a state trooper who took me up; it was the governor of the state who did it to me; he controls every judge in the state; my boss was his best friend. Who could I trust?" she said. "Anyway, who's going to hire me again if I'm hollering sexual harassment?"

It was not until they moved to California in the summer of 1993 that they felt safe. Even so, Paula would not have come forward if it had not been for David Brock's Troopergate article in the December 1993 issue of *The American Spectator*, which set off the chain of events by suggesting, erroneously, that a woman called "Paula" had been a willing mistress of the governor.

The press continued to treat her case with derision until Stuart Taylor wrote a 27-page article in *The American Lawyer* in November 1996 asserting the merits of her case. Confronted by Taylor's body of facts, and chastened by his accusations of both ideological and class bias, the media then performed a lockstep cartwheel and started chirping in unison that her claims had some validity after all. Nothing had changed in the nature of the case. The same witnesses were telling the same story that they had told from the beginning. Their affidavits had been available for two years. All that had changed was journalistic fashion.

If *The Washington Post* had run the story, Bill Clinton would not be facing a court date on May 27, 1998, on charges of sexual harassment. Paula was adamant that Clinton be held to account for his affront, but the accounting did not require a legal stamp. It would have been enough to shame him in the public square. True, her desire for punitive retaliation was growing by the day as the White House tried to blacken her name. It drove her to fury that Clinton's surrogates could simply call her a liar and get away with it. "It's got to get out. People have got to know what he did to me," she said "What's right is right." But she was wavering during the days and weeks before she filed the lawsuit.

"Maybe I'm just not strong enough for this," she confided. "Steve wants to go all the way. It's me that's dragging my feet. Clinton's got so much power. He can manipulate people, and it really upsets me. I've had some fear for retaliation against my family and my little boy. What do you think they'll do?"

"They'll attack your reputation, but they won't hurt you," I told her. "It's far too late for anything like that."

"Look what happened to Vince Foster. I really don't know if I'd be scared for my life if I get into this."

"And Steve?"

"He's not scared of anybody. He wants to sue the crap out of Bill Clinton."

In the end *The Post* ran a diluted version of the story, but only after the impending lawsuit had propelled Paula Jones into the news headlines. By then Michael Isikoff had already been suspended for two weeks after a shouting match in the newsroom with the national editor, Fred Barbash. He later left the newspaper to join *The Post*'s sister publication *Newsweek*. "Having done the reporting, I felt to not publish the story was withholding information from the readers," he later told *The American Journalism Review*.

Clinton's lawyers came close to stopping the lawsuit with an eleventh hour offer stating that the president had "no recollection" of meeting Paula Jones in "a room" but did "not challenge her claim that we met there.... I regret any untrue assertions that may have been made about her."

It could have been the basis of a settlement. Paula's legal team agreed to delay the suit to think about it overnight. Then the White House leaked to CNN that Paula Jones had delayed filing because she knew her case was hopeless. It was the propaganda reflex, once again. Incensed, Paula filed the lawsuit the next day. James Carville responded on the airwaves with his famous quip: "Drag a hundred dollars through a trailer park and there's no telling what you'll find." It went downhill from there.

They underestimated Paula Jones. Perhaps they thought she would wither under fire, perhaps they thought they could stall until eternity. Instead they have turned her into an implacable enemy, armed with the subpoena power of legal discovery.

"May God have mercy on Bill Clinton, because Paula is not going to have any," Steve told me, when the Supreme Court upheld the ruling by 9 to 0 that the president, not being a monarch, could not claim immunity from civil suits. "After the things they've put us through for the past two years—calling Paula a trailer-park whore—he can't expect much, can he?"[10]

In a belligerent mood, Steve warned that he was going to use subpoena power to reconstruct the secret life of Bill Clinton. Every state trooper used by the governor to solicit women was going to be deposed under oath. "We're going to get names; we're going to get dates; we're going to do the job that the press wouldn't do," he said. "We're going to go after Clinton's medical records, the raw documents, not just opinions from doctors, and we're going to find out if he ever overdosed on cocaine; we're going to find out everything."

An offer to settle would not be enough any longer. When Clinton's lawyers agreed to pay $700,000 along with a fudged apology in September 1997, Paula Jones refused. Her own lawyers pressed her hard to take the money and declare victory, warning that they could not continue representing her any longer. She still refused. A full apology, or nothing, she told them. Best of all, a trial, for by now she was determined to break the president of the United States.

Two weeks earlier, on August 22, 1997, Judge Susan Webber Wright had ruled that Paula Jones had "sufficiently alleged that the then-governor's actions were based on an intent to harass because of her status as a woman," while at the same time dismissing Paula's claims for defamation.

At first blush this looked like a partial victory for the president. In fact it was a disaster. Clinton's mounting legal fees were being covered by his personal liability insurance. State Farm and the Chubb Group had already paid out more than $1.5 million, but those payments were triggered by the defamation component of the case. The underwriters are not obliged to pay costs in a sexual harassment suit because the offense is considered "intentional" rather than "negligent" behavior. State Farm withdrew after the ruling by Judge Wright, and Chubb was expected to follow.

Huge sums of money have been wasted on power lawyers when the case could have been resolved so easily at the beginning with an honest word of apology. Three and a half years later it threatens Clinton with acute humiliation, collateral revelations, and personal bankruptcy. By any accounting, the penalty is now out of all proportion to the original offense. Clinton did not assault Paula Jones. He did not use force. He certainly did not try to rape her. When she rebuffed his squalid proposition, he said: "I don't want to make you do anything you don't want to do." In the opinion of many, it is questionable whether it constituted sexual harassment in the first place.

Of all the sins committed by Bill Clinton during his ascent to power, this was surely one of the most picayune. Yet it would not surprise me if he escaped retribution for everything else he has done, only to see his life ruined by the country girl from Lonoke. Fate has a strange way of meting out justice.

AMERICA'S HOPE

I EXPECT THAT Bill Clinton will drift into café society at the end of his eight-year term, with one foot in Hollywood and another at Pebble Beach, not quite disgraced, but not exalted, either. Over time, history will exact its toll, even if he is never held to full account for his offenses. President Nixon, I think, will look better in the end.

But if Clinton eludes justice, at least it can be said that his destructive influence has been checked. The common citizens of the United States have fought battles of resistance across a wide front. They have not always prevailed, but even in defeat they have helped to expose the malice and dishonesty of his agents. Linda Ives has not achieved justice for her murdered son, but she has landed so many punches that the FBI is reeling and on the ropes. Terry Reed has not been able to prove who was behind the campaign of persecution against him, but his quixotic lawsuit brought to light the incontrovertible fact that Governor Clinton's right-hand man was sent to assassinate him. The late Glenn Wilburn did not live long enough to learn why the FBI and U.S. Justice Department are suppressing the truth in the Oklahoma bombing, but he demonstrated beyond doubt that the "OKBOMB" investigation is a sham. With time, I believe, the lawsuit that he bequeathed to the nation will reveal exactly what the Clinton administration is trying to hide.

Countless others have fought their little corner against abuse of power. The cumulative effect of all these individual acts of courage is decisive for a democracy. A lesser nation would have succumbed to Clintonism, a little at a time, from complacency and servile nature. Americans are too high spirited. They have shown that it is impossible to graft the practices of a banana republic onto their political culture. It makes me feel almost proud to witness such defiance.

The protagonists have come from all walks of life, but mostly they have been simple people. While credentialed officials looked the other way or colluded at the edges, it was the construction worker, the paramedic, the man-in-the-white-van who refused to change their testimony in the Foster case. The well-connected, privately-educated prosecutors on the staff of the Independent Counsel went along quietly with the coverup; the Hispanic son of migrant farm workers resigned on principle.

The American elite, I am afraid to say, is almost beyond redemption. Moral relativism has set in so deeply that the gilded classes have become incapable of discerning right from wrong. Everything can be explained away, especially by journalists. Life is one great moral mush—sophistry washed down with Chardonnay.

The ordinary citizens, thank goodness, still adhere to absolutes. A lie is an abomination. A vow is sacred. Injustice cannot be excused. It is they who have saved the republic from creeping degradation while their "betters" were derelict.

As I bid a fond farewell to America, I commend these words from Bill Clinton's fine speech to the Democratic Convention in Atlanta in August 1992:

"We have seen the folks in Washington turn the American ethic on its head. For too long, those who play by the rules and keep the faith have gotten the shaft. And those who cut corners and cut deals have been rewarded."

It makes you want to cry, doesn't it?

NOTES

ABOUT THE NOTES

For reasons of readability, I have limited my use of endnotes to situations in which I consider them to be absolutely essential. Therefore, for each chapter I offer a bibliographical note highlighting my main sources for that chapter. I have supplemented the bibliographic note with endnotes only when I cite official documents, such as those of the ATF, the FBI, or the Park Police; when I cite court documents or other information obtained from court proceedings; or when I have obtained information through personal interviews. In addition, I occasionally offer explanatory endnotes to the reader.

INTRODUCTION

I am indebted to Carol Moore's well-documented work, *The Davidian Massacre: Disturbing Questions About Waco Which Must Be Answered* (1995).
   1. There was an in-depth study by Failure Analysis, a firm of experts that prepared its findings for the House investigation of Waco. In the end the firm's work was never used because it had been sponsored by the NRA.

CHAPTER 1

Many have commented on how the Oklahoma bombing helped President Clinton politically, including President Clinton himself, as reported in a November 1996 Reuters News Service story.

1. *Brady* was a landmark case that set the standard for what evidence the prosecution has to provide the defense.
2. Writ of mandamus, Timothy McVeigh defense team.
3. Inspector General's report. It noted that the blast might have been an ANFO bomb but it was also consistent with a dynamite explosion. Residue of nitroglycerine was found at the crime scenes, and so was a dynamite wrapper. Yet the FBI failed "to address the possibility that the main charge consisted of dynamite."
4. Ibid. There was no science to back any of this up. The FBI labs never measured "the radius of the curvature of the fragments" so it was "virtually impossible" to know where the plastic came from.
5. Ibid.
6. For evidence about the controversy over harassment, see the Inspector General's report.

CHAPTER 2

For this chapter, I am of course particularly indebted to the crusading efforts of Glenn and Kathy Wilburn. And I must commend the gritty, heroic reporting of John "J. D." Cash and *The McCurtain Daily Gazette*. ABC's *20/20* was a valuable resource. Other sources: *The Panola* (TX) *Watchman, The Oregonian*, and CNN.

1. The Wilburns later inspected the records kept by the manager of the daycare center. No law enforcement agent had ever put a child in the crèche.
2. Patriot's Day commemorates the battles of Lexington and Concord, April 19, 1775.
3. ATF press release, May 24, 1995.
4. Joseph Hartzler court documents.
5. At the meeting, Franey had his right arm bandaged. He claimed to have been wounded in the blast. But Wilburn discovered a photograph of Franey after the blast, doing rescue work in the building. He was carrying a heavy box in his right arm. His left arm was free.
6. Author interview with Edye Smith, April 1996.
7. Author interview with Glenn Wilburn, April 1996.
8. After stonewalling for months, the Fire Department later admitted that it did get a warning. The spokesman issued a statement saying it concerned a possible sarin gas attack, similar to the deadly attack on the Tokyo subway. If so, why did the Fire Department deny that there was a warning for so long? And what happened to the dispatch tapes?
9. FBI 302 report, statement of Renée Cooper.
10. Exhibit H, petition for writ of mandamus for Timothy McVeigh, Tenth Circuit, U.S. Court of Appeals, March 25, 1997.
11. FBI 302 report, statement of Deputy Bill Grimsley.
12. Author interview with J. D. Cash, August 1997.
13. Koskoff, Koskoff & Bieder: amended claim for damage, April 17, 1997.

14. District Court of Oklahoma County, CJ-97 2661: petition for wrongful death.

CHAPTER 3

Published sources: *The Junction City Daily Union*, *The Daily Oklahoman*, *The Denver Post*, and the Associated Press. Daina Bradley's baby face description of the second man she saw occurred in trial testimony.
1. Author interview with Hoppy Heidelberg, April 1995.
2. Pre-trial hearings for Timothy McVeigh, February 18, 1997.
3. FBI 302 report, April 20, 1995.
4. McVeigh trial, May 23, 1997: cross-examination of FBI Agent Rozycki.
5. McVeigh trial, May 23, 1997: cross-examination of FBI Agent Hersley.
6. Author interview with Glenn Wilburn, February 1997.
7. FBI 302 report, statement of Vicki Beemer, April 19, 1995.
8. McVeigh trial, May 22, 1997.
9. McVeigh trial; author interview with Nancy Jean Kindle, May 1996.
10. Author interview with Tonya, June 1996. She did not want her surname revealed.
11. McVeigh trial, May 22, 1997.
12. Writ of mandamus submitted by McVeigh defense team.
13. Author interview with Hilda Sostre, June 1996.
14. Author interview with Barbara Whittenberg, June 1996.
15. Author interview with Barbara Whittenberg, May 1996.
16. Author interview with David King, May 1996.
17. Wilburn archive: tape of Kyle Hunt.
18. Wilburn archive: tape of Dave Snider.
19. McVeigh trial, May 23, 1997.
20. McVeigh trial, May 23, 1997.
21. FBI 302 report, May 3, 1995; FBI 302 report, May 21, 1995.
22. FBI 302 report, statement of Daina Bradley.
23. Author interview with Mike Vanderboegh, January 1997.

CHAPTER 4

Information on the Christian Identity religion came from *The Christian Research Journal* (Fall 1992). J. D. Cash introduced me to Elohim City.
1. FBI memo of Special Agent Sorrows, May 10, 1995.
2. Carol Howe's ATF notes.
3. Carol Howe's ATF notes.

CHAPTER 5

J. D. Cash's work for *The McCurtain Daily Gazette* established a groundwork for my research for this chapter. My research also included articles from *The*

Denver Post and a documentary presented by the Canadian Broadcast Company on October 22, 1996. Specific information about Mapco Incorporated can be found on the company's website (http://www.mapcoinc.com).

1. ATF informant agreement, CI 53270-183.
2. Tulsa police report, August 22, 1994.
3. Ibid.
4. Testimony of Carol Howe at her trial; letter from Carol Howe to her father.
5. White Aryan Resistance (hereinafter "WAR") Report #001, August 30, 1994.
6. Expert testimony of former ATF official Robert Sanders at Howe trial.
7. WAR Report #003, October 26, 1994.
8. WAR Report #002, September 26, 1994.
9. WAR Report #004, November 29, 1994; Carol Howe's handwritten notes.
10. WAR Report #005, January 1, 1995.
11. Ibid.
12. WAR Report #006, February 28, 1995.
13. Ibid.
14. ATF WAR file, Report #004, November 29, 1994.
15. Howe trial, August 1997.
16. Kathy Wilburn interviewed Howe in late August 1997. At that point Howe had withdrawn from the press, but she continued to talk to Kathy Wilburn.
17. FBI memo of Special Agent James Blanchard, April 21, 1995.
18. Criminal Alien Information, INS, January 9, 1995.
19. Trooper Safety Alert, Angela Finley of the ATF.
20. WAR Report #006, February 28, 1995.
21. ATF deactivation request #001, March 3, 1995.
22. Testimony of Carol Howe at her trial.
23. Ibid.
24. WAR Report #007, May 22, 1996.
25. FBI memo of Special Agent James Blanchard, April 21, 1995.
26. McVeigh motion for a new trial, filed July 7, 1997, p. 72.
27. McVeigh trial, May 12, 1997.
28. Mahon told me that he had met McVeigh many times, contradicting news accounts that the two men had never met.
29. McVeigh's defense team accused the FBI of malfeasance in the writ of mandamus. "We believe that this information was deliberately misspelled in order to disguise or hide it from a computer search by the defense counsel."
30. ATF memo to Dallas Field Division, April 22, 1996.
31. Under cross-examination at the Howe trial, Rickel admitted receiving the call.
32. Howe trial, July 1997.
33. Exhibit at the Howe trial.
34. Testimony of Special Agent Pete Rickel at the Howe trial.
35. Author interview with Roger Charles, former ABC assistant producer, July 1997.

CHAPTER 6

As with the other chapters on the Oklahoma bombing, *The McCurtain Daily Gazette* proved to be an invaluable resource. Other sources: ABC's *Good Morning America*, *The Denver Post*, and *The Los Angeles Times*.

1. FBI memo of Special Agent James Blanchard on Carol Howe debriefing 174A-OC-56120 JRB/csc, April 21, 1995.
2. Author interview with Andreas Strassmeir, May 1996.
3. German federal directory.
4. Author interview with Lt. Col. Vincent Petruskie, May 1996.
5. Non-Immigrant Information System Basic Display Data.
6. Author interview with Petruskie, May 1996.
7. Author interview with a confidential source from the Texas Light Infantry, July 1996.
8. Author interview with Kirk Lyons, May 1996.
9. FBI Memo of Special Agent Travis K. Sorrows, May 10, 1995.
10. Author interview with Kenny Pence, May 1996.
11. Writ of mandamus, Tenth Circuit, March 25, 1997.
12. FBI Memo, May 10, 1995.
13. Author interview with Petruskie, May 1996.
14. Author interview with Joan Millar, June 1996.
15. FBI, April 21, 1995.
16. ATF WAR investigation file, Report #004, November 29, 1994; WAR Report #005.
17. The call was made on the pre-paid card of Daryl Bridges, which the government claims was used by McVeigh. It was also used by Nichols at times, but this call originated from the Imperial Motel in Kingman, where McVeigh was staying.
18. Author interviews with Kirk Lyons and Dave Holloway, May 1996.
19. Author interview with Katina Lawson, June 1996.
20. The tape would normally have been discarded, but it was kept by pure chance because there was an incident later that night. J. D. Cash's story came out in *The McCurtain Daily Gazette*, September 26, 1996.
21. FBI memo, April 28, 1995.
22. Confidential intelligence source.

CHAPTER 7

J. D. Cash's work for *The McCurtain Daily Gazette* was an essential source for my research. Other sources: Kevin Flynn's and Gary Gerhardt's *Silent Brotherhood* (New York: Free Press, 1989) and *The Philadelphia Inquirer*.

1. The Order, "Declaration of War," December 25, 1984.
2. Bruders Schweigen Manual, Membership and Structure.
3. Author interview with Dennis Mahon, July 1997.
4. FBI Evidence Recovery Log.

5. FBI 302 report, statement of Kevin McCarthy, June 14, 1996. Special Agent Paul Henderson: "Approximately three days before the bombing McCarthy and Stedeford left the Strassmeir residence to travel to Pittsburgh, Kansas."

6. This was the story he told when Josh Friedman from *Newsday* interviewed him at Elohim. Carol Howe's notes show that it took her some time to find out his true name, and where he came from.

7. Glenn also had ABC News and *The New York Times* at work on the mission.

8. Author interview with Connie Smith, 1996.

9. Katina subsequently lost touch with Lindy Johnson. We were unable to locate her.

10. Her FBI statement does not reflect this. Either she is changing her story, or the FBI—once again—has suppressed relevant witness testimony.

11. Author interview with Joan Millar, July 1996.

12. Author interview with Andreas Strassmeir, May 1996.

13. Author interview with George Eaton, June 1996.

14. Author interview with Kathy Wilburn, July 1997.

CHAPTER 8

In September 1997 I offered Kenneth Starr the opportunity to respond to the issues which I raise in this book. I submitted a written list of questions to Mr. Starr. In response, Jackie M. Bennett, Jr., Deputy Independent Counsel, wrote a brief letter stating that "we will be unable to accommodate you with answers."

I owe a great debt to my gentle friend Hugh Sprunt, who became involved in the Foster case as a private citizen because his own grandfather had shot himself with a .38 caliber revolver. An accountant, educated at Stanford and MIT, he has done extraordinary work examining the primary documents released by the Senate Banking Committee in late January 1995. "I figured that the journalists up in Washington would be going through the books just as I was," he told me. "I kept expecting to pick up the newspaper one day and see a big exposé, but nobody was doing anything." So, American that he is, he took matters into his own hands.

The Sprunt Report—properly, the Citizen's Independent Report—is a meticulous deconstruction of the Fiske Report, showing that it distorted witness testimony in a systematic fashion. The final version was released in July 1995 and sent to every member of the Whitewater Committee, to Bill and Hillary Clinton, and to the Office of the Independent Counsel. It cost Sprunt about $5,000, which he paid out of his own pocket. I have it on good authority that the investigation of Kenneth Starr is seriously afraid of Hugh Sprunt. For that reason it is relying heavily on secret grand jury testimony to sustain its final report on the death of Foster. The transcripts will never be made available to the public, which ensures that Sprunt will not be able to check the report against witness statements.

Published sources: *The Legal Times*, *Strategic Investment*, and Reuters News Service.

1. Task list compiled by Associate White House Counsel Jane Sherburne, December 13, 1994. Provided to House Government Reform and Oversight Committee. First reported by Philip Weiss in *The New York Observer*, May 26, 1997.
2. Senate Whitewater Special Committee (henceforth "SWSC") Deposition of Webster Hubbell, July 13, 1995.
3. Report from the 1994 Senate Hearings Related to Madison Guaranty S&L and the Whitewater Development Corporation-Washington, DC Phase (henceforth "Green Books"), p. 741. Deposition of Captain Charles Hume, July 22, 1994.
4. Author interview with Luca Dalla Torre, June 1995.
5. FBI agent's handwritten notes and FBI 302 statement of William Kennedy dated May 6, 1994.

CHAPTER 9

Published sources: Ronald Kessler's *The FBI* (New York: Pocket Books, 1993), Peter Boyer's article entitled "Life After Vince," appearing in the September 11, 1995 issue of *The New Yorker*, Ellen Joan Pollock's April 4, 1994, *Wall Street Journal* piece, "Fiske Is Seen Verifying Foster Killed Himself," and the Sprunt Report.

1. Many people are already aware of the witness's identity. His name has been disclosed in a number of news articles. However, my interviews with him were conducted on the basis of strict confidentiality over the last two years, so I will abide by that agreement to protect his privacy from a wider public.
2. He was not the only witness who noticed this. Detective John Rolla said he saw "brush that had been trampled out. No other indications of struggle." That was the version in his handwritten notes of the FBI interview (notes 192). This was left out of the FBI 302, which instead stated that "there were no signs of struggle."
3. Green Books: deposition of Kevin Fornshill, July 12, 1994.
4. Ibid.
5. FBI 302 report, statement of Todd Hall, March 18, 1994.
6. FBI 302 report, statement of Todd Hall, April 27, 1994.
7. Author interview with a confidential grand jury source, January 1996.
8. Fornshill deposition.
9. Ibid.
10. Author interview with a member of the Fairfax County rescue squad, March 1995.
11. Green Books, p. 491: Senate deposition of Detective Cheryl Braun, July 23, 1994.
12. Green Books, p. 871: Senate deposition of Richard Arthur, July 14, 1994.

13. Ibid.
14. Robert Bryant, FBI special agent in charge, Washington Metropolitan Office, August 10, 1993.
15. Author interview with Alice Sessions, February 1995.
16. Author interview with Alice Sessions.
17. Green Books, p. 398: Senate deposition of Detective John Rolla, July 21, 1994.
18. Ibid.
19. Ibid.
20. Green Books, p. 2153: interview with Lisa Foster, July 29, 1993, Supplemental Criminal Incident Record.
21. Green Books, p. 2227: notes of Captain Hume, July 29, 1993.
22. Fiske Report, p. 38.
23. Author interview with Lee Bowman, April 1995.
24. Green Books, p. 1806. FBI 302 report, statement of Lee Foster Bowman, June 28, 1994
25. Ibid.
26. Green Books, p. 1633. FBI 302 report, interview with Lisa Foster, May 9, 1994.
27. The Fiske Report finessed the deception by ignoring the color of the gun. But the 1994 Senate Report 103-433 Vol. I states baldly: "Mrs. Foster examined the revolver recovered from Mr. Foster's hand... a silver-colored handgun."
28. Green Books, p. 1903. FBI Lab memo, May 9, 1994.
29. Green Books, p. 2056: The National Tracing Center of the ATF says that the gun could not be traced because it "was manufactured prior to 1945."
30. Fiske Report, p. 57: There was microscopic residue of gunpowder in the soft palate obtained from the autopsy.
31. Fiske Report, p. 44.

CHAPTER 10

In my research for this chapter I benefited from the work of Christopher Ruddy of *The Pittsburgh Tribune-Review* and from the Sprunt Report. Other sources: *Newsweek*, David Halperin's work for *The Nation*, and Ralph Nader's and Wesley J. Smith's *No Contest: Corporate Lawyers and the Perversion of Justice in America* (New York: Random House, 1996). On January 6, 1995, Lisa Howard of the Scripps-Howard News Service published one of the earliest stories reporting that Starr had concluded his investigation into Foster's death.
1. Author interview with a confidential informant in March 1995.
2. Author interview with a confidential source inside the Starr investigation (Office of the Independent Counsel, hereinafter referred to as "OIC").
3. Fiske Report, p. 44.
4. Fiske Report, p. 45.
5. Green Books, p. 63: Senate testimony of Dr. Charles Hirsch, July 29, 1994.

6. Fiske Report, Exhibit 2.
7. Ibid.
8. Author interview with a confidential source at OIC.
9. Author interview with Victor Ostrovsky, former Mossad agent.
10. Green Books, p. 425: Senate deposition of Detective John Rolla, July 21, 1994.
11. FBI 302 report, statement of Officer Franz Ferstl, May 2, 1994.
12. Green Books, p. 652: Senate deposition of Peter Simonello, July 14, 1994.
13. Green Books, p. 631: Simonello deposition.
14. Green Books, p. 658: Simonello deposition.
15. Fiske Report, Exhibit 1, p. 13.
16. Green Books, p. 2112: FBI property receipt.
17. Haut Report, July 20, 1993. Office of Chief Medical Examiner.
18. Green Books, p. 892, deposition of Richard Arthur, July 14, 1994.
19. Author interview with a confidential source at OIC.
20. FBI 302 report, statement of Corey Ashford, February 26, 1994.
21. FBI 302 report, second statement of Corey Ashford, April 27, 1994.
22. FBI 302 report, statement of Roger Harrison, March 11, 1994.
23. EMS Incident Reports list exact times of each crew.
24. Green Books, p. 891 Arthur deposition, July 14, 1994.
25. Ibid, p. 885.
26. Green books, p. 996, deposition of Sgt. George Gonzalez, July 20, 1994.
27. FBI 302 report, statement of Dr. Julian Orenstein, April 14, 1994.
28. Author interview with Orenstein, May 1995.
29. FBI Notes, p. 287, notes on interview with Orenstein.
30. FBI 302 report, statement of Detective Rolla, April 27, 1994.
31. FBI notes, p. 196.
32. The investigator, an Arkansas native, was carrying out an investigation for *The Sunday Telegraph*. Wittenberg clearly did not realize that he was being taped.
33. Green Books, p. 2128.
34. Green Books, p. 370: Autopsy report, gunshot wound chart.
35. Senate testimony of Dr. James C. Beyer, July 29, 1994.
36. Green Books, p. 138: Senate Resolution 229, June 19, 1994.
37. Author interview with Beth Burkett, September 1995.
38. Author interview with a confidential source in OIC.
39. Blackbourne worked as the deputy chief medical examiner in Washington, D.C., under Dr. James Luke, the leading pathologist in the Fiske investigation. Why did Starr choose a man from the same incestuous group?

CHAPTER 11

1. Josie and Duncan are not their real names. I have disguised their identity after Josie pleaded with me, alarmed about the consequences for their marriages. Their true names can be discovered in the archive of official docu-

ments, but only true researchers are likely to get that far. The narrative is
drawn from a mixture of their FBI statements and an interview with Josie
in September 1995.

2. Author interview with Josie, September 1995.

3. Park Police Supplemental Criminal Incident Report by Detective John
   Rolla.

4. Author interview with Josie, September 1995.

5. Fiske Report, p. 11: Exhibit 1, FBI documents.

6. Green Books, p. 67: Senate testimony of Special Agent Larry Monroe, July
   29, 1994.

7. Fiske Report, p. 35.

8. FBI 302 report, statement of Patrick Knowlton, April 15, 1994.

9. Interestingly, this contradicts the jacket being folded over the passenger
   seat, as in the Fiske report.

10. FBI 302 report, statement of Patrick Knowlton, May 11, 1994.

11. Park Police vandalism report on Knowlton.

12. Author interview with Mary McClaren of the U.S. Attorney's Office,
    October 1995.

13. The Defense Department document is reproduced in the appendix.

14. The sketch is reproduced in the appendix.

15. Park Police evidence receipt.

16. FBI 302 report, statement of Lisa Foster, May 9, 1994.

17. FBI notes, statement of William Kennedy.

18. Green Books, p. 2153: Park Police interview with Lisa Foster.

19. Fiske Report, p. 25.

20. FBI 302 report, statement of Lisa Foster, May 9, 1994.

21. Green Books, p. 50: Senate testimony of Larry Monroe, July 29, 1994.

22. Green Books, p. 2390: Park Police photographs.

23. Green Books, p. 1522: FBI 302 report, statement of Jeanne Slade, April 4,
    1994.

24. Green Books, p. 1422: EMS narrative report.

25. Author interview with Dr. Donald Haut, March 1995. This is confirmed by
    the handwritten notes of Dr. Haut's FBI interview. It says "red compact."

26. Green Books, p. 1628: FBI 302 report, statement of Franz Ferstl, May 2,
    1994.

27. Green Books, p. 393: Senate deposition of Detective John Rolla, July 21,
    1994.

28. Green Books, p. 2189: Park Police evidence control receipt.

29. Fiske Report, p. 13: Exhibit 1, FBI documents.

30. Green Books, p. 153: Park Police supplemental criminal incident report.

31. The hospital staff are adamant that Kennedy arrived before the Park Police.
    The Park Police themselves cannot get their story straight. In his FBI state-
    ment Detective Rolla said he went to the hospital "after we made a death
    notification, to recheck him." But his colleague Cheryl Braun contradicts
    this in her Senate deposition, saying they went to the morgue first, then to
    the Foster house in Georgetown.

Kennedy says that he was notified about the death at 8 PM (SWSC deposition July 11, 1995). He was negotiating with Livingstone and the Park Police on mobile telephones while the body was en route to the morgue. It appears that Kennedy set out for the hospital while the body was still en route. It arrived at 8:31, according to hospital logs.

Kennedy says that he was there for almost two hours before sorting things out. This does not square with the recollections of the hospital staff. The chronology is highly confused. The conclusion of this author is that Kennedy reached the morgue early that evening, before the Park Police.

32. Author interview with a confidential source, June 1997.
33. Green Books, p. 443: deposition of Detective John Rolla.
34. House hearings on Travelgate, p. 198.
35. Ibid. Zeliff, p. 429
36. SWSC deposition of William Kennedy, July 11, 1995. Technically the invitation came from Hillary Clinton.
37. SWSC deposition of Craig Livingstone, July 10, 1995.
38. SWSC deposition of William Kennedy, July 11, 1995.
39. FBI Notes, p. 238, statement of William Kennedy.

CHAPTER 12

Published sources: *The Washington Post* and United Press International.
1. OIC subpoena signed by John Bates.
2. The details are catalogued in Knowlton's "Witness Tampering Report."
3. *Knowlton* v. *United States*, U.S. District Court for the District of Columbia, case number 96-2467.
4. Author interview with Patrick Knowlton, October 1995.
5. Patrick had requested frequent breaks during his testimony so that he could step outside and write down the questions, giving us a record, of sorts, of the secret proceedings. Cavanaugh asked him if he had received a fax the day before. This was highly suspicious. I had sent Patrick a fax of "Rule 6" explaining that grand jury secrecy laws did not apply to the witness—only the jurors and court officers. How did they know about this? Were they monitoring his fax machine?

I complained to one of Starr's prosecutors: "I damn well hope you've got a court order for the wire-tap on Knowlton's phone."

"That's an outrageous thing to say," was the reply.
6. This is all outlined in detail in the Witness Tampering Report.
7. *Knowlton* v. *United States*.

CHAPTER 13

Published sources: *The Mertonian*, *The Albuquerque Journal*, *The American Spectator*, and Elizabeth Drew's *On the Edge: The Clinton Presidency* (New York: Simon and Schuster, 1994).
1. Green Books, p. 2527: Detective John Rolla's notebook.

2. Senate deposition of Detective Rolla, July 21, 1994.
3. Author interview with Reed Irvine, June 1995.
4. Green Books, p. 2517: Park Police evidence receipt.
5. Senate deposition of Rolla.
6. FBI 302 report, statement of Lisa Foster.
7. Green Books, p. 2551: US Secret Service.
8. Author interview with Pat Gavin, April 1995.
9. Author interview with David Watkins, January 1996.
10. Author interview with David Watkins, January 1996: He is adamant that Foster had exhibited no signs of clinical depression.
11. Green Books, p. 1421: EMS incident report.
12. FBI 302 report, statement of William Bianchi, March 17, 1994.
13. FBI handwritten notes, p. 28.
14. FBI 302 report, statement of Victoria Abbott Jacobs, March 11, 1994.
15. FBI handwritten notes, p. 28.
16. FBI 302 report, statement of William Bianchi.
17. Ibid.
18. Author interview with a confidential source, March 1995.
19. Author interview with Dr. Donald Haut, April 1995.
20. FBI 302 report, statement of Dr. Donald Haut, April 14, 1994: "Haut recalls that the USPP [United States Park Police] had an Arkansas driver's license belonging to Foster and it was known that he was employed at the White House."
21. FBI Notes, p. 251, Cheryl Braun.
22. FBI 302 report, statement of Detective John Rolla. Also, Senate deposition of Rolla.
23. FBI 302 report, statement of Richard Arthur, March 21, 1994.
24. FBI Notes, p. 252, Cheryl Braun.
25. FBI 302 report, statement of Cheryl Braun, April 28, 1994.
26. FBI notes, p. 251, Cheryl Braun.
27. The Park Police cannot keep their story straight, even on this elementary point. When I interviewed the shift commander, Pat Gavin, he inadvertently contradicted Cheryl Braun, saying that it was John Rolla who called to tell him about the discovery of the White House ID. Gavin failed to appear for Senate testimony in July 1994. No explanation given.
28. Author interview with Roger Perry, January 1995.
29. Ibid.
30. Author interview with Larry Patterson, April 1995.
31. Author interview with Lynn Davis, April 1995.
32. Affidavit of Helen Dickey.
33. SWSC deposition of Helen Dickey, February 12, 1996: comment by majority counsel Viet Dinh.
34. SWSC Archive of Documents: Letter to Robert Giuffra dated September 30, 1995.
35. SWSC Helen Dickey deposition.

36. Ibid.
37. SWSC archive: "Movements to/from Living Quarters."
38. Author interview with Senator Al D'Amato, May 1994.
39. SWSC deposition of Henry O'Neill, June 23, 1995.
40. SWSC deposition of Maggie Williams, July 7, 1995.
41. Senate testimony of Patsy Thomasson.
42. As with the peripatetic gun, so too is there a peripatetic briefcase. Several witnesses saw the briefcase in the Honda at Fort Marcy Park, but the U.S. government denies it was there.
43. The Freeh family are deeply involved in Opus Dei. Louis Freeh's brother was a "Numerary" in the Order.
44. SWSC deposition of Mack McLarty, July 6, 1995.
45. Fiske also "disappeared" the FBI 302 of Tom Castleton, an intern in the White House Counsel's Office who saw Foster leaving with his briefcase.
46. FBI notes, p. 384: statement of Bruce Lindsey.
47. Green Books, p. 1800: FBI 302 report, statement of Bruce Lindsey.
48. SWSC deposition of Linda Tripp.
49. SWSC deposition of Betsy Pond.
50. SWSC deposition of Betsy Pond.
51. SWSC deposition of Lisa Caputo, July 10, 1995.
52. SWSC deposition of Maggie Williams, July 7, 1995.
53. SWSC deposition of Betsy Pond, p. 51.
54. SWSC deposition of Tom Castleton, June 27, 1995.
55. SWSC deposition of Deborah Gorham.
56. SWSC deposition of Betsy Pond.
57. SWSC deposition of Deborah Gorham.
58. SWSC deposition of Patsy Thomasson, July 25, 1995.
59. Author interview with David Watkins, January 1996.
60. The logs misspell a number of names. In one case it wrote "Thomison," in another "Tomlinson," but there was nobody on the White House staff by these names, certainly nobody with routine access to room 015-018. It clearly refers to Thomasson. ("Nussbaum" is sometimes spelled "Naussbaum," for example.)
61. FBI 302 report, statement of Maggie Williams.

CHAPTER 14

Christopher Ruddy's tenacious reporting for *The New York Post* and *The Pittsburgh Tribune-Review* was essential to my research for this chapter. Other sources: ABC News, *The New York Daily News*, *Editor & Publisher* magazine, *The Wall Street Journal*, *The New York Times Magazine*, *The New York Observer*, and Hannah Arendt's *The Origins of Totalitarianism* (New York: Harcourt, Brace & World, 1966).

1. Newt Gingrich did in fact appoint Congressman Steve Schiff of New Mexico to investigate the death. Schiff kicked the ball into touch, saying

that he would wait to see what Kenneth Starr did. It nullified the whole purpose, which was to keep Starr honest by running a parallel probe. But by then Gingrich was fighting for his political life. The matter was quietly dropped.

2. One of the journalists was Phil Weiss from *The New York Times Magazine* and *The New York Observer*. It backfired badly when he started looking more deeply into the subject and began to write some harsh articles of his own about corruption by the Clinton machine.

3. Author interview with Chris Ruddy, May 1997.

4. The Fiske Report makes much of the presence of mica particles on Foster's shoes and clothing, but this is meaningless. Mica floats in the air and settles on leaves and vegetation. It does not indicate whether Foster walked to the spot, or was carried—only that the body was lying on foliage.

5. Author interview with a confidential source.

6. Author interview with Jim Davidson, May 1997.

7. Green Books: Senate deposition of Pete Simonello.

8. Affidavit of Reed Irvine: When shown blown-up samples of the exemplar and the suicide note Lockhart concluded that the two were incompatible.

9. Green Books, p. 2047: FBI lab report, June 13, 1994.

10. SWSC deposition of Deborah Gorham, July 31, 1995. Foster's secretary said that he did not usually rip up his notes for the burnbag. He rolled up the paper and tossed it.

11. SWSC deposition of Louis Hupp, July 14, 1995. Brett Cavanaugh from the OIC was present. He left the room to consult with Mark Touhey and was told that the witness was not to answer.

12. SWSC deposition of Pete Markland, June 28, 1995.

13. SWSC deposition of Linda Tripp.

14. SWSC deposition of Deborah Gorham, July 31, 1995.

15. SWSC archive of support documents.

16. SWSC deposition of Webb Hubbell, July 13, 1995.

17. FBI Notes, p. 281: FBI interview of Lisa Foster.

18. Green Books, p. 2665: Letter on Swidler & Berlin letterhead.

19. Author interview with Joe Farah, May 1997.

20. Green Books, p. 2187: Park Police Evidence/Property Control Receipt, July 20, 1993.

21. Green Books, p. 2191: Park Police Evidence Receipt, July 21, 1993.

22. Green Books, p. 1658: FBI 302 report, statement of Dr. Donald Haut.

CHAPTER 15

Published sources: *The New York Times, The Los Angeles Times, The American Spectator, Newsweek*, Peter Boyer's interview with Lisa Foster, published in the September 11, 1995 issue of *The New Yorker*, and James Stewart's *Blood Sport: The President and His Adversaries* (New York: Touchstone, 1996).

1. SWSC deposition of Webster Hubbell, July 13, 1995.

2. FBI 302 report, statement of Lisa Foster, April 12, 1994.
3. Park Police interview with Lisa Foster, July 29, 1993.
4. FBI 302 report, statement of William Kennedy, May 6, 1994.
5. FBI 302 report, statement of Dr. Larry Watkins, May 16, 1994. This was misrepresented in the Fiske Report.
6. FBI 302 report, statement of Lisa Foster, May 9, 1994.
7. SWSC deposition of Tom Castleton, June 27, 1995: comment by majority Counsel Michael Chertoff.
8. FBI 302 report, statement of Lisa Foster, April 12, 1994.
9. SWSC deposition of Deborah Gorham, June 23, 1995.
10. Author interview with Boyden Gray, March 1996.
11. SWSC deposition of Linda Tripp, July 11, 1995, p. 52.
12. Green Books, p. 1613: FBI 302 report, statement of William Kennedy.
13. Author interview with a confidential source.
14. SWSC deposition of Webster Hubbell, July 13, 1995.
15. FBI 302 report, statement of Lisa Foster, April 12, 1994.
16. FBI 302 report, statement of Webster Hubbell, April 13, 1994.
17. FBI 302 report, statement of Deborah Gorham, April 19, 1994.
18. Lisa Foster went through the accounts later and claimed that the credit union had made a mistake with every withdrawal. The sums were actually $35 each. This does not pass the smell test. Foster had $292 in cash in his wallet when he died.
19. FBI 302 report, statement of Marsha Scott, June 9, 1994
20. FBI 302 report, statement of Linda Tripp, April 12, 1994.
21. FBI notes of Marsha Scott, p. 353: This is subtly different.
22. SWSC ancillary documents.
23. FBI 302 report, statement of Marsha Scott, June 9, 1994.
24. FBI 302 report, statement of Marsha Scott, May 12, 1994.
25. Green Books, p. 1829: deposition of President Clinton June 12, 1994.
26. July 21, 1993. Presidential Documents 1351,1411.
27. Author interview with Luca Dalla Torre, Swiss exchange student staying at the Fosters' home.
28. Ibid.
29. FBI 302 report, statement of Bruce Lindsey, June 22, 1994.
30. Deposition of Hillary Clinton, June 12, 1994.
31. Confidential interview with a family member.
32. Park Police interview with Lisa Foster, July 29, 1993.
33. Confidential interview with a family member.
34. Fiske Report, p. 9.
35. FBI 302 report, statement of Dr. Larry Watkins, May 16, 1994.
36. FBI 302 report, statement of Deborah Gorham, April 19, 1994.
37. Fiske Report, p. 24.
38. Deposition of Detective John Rolla, July 21, 1994.
39. Park Police interview, August 22, 1993.
40. Author interview with David Watkins, January 30, 1996.

41. FBI 302 report, statement of Webster Hubbell, April 13, 1994.
42. FBI 302 report, statement of James Lyons, May 12, 1994.
43. FBI 302 report, statement of Nancy Hernreich, June 9, 1994.
44. FBI 302 report, statement of Beth Nolan, June 7, 1994.
45. FBI 302 report, statement of Lorraine Cline, May 18, 1994.
46. FBI 302 report, statement of Susan Thomases, June 14, 1994.
47. FBI 302 report, statement of Sheila Anthony, April 28, 1994.
48. Confidential interview with a family member.
49. FBI 302 report, statement of Dr. Hedaya, May 17, 1994. In the handwritten notes of the interview there are multiple references to Top Secret issues.

CHAPTER 16

Published sources: *The Washington Post* and *The American Spectator*, Meredith Oakley's *On The Make: The Rise of Bill Clinton* (Washington, DC: Regnery Publishing, 1994), Roger Morris's *Partners In Power: The Clintons and Their America* (New York: Henry Holt and Company, 1996), and David Maraniss's *First in His Class* (New York: Simon & Schuster, 1995).

1. Author interview with Gary Parks, February 1994.
2. Author interview with Jane Parks, April 1994.
3. Composite of the police report, family interviews, and witness observations. It differs somewhat from the police version, which is incomplete.
4. Parks already had the contract for the building, which was owned by *The Democrat-Gazette*, so the campaign inherited Parks. But Parks later expanded his role by displacing the Pinkerton security guards and taking over everything.
5. Author interview with Walter Pincus, February 1996.
6. Confirmed by Little Rock Police Department Sgt. Clyde Steelman in an interview. There is no police report of the burglary but Steelman said: "The files were taken, the family is not lying to you."
7. The identity of the witnesses is known to the author, but their information was provided under strict confidentiality.
8. Author interview with a confidential informant from the Arkansas State Police, June 1994.
9. Author interview with John D. McIntire, March 1994.
10. Two hour surveillance tape filmed at the apartment of Rodney Myers, viewed by the author; transcripts.
11. Author interview with a confidential source from the House Banking Committee investigation into money-laundering in Arkansas.
12. The tape is hard to make out because of background noise, but Detective Bunn was traveling with Roger Clinton in the car and insists that he heard the words clearly at the time.
13. Author interview with a confidential source.
14. Author interview with Jane Parks, April 1994.
15. Author interview with Harvey Bell, September 1996.

16. Author interview with Lee Bowman, July 1994.
17. Author interview with Jane Parks.
18. The pretense, still maintained by a few in the media, that Bill Clinton abided by the usual conventions of married life is so preposterous, after so much evidence to the contrary, that I will take it for granted that I don't need to address the issue here.
19. I presume that this is a misunderstanding. Foster must have been buying one of those $10 or $20 phone cards sold at many convenience stores.
20. Deposition of President Clinton, June 12, 1994.
21. Author interview with Lee Bowman.
22. Green Books, p. 2157: Park Police incident report of interview with James Lyons.
23. FBI 302 report, statement of James Lyons, May 12, 1994.
24. The checks were paid to American Industrial Services, but the main company was called American Contract Services.
25. American Contract Services company records.
26. Ibid.
27. In late 1996 Jane Parks met with two prosecutors from Starr's OIC. No FBI agents were present. No notes were taken. It was off-the-record in a Little Rock park. They mentioned to Jane that telephone records showed several calls to Webb Hubbell. They also seemed to know that Parks and Foster had been seen lunching at a restaurant in Mena.

CHAPTER 17

Sources: *Obstruction of Justice*, Integrity Film's 1996 documentary. Also: *The Benton Courier*, *The Democrat Gazette*, and Meredith Oakley's *On the Make*.

1. Author interview with Jean Duffey, May 1994.
2. The U.S. Attorney, Charles Banks, subsequently gave a press conference saying that one of the witnesses—he was referring to Sharlene—had refused to submit to a polygraph test. But this was not true. As Jean Duffey's March 1, 1991, diary entry confirms, Sharlene had told the assistant U.S. Attorney Kevin Alexander—Govar's replacement—that she was happy to do the polygraph but could not get to Little Rock that week. Her sister was recovering from surgery and Sharlene had to look after her shop. She asked whether the test could be scheduled for the following week. Alexander was abusive. Sharlene called him the next week to arrange a time for the polygraph. But Alexander never returned her call.
3. Govar talked of resigning at the time, but decided to stay on and fight from the inside. He later told Phil Weiss of *The New York Observer* that the "federal system failed Jean Duffey."
4. The diary for January 7 reads: "She was more frightened today than I have ever seen her. She says what worries her the most is that they realize that she knows an enormous amount about a lot of important people and although she has not told everything she knows, they do not know what she

is telling and what she isn't. I asked her for a specific. She told me about a
time she went to a party in Hot Springs with Roger Clinton. He picked her
up in the governor's limo and Bill Clinton was at the party. She said Bill was
very intoxicated and she saw him 'do a line' and then stumble into a garbage
can." The version is slightly different, but Duffey said she wasn't taking
notes and wrote it up later that day. She now thinks she mixed up the different incidents that Sharlene had told her.

5. Author interview with Gary Martin, DEA agent, Little Rock, June 1994.
6. It was revealed in the Circuit Court, Hot Springs County, CR 94-160, page
   25, that Potts was a defendant informant, "working off" criminal charges.
7. The details are disputed. In her appeal, Wilson accused the informant of
   signing a false affidavit.
8. U.S. Supreme Court, *Wilson* v. *Arkansas*, case number 94-5707, May 22,
   1995.
9. Author interview with Margie Wilson, June 1994.
10. Author interview with Sharlene Wilson, June 1994.
11. Investigator's notes from Undercover Officer Scott Lewellen: his interview
    with the parents of the late Don Henry, January 2, 1991.
12. Police interviews from the Duffey investigation.
13. Author interview with Arkansas State Trooper L. D. Brown, June 1997.
    Brown was assigned to the case.
14. Author interview with Linda Ives, June 1994.
15. Autopsy report.
16. Author interview with L. D. Brown, July 1997.
17. Author interview with Linda Ives, June 1994.
18. Author interview with Linda Ives, June 1997.
19. At this point Sharlene Wilson was not telling Duffey everything she knew
    about the operation.
20. Neither I nor my American editors have been able to penetrate this, appar-
    ently, Arkansan expression.
21. Scott Lewellen's investigation notes.
22. He was later appointed Chief of Police for Alexander.
23. Author interview with Linda Ives, who was taken to the site by the witness.
24. Author interview with FBI Agent Phyllis Cournan, May 1994.
25. Author interview with Sharlene Wilson, May 1994.
26. Author interview with Linda Ives, December 1995.
27. Ibid.

CHAPTER 18

Sources: *The Wall Street Journal*, *The Los Angeles Times*, the Associated Press,
Time, *Business Week*, CBS's *60 Minutes*, James Stewart's *Blood Sport*, Roger
Morris's *Partners in Power*, and Virginia Kelley's *Leading with My Heart* (New
York: Simon & Schuster, 1994).

1. Author interview with Rex Armistead, May, 1995.

2. Criminal Investigative Section memo, dated March 22, 1976, written by Doug Fogley. (Fogley later became a close ally of Don Tyson.)
3. Documents from the Criminal Investigations Division, dated February 5, 1980.
4. Author interview with Beverly Weaver, June 1994.
5. Ibid.
6. Author interview with Michael Fitzhugh, September 1994.
7. Memo from J. N. Delaughter to Major Doug Stephens, dated July 19, 1988.
8. Author interview with J. N. Delaughter, April 1994.
9. Author interview with Michael Fitzhugh, September 1994.
10. Author interview with Colonel Goodwin, September 1994.
11. Author interview with J. N. Delaughter, April 1994.
12. Author interview with Trooper Larry Patterson, June 1994.

CHAPTER 19

The Albuquerque Journal published excellent articles on this subject. Other sources: *The Arkansas Democrat-Gazette, The Pittsburgh Tribune-Review, The Whitley Republican, The Louisville Courier-Journal, The Wall Street Journal,* and *The Washington Times.*
1. Statement of Patty-Anne Smith to Arkansas State Police, September 15, 1986.
2. Author interview with Patty-Anne Smith, June 1994.
3. In a hilarious confession to the FBI, Senator Locke later said that he found himself in bed with an unknown female after snorting "bump amounts" of cocaine and "could not perform his manly duties." The experience was so shocking that he never used cocaine again.
4. Statement of Michelle Cochran to Arkansas State Police.
5. Statement of Gina Hartsell to Arkansas State Police, September 22, 1986.
6. Author interview with J. N. Delaughter, April 1994.
7. Statement of Patty-Anne Smith to Arkansas State Police. She was not the only one to be threatened. Jacquelyn Teel told the Arkansas State Police that Chuck Berry had warned her "never to discuss anything about his or Dan Lasater's business.... He made it very clear that anyone, no matter how close they were to him, will be taken care of if they crossed him." Berry was found dead in a motel room in Dallas in 1995.
8. Author interview with Patty-Anne Smith, June 1994.
9. See, for example, the Lasater Deposition to the SWSC, February 22, 1996.
10. Deposition of Corporal Barry Spivey, August 9, 1995, *Reed* v. *Young* LR-C-94-634.
11. Arguments by Lasater's defense lawyer at his sentencing, December 18, 1986, LR-CR-86-158
12. FBI 302 report, statement of Dan Lasater, November 14, 1986.
13. Statement of Michael Drake to Arkansas State Police.

14. FBI 302 report, statement of Dan Lasater, November 14, 1986.

15. Statement of Michael Drake to Arkansas State Police.

16. Document from Regional Organized Crime Information Center in Nashville, dated May 15, 1986, noted a request by the Attorney General's Office of New Mexico for criminal intelligence on Dan Lasater "in reference to narcotics trafficking via aircraft with possible ties to organized crime."

17. Deposition of Dan Lasater, SWSC, February 22, 1996.

18. The contact was Maurice Rodriguez. Roger had requested $16,000 to $20,000 but Lasater told the FBI he only paid $8,000. Roger then pocketed half the money for himself.

19. FBI 302 report, statement of Dan Lasater.

20. Author interview with a confidential informant.

21. Author interview with Ron Davis, March 1994.

22. Statement of Dan Lasater to FBI, 1986.

23. Ibid.

24. DEA file GJ-83-Z001, dated March 12, 1984.

25. FBI 302 report, statement of State Senator George Locke, October 10, 1986.

26. Report by Little Rock Police detective Tom James. Also, Police interview with pilot Ronald Ziller, September 8, 1986.

27. FBI 302 report, statement of Dan Lasater. He was mixing up his terminology, of course. There is no "governor of Belize." The country is a sovereign state with a prime minister.

28. FBI 302 report, statement of Dan Lasater.

29. Investigation notes of Russell Welch, p. 51. Welch mistakenly thought it was in Venezuela.

30. Author interview with Basil Abbott, June 1994.

31. FBI 302 report, statement of George Locke.

32. FBI 302 report, statement of Dan Lasater.

33. Ibid.

34. FBI 302 report, statement of George Locke.

35. Michael Drake, memo of interview, October 14, 1986

36. Author interview with J. N. Delaughter, May 1994.

37. Author interview with Dick Lyneis, December 1994.

38. SWSC deposition of Patsy Thomasson, February 23, 1996.

39. Interview with a confidential informant, June 1994.

40. SWSC deposition of Patsy Thomasson, July 25, 1995.

41. Author interview with Dennis Patrick, April 1994.

42. Lasater & Company, Patrick & Associates account number 61-1041943. Some of these account statements are reproduced in the appendix.

43. The bank official was Gerenthia Calloway, the account number was 00-5674.

44. Author interview with ATF officer John Simms, Lexington, Kentucky, April 1994.

45. This is the version recounted by Patrick. It occurred at the ATF offices in London, Kentucky.

46. Deposition of Danny Starr Burson, U.S. District Court, Eastern District of Kentucky, October 15, 1986, Civil Action 85-497.

47. This was in a sworn statement taken by his lawyer in Grand Prairie, Texas, on January 13, 1986, at 3 AM. It was an effort to belittle the attack on Dennis, but the slip about Steve and Little Rock was revealing. Burson later changed his story, omitting any reference to this. A copy of the document was later slipped to Dennis by somebody sympathetic to his case.

48. Author interview with John Simms, May 1994.

49. The author has heard the tape. Josey was extremely distraught, saying that he too had been a victim of something much larger. He promised to tell Dennis what really happened, but not on a prison telephone.

50. Spring 1987. Dennis taped the conversation.

51. May 1994. It was also taped.

52. This report was sent anonymously.

53. Dennis was tipped off at the time by a friend in the local sheriff's department.

54. The meeting was attended by Officer Rick Moseley, who later told Dennis what had happened.

55. Author interview with Steve Love, May 1994.

56. ADFA also issues bonds for housing, displacing the old Arkansas housing authority.

57. Documents released as a result of a Freedom of Information Act (FOIA) lawsuit by Mark Swaney versus ADFA.

58. Author interview with Mark Swaney, July 1997.

59. Wilson said that ADFA needed to issue the bonds "before the cap expired." He was afraid that the federal law allowing issuance of these bonds was going to expire.

60. "The Reoffering Memorandum does not include $2,085,000 principal amount of the Bonds which are being retained by the Owners thereof."

61. ADFA minutes, December 17, 1987, released as a result of a FOIA lawsuit by Mark Swaney.

62. Letter August 18, 1992, from Delaware Supervising Insurance Examiner to ADFA.

63. SWSC depositions of Dan Lasater. He nominated Bill Mathis, Mort Hardwicke, Donny Spears, Margaret Davenport-Jacks, James Branyan, George Wright, Jr., Jim Tom Bell, and Ed Williams. The Committee also obtained message slips from some of Lasater's calls to the Mansion.

64. As an experiment, I tried to audit the $175 million July 1985 issue of Single Family Mortgage Revenue Bonds. The explosion of housing issues in 1985 seemed excessive. The money was transferred in blocks to private banks, which then commingled funds from other sources. It was absolutely impossible to track the money flow—which I believe was the purpose.

65. Author interview with Bill Wilson, July 1994.

66. Lasater & Company participated in the underwriting of $660 million of ADFA and other state bond issues before Lasater was convicted in 1986 (as reported in the May 7, 1994, issue of *The Economist*). Usually there would be a group of five underwriters, managed by Paine Webber. ADFA refused to tell me how much of the pie was cut for Lasater, insisting vaguely that it was less than 5 percent. Mark Swaney says that records he reviewed indicate the figure was much higher in the 1985 period.

67. *First American* v. *Lasater*, U.S. District Court, Little Rock, October 9, 1985.

CHAPTER 20

Published sources: *The Wall Street Journal*, and Richard Secord's *Honored and Betrayed: Irangate, Covert Affairs, and the Secret War in Laos* (New York: Wiley, 1992).

1. I wrote an entire piece on the incident, which *The Washington Post*'s rival *The Washington Times* picked up and ran on the front page.

2. The quotes from Debbie Seal are based on a series of interviews conducted by the author between 1995 and 1997.

3. In a deposition to the House Subcommittee on Crime, March 11, 1988, DEA agent Ernest Jacobsen was asked if there was a "national security defense" in the case.

4. LeBlanc testimony at DEA, Baton Rouge, April 2, 1986.

5. Author interview with Debbie Seal, June 1997. She knew that it was June because she kept a piece of paper with the name and number of a babysitter. It was a receipt with a date on the other side.

6. Jacobsen deposition.

7. Testimony of Billy Bottoms to the House Subcommittee on Crime, June 20, 1988.

8. Deposition of Russell Welch at the Arkansas Attorney General's office, June 21, 1991.

9. Testimony of Barry Seal, October 7, 1985.

10. Sheriff Al Hadoway of the Arkansas State Police, May 1, 1986.

11. Duncan IRS investigation. Seal bought N62856 from Air America Inc. in May 1982. Contrary to news reports, this had nothing to do with the famous CIA front also called Air America.

12. Jacobsen deposition.

13. Seal told the Arkansas State Police and the IRS that the only laundering done at Mena was to cover local expenses.

14. Statement of Billy Earle, Jr., to the Arkansas State Police, October 10, 1985.

15. Testimony of Barry Seal, October 7, 1985.

16. This was a calculation by the Louisiana Attorney general in a letter to the United States Justice Department, dated March 3, 1986.

17. Jacobsen deposition.

18. Ibid. There is some dispute over whether it was Somoza's house, (the DEA version) or the property of a former diplomat.

19. Duncan interview of Peter Emerson, June 9, 1988. Emerson was Seal's flight engineer on the C-123.

20. Jacobsen deposition.

21. Ibid. The DEA had the fuel analyzed, just to be sure that Seal really had landed in Nicaragua and not somewhere else.

22. I am not entirely convinced that this incident took place on Nicaraguan soil. It strikes me as odd that the *Frente Sandinista* would let a U.S. military C-123 come and go.

23. Deposition of Ronald J. Caffrey, DEA cocaine chief, before the House Subcommittee on Crime, March 15, 1988.

24. Deposition of Ronald J. Caffrey. Also in the report issued by the Kerry Committee.

25. Defense motion in U.S. District Court, Louisiana, case 84-77.

26. Testimony of Richard Secord to the Iran-Contra Committee, May 5, 1987.

27. Another slip was leaving a paper trail mentioning four C-123s for "delivery to Tucson." In his testimony to the Iran-Contra Committee (May 5, 1987), Secord said he had only two Fairchild C-123K transports. But there were in fact a total of four C-123s used in the resupply network.

28. Author interview with Joe Cadiz, September 1997.

29. Department of Transportation, aircraft bill of sale. Conveyance recorded July 27, 1983.

30. FAA Aircraft Registry.

31. Jacobsen deposition.

32. Ibid.

33. Author interview with a confidential source from the House Banking Committee.

34. Jacobsen deposition.

CHAPTER 21

Both R. Emmett Tyrrell, Jr.'s *Boy Clinton: The Political Biography* (Washington, DC: Regnery Publishing, 1996) and Terry Reed's and John Cummings's *Compromised: Clinton, Bush and the CIA* (New York: Spi, 1994) have been important sources. Terry Reed has been of great help in providing me with depositions from his lawsuit. Other published sources: James Stewart's *Blood Sport* and Richard Secord's *Honored and Betrayed*.

1. Deposition of Ernest Jacobsen before the House Subcommittee on Crime, March 11, 1988.

2. Deposition of L. D. Brown, *Terry K. Reed, Et Al* v. *Raymond Young, Et Al*, LR-C-94-634, U.S. District Court, Eastern District of Arkansas.

3. Interview with L. D. Brown, December 1985.

4. Brown deposition, *Reed* v. *Young*.

5. Walsh Report, page 485; Congressional Iran-Contra Report.
6. Author interview with L. D. Brown, July 1997.
7. Interview with a confidential source from the House Banking Committee, June 1997.
8. Deposition of Ken Maddox, *Brotherton* v. *Reed*, Case 94-2071, June 25, 1996.
9. Walsh Report, p. 296.
10. Walsh Report, p. 161.
11. The First Boland Amendment allowed the CIA to spend $24 million to support the Contras, provided it was not to overthrow the government of Nicaragua. This was made much more restrictive in the Second Boland Amendment passed in October 1984, which limited the CIA to gathering intelligence only. But the wording was a compromise, drafted to avoid a veto by President Reagan. It left some wiggle room for the White House. It was in force from October 1984 to October 1986.
12. Iran-Contra Report, pp. 34-35.
13. Walsh Report, grand jury testimony of Donald Gregg, October 23, 1987.
14. Walsh Report, p. 487.
15. Author interview with L. D. Brown, July 5, 1997.
16. Deposition of Tommy Goodwin, CIV-94-2071, Brodix v. Reed, June 24, 1996. This is supported by testimony from other sources. Ken Maddox, an undercover narcotics agent working for the DEA, FBI, and drug task force talked about military training at Nella.
17. The FBI was worried about the legality of CIA activity in the U.S. They claimed that North was based in Toronto, coordinating a Finnish connection.
18. Anne Ellet interview with Joe Dunlap of the Kansas public defenders office.
19. Deposition of Michelle Tudor, *Reed* v. *Young*, July 25, 1995.
20. Iran-Contra Report.
21. There is extensive police documentation of suspicious activities at Nella, e.g. DEA October 28, 1986. "The farm on which the airstrip has been the object of a DEA/Arkansas State Police investigation in 1983 and 1984 as a possible smuggling field for the Barry SEAL organization." In addition, in his deposition of June 21, 1991, Arkansas State Trooper Russell Welch talks of "air traffic at the Nella airport" and movements by "camouflaged subjects."
22. Author interview with a confidential source, July 1997. For obvious reasons Bottoms now denies all involvement. But he confessed his role in a meeting with three people, including a veteran law enforcement official.
23. Deposition of Trooper Larry Patterson: "Tommy Goodwin was in the Lincoln, I was driving, the governor was in the front seat. Bill Clinton turned to Tommy Goodwin in the backseat and said verbatim 'Tommy, I want to know what the hell is going on at Mena.' Goodwin said 'Governor, I have been told by Senator Pryor and Senator Bumpers to stay out of Mena.'"

24. Press conference, October 7, 1994.
25. Deposition of Bill Duncan, taken by Arkansas Congressman Bill Alexander.
26. Memo from Lieutenant Doug Williams to Capt. Doug Stephens, *re:* Rich Mountain Aviation, dated January 7, 1987.
27. Deposition of Russell Welch, June 21, 1991.
28. Welch's handwritten diary, 1987.
29. FBI teletype, Little Rock office, October 10, 1987.
30. EPIC's lawyer would refute this in Reed's criminal case.
31. Cover sheet of the FBI file on Terry Reed.
32. Deposition of Barry Spivey, *Reed* v. *Young.*
33. Memo from Robin Fowler to US Attorney, June 5, 1990.
34. Deposition of Bill Duncan, p. 34.
35. Order of the U.S. District Court, Eastern District of Arkansas, case LR-C-94-6343.

CHAPTER 22

Published sources: *The Washington Post, The American Lawyer,* and *Newsweek.*
1. Author interview with Gene Wirgess, March 1994.
2. Author interview with Danny Traylor, March 1994.
3. Author interview with Paula Jones, March 1994.
4. Author interview with Sally Perdue. I had been talking to Perdue since January 1994, but this occurred in May 1994.
5. The threat was made at the Cheshire Inn by a man named Ron Tucker. The witness was Denison Diel, who signed an affidavit detailing the conversation. There is further corroboration. Tucker was heard talking about the subject on the telephone at his job at the Marion Mining Bolt Company in Kentucky. When confronted by his boss, Tucker said that he had been asked by someone in the Democratic Party in St. Louis to "shut the woman up."
6. Affidavit of Pamela Blackard, February 7, 1994.
7. Author interview with Debra Ballantine, March 1994.
8. Author interview with Delmar Corbin, March 1994.
9. Author interview with Lydia Cathey, March 1994.
10. Interview with Steve Jones, May 1997.

APPENDIX A
OKLAHOMA

(A) Carol Howe.

ORT OF INVESTIGATION (Law Enforcement)

☐ ROUTINE
☒ SENSITIVE   ☐ SIGNIFICANT | 3 pages

Special Agent in Charge
Dallas District Office

1. MONITORED INVESTIGATION INFORMATION (Number and Branch)
53270-183
FY 95   53270-183

F INVESTIGATION
CONFIDENTIAL INFORMANT APPROVAL REQUEST

5. INVESTIGATION No. (Include Suspect No.)
53270-94-01248

F REPORT *(Check applicable boxes)*

ELIMINARY		COLLATERAL *(Request)*		7. BUREAU PROGRAM		8. PROJECT(S)	
				TITLE I		TARGETED OFFENDE	
				TITLE II	FIREARMS	TERRORIST/EXTREM	
ATUS		COLLATERAL *(Reply)*		TITLE VII		OCD	
				TITLE II	EXPLOSIVES	ITAR	
AL		INTELLIGENCE		TITLE XI		SEAR	
				TOBACCO		OMO	
PPLEMENTAL		REFERRAL *(Internal)*		ALCOHOL		OTHER *(Specify)* X	
S:						CI REQUEST	

1. Name: _Carol Elizabeth Howe_

2. Aliases: _"Lady MacBeth" TIT and TOOT_

3. Residence address(es): _7100 S. Riverside_
Tulsa, Oklahoma

4. Residence Phone #(s): _(918) 488-8223_

5. Business Address(es): _unemployed_

6. Business Phone #(s): _____

7. Physical Description: Race _W_ Sex _F_ Ht. _5'1"_

Hair _BLND_ Eyes _GRN_ Wt. _112_

Tattoos/Marks/Scars _T-swastika lft shldr; pentagram_
rt. ankl; S- lft. foot

Photograph Attached: Yes _X_
No _____
(If no, reason for
requesting waiver)

DEFENDANT'S
EXHIBIT
4
97-cr-5-B-(H...)

TED BY *(Name)*	11. TITLE AND OFFICE	12. DATE
Carol Figley	_S/A Tulsa, Oklahoma_	_05/18/95_
VED BY *(Name)* _David FL. Roberts_	14. TITLE AND OFFICE	15. DATE

(B) ATF confidential informant document for Carol Howe.

174A-OC-56120
JRB/csc

1

        The following investigation was conducted by
Special Agent (SA) JAMES R. BLANCHARD, II, and SA ANGIE FINLEY,
Alcohol, Tobacco and Firearms (ATF), on April 21, 1995:

        SA BLANCHARD and SA ANGIE FINLEY, ATF, talked with
SA FINLEY's confidential source "CAROL". CAROL stated she
believes in 1994, she saw an individual resembling the composite
of UNSUB #1 in a white separatist paramilitary camp called "Elohm
City" (phonetic) (EC). This camp is located around Stillwell,
Oklahoma. CAROL knows this person as "PETE." CAROL has seen an
individual named "TONY" resembling the composite of UNSUB #2.
TONY is PETE's brother, and is not well liked at EC. TONY would
do as his brother directed, however.

        When CAROL saw the television pictures of TIMOTHY JAMES
MCVEIGH, she said MCVEIGH doesn't look like "PETE." CAROL
recalled that she did see a person who looked like MCVEIGH in a
photograph in a photo album she saw at a 1994 Klan Rally.

        CAROL began going to EC around June of 1994. She
learned about EC when she called a racist hotline in May, 1994.
CAROL met the hotline operator/owner DENNIS MEHAUN (phonetic) who
would visit EC to engage in paramilitary training. CAROL began
firearms training at EC.

        CAROL learned that EC is operated by BOB LAMAR. EC's
"Chaplain" is ZERA PATTERSON. EC's Security Officer is ANDY
STRASMEYER, an illegal alien from Germany, who is a former West
German Infantry Officer.

        STRASMEYER speaks English fluently, but has a German
accent. STRASMEYER has talked frequently about direct action
against the U.S. Government. He is trained in weaponry and has
discussed assassinations, bombings and mass shootings.
STRASMEYER frequently talks about direct action against the U.S.
Federal Government. CAROL has not seen PETE ever training at EC,
but is friends with STRASMEYER.

        CAROL has heard frequent anti-Federal government
philosophy. CAROL described EC residents as being ultra-militant
white separatists. Many of the younger members practice Odinism,
the worship of the Norse God Odin. There is much required
reading at the compound such as Mien Kamph, The Silent
Brotherhood and The Turner Diaries. The Turner Diaries is a book
which described the idea of driving a delivery truck loaded with
explosives into the delivery area of a Federal building and
detonating it at 9:30 a.m.

000632

                        P25972

                174A-OC-56120-E-427

EXHIBIT "D"

(C) FBI debriefing of Carol Howe at the Oklahoma Command
Center two days after the Oklahoma bombing. No agency of the
United States has interviewed Dennis Mahon (misspelled
"MEHAUN"), whom she implicates in the bombing.

174A-OC-56120

<u>2</u>

Many EC residents have sympathies to DAVID KORESH and even have a Branch Davidian flag hanging in the EC church. CAROL has heard a lot of discussion of hatred toward the U.S. Government for the WACO raid, and that EC could be the government's next victim. Although some EC members have suggested that they should strike the government first, CAROL has heard of no specific plans for vengeance.

EC receives funds from a Neurosurgeon, Dr. PETER LIPRON, who resides in Lawton, Oklahoma. LIPRON has associated with MEHAUN and various "militia" movements in Oklahoma. LIPRON has purchased communication equipment and medical supplies for EC.

MEHAUN has talked with CAROL about targeting federal installations for destruction through bombings, such as the IRS Building, the Tulsa Federal Building and the Oklahoma City Federal Building. MEHAUN has also discussed a plan for destroying power lines from Oklahoma City to Catousa, Oklahoma, during the hottest time of the summer. MEHAUN reasons this will create a panic, and without air conditioning, mass race riots would begin.

MEHAUN resides at 1448 N. College, Tulsa, Oklahoma. MEHAUN and STRASMEYER has taken three trips to Oklahoma City in November, 1994, December, 1994, and February, 1995. CAROL only accompanied the group once, in December, 1994. CAROL remembered visiting a church on the NW or NE 10th. They also visited the "Jesus is Lord" salvage yard on Northwest 10th operated by JOE CECIL.

EC has computer equipment, food, agricultural resources, two fishponds, reservoirs, livestock and weapons. CAROL said EC has 308 rifles, MAC 90s, mini-14s, and various fully automatic weapons. STRASMEYER once bragged about having an M-60 automatic machine gun, but later denied it.

April 18th is the anniversary of the WACO raid and April 19th is HITLER's birthday. CAROL said EC residents are very conscious of these dates.

CAROL attempted to use ATF equipment to make a consensually recorded telephone call to MEHAN on April 21, 1995, but was unsuccessful in reaching him. SA FINLEY supervised CAROL in these attempts.

P25973

000633

RCS ATF R 3270.1

DEPARTMENT OF THE TREASURY- BUREAU OF ALCOHOL, TOBACCO AND FIREARMS	1. INVESTIGATION IS		Page 1 of
REPORT OF INVESTIGATION (Law Enforcement)	☐ ROUTINE ☒ SENSITIVE ☐ SIGNIFICANT		_3_ pages

2. TO:	3. MONITORED INVESTIGATION INFORMATION (*Number and Branch*)
Special Agent in Charge	CIP: DALLAS FY-95
Dallas Field Division	FIREARMS VIOLATIONS
	REPORT 005

4. TITLE OF INVESTIGATION	5. INVESTIGATION No. (*Include Suspect No.*)
White Aryan Resistence, W.A.R.	53270-94-0124-B

6. TYPE OF REPORT(*Check applicable boxes*)			7. BUREAU PROGRAM		8. PROJECT(S)	
	PRELIMINARY	COLLATERAL (*Request*).	X	TITLE I		TARGETED OFFENDER
			X	TITLE II	FIREARMS	X TERRORIST/EXTREMIST
X	STATUS	COLLATERAL (*Reply*)		TITLE VII		OCD
			X	TITLE II	EXPLOSIVES	ITAR
	FINAL	INTELLIGENCE		TITLE XI		SEAR
				TOBACCO		OMO
	SUPPLEMENTAL	REFERRAL (*Internal*)		ALCOHOL		OTHER

9. DETAILS:

This is a 30 day status report in the investigation of the White Aryan Resistance and the violations of federal firearms and conspiracy laws in various counties in both the Northern and Eastern Judicial Districts of Oklahoma.

On December 9, 1994 CI-183 went to Elohim City for a three-week visit.

On December 19, 1994 this agent learned the identity of "Andy" who is said to be the head of security at Elohim City. He is actually Andreas Karl Strassmeir, a West German, DOB 051759. This agent then contacted INS in Oklahoma City and was informed that according to their records, Strassmeir is an illegal alien. Strassmeir entered the United States in May of 1991 and was scheduled to leave August of 1991, however, according to records Strassmeir has not left the country. It should be noted that Strassmeir always carries a .45 pistol.

On January 1, 1994 CI-183 returned to Tulsa. This agent received the following information:

Strassmeir is said to have worked for the C.A.U.S.E. foundation in Houston, Texas during a visit in 1987 or 1988. He also has access to prescription drugs, i.e. he maintains the "pharmacy" in which 183 viewed an ampule of xylocaine, an anesthetic. 183 watched as the xylocaine was injected into the face of a man who was having one of the women perform surgery to remove a scar he had. They told 183 the reason for the surgery was to keep the man from being identified by his scar. Zera Patterson IV told 183 that Strassmeir had questionable weapons connections. Strassmeir told 183 about a required equipment list for each resident at EC. The list

10. SUBMITTED BY (*Name*) Angela Finley	11. TITLE AND OFFICE S/A, Tulsa, Oklahoma	12. DATE 01/11/9
13. REVIEWED BY (*Name*) David E. Roberts	14. TITLE AND OFFICE RAC, Tulsa, Oklahoma	15. DATE 1/16/9
16. APPROVED BY (*Name*) Lester D. Martz	17. TITLE AND OFFICE Special Agent in Charge	18. DATE / /

ATF EF 3270.3 (5-90)

(D) ATF debriefing of Carol Howe about Elohim City and her investigation of Andreas Strassmeir.

DEPARTMENT OF THE TREASURY BUREAU OF ALCOHOL, TOBACCO AND FIREARMS **REPORT OF INVESTIGATION - CONTINUATION SHEET** (Law Enforcement)		PAGE __2__ OF __3__ PAGES
TITLE OF INVESTIGATION White Aryan Resistance, W.A.R.	INVESTIGATION NO. 53270-94-0124-B	

DETAILS *(Continued)*

had required gear for patrols, maneuvers and combat. Each household is required to be stockpiling ammunition and it is recommended that there are 400 to 500 rounds per firearm. Each person is required to have a gas mask and spare filters. Certain individuals are trained for sniping and others are specifically trained to do combat. Strassmeir alleges that he makes weapon and firearm purchases for those who cannot buy for themselves, i.e. because of age, background, etc.

183 was not allowed to participate in the combat maneuvers, however, 183 stated that these maneuvers were taking place the day he/she arrived at EC and that the people were camping outside in 14 degree weather. 183 stated that during the maneuvers, participants were forced to swim in a creek in these frigid temperatures. The leader of these maneuvers is Strassmeir and 183 stated that he reported his dissatisfaction with his "troops" to Millar. Millar responded by calling the "troops" to stand during Sabbath meeting and yelling at them for an unsatisfactory performance.

183 met Keith Bowel, former CSA who stated that many members of CSA have stayed together and are living in Sparta, Mo. Ellison is still planning to visit EC in April and is expected to round up his followers in order to reconstruct CSA.

During the Sabbath meeting, Millar gave a sermon soliciting violence against the US Government. He brought forth his soldiers and instructed them to take whatever action necessary against the US Government. It is understood that ATF is the main enemy of the people at EC. He further stated that they would be gaining territory and expanding through the midwest. He stated that certain groups from Texas, Missouri, Arkansas and Oklahoma will be uniting as one front to fight the government. He told 183 that EC considers itself a separate nation of Israelites which happens to be located in the continental United States. He explicitly told 183 that they were preparing to fight a war against the government. He also stated that they had been close friends of the Weavers and that they agreed with what they did. He stated that they were friends with some of the Branch Dividians in Waco, Texas and that the Branch Dividians have set up another community in Colorado.

Millar has an office in his trailer and 183 noted that there are three large computer systems in this small area. Millar does not allow access to this area. It is unknown what these computers are used to do.
It is expected that one use for the computers is for Millar's trucking company, RBJ Trucking, which is reported to have a garage in VanBuren, Arkansas.

2

DEPARTMENT OF THE TREASURY
BUREAU OF ALCOHOL, TOBACCO AND FIREARMS

REPORT OF INVESTIGATION - CONTINUATION SHEET
(Law Enforcement)

PAGE	3
OF	3 PAGES

TITLE OF INVESTIGATION	INVESTIGATION NO.
White Aryan Resistence, W.A.R.	53270-94-0124-B

DETAILS *(Continued)*

183 spoke with an individual named " Mike" who is actually William Brescia and has ties to the Posse Comitatus in Pennsylvania. Mike is interested in obtaining 183's Tec-9 and stated that it is an easy firearm to convert. Zera Patterson IV told 183 that he knew that Mike would convert the firearm if 183 gave it to him.

183 met a woman named Teresa, who stated that she was a former CSA. Teresa stated that Ellison will have a militia with fully automatic firearms and that he intends to have fewer followers to insure a stronger community. 183 was told that he/she would be welcome to become part of CSA upon the return of Ellison.

183 was invited to stay at EC by Millar. 183 stated that Millar was disappointed that he/she could not stay. 183 has made many friends and has become romantically involved with one individual. 183 and this individual have formed a very close relationship and 183 has become privy to much more information based on the status of this individual. This individual stated that he/she has had a message from God to court and marry 183.

183 was able to obtain a partial telephone registry of numbers that have been called from EC. These numbers were forwarded to headquarters and the response is pending. It is known that one of the numbers belongs to Joe Cecil, who is a multiple convicted felon living in Oklahoma City, Oklahoma. This agent was contacted regarding one of the license tags on a vehicle at EC. It is owned by Robert McHenry, who is a convicted felon. He has a three year felony conviction for transporting illegal aliens.

On January 6, 1995 183 traveled to EC. 183 was allowed to move about without supervision and discovered an area in one of the metal buildings that contained reloading equipment, hundreds of shotgun shells and many boxes of shotgun primers. 183 stated that there is a huge camouflage tarp that is folded in this area and that if the tarp were to be stretched it would be the size of a giant circus tent. 183 stepped on part of the tarp and stated that there was something under it. 183 strongly suspected that the tarp was concealing some type of storage area and due to the other items found in this area, 183 believes it to be a storage for ammunition or weapons. 183 also found many boxes which contained one large screw or bolt, approx. 5 to 6 inches long and 1 1/2 to 2 inches diameter with a nut on each. It is not known what these are, however, they are scattered among the reloading equipment.

It is requested that CI 183 return to Elohim City for a three month period, which is the next step in becoming a permanent resident. 183 believes that he/she will be included in the combat maneuvers upon returning.

This investigation to remain open.

3

ATF SE 3730 1 (5-90)

RCS ATF R 3270.1

DEPARTMENT OF THE TREASURY- BUREAU	ALCOHOL, TOBACCO AND FIREARMS	1. I. IGATION IS		Page 1 of
REPORT OF INVESTIGATION (Law Enforcement)		☐ ROUTINE ☒ SENSITIVE ☐ SIGNIFICANT		2 pages

2. TO: Special Agent in Charge Dallas Field Division	3. MONITORED INVESTIGATION INFORMATION(*Number and Branch*) CIP: DALLAS FY-95 FIREARMS VIOLATIONS REPORT 007

4. TITLE OF INVESTIGATION White Aryan Resistance, W.A.R.	5. INVESTIGATION No. (*Include Suspect No.*) 53270-94-0124-B

6. TYPE OF REPORT(*Check applicable boxes*)

				7. BUREAU PROGRAM			8. PROJECT(S)	
	PRELIMINARY		COLLATERAL (*Request*).	X	TITLE I			TARGETED OFFENDER
				X	TITLE II	FIREARMS	X	TERRORIST/EXTREMIST
X	STATUS		COLLATERAL (*Reply*)		TITLE VII			OCD
				X	TITLE II	EXPLOSIVES		ITAR
	FINAL		INTELLIGENCE		TITLE XI			SEAR
					TOBACCO			OMO
	SUPPLEMENTAL		REFERRAL (*Internal*)		ALCOHOL			OTHER (*Spec*)

9. DETAILS:

This is a 30 day status report in the investigation of the White Aryan Resistance and the violations of federal firearm, explosive and conspiracy laws in both the Northern and Eastern Judicial Districts of Oklahoma

On April 20, 1995 this agent was contacted by CI-53270-183 in regard to the bombing in Oklahoma City, Oklahoma. CI-183 stated that he/she believed suspect #2 resembled one of the residents of Elohim City, Tony Ward.

On April 21, 1995 this agent, along with Special Agent John Risenhoover, traveled to Tulsa to pick up CI-183 and transport him/her to Oklahoma City. CI-183 was debriefed by Special Agents from ATF and FBI. A lead sheet was then completed. It was then determined that CI-183 would be sent to Elohim City to obtain any intelligence relating to the bombing.

On April 29, 1995 CI-183 met with area W.A.R. leader, Dennis Mahon, and obtained several video tapes regarding the movement. CI-183 stated that they discussed alibi's for April 19, 1995 and the components of the explosive. CI-183 stated that Mahon mentioned the name of a man familiar in explosives who lives in Illinois. Mahon used the name, Pierson, however, he was not sure. CI-183 stated that Mahon could have been referring to Paulson because he cannot remember people's names.

On May 1, 1995 CI-183 traveled to Elohim City and stayed for three days.

On May 3, 1995 this agent met with CI-183 and debriefed him/her. This agent then took CI-183 to Oklahoma City to meet with ATF and FBI agents for further debriefing. CI-183 stated that while he/she was inside, a news crew was also there doing a story and that he/she was asked to stay out of

10. SUBMITTED BY (*Name*) Angela Finley	11. TITLE AND OFFICE S/A Tulsa, Oklahoma	12. DATE 05/22/9
13. REVIEWED BY (*Name*) David E. Roberts	14. TITLE AND OFFICE RAC Tulsa, Oklahoma	15. DATE 5B1K
16. APPROVED BY (*Name*) Lester D. Martz	17. TITLE AND OFFICE Special Agent in Charge	18. DATE / /

ATF EF 3270.2 (5-90)

(E) ATF debriefing of Carol Howe regarding John Doe Two and her discovery of a "big secret" at Elohim City.

<table>
<tr><td>⌐</td><td>ᴧTMENT OF THE TREASURY
BUREAU OF ALCOHOL, TOBACCO AND FIREARMS</td><td>PAGE __2__</td></tr>
<tr><td colspan="2" style="text-align:center">REPORT OF INVESTIGATION - CONTINUATION SHEET
(Law Enforcement)</td><td>OF __2__ PAGES</td></tr>
</table>

TITLE OF INVESTIGATION	INVESTIGATION NO.
White Aryan Resistance, W.A.R.	53270-94-0124-B

DETAILS *(Continued)*

sight. CI-183 was excluded from the daily worship meetings due to the media attention. CI-183 did speak to an individual who stated, "There is a big secret out here." CI-183 also was informed by Zara Patterson IV that James Ellison was now residing at Elohim City, however, CI-183 did not see him. Ellison was the former leader of the Covenant, Sword and Arm of the Lord in Arkansas. CI-183 stated that he/she viewed the freshly dug grave of Snell, the man executed in Arkansas on April 19, 1995 for the slaying of an Arkansas trooper. CI-183 was informed that Robert Millar had attended the execution and transported the body to his compound for burial. CI-183 stated that individuals spoken with were supportive of the bombing of the building in Oklahoma City.

On May 18, 1995 this agent met with CI-183 to discuss returning to Elohim City in order to determine what the "big secret" is and to attempt to identify suspect #2.

On May 22, 1995 this agent was contacted by CI-183 who stated that he/she had been contacted the previous day and informed that he/she had better not go to Elohim City. CI-183 stated that the person called again on this day and gave him/her the same warning. CI-183 did not reveal the source at this time. CI-183 then stated that he/she had seen the numerous television broadcasts about Elohim City and was too frightened to go.

On May 24, 1995 this agent was informed by RAC, David Roberts that Robert Millar suspected CI-183 of being a confidential informant. It was determined that CI-183 would not be sent to Elohim City at this time or in the future.

This investigation to remain open.

2

RCS ATF R 3270.1

DEPARTMENT OF THE TREASURY- BUREAU OF ALCOHOL, TOBACCO AND FIREARMS	1. INVESTIGATION IS		
REPORT OF INVESTIGATION (Law Enforcement)	☒ ROUTINE		Page 1 of
	☐ SENSITIVE ☐ SIGNIFICANT		**2** pages

2. TO:	3. MONITORED INVESTIGATION INFORMATION(*Number and Branch*)
Special Agent in Charge Dallas Field Division	CIP: DALLAS FY-96 NON CIP REPORT 001

4. TITLE OF INVESTIGATION	5. INVESTIGATION No. (*Include Suspect No.*)
Disclosure of Confidential Informant	53270-96-0001-X

6. TYPE OF REPORT(*Check applicable boxes*)

				7. BUREAU PROGRAM		8. PROJECT(S)
PRELIMINARY		COLLATERAL (*Request*).	X	TITLE I		TARGETED OFFENDER
				TITLE II	FIREARMS	TERRORIST/EXTREMIST
STATUS		COLLATERAL (*Reply*)		TITLE VII		OCD
				TITLE II	EXPLOSIVES	ITAR
FINAL		INTELLIGENCE		TITLE XI		SEAR
				TOBACCO		OMO
SUPPLEMENTAL	X	REFERRAL (*Internal*)		ALCOHOL	X	OTHER (*Specify*) CI DISCLOSURE

9. DETAILS:

This referral is to inform Dallas Division about the disclosure of ATF informant 53270-183 by FBI Special Agent James R. Blanchard II during the OKBOMB investigation.

On March 29, 1996 this agent received a telephone call from S/A Harry Eberhardt. S/A Eberhardt stated that the identity of CI 53270-183 had been severely compromised. S/A Eberhardt stated that a report released by FBI agent James R. Blanchard II contained the formal name of CI 53270-183 and enough information to reveal the identity CI 53270-183 without his/her name being used. S/A Eberhardt stated that the report had been given to Timothy McVeigh's defense attorneys during discovery in January 1996. S/A Eberhardt stated that he had attempted to relay this matter to FBI ASAC Jack McCoy, however, ASAC McCoy showed little concern and denied that S/A Blanchard was at fault. S/A Eberhardt stated that he became irate because it was apparent that nothing was going to be done in an effort to rectify the problem or at least provide help for the safety of CI 53270-183.

On this same date, this agent immediately telephoned CI 53270-183 and informed him/her that their name had been disclosed and that he/she should take every precaution for their safety. CI 53270-183 stated that he/she was still involved with members of the militia and White Aryan Resistance who know where he/she lives. CI 53270-183 also stated that he/she suspected that they were being followed on several occasions and have had strange telephone calls and visitors. This agent offered to relocate CI 53270-183 temporarily for the weekend, however, he/she stated that they would be in a safe place. This agent told the CI that anything and everything will be done to insure his/her safety.

DEFENDANT'S EXHIBIT

10. SUBMITTED BY (*Name*) Angela Graham	11. TITLE AND OFFICE S/A Tulsa, Oklahoma	DATE 04/01/96
13. REVIEWED BY (*Name*) David E. Roberts	14. TITLE AND OFFICE RAC Tulsa, Oklahoma	15. DATE / /
16. APPROVED BY (*Name*) Lester D. Martz	17. TITLE AND OFFICE Special Agent in Charge	18. DATE / /

ATF EF 3270.2 (5-90)

(F) ATF report complaining that Carol Howe has been "severely compromised" by the FBI.

DEPARTMENT OF THE TREASURY
BUREAU OF ALCOHOL, TOBACCO AND FIREARMS

125 West 15th Street, Suite 500
Tulsa, Oklahoma 74119-3822

April 22, 1996

Refer to

MEMORANDUM TO: Special Agent in Charge
Dallas Field Division

THRU: David E. Roberts, Resident Agent
Tulsa Field Office

FROM: Special Agent Angela Graham
Tulsa Field Office

SUBJECT: Threat Assessment for CI 53270-183

This informant is involved with the OKC bomb case which is pending
prosecution in Denver and was the key in identifying individuals at
Elohim City, which is tied to the OKC bomb case. The majority of
the associates of CI 52705-183 are militia members.

CI 53270-183 has no criminal record.

The threat to CI 5270-183 comes from the release of his/her
identity by the FBI to Timothy McVeigh's defense attorney. CI
53270-183 told this agent that s/he has been receiving suspicious
phone calls; has been followed on numerous occasions; and has had
frequent unidentified visitors. CI 53270-183 stated that Dennis
Mahon, area leader of White Aryan Nation has stated that he knew
there was a snitch he had been dealing with in the past. This CI
thought he was referring to him/her.

The FBI is the lead agency on this case, however, many other
federal state and local agencies are involved. Individuals who
pose immediate danger to CI 53270-183 are: (1) Dennis Mahon, (2)
members of Elohim City, and (3) any sympathizer to McVeigh, i.e.,
militias.

CI 5270-183 has expressed a great deal of concern for his/her
safety, although s/he is in fear because of serious threats made by
former and current associates regarding the discovery of a
"snitch".

TOTAL P.03

(G) ATF document assessing the threats to Carol Howe. Note that
the ATF states that Elohim City "is tied to the OKC bomb case."
Note also the last paragraph, in which the ATF defends the credibility of Carol Howe.

This agent has known CI 53270-183 for approximately two years and can assert that this informant has not been overly paranoid or fearful during undercover operations. This agent believes that s/he could be in serious danger when associates discover his/her identity.

Angela S. Graham

(H) Andreas Strassmeir.

~~LIMITED OFFICIAL USE~~ UNCLASS

INCOMING TELEGRAM

D147

R

DEPARTMENT OF STATE
DIPLOMATIC SECURITY

PAGE 01   BONN 06562 2812642   --   3264 328314   DS6949
ACTION DS-33

INFO DSS-01 PII-01 /002 A1 CM

INFO LOG-00   OASY-30 TEDE-00 ADS-00   ASDS-0: DSCC-00   /001W
------------------------------C046FE 2812042 /38

P 2812342 APR 95
FM AMEMBASSY BONN
TO SECSTATE WASHDC PRIORITY 8342

LIMITED OFFICIAL USE BONN 06562

DS CHANNEL

FOR DS/ICI/PII

E. O. 12356: N/A
TAGS: ASEC
SUBJECT: CT03-0495-100-0283 OKLAHOMA CITY BOMBING

REF: S/A HUDSPETH E-MAIL AND TELCON OF 4/27/95

1.   PER REFERENCED REQUEST, GERMAN POLICE INTELLIGENCE AND
CRIMINAL HISTORY CHECKS HAVE BEEN CONDUCTED ON ANDREAS
CARL (STRASSMEIR); DOB: 05/17/59, BERLIN, GE; GERMAN
PASSPORT NUMBER G7572322, WITH THE FOLLOWING RESULTS:

--FRG POLICE INTELLIGENCE CHECK, NO RECORD - 04/27/95

--FRG CRIMINAL HISTORY CHECK, NO RECORD - 04/27/95

--BFV BUNDESAMT FUER VERFASSUNGSSCHUTZ - FEDERAL OFFICE
FOR PROTECTION OF THE CONSTITUTION), NO RECORD - 04/27/95

--FRG RESIDENCE REGISTRATION RECORDS, CHECKED ON 04/27/95,
REFLECT THAT (STRASSMEIR), FROM 10/23/86 TO 07/13/89,
RESIDED IN HAMBURG AT 545 CUXHAVENER STRASSE, 2114S HAMBURG

ANOTHER HAMBURG ADDRESS WAS ALSO LISTED ON THE RECORD CARD
ANOTHER HAMBURG ADDRESS WAS ALSO LISTED ON THE RECORD CARD
AS 13 STOLTENSTRASSE, HAMBURG (FRG ARMY BARRACKS OR SCHOOL)

PRIOR TO 10/86, (STRASSMEIR) WAS REGISTERED AS LIVING IN
BERLIN AT 50 NASSAUERSTRASSE, 1000 BERLIN 31, AND HIS POB
WAS INDICATED AS BERLIN, GE.

--LKA HAMBURG (LANDESKRIMINALAMT - STATE LEVEL CRIMINAL
INVESTIGATIONS OFFICE), NO RECORD - 04/28/95

2.   FRG MILITARY RECORD CHECKS AND BERLIN POLICE CHECKS
HAVE BEEN REQUESTED, BUT ARE PENDING. RESULTS WILL BE
PROVIDED SEPTEL.

3.   THE ABOVE INFORMATION IS PROTECTED UNDER GERMAN
DATENSCHULTZ (PRIVACY ACT) LAWS, PLEASE PROTECT
ACCORDINGLY.   ALSO, AT THE DISCRETION OF DS/ICI/PII, THIS
CABLE MAY BE DOWNGRADED TO "UNCLASSIFIED" FOR LAW
ENFORCEMENT PURPOSES.
REDMAN

UNCLASS

~~LIMITED OFFICIAL USE~~

(I) State department telegram: background check on Andreas Strassmeir.

APPENDIX B

VINCE FOSTER

(A) Vince Foster's car registration, confirming that it was a grey 1989 Honda.

2527

(B) Park Police Detective Rolla's notes, noting a grey Honda and the phone number of Lt. Walter, Secret Service.

1658

FD-302 (Rev. 3-10-82)

CONFIDENTIAL

- 1 -

FEDERAL BUREAU OF INVESTIGATION

Date of transcription   5/17/94

Dr. DONALD DAVID HAUT, Medical Examiner, Fairfax County, Virginia, was interviewed at his office, 312 South Washington Street, Alexandria, Virginia. After being apprised of the identities of the interviewing agents and the purpose of the interview, HAUT thereafter provided the following information:

As Medical Examiner, HAUT advised that he is paid on a case by case basis. When not serving in his capacity as a medical examiner for Fairfax County, HAUT is a private physician. HAUT noted that physicians in private practice are selected to assist the forensic pathologists in a specific district. The function of the medical examiner is to investigate any death from unnatural causes or any death that is unattended by a physician. According to HAUT, there are usually two to three medical examiners working at any given time.

HAUT has responded to the scene of approximately 12 suicides in the course of his tenure as a medical examiner. Of the twelve, half were gunshot wounds to the head. At least one or two of those gunshot wounds were to the mouths of the victims.

In the course of the interview, HAUT was shown a series of photographs taken at the scene of the death of VINCENT W. FOSTER, JR. After reviewing the photographs, HAUT did not recall seeing blood on the decedent's shirt or face and no blood was recalled on the vegetation around the body. HAUT does not recall the body being photographed while he was at the death scene. He does recall lifting the body by the right shoulder and remembers receiving some assistance in doing so. He could not recall the individual providing that assistance. The purpose of lifting the right shoulder of the body was to check for an exit wound. HAUT had received no indication by U.S. Park Police (USPP) personnel that the body had been moved. HAUT could not provide any insight regarding the lateral blood flow as depicted in the photographs on FOSTER's face. HAUT did not recall seeing anyone touch the body while he was at the death scene. HAUT recalls arriving at the death scene at approximately 6:45 pm on July 20, 1993; he recalls there being moderate traffic in the area as he drove to Fort Marcy Park on the George Washington Memorial Parkway.

Investigation on	4/14/94	at Alexandria, Virginia	File # 29D-LR-35063 SUB A

OIC 000299

by _____ Date dictated   5/16/94 .

This document contains neither recommendati   ...—lusions of the FBI. It is the property of the FBI and is loaned to your agency; it and its contents are not to be distributed outside your agency.

(C) Dr. Haut's FBI statement that he arrived on the scene at 6:45 and found no blood on or around Foster's body.

1383

FD-302a (Rev. 11-15-83)

29D-LR-35063

CONFIDENTIAL

Continuation of FD-302 of ___Richard M. Arthur_____ , On ___3/16/94___ , Page ___3___

    ARTHUR estimated that from where the couple was they could
have heard a shot, but would not have been able to observe
anything in or heard voices from the vicinity of where FOSTER was
found.

    As ARTHUR returned to the parking area, GONZALES and
HALL were running back also from the lefthand path and yelled
that they had found the body. ARTHUR went down the path to take
a look. He located FOSTER's body somewhat off the path, located
such that if you were just walking the path you could miss it.
Police were following ARTHUR to the scene. In ARTHUR's
judgement, FOSTER was obviously dead and so he did not check for
a pulse. He noted that the body was lying perfectly straight--
like it was "ready for a coffin". A gun was lying on the ground
under his right hand, with the barrel partially under FOSTER's
thigh. He remembers the gun as being an automatic weapon of
approximately .45 caliber. He noted what appeared to be a small
caliber bullet hole in FOSTER's neck on the right side just under
the jaw line about half way between the ear and the tip of the
chin. He did not note anything else he thought might be a bullet
hole. He did not touch the body and remained at a distance of
two to four feet from it. He did not observe anybody touch the
body. He did not observe anybody move the gun. As he left to
return to the parking area, the U.S. Park Police were roping off
the scene.

    Once back in the parking area, the U.S. Park Police
took all the EMT's names. He observed them gaining access to a
cream colored car with a suit jacket and tie in it, looking for
identification of some sort. ARTHUR was on the scene
approximately 30-40 minutes.

    ARTHUR does not recall seeing any footprints or
disturbed earth around FOSTER's body. The deceased's clothes
were not disheveled, the hill area was clean and there was
nothing that struck him as unusual, except for the following
things, which make him doubt that it was a suicide: the straight
attitude of the body, the apparent caliber of the gun appeared
bigger that the hole he thought he had observed just under the
jawline, and that he remembered the barrel of the gun as being
under FOSTER's thigh (possibly half-way). It also struck him as
odd that the person who called authorities did not remain there

OIC 000038

(D) FBI statement of Richard Arthur, emergency medical service
technician, referring to Foster's neck wound from a small caliber
bullet.

2128

NATIONAL PARK SERVICE
SUPPLEMENTAL CRIMINAL INCIDENT RECORD
1 JUVENILE CASE ☐

GWMP Ft. Marcy

DID IT OCCUR? MO 0 7 DAY 2 0 YR 9 3 YEAR 9 3 · 0 3 0 5 0 2

ATURE OF INCIDENT: Death Investigation

RECLASSIFICATION OF INCIDENT

RESULTS OF INVESTIGATION

On 7/21/93 Sgt. [Rule,] I.D.Tech's [Johnson] and [Hill,] and the undersigned responded to the officer of the Medical Examiner in Fairfax Va. At this time we met with Dr. Byer. After briefing him with the available information surrounding the crime scene and the victim he started the autopsy on the victim. Prior to our arrival the victim's tongue had been removed as well as parts of the soft tissue from the pallet. Dr. Byer stated that there was evidence of gunpowder residue on the soft tissue but not on the tongue.

Dr. Byer pointed out what he thought to be gunpowder residue on the right hand forefinger of the victim. I supplied him with a picture of the crime scene in which the suspected residue was evident.

During the autopsy Dr. Byer noted that the bullet trajectory was "upward and backward" exiting in the center line of the back of the head. Dr. Byer stated that X-rays indicated that there was no evidence of bullet fragments in the head.

Dr. Byer stated that it appeared that the victim had eaten a "large" meal which he believed to have occurred within 2-3 hours prior to death. He was unable to state positively what type of food was consumed but stated the it might have been meat and potatoes.

The cause of death was determined to be "perforated gunshot wound in and out". The point of entry was in the back of the mouth with the exit in the back of the head.
Autopsy concluded at 1105 hrs.

Hair and blood samples as well as fingerprints were taken from the victim by Dr. Byer and turned over to I.D.Tech [Johnson.] In addition, I.D. took custody of the victim's clothing.

WARRANT(S)
☐ YES ☐ NO   ☐ LATENTS ☐ PHOTOS   ID TECH NOTIFIED   INVESTIGATOR NOTIFIED   12   PAGE OF PAGES

STATUS ☐ OPEN ☐ SUSPENDED ☐ CLOSED ☐ ARREST ☐ EXCEPTION ☐ UNFOUNDED

REPORTING OFFICER BADGE NO DATE IS INVESTIGATOR BADGE NO DATE IS SUPERVISOR BADGE NO DATE

(E) Dr. Beyer's statement to the Park Police that his X-rays found no evidence of bullet fragments in Foster's skull. Beyer later testified before the Senate Banking Committee that he never took any X-rays.

```
*01    BICKETT.SCOTT.JEFFREY              SSN=341606737   DB=620605   SB=IL   CB=US
    02    DOSSIER     LOCATION=DDIS      YEAR INDEXED=82     NUMBER=357DJ613721F3F
                      CONTEXT=SUBJECT    RETENTION=15 YRS   CLOSED DATE=
    03    NAC-HIST    DATE=830131  AGCY=DCII        FBI-HQ     FBI-T
    04    CLEARANCE AGCY=ACCF     ELIG=F   GRANTED=841115   ACCESS=     REV ACT=SCI
                      TYPE INV=SBI     DATE INV=830419   CAT=Z   CZIP=Z   SEP=
                      FILES=>DDIS=1   AIRR=1   ACRD=0   FOSI=0   NNIS=0   OTHER=
```

(F) Intelligence document that links the man who attacked Patrick Knowlton's car to the FBI and the Defense Department.

(G) Suspect sketch of the menacing man Knowlton saw in Fort Marcy Park, done for *The Sunday Telegraph*.

Secret Service
Alarm logs.

4214

MR. WATKINS OFFICE

07/20/93	02:21	O'NEILL	UD
	02:21	CC	UD
	02:30	O'NEILL	UD
	02:30	CC	UD
	04:47		
	04:48	CC	UD
	04:48		
	07:16	THOMASON	STAFF
	07:16	CC	UD
	19:05	THOMISON	STAFF
	19:05	THOMISON	STAFF
	19:10	MIG GROUP	USSS
	19:44	TOMLINSON	STAFF
	19:44	MIG GROUP	USSS
	22:48	THOMASON	STAFF
	22:48	CC	UD
07/21/93	00:11	THOMPSON	STAFF
	00:12	THOMPSON	STAFF
	00:12	CC	UD
	03:15	O'NEILL	UD
	04:54	CC	UD
	07:22	UIE	STAFF
	07:22	CC	UD
	20:55	NORTHCUTT	STAFF
	20:55	NORTHCUTT	STAFF
	20:55	CC	UD

6495

(H) Secret Service Alarm logs for the night of Foster's death. Note the multiple appearances of Patsy Thomasson (her name is misspelled). Also note the appearance of the "MIG GROUP"—a confidential technical branch of the Secret Service.

1778

FD-302a (Rev. 11-15-83)

29D-LR-35063 SUB A

Continuation of FD-302 of __SUSAN T. THOMASES__ , On __6/14/94__ , Page __2__

CLINTON administration, got to know VINCENT FOSTER fairly well.

She last saw VINCENT FOSTER on Wednesday or Thursday before his death. She believes that they had lunch together with some other people in Washington. She recalls him mentioning he planed to take a weekend trip to the eastern shore of Maryland. She noted no change in his demeanor or physical appearance but was aware that he was working very hard and was under considerable pressure. His death came as a complete shock to her and she can offer no reason or speculation as to why he may have taken his life.

Ms. THOMASES continues to regard HILLARY and BILL CLINTON as friends and visits with them from time to time when she is in Washington.

OIC 000418

(I) Susan Thomases's FBI statement that Foster's death came as a complete shock—a glaring contradiction to what she later told *Blood Sport* author James Stewart.

APPENDIX C

ARKANSAS

(A) Kevin Ives.

REPORT OF INVESTIGATION   Page 1 of 3

| 1. PROGRAM CODE | DESTROY | 2. CROSS FILE | 3. FILE NO. GFMQ-84-4046 | 4. G-DEP IDENTIFIER DA1-CO |

5. BY: S/A Anthony J. Coulson
AT: Tucson, Arizona

6. FILE TITLE
TYSON, Donald J. et al

7. ☐ Closed ☐ Requested Action Completed
☐ Action Requested By:

8. DATE PREPARED
July 9, 1984

9. OTHER OFFICERS:
Tucson Police Detective Roy LeBlanc

10. REPORT RE:
Debriefing of SMQ-84-0019 Re: Donald TYSON Drug Trafficking Organization

DETAILS:

DRUG-RELATED INFORMATION.

1. On July 5, 1984, SMQ-84-0019 telephoned S/A Anthony Coulson at the Tucson District Office concerning narcotic trafficking by Donald J. TYSON in and around the area of Fayetteville, Arkansas. The Cooperating Individual (CI) had information concerning heroin, cocaine and marijuana trafficking in the States of Arkansas, Texas, and Missouri by the TYSON Organization. On that same day, S/A Coulson and Tucson Police Detective Roy LeBlanc met with SMQ-84-0019 to debrief that CI. The CI advised S/A Coulson that in January, February and March of 1978 the CI had contact with Alex MONTEZ and Donald KEMP, who are believed to be Lieutenants for Donald TYSON. The CI stated that MONTEZ owns a restaurant named CASA MONTEZ and distributes cocaine from that restaurant.

2. The CI got involved with the TYSON Organization through James and Harmon CURRY. The CURRY brothers are believed to be smugglers for Donald TYSON. The CI stated that Harmon CURRY, AKA BUTTER, used the CI's vehicle to smuggle marijuana and cocaine throughout Arkansas. Harmon CURRY is believed to be living in Cement, Oklahoma, working for a construction/excavation company approximately forty miles from Oklahoma City.

3. The CI stated that a Jacqueline SMITH, who used to live in Fayetteville, Arkansas, married to George SMITH, had an affair back in 1978 with Donald KEMP. It was from SMITH that the CI learned of a location called "THE BARN" in which TYSON used as a "stash" location for large quantities of marijuana and cocaine. "THE BARN" area is located between Springdale and Fayetteville, Arkansas and, from the outside, the appearance of "THE BARN" looks run down. On the inside of "THE BARN" it is quite plush. The CI also learned that Donald TYSON has all of the narcotics related meetings at the Ramada Inn in Fayetteville, Arkansas, and those meetings are usually concerning the business in and around "THE BARN."

11. DISTRIBUTION:	12. SIGNATURE (Agent)	13. DATE
REGION Little Rock R.O	ANTHONY J. COULSON, Special Agent	8-10-84
DISTRICT ARI, PDFR, OIE	14. APPROVED (Name and Title)	15. DATE
OTHER HQS-OC-Direct	W. T. FERNANDEZ, Group Supervisor	8/11/84

DEA Form – 6 (May 1980)   RMB/8/10/84

DEA SENSITIVE
DRUG ENFORCEMENT ADMINISTRATION
This report is the property of the Drug Enforcement Administration.
Neither it nor its contents may be disseminated outside the agency to which loaned.
Previous edition may be used.

(B) DEA report on the "Donald TYSON Drug Trafficking Organization."

	1. FILE NO.	2. G-DEP IDENTIFIER
REPORT OF INVESTIGATION *(Continuation)*	GFMQ-84-4046	DA1-CO
	3. FILE TITLE	
4. Page 2 of 3	TYSON, Donald J. et al	
5. PROGRAM CODE	6. DATE PREPARED July 9, 1984	

4. The CI stated that James CURRY was the leader of the brothers which included not only Harmon CURRY, but William CURRY, AKA BUN. The CI informed S/A Coulson that all three CURRY brothers had been arrested in and around September 1977 on a narcotics related charge, but the CI did not know the disposition on that particular arrest. In March 1978, Jacqueline SMITH, in a state of intoxication, stated to the CI, "Daddy Don (Donald TYSON) can put out the word to take care of you, and Alex MONTEZ will leave you in a culvert, but somebody else will take the blame for it." SMITH then stated, "Don (KEMP) couldn't have done it because I was with him." The CI stated that around that time a female who worked at a forge (tool making business in the Fayetteville area) was found in a culvert near Highway 71 outside of Fayetteville, Arkansas.

5. The CI advised that the CURRY brothers are fluent in the Spanish language, and James and Harmon CURRY have lived in El Paso, Texas, and have several contacts with Mexican sources of supply for marijuana in Juarez, Chihuahua, Mexico. A male, only known as Richard (LNU), who is not a relative and who married Don and Donna Hendricks' daughter, was living with James CURRY and was a heavy narcotics user. Richard (LNU) did all of his narcotics business at the University of Arkansas. James CURRY talked frequently to the CI concerning Richard's (LNU) abusing narcotics and how that would draw attention to CURRY's narcotics businesses.

6. The CI traveled back to Arkansas in July 1978, and at that time Jacqueline SMITH appeared very nervous that the CI was back in Arkansas. Subsequently, it was learned by the CI that Jackie SMITH moved to Las Vegas, Nevada, and worked or was associated with a Casino there. Before Jacqueline SMITH left for Las Vegas, she (SMITH) wanted the CI to meet a lawyer who was associated with Donald TYSON. This attorney was in his mid fifties, was short and overweight, and his office was across from Donald KEMP's office in Fayetteville, Arkansas.

7. The CI believes that Donald KEMP has since moved to Oklahoma. The CI learned in November 1982 from the CI's relatives that "THE BARN" is still operating.

8. At this time, attempts will be made by the CI to recontact Harmon CURRY to negotiate with Harmon CURRY to transact an amount of cocaine here in Tucson, Arizona.

NON-DRUG RELATED INFORMATION.

    None.

I-4089

REPORT OF INVESTIGATION *(Continuation)*	1. FILE NO. GFMQ-. 4046	2. G-DEP IDENTIFIER DA1-CO
	3. FILE TITLE TYSON, Donald J. et al	
4. Page 3 of 3		
5. PROGRAM CODE	6. DATE PREPARED July 9, 1984	

INDEXING:

1. TYSON, Donald J.: NADDIS #470067.

2. MONTEZ, Alex Franco: NADDIS #408244.

3. SMITH, Jacqueline: NADDIS #998530.

4. KEMP, Donald: NADDIS negative. Resides in Oklahoma. NFI.

5. CURRY, James: NADDIS negative. Resides in Fayetteville, Arkansas. NFI.

6. CURRY, Harmon, AKA BUTTER: NADDIS negative. Is a white male, believed to reside in Cement, Oklahoma. Possible DOB: 1/25/55. NFI.

7. CURRY, William, AKA BUN: NADDIS negative. Is a white male, believed to reside in Rogers, Arkansas. NFI.

8. (LNU), Richard: NADDIS negative. Address negative. NFI.

9. CASA MONTEZ, XR: NADDIS #408278.

OB 1-18-83

REPORT OF INVESTIGATION

Page 1 of 1

1. PROGRAM CODE	2. CROSS FILE	RELATED FILES	3. FILE NO. GFGJ-83-9052	4. G DEP IDENTIFIER DA1-CO

5. BY: H. Dean Gates, S/A
   AT: Oklahoma City, Oklahoma

6. FILE TITLE
   REFERRALS FROM STATE LAW ENFORCEMENT
   AGENCIES

7. ☐ Closed ☒ Requested Action Completed
   ☐ Action Requested By:

8. DATE PREPARED
   December 14, 1982

9. OTHER OFFICERS:

10. REPORT RE:

Identification of associate of Jerry PRIDEAUX.

DETAILS:

1. Reference is made to DEA-6 by S/A Robert Morris, Little Rock, Arkansas, dated 11/30/82 concerning the arrest of Jerry BLACKWELL and Tina JONES.

2. On December 14, 1982, S/A Gates had a telephone conversation with Detective Sgt. Frank Myres of the Tulsa Police Department concerning Jerry PRIDEAUX. Sgt. Myres advised that he had received information from confidential sources indicating that PRIDEAUX' source for cocaine is a Don TYSON, who owns TYSON INDUSTRIES in Springdale, Arkansas. Sgt. Myres also advised that his source said that TYSON smuggles cocaine from Colombia, South America inside race horses to Hot Springs, Arkansas. No further amplification or clarification as to exactly how the drugs were concealed in the horse was made. It was unknown by Sgt. Myres and S/A Gates that horses were brought to the race tracks at Hot Springs from Colombia.

3. Sgt. Myres' source also stated that a Dale LNU is a runner for TYSON and drops cocaine to PRIDEAUX. Sgt. Myres' source was under the impression that Dale LNU lives in Stilwell, Oklahoma rather than the Sallisaw area where, accoridng to the referenced report Dale WARD resides.

4. Sgt. Myres advised that PRIDEAUX has been a target by the Tulsa PD for several years and in fact PRIDEAUX has been arrested numerous times for illegal gambling. PRIDEAUX owns the STING BAR, 9421 East 31st, Tulsa, Oklahoma, telephone 918/627-9988 and is part owner of the PARADOX CLUB, 6214 South Lewis, Tulsa, Oklahoma, telephone 918/742-9386.

INDEXING SECTION:

1. PRIDEAUX, Jerry - NADDIS 1427803, DOB 12/04/34, Tulsa PD# 39086, OSBI# 85101.

2. TYSON, Don J. - NADDIS 470067, aka "CHICKEN MAN", owns Tyson Industries, Springdale, Arkansas.

3. WARD, Dale - NADDIS 1427854.

11. DISTRIBUTION:	12. SIGNATURE (Agent)	13. DATE
REGION	H. Dean Gates, S/A	1-18-8
DISTRICT Dallas, Little Rock	14. APPROVED (Name and Title)	15. DATE
OTHER ARL OC	Mel B. Ashton, RAC	1/18/83

DEA Form — 6
(May 1980)

Sandler
Best
Lt Pife
Weaver

I-17927 (DALE WARD)
SEE: I-17927 (JERRY PRIDEAUX). SEE: T-2953 (DON TYSON)

CRIMINAL INVESTIGATION SECTION

INTELLIGENCE

```
CIS - 3C
DATE:                          3/22/76
DICTATED BY:                   INV. DOUG FOGLEY
COUNTY:                        Washington
SOURCE OF INFORMATION:         Sheriff HERB MARSHALL
TOPIC OF INFORMATION:          Criminal Activity
DATE TYPED:                    3/25/76
COPIES TO:                     CAPT. GEORGE MOYE
                               LT. CARROLL EVANS
                               INV. FOGLEY
```

VERY CONFIDENTIAL

This information was related to this agent on the morning of March 22, 1976 by Sheriff HERB MARSHALL.

No dissemination is to be made of this information other than to this agent, Captain MOYE and Lieutenant EVANS.

Several hotels in the southern United States including Arkansas are owned by the Teamsters Union as legitimate businesses which the various factions of the somewhat questionable Teamsters Union use to "clean" their money. Two such hotels are the Downtowner Inn in Fayetteville and the Aristocrat Hotel in Hot Springs. The Teamsters Union goes out of its way to keep these hotels highly legitimate and of unquestionable reputation. The manager or overseerer employed by the Teamsters Union for the two hotels in Arkansas (plus others) is BOB FORSHEE, a white male. Recently a private club called the Brass Monkey was established in the basement of the Downtowner Inn in Fayetteville, Arkansas. This club of somewhat questionable reputation has lately caused the Teamsters certain anxiety about it being in one of their hotels. The club is leased and the license holder for the private club are DON TYSON, a white male and BILLIE SNYDER, a white female.

DON TYSON needs no introduction to the State Police CID or for that matter any law enforcement agency in Northwest, Arkansas. He is an extremely wealthy man with much political influence and seems to be involved in most every kind of shady operation especially narcotics, however, has to date gone without implication in any specific crime. TYSON likes

FILE NUMBER: W I-2465

(C) State Police criminal investigation documents linking Tyson to "every kind of shady operation especially narcotics."

PAGE NO. __2__

to think of himself as the "King of the Hill"
in Northwest, Arkansas and quite possibly this
might not be erroneous.

BILLIE SNYDER is a very close friend of
DON TYSON, is financially comfortable by anyone's
means and also has a great deal of influence both
financial and political in the Northwest, Arkansas
area. BILLIE SNYDER is on a first name basis with
many of Arkansas' top politicians.

Since TYSON and SNYDER have been working·
the Brass Monkey, prostitution and gambling have ·
run rampant in the club. Two employees,RED SMITH
and FNU TAYLOR allegedly push drugs from behind the
bar. Needless to say, this situation causes the
Teamsters a certain amount of worry since the hotels
are used as a legitimate front and their reputation
must be kept above reproach.

According to Sheriff HERB MARSHALL, the
representative of the Teamsters Union have advised
TYSON and SNYDER to vacate the premises·of the club
in the Downtowner Inn in Fayetteville. Allegedly
TYSON and BILLIE SNYDER slightly refused in very
blunt terms.

The Teamsters Union dispatched "an investigator"
from the St. Louis Office named Mr. WAYRICK who
is an attorney employed by the Union to "correct ·
the situation".

It is the opinion of Sheriff MARSHALL and Mr.
BOB FORSCHEE, District Manager for the hotels,
that if simple reasoning does not cause the TYSON-
SNYDER partnership to vacate the premises "other
methods" will be employed by the Teamsters Union to
accomplish these ends.

Since law enforcement will not become involved
until a crime has occurred, it was decided by ·
Sheriff MARSHALL that he would wait to see what
happened in the above described situation.

It is the personal opinion of this investigator
that knowing TYSON and his pride, he will slightly
ւefuse to vacate the premises and in knowing the
Teamsters Union, it will more or less be insisted
.upon above TYSON's objections. The reason this

FILE NUMBER: CRIME: Criminal Activity

PAGE NO. ___3___

intelligence report is dictated is to document
the information already obtained on the situation
for a possible future use. It is felt that it will
be interesting to see what transpires from the
situation as whether or not TYSON thinks that he
is a big leaguer. He is most assuredly dealing
with the "big boys" now in the form of the
Teamsters Union.

TO: _Fogley_____ DATE _____
TO: _Coase_____ DATE _____
TO: _____ DATE _____
TO: _CF009_____ DATE _____
TO: _____ DATE _____
TO: _____ DATE _____
TO: _____ DATE _____
TO: _____ DATE _____
TO: _____ DATE _____
TO: _____ DATE _____

FILE NUMBER: CRIME: Criminal Activity

NO DISSEMINATION
CRIMINAL INVESTIGATION DIVISION

INTELLIGENCE

CID - 3C
DATE:
DICTATED BY: *January 21, 1981*
COUNTY: *SERGEANT HALE*
SOURCE OF INFORMATION: *WASHINGTON*
TOPIC OF INFORMATION: *CONFIDENTIAL INFORMANT*
DATE TYPED: *DRUG AND STOLEN PROPERTY DEALERS*
COPIES TO: *January 17, 1981*

NO DISSEMINATION

  *The following information was received from Inmate JAMES DAVIS
at the Tucker Unit of the Arkansas Department of Corrections. The
informant has been confined since 1978 and the reliability of his
information is not known at this time, but he states he had been
updated on happenings with in the county by other inmates.*

  *The dissemination of this information should remain within
confidential sources.*

  *The inmate states that <u>DON TYSON</u>, white male, in his 50's,
that lives in Springdale and operates the Tyson Chicking Processing
Plant in that city is involved in drug traffic and stolen property.
The informant states that TYSON has been operating · a Crystal
Methamphetamine lab that was located at the Swepco Generator Plant
in a small shed located on Highway 68 west of Springdale between
Siloam Springs and Gentry. The security on this drug lab was over
seen by <u>BILL ELVINS</u> and his son, <u>BILL, JR.</u>. The above two are
affiliated with a security company there in Springdale. The plant
was moved approximately 4 months ago to Baldwin, Arkansas and set
up in a mobile home behind the Speedy-Mart Store. Most of the products
of this drug lab are being passed on the campus of the University
of Arkansas at Fayetteville. TYSON brings in his supplies for his
lab in his trucks that haul frozen chickens.*

  *An assosicate of TYSON was now ex-sheriff <u>HERB MARSHALL</u>. Ex-
sheriff MARSHALL was to have been furnishing confiscated weapons
to TYSON for sale. The information is that in July, 1980, ex-sheriff
MARSHALL confiscated a large amount of guns in a mobile home and
that these guns were turned over to TYSON.*

  *Also involved with the stolen guns is <u>JOE FRED STARR</u>, white male,
approximately 57 years of age, operator of Springdale Farms.
STARR also is involved in purchasing Cocaine and Marijuana and hires
the runners to distribute it. STARR and TYSON work together in the*
FILE NUMBER:

I-4835

I-3.5(66.4 ??)

ASP-3

PAGE NO. ___2___

narcotics and stolen gun dealings.

Inmate DAVIS stated he has information that the gun that was confiscated from him, that he used in the shooting which he was convicted of, was used also in an armed robbery of the Monteray (phonetic) Seafood Cafe. The robbery was committed by a black male, who is now said to be serving time in Cummins for the crime.

The stolen guns are often said to end up in the "71" Gun Shop in Fayeteville.

CLINT SPENCER, white male, approximately 60, 185 pounds, operator of the Spencer Bonding Agency in Fayetteville is said to work for TYSON as a hit man. Drug dealers that owe TYSON money were tracked down by SPENCER and said to have been found missing and to be heard of again.

Runners for TYSON are said to be ; 1. RICK DOLAN, white male, 23, 6'4", 170 lbs. 2. BOBBY CARSLIE, white male, 45, 6', 180 pounds (said to be Mayor of Farmington). 3. CHARLES AGEE, white male, 60, 5', 190 pounds, manager of the IGA Grocery, Fayetteville. 4. LARRY HASKINS, white male, 26, 5'10", 175 lbs., was the jailer at the Washington County Jail. 5. MORTON MARSHALL, white male, 24, 5'8", 220 lbs., also jailer at the Washington County Jail.

Also information that the Am-Vet's Club in Fayeteville, Highway 62 west, has the same ownership as TOMMY'S Lounge in Sprindgale, being CHUCK last name unknown, white male, 6'5", 280 lbs., was paying the Washington County Sheriff's Office for protection in the past and some of TYSON'S drugs goes through these clubs.

NO DISSEMINATION

TO: _____ DATE 1:30
TO: _____ DATE 1:30
TO: _____ DATE _____
TO: _____ DATE _____
TO: _____ DATE _____
TO: _____ DATE _____
TO: _____ DATE _____
TO: _____ DATE _____
TO: _____ DATE _____
TO: _____ DATE _____

FILE NUMBER: CRIME:

FD-302a (Rev. 11-15-83)

LR 245F-2

After obtaining the $300,000, he flew to Lexington, Kentucky, and turned over the money to JIMMY LAMBERT at the airport. The money was carried in a paper sack, and the $300,000 amount was paid back within six months without any payment on the interest. Mr. LASATER said he paid the interest on the amount himself when he paid off the $300,000 note.

When the note was due, the money was wired to him in care of his bank account at what was then FIRST NATIONAL BANK in Little Rock.

Mr. LASATER advised he first met TONY ANAYA in October 1984 when Mr. ANAYA was governor of New Mexico and was a guest speaker at a barbecue during the inaugural opening of ANGEL FIRE RESORT in New Mexico. Mr. ANAYA has never done him any personal favors even though he may have been responsible for blacktopping a road between Mora and Black Lake, New Mexico. It was not done as a favor to him. The road was paved sometime during the summer of 1985, and even though it benefited employees of ANGEL FIRE, there were no improprieties on his part or the governor's part.

He explained that the 8,900-foot runway at the ANGEL FIRE RESORT, New Mexico, was already under construction when he purchased the resort. There were 110 acres donated to the county during the construction of the runway, but there were no improprieties on his part or the governor's part regarding this transaction.

Mr. LASATER says he does recall that ODIS ECKLES has talked to Governor ANAYA about a consultant job upon the governor's leaving office sometime at the end of the year 1986. Mr. LASATER identified ECKLES as a consultant for the ANGEL FIRE RESORT Company but that nothing improper surrounded his offer to the governor.

Mr. LASATER stated CLARENCE STRAHAN was an employee who formerly worked for GEORGE HALL at the CAPITAL CLUB in Little Rock, and he became familiar with STRAHAN who worked as a bartender and waiter at several of the company parties. He personally hired STRAHAN as a personal valet on his aircraft, THE CHALLENGER, which he sold in December 1985. STRAHAN started his employment in July 1984. He is presently employed as a salesman for LASATER AND COMPANY. Mr. LASATER

(D) FBI statement of Dan Lasater confessing, among other things, that he took cocaine with Roger Clinton, whom he hired at the request of Governor Clinton.

FD-302a (Rev. 11-15-83)

LR 245F-2

Continuation of FD-302 of _____ DANNY RAY LASATER _____ . On __10/14/86__ . Page __20__

stated that he has seen CLARENCE STRAHAN use cocaine approximately
five times and that STRAHAN has had the responsibility
of holding his (LASATER's) cocaine on numerous occasions.
He stated that CLARENCE STRAHAN has bought cocaine for
him approximately three or four times but that the money
used for the purchase always came from himself.

Mr. LASATER admitted doing cocaine with GEORGOE
HALL and HERBIE DOUGLAS in the past, with one of the occasions
occurring at the KING ARTHUR'S CLUB on Markham in 1982
or early 1983. He did not recall to whom the cocaine belonged
at the time.

He is familiar with LARRY KELLY, but he has never
done cocaine with KELLY, and he has never given KELLY any
cocaine.

He is unfamiliar with an individual by the name
of BUD GUY. Mr. LASATER advised that he has snorted cocaine
with DON BUZANOWSKI, who worked in the Fort Lauderdale,
Florida, office. He snorted cocaine with him on one or
two occasions and has given him cocaine in bump amounts.

He is only slightly familiar with OMAR BUTTARI
as BUTTARI worked in the Fort Lauderdale, Florida, office.
He had no drug dealings with BUTTARI.

He is familiar with TOM CARTER, with whom he
has snorted cocaine on several occasions in which the cocaine
would be both his and TOM CARTER's at the time.

Mr. LASATER related that he has given PAULA COLLINS
cocaine ranging from fifteen (15) to twenty-five (25) times
in small amounts. He denied ever ordering CHUCK BERRY
to give PAULA COLLINS cocaine but was aware that BERRY
had given her cocaine in the past. He knows PAULA COLLINS
as being the former wife of DAVID COLLINS.

Regarding ROGER CLINTON, Mr. LASATER advised
he met CLINTON through MITCHELL WOOD sometime around 1981
or 1982 during the time CLINTON played in a band in the
Hot Springs area. CLINTON was employed by him at one time
in which Governor BILL CLINTON requested LASATER to hire
him. ROGER CLINTON was employed as a stable hand at his
Ocala, Florida, horse farm. Mr. LASATER stated he has
done cocaine with ROGER CLINTON, and they have shared their
personal supplies of cocaine as each of them always had
it with them.

Appendix C

FD-302a (Rev. 11-15-83)

LR 245F-2

Continuation of FD-302 of _____ DANNY RAY LASATER _____ .On 10/14/86 , Page ____ 21

> In regard to the $8,000 loan made to ROGER CLINTON,
Mr. LASATER advised that ROGER CLINTON approached him about
borrowing $16,000 or $20,000 as Mr. CLINTON explained that
someone had stolen his stash of cocaine which belonged
to SAM ANDERSON at the time. The cocaine, as he recalls,
was supposed to have been in a car that was broken into.
He advised CLINTON came to him and said that someone was
putting the heat on him and something might happen to his
brother and his mother. The loan was not for that large
amount, but he consented to loan CLINTON $8,000. He did
not handle the transaction personally but thinks that it
was taken care of by one of his employees in the company.
The transaction was done with a check, and it was requested
that CLINTON turn over his car title for collateral. He
denied ever buying cocaine from ROGER CLINTON.

> LASATER may have met MAURICE RODRIGUEZ on one
occasion at the end of the race season in Hot Springs,
Arkansas. It was possibly during the spring of 1983.

> Mr. LASATER related that he would estimate that
his company has contracted with the state of Arkansas less
than one-tenth (1/10) of 1% of the bond business. He denied
any allegation of improprieties regarding himself or his
company with the governor of Arkansas, BILL CLINTON.

> He advised that BILL CLINTON had been at his
house on one occasion for a Christmas party and was there
only thirty (30) minutes. He also attended a Christmas
party at the LITTLE ROCK COUNTRY CLUB and was there approximately
thirty (30) minutes. He was present for the opening of
PULLEYBONE'S, a local restaurant, and was there approximately
thirty (30) minutes also.

> Concerning the contract surrounding the bond
issue pertaining to the communication system for the Arkansas
State Police, Mr. LASATER advised that representatives
of the E. F. HUTTON COMPANY represented LASATER AND COMPANY
during meetings with the CLINTON staff. There were no
improprieties surrounding these meetings, and very few
people associated with LASATER AND COMPANY had any dealings
with Mr. CLINTON's personnel.

ASP-6   CRIMINAL INVESTIGATION DIVISION
                    DESCRIPTION OF SUBJECT

NAME: Patricia Anne Smith

ALIAS: Pattie Anne, Muffin, Precious   S.S.# ████████

ADDRESS: P.O. Box 4169 N State line 89449   PHONE: 916 542 0900

RACE: W   SEX: F   DOB: 5/26/66   WHERE BORN: L R, AR.

HEIGHT: 5'8"   WEIGHT: 104   COMPLEXION: fair   HAIR: blonde   EYES: green

SCARS & MARKS: surgical - apindxy - 2 one on each side

PECULIARITIES: NONE

OCCUPATIONS: seating hostess, Time share sales

EMPLOYER: Tahoe Beach and Ski Club

EDUCATION: 12th grade drop out.

MARITAL STATUS: Single

RELATIVES: Mary E. Smith, James F. Smith

VEHICLE: 1986 Suzuki Samari (Red)

DATE ARRESTED: _____ PLACE ARRESTED: _____

RECORD FROM: _____ CHARGE: _____

DISPOSITION: _____

PHOTOGRAPHED: _____ DATE: _____ AGENCY: _____

FINGERPRINTED: _____ DATE: _____ AGENCY: _____

ASPOL NUMBER: _____ FBI NUMBER: _____

FILE NUMBER: 58-689-86   INVESTIGATOR: DE LAUGHTER

(E) Patty-Anne Smith, the young girl "introduced to cocaine use by Dan Lasater."

Lasater & Company
INVESTMENT BANKERS

312 Louisiana Street • Little Rock, Arkansas 72201
501/376-0069 • National Wats 1-800-643-8072 • Arkansas Wats 1-800-482-8496

SIPC

ORIGINATOR NO.	DEL. VIA	OFFICE-ACCOUNT-TYPE-RR	TRANS. NO.	CODES TR	CAP	SETT	TRADE DATE	SETTLEMENT DATE	AS OF
01	F	1-35067-1-2 271	2844	7	6	8	9/23/85	9/26/85	9/23/85

IDENTIFICATION NO.	ACCOUNT NAME	C.H. NUMBER	SPECIAL DELIVERY INSTRUCTIONS

SS# 61-1041943

PATRICK & ASSOCIATES
ATTN DENNIS PATRICK
ROUTE #4, BOX 890

WILLIAMSBURG   KY 40769

ABA #0260-0588-5
SECURITY NYC/SPCS/LASATER

00000

	QUANTITY	CUSIP NUMBER	SECURITY DESCRIPTION
YOU SLD	11625000.00	313401FJ5	FHLMC GROUP #16-0055 AMORTIZED PAR 8,116,654.05 9.250 9/01/2008 DTD 9/01/1978

PRICE	PRINC. AMOUNT	INTEREST	COMM.	TAX	S.E.C. FEE	MISC. AMOUNT	NET AMOUNT
91 11/32	7414056.18	52138.23					7466194.41

WE CONFIRM THE ABOVE TRANSACTION. SEE REVERSE FOR TERMS OF AGREEMENT AND EXPLANATION OF ITEMS MARKED. PLEASE RETAIN THIS CONFIRMATION FOR INCOME TAX PURPOSES.

Lasater & Company
INVESTMENT BANKERS

312 Louisiana • Little Rock, Arkansas 72201
501/376-0069 • National Wats 1-800-643-8072 • Arkansas Wats 1-800-482-8496

SIPC

ORIGINATOR NO.	ACCOUNT	RR	TRAN. NO.	CODES TR	CAP	SETT	TRADE DATE	SETTLEMENT DATE	AS OF
01	1-35067-1-2	271	93706	7	2	7	12/23/85	1/21/86	1/07/86

IDENTIFICATION NO.	TELEPHONE NO.	SPECIAL DELIVERY INSTRUCTIONS
61-1041943	606-549-2973	PAIROFF 12/27 @ 96 09/32 BEY 100-9.73 8-9.60 CORR #8034

PATRICK & ASSOCIATES
ATTN DENNIS PATRICK
ROUTE #4, BOX 890

WILLIAMSBURG   KY 40769

	QUANTITY	PRICE	YIELD	▼ CUSIP NUMBER ▼	SECURITY DESCRIPTION
YOU BOT	5,000,000.00	96 00/32		362011AC3	GNMA POOL #0000 AMORTIZED PAR 5,000,000.00

PRINC. AMOUNT	INTEREST
4,800,000.00	

NET AMOUNT
4,800,000.00

AS/OF 1/07/86 9.000

(F) Dennis Patrick's account statements from Lasater & Company, indicating the millions of dollars flowing through his account.

Repair Description		Amount
Date 2/1/1984		
Make & Model 54674 C123		
Work Order No 0534		
Name BARRY SEAL		
Labor to make crate for shipping - 1.69 hr. @ $28.00	47	32
Labor to install L/H engine - 8.00 hr. @ $28.00 per hr.	225	12
Labor to remove engine - 18.00 hr. @ $28.00 per hr.	504	00
Labor to remove prop gove. - 17.75 hr. @ $28.00 per hr.	497	00
Labor to tear down prop & load in aircraft - 6.08 hr. @ $28.00	170	24
Labor to pre-flight aircraft - 2.38 hr. @ $28.00 per hr.	66	64

Total of Attached Sheets

TOTAL PARTS

OUTSIDE WORK

TOTAL OUTSIDE WORK

Total Labor
Total Part
Outside Work
Freight
Gas & Oil
Tax
Total Amount

(G) Rich Mountain repair receipts for Barry Seal's "No Problema," indicating Seal operated the "phantom plane" as early as February 1984.

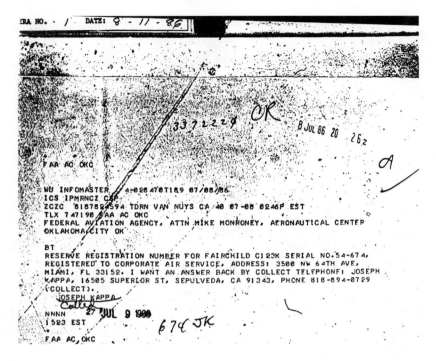

RA NO. / DATE: 8 - 11 - 86

F AA AC OKC

WU INFOMASTER 4-028 470T189 07/08/86
ICS IPMRNCZ CSP
ZCZC 818788594 TDRN VAN NUYS CA 40 07-08 0246P EST
TLX 747190 FAA AC OKC
FEDERAL AVIATION AGENCY, ATTN MIKE MONRONEY, AERONAUTICAL CENTER
OKLAHOMA CITY OK

BT
RESERVE REGISTRATION NUMBER FOR FAIRCHILD C123K SERIAL NO. 54-674,
REGISTERED TO CORPORATE AIR SERVICE, ADDRESS: 3500 NW 64TH AVE,
MIAMI, FL 33152. I WANT AN ANSWER BACK BY COLLECT TELEPHONE: JOSEPH
KAPPA, 16505 SUPERIOR ST, SEPULVEDA, CA 91343, PHONE 818-894-0729
(COLLECT).
JOSEPH KAPPA
NNNN 27 JUL 9 1986
1523 EST
F AA AC OKC

(H) The first official document with the serial number of "No Problema."

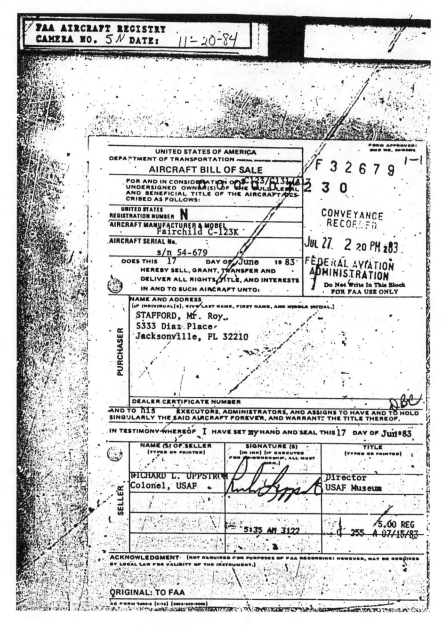

(I) The paper trail of "Fat Lady" registrations.

FAA AIRCRAFT REGISTRY.
CAMERA NO. 5 N DATE: 11-20-84

FORM APPROVED OMB NO. 04-R0076

UNITED STATES OF AMERICA
DEPARTMENT OF TRANSPORTATION - FEDERAL AVIATION ADMINISTRATION

4-1

AIRCRAFT REGISTRATION APPLICATION

CERT/ ISSUE DATE

UNITED STATES
REGISTRATION NUMBER **N 010 1 3 9 6**

AIRCRAFT MANUFACTURER & MODEL
Fairchild C-123K

B 10 26 83

AIRCRAFT SERIAL No.
54-679

FOR FAA USE ONLY

TYPE OF REGISTRATION (Check one box)

[ ] 1. Individual [ ] 2. Partnership [X] 3. Corporation [ ] 4. Co-Owner [ ] 5. Gov't.

NAME OF APPLICANT (Person(s) shown on evidence of ownership. If individual, give last name, first name, and middle initial.)

DOAN HELICOPTER, INC
P O BOX 821
Daytona Beach, Florida 32015

ADDRESS (Permanent mailing address for first applicant listed.)

Number and street: **Big Tree Road**

Rural Route: _____ P. O. Box: **821**

CITY	STATE	ZIP CODE
Daytona Beach	Florida	32015

[ ] CHECK HERE IF YOU ARE ONLY REPORTING A CHANGE OF ADDRESS

ATTENTION! Read the following statement before signing this application.

A false or dishonest answer to any question in this application may be grounds for punishment by fine and/or imprisonment (U.S. Code, Title 18, Sec. 1001).

CERTIFICATION

WE CERTIFY that the above described aircraft (1) is owned by the undersigned applicant(s), who is/are citizen(s) of the United States as defined in Sec. 101(13) of the Federal Aviation Act of 1958; (2) is not registered under the laws of any foreign country; and, (3) legal evidence of ownership is attached or has been filed with the Federal Aviation Administration.

NOTE: If executed for co-ownership all applicants must sign. Use reverse side if necessary.

SIGNATURE	TITLE	DATE
Harry S Doan	President	8/18/83
SIGNATURE	TITLE	DATE
SIGNATURE	TITLE	DATE

EACH PART OF THIS APPLICATION MUST BE SIGNED IN INK

NOTE: Pending receipt of the Certificate of Aircraft Registration, the aircraft may be operated for a period not in excess of 90 days, during which time the PINK copy of this application must be carried in the aircraft.

AC FORM 8050-1 (8-78) (0082-00-628-9004)

(J) "No Problema": the phantom plane.

IN THE UNITED STATES DISTRICT COURT
EASTERN DISTRICT OF ARKANSAS
WESTERN DIVISION

TERRY K. REED, ET AL.   PLAINTIFFS

     v.   Civil No. LR-C-94-634

RAYMOND YOUNG, ET AL.   DEFENDANTS

ORDER

     Pending before the Court is defendants' [Raymond (Buddy) Young and Tommy L. Baker] December 4th motion in limine to exclude the following matters:.......These general areas will be referred to as the "Mena " evidence or documents.

......Even if the Court were to find that the complaint adequately states sufficient facts to make the allegations......relevant to the alleged overt actions of these defendants, the probative value is substantially outweighed by the dangers of unfair prejudice, confusion of issues, the potential for misleading of the jury and considerations of undue delay and waste of time. The following description will control: [may not be introduced into evidence or made part of the court record]

     Any reference to the plaintiffs' [Terry and Janis Reed] participation in programs, operations or missions sponsored by the Federal Bureau of Investigation or the Central Intelligence Agency or any other agency of the United States government, covert or otherwise, as well as any organization sponsored by or aligned with the United States government specifically including, but not limited to, any programs, operations or missions conducted in southwest Arkansas regarding the training of Nicaraguan nationals, the funding and support for any factions involved in the Nicaraguan conflict and any contact or communications with operatives or officials of the above-named agencies or organizations. Any reference to President or Governor Bill Clinton and/or Hillary Clinton and the Mena or Nella Airports. Any references to Barry Seale [sic] and any alleged drug smuggling operation or other references to the Mena and Nella Airports, or to a business relationship of Barry Seale [sic] and Dan Lasater, Lasater and Company and the Arkansas Development and Finance Authority (ADFA) and ADFA's former Director, Bob Nash.

     ....IT IS SO ORDERED THIS _____8th_____ day of March, 1996.

                       _____George Howard , Jr._ [signed]_
                       UNITED STATES DISTRICT JUDGE

(K) Judge George Howard's order barring Mena evidence in the Terry Reed case.

INDEX

445

26–31; Parks murder, 249–251;
Rolla interview, 146; Scott
interview, 224, 225; Strassmeir
arrest and, 63; Thomasson and,
298; Vanderboegh and, 36
Federal Savings and Loan
Insurance Corporation, 311
Ferguson, Danny, 358, 359
Ferstl, Franz, 124, 166
Fifth Estate, 88
Finley, Angela: damage assessment
memo, 68–69; Howe and,
54–55, 56, 60–61, 64, 71; notes
and reports, 60–61, 66, 73;
Strassmeir arrest and, 63
First American Savings and Loan,
Oak Brook, Illinois, 311–312
1st Alabama Cavalry Regiment,
35–36
Fiske, Robert, 113, 121–122, 129,
147, 189–190, 193
Fiske Report, 138–139, 159, 183,
228; Confidential Witness
and, 123; gun, 130–131; missing
bullet, 133, 134; no shot heard,
157; suicide ruling, 122, 209
Fitzhugh, Michael, 280
Fitzpatrick, Neal, 74
*Fools for Scandal: How the Media
Invented Whitewater*,
187
Fornshill, Kevin, 124–126
Fort Marcy Park crime scene, 112;
Confidential Witness and,
119–120; exploration of, 134;
Fairfax County Emergency
Medical Services, 124–125; gun,
absence of, 120; gun,
appearance of, 125; gun in

hand, 127, 207, 209; lack of
blood, 144, 207, 217–218;
photos, 122, 125, 140, 141–142,
209;
disappearance, 126, 141;
inconsistencies, 126;
tampering, 140, 141–142;
Rodriguez and, 135–136; U.S.
Park Police, 124–125
Fort Marcy Park parking lot:
Josie's and Duncan's story,
155–158; Knowlton's story,
158–164; woman in blue
Mercedes, 166. *See also* Foster's
Honda Accord
Fortier, Michael, 67
Foster, Lisa: Easton trip, 223, 248;
FBI interview, 131–132, 165,
221, 223, 227; gun and, 130;
Hamilton and, 115, 116;
husband's death, 122, 129–130,
228–229; *New Yorker*
interviews, 130, 132; suicide
note and, 213, 214; Waco
comments, 221
Foster, Vincent, 139, 362; affair
with Hillary Clinton, 333;
Bell and, 244–245; call from
Clinton, 225–226; character,
116–117; credit union visit, 224;
Easton trip, 223, 248; First
American case, 311; Kennedy
and, 169; missing keys,
167–170, 191; office alarm
system, 195; office safe, 195,
196, 221; office typewriter, 214;
Parks and, 245–249; plans for
evening, 129; purported
depression, 219–220, 226, 231;